The people who came from
France to interview me gave me
these, along with some supremely
delicious chocolate. You came from
so far away! Thank you so much!
Someday I'll go to France too.
Someday... Someday!!

—*Yūki Tabata, 2018*

YŪKI TABATA

was born in Fukuoka Prefecture
and got his big break in the 2011
Shonen Jump Golden Future Cup
with his winning entry, *Hungry*
al fantasy
015.

BLACK CLOVER
VOLUME 16
SHONEN JUMP Manga Edition

Story and Art by YŪKI TABATA

Translation ❧ SARAH NEUFELD,
HC LANGUAGE SOLUTIONS, INC.

Touch-Up Art & Lettering ❧ ANNALIESE CHRISTMAN

Design ❧ SHAWN CARRICO

Editor ❧ ALEXIS KIRSCH

BLACK CLOVER © 2015 by Yuki Tabata
All rights reserved.
First published in Japan in 2015 by SHUEISHA Inc., Tokyo.
English translation rights arranged by SHUEISHA Inc.

The stories, characters and incidents mentioned in
this publication are entirely fictional.

Printed in the U.S.A.

Published by VIZ Media, LLC
P.O. Box 77010
San Francisco, CA 94107

10 9 8 7 6 5 4 3 2 1
First printing, July 2019

viz.com

shonenjump.com

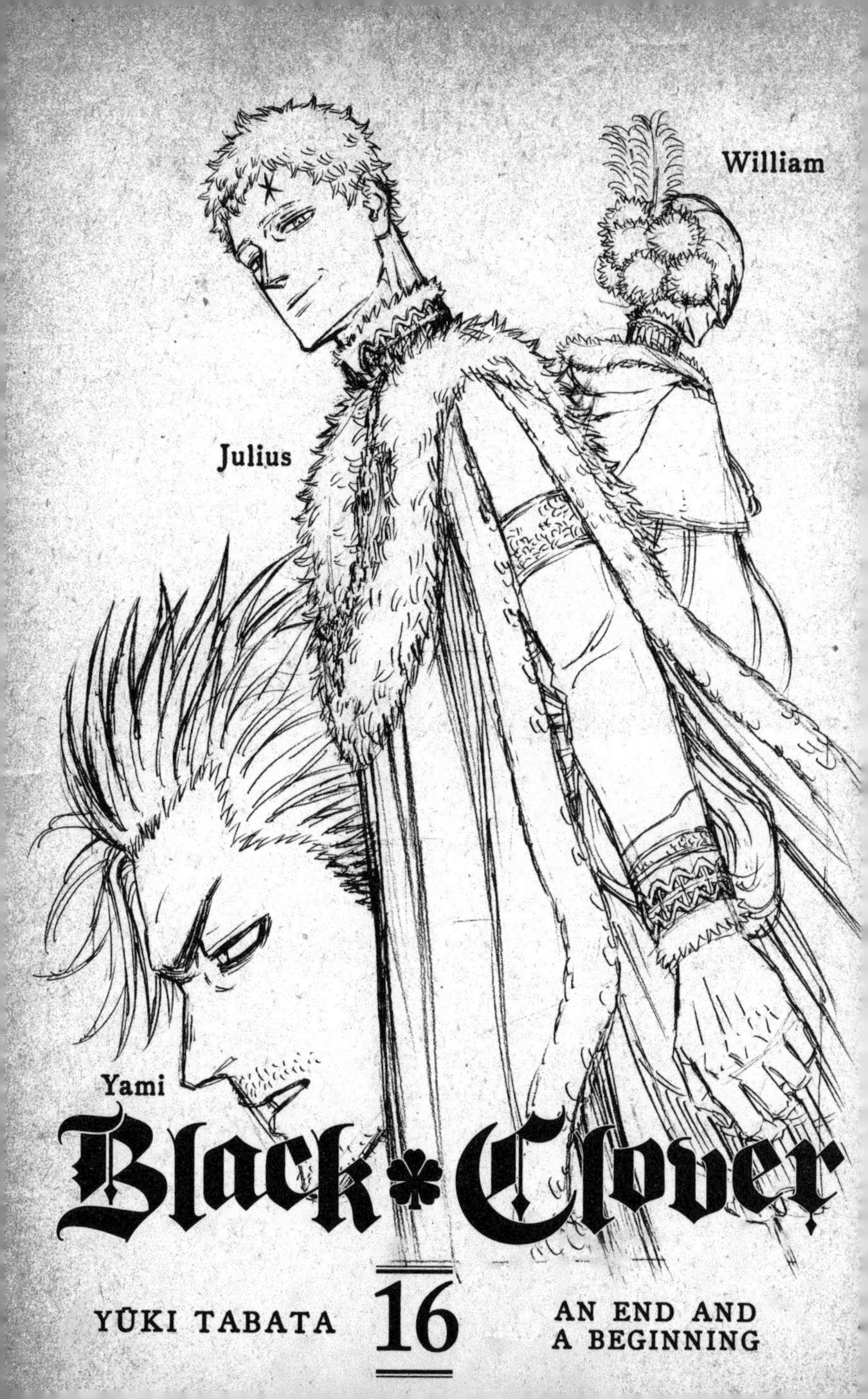
William
Julius
Yami

Black Clover

YŪKI TABATA

16

AN END AND A BEGINNING

Yuno

Member of:
The Golden Dawn Magic: Wind

Asta's best friend, and a good rival who's also been working to become the Wizard King. He controls Sylph, the spirit of wind.

Asta

 Member of: The Black Bulls
Magic: None (Anti-Magic)

He has no magic, but he's working to become the Wizard King through sheer guts and his well-trained body. He fights with an anti-magic sword.

Yami Sukehiro

 Member of:
The Golden Dawn
Magic: Dark

A captain who looks fierce and has a hot temper, but is very popular with his brigade. They have a deep-rooted confidence in him.

Noelle Silva

 Member of:
The Black Bulls
Magic: Water

A royal. She feels inferior to her brilliant siblings. Her latent abilities are an unknown quantity.

Gauche Adlai

 Member of:
The Black Bulls
Magic: Mirror

A former convict with a blind, pathological love for his little sister.

Zora Ideale

 Member of:
The Black Bulls
Magic: Ash

He idolizes his father, who was a Magic Knight, and he's particularly good at trap spells.

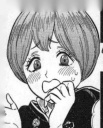

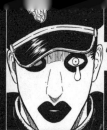

Gordon Agrippa

Member of: The Black Bulls
Magic: Poison

Incredibly bad at communicating. He wants to get closer to everybody else, but he can't say it.

Grey

Member of: The Black Bulls
Magic: Transformation

She has a shy personality, and can transform to look like whoever she's with.

Mereoleon Vermillion

Member of: The Crimson Lion Kings
Magic: Flame

The captain of the Royal Knights. She h a stormy personality, and her high combat abilities are universall acknowledged.

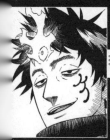

Raia

Member of: The Eye of the Midnight Sun
Magic: Copy

The final member of the Third Eye. Once he touches his opponent's grimoire, he's able to copy their magic.

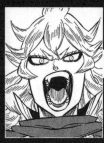

Julius Novachron

Wizard King

The strongest man in the Clover Kingdom. Also a peerless magic fanatic. Hugely popular with the kingdom's citizens.

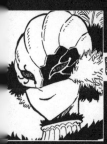

William Vangeance

Member of: The Golden Dawn
Magic: World Tree

The captain of the kingdom's strongest brigade. He has a cursed scar beneath his mask, and a deep respect for the Wizard King.

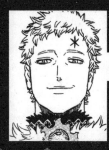

STORY

In a world where magic is everything, Asta and Yuno are both found abandoned on the same day at a church in the remote village of Hage. Both dream of becoming the Wizard King, the highest of all mages, and they spend their days working toward that dream.

The year they turn 15, both receive grimoires, magic books that amplify their bearer's magic. They take the entrance exam for the Magic Knights, nine groups of mages under the direct control of the Wizard King. Yuno, whose magic is strong, joins the Golden Dawn, an elite group, while Asta, who has no magic at all, joins the Black Bulls, a group of misfits. With this, the two finally take their first step toward becoming the Wizard King…

The Royal Knights–a band of elites, captained by Mereoleona–invade the Eye of the Midnight Sun's hideout, where they find a formidable enemy in Raia. Meanwhile, the Black Bulls hideout is also under attack by the Eye of the Midnight Sun. Gauche and the others had been driven into a corner when a mysterious young guy who introduces himself as Henry suddenly appears and launches a counterattack!!

CONTENTS

BLACK ❀ CLOVER

16

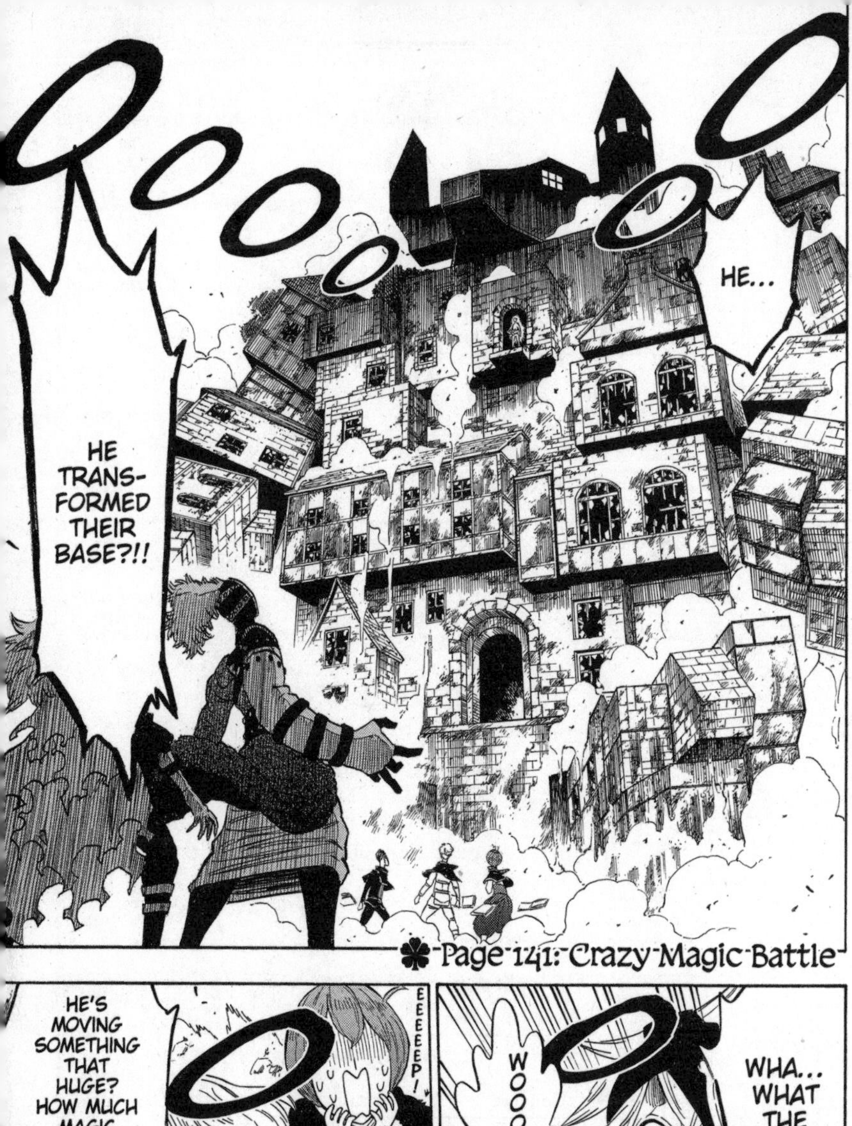
ROOOOOO
HE...
HE TRANSFORMED THEIR BASE?!!

Page 141: Crazy Magic Battle

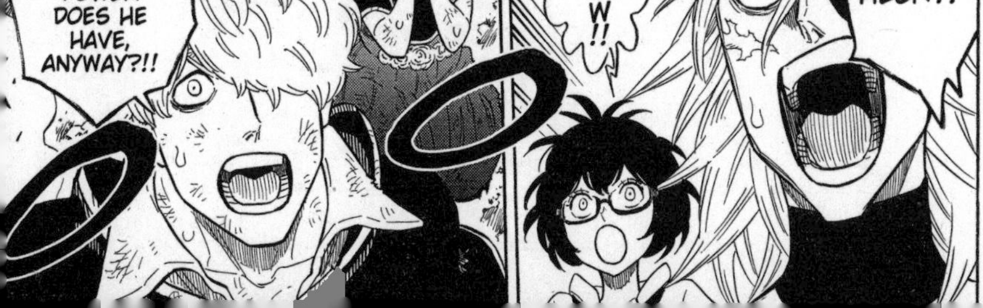
WHA... WHAT THE HECK?!
WOOOOOW!!
EEEEEEEP!
HE'S MOVING SOMETHING THAT HUGE? HOW MUCH MAGIC POWER DOES HE HAVE, ANYWAY?!!

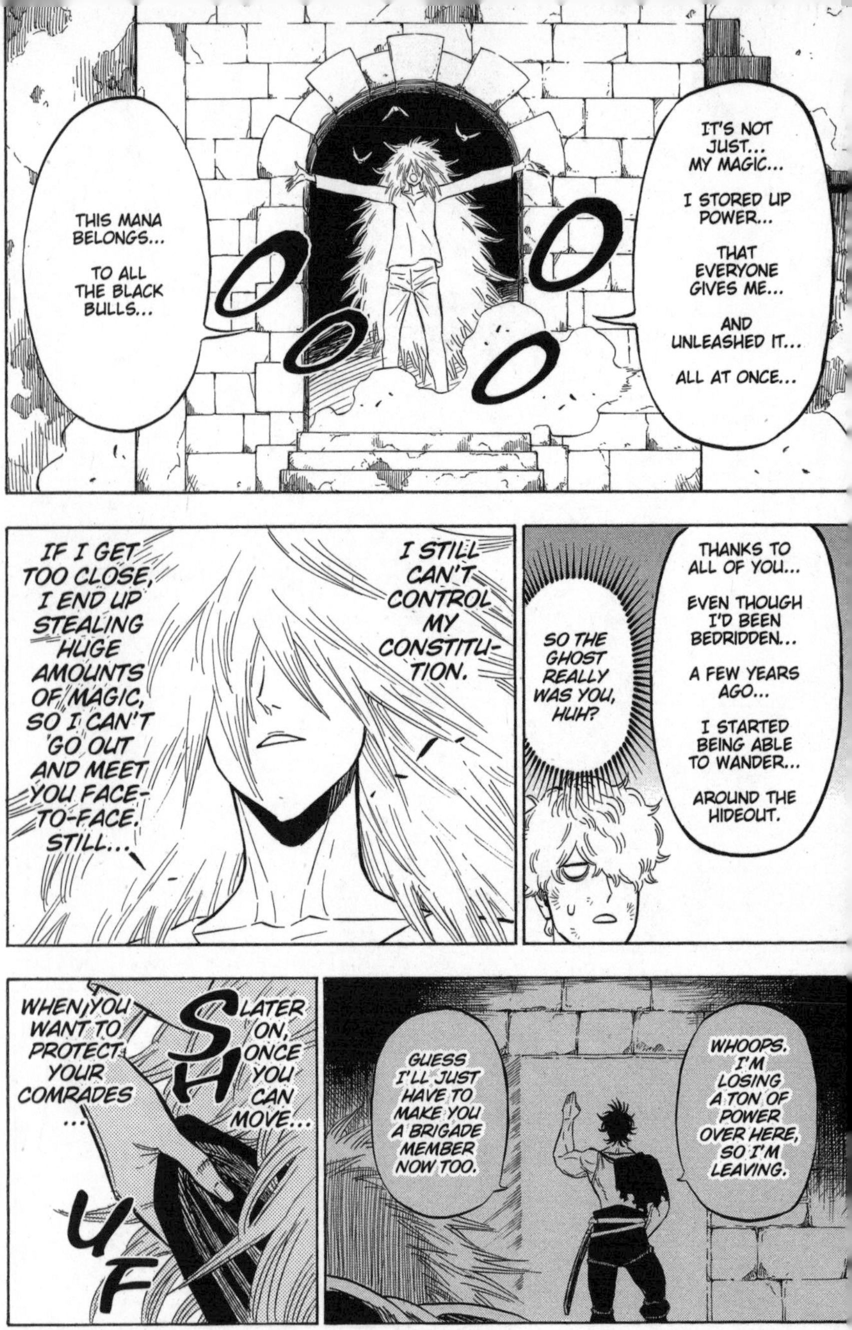
IT'S NOT JUST... MY MAGIC... I STORED UP POWER... THAT EVERYONE GIVES ME... AND UNLEASHED IT... ALL AT ONCE...
THIS MANA BELONGS... TO ALL THE BLACK BULLS...
THANKS TO ALL OF YOU... EVEN THOUGH I'D BEEN BEDRIDDEN... A FEW YEARS AGO... I STARTED BEING ABLE TO WANDER... AROUND THE HIDEOUT.
SO THE GHOST REALLY WAS YOU, HUH?
I STILL CAN'T CONTROL MY CONSTITUTION.
IF I GET TOO CLOSE, I END UP STEALING HUGE AMOUNTS OF MAGIC, SO I CAN'T GO OUT AND MEET YOU FACE-TO-FACE. STILL...
WHOOPS. I'M LOSING A TON OF POWER OVER HERE, SO I'M LEAVING.
GUESS I'LL JUST HAVE TO MAKE YOU A BRIGADE MEMBER NOW TOO.
LATER ON, ONCE YOU CAN MOVE...
SH
WHEN YOU WANT TO PROTECT YOUR COMRADES...
UF

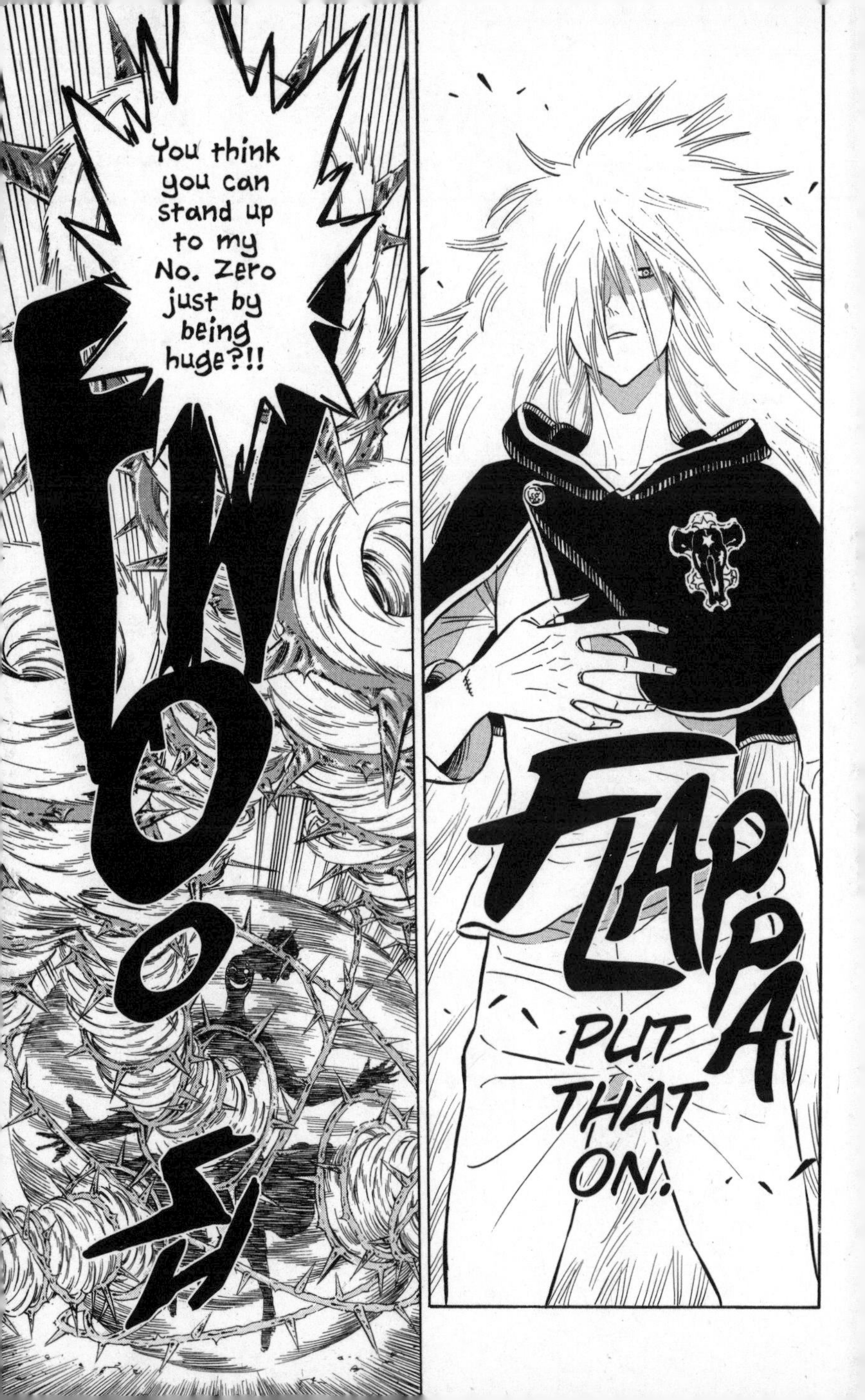
FLAPPA
PUT THAT ON.
You think you can stand up to my No. Zero just by being huge?!!

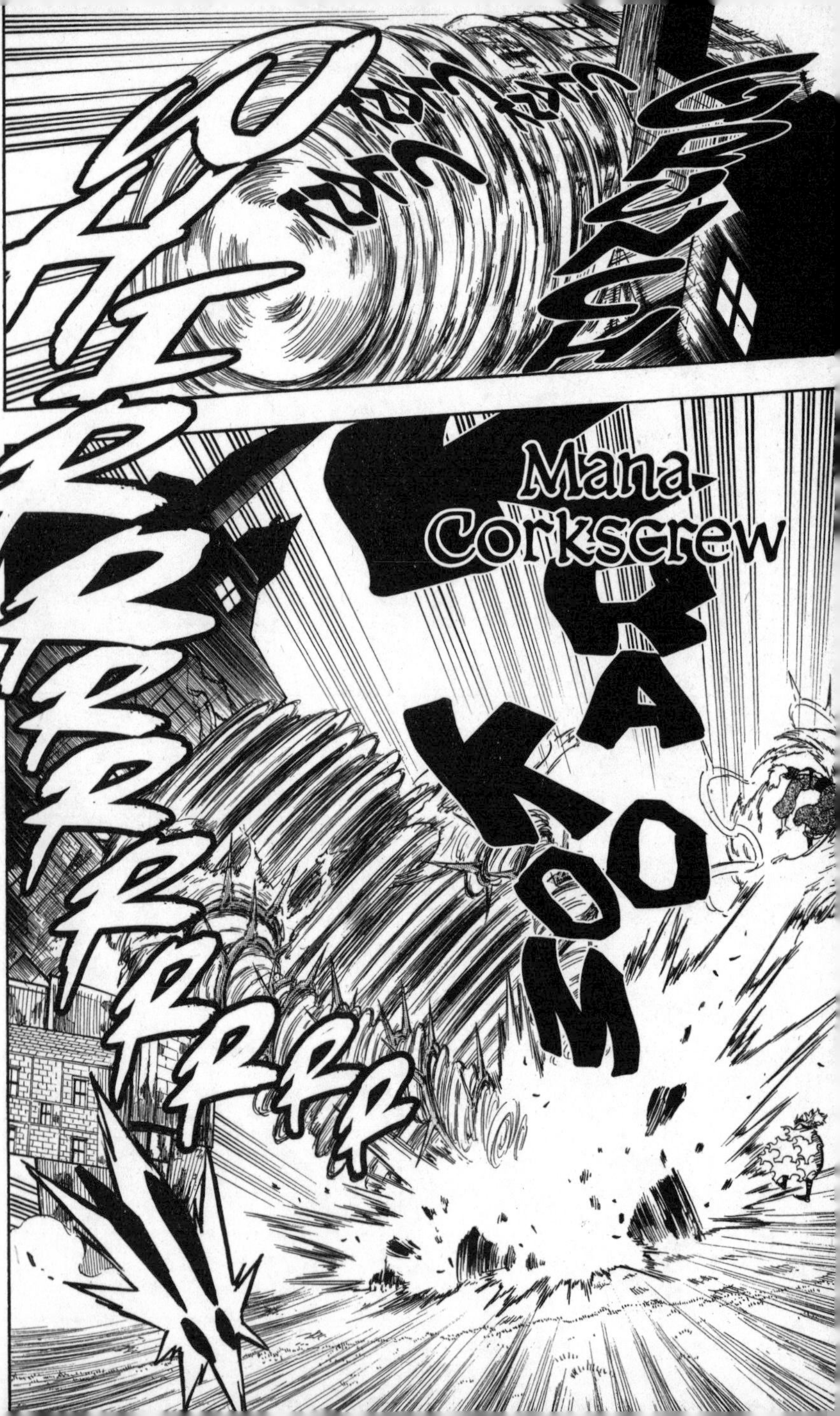
Mana Corkscrew
KAKOOM

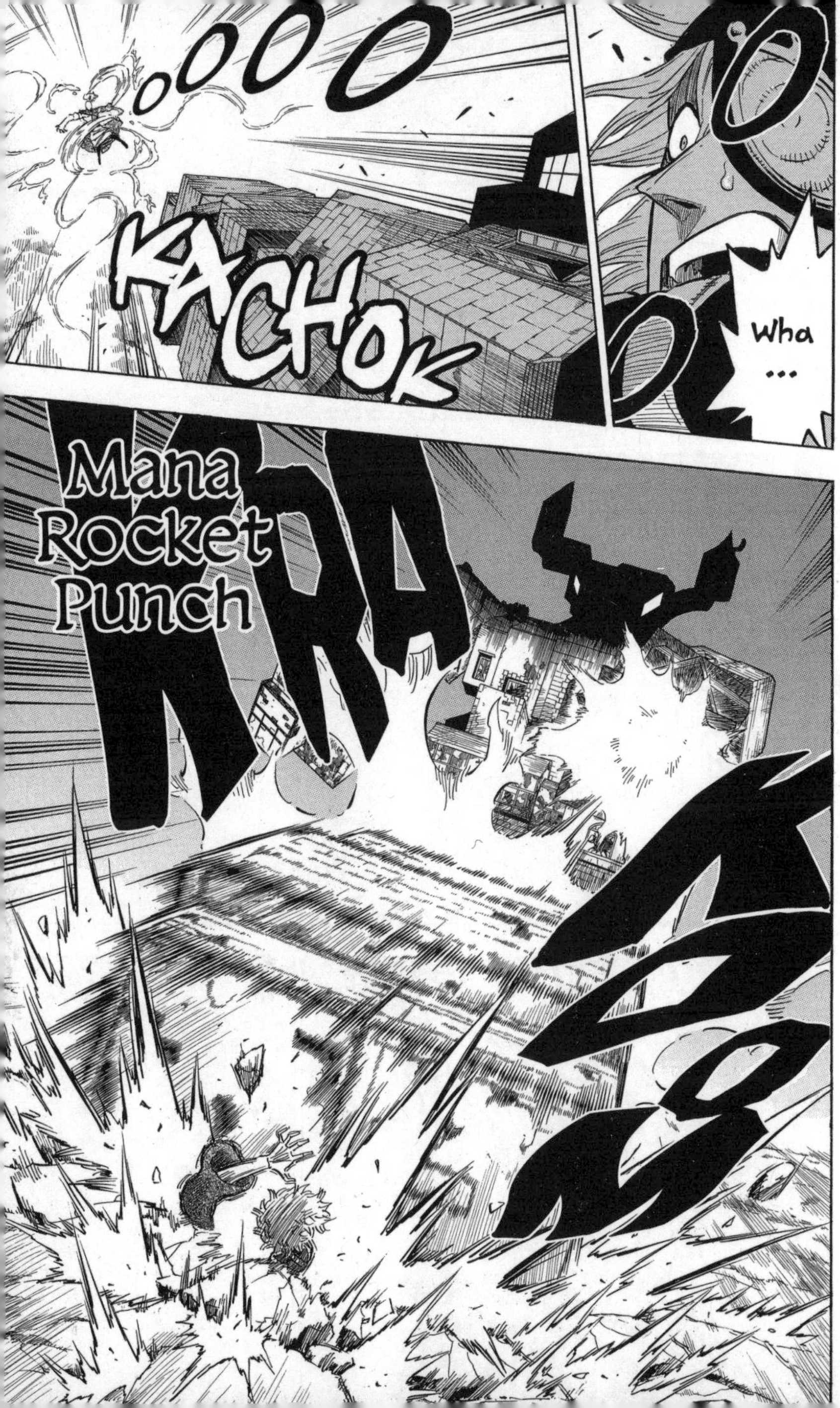
Wha ...
KACHOK
Mana Rocket Punch

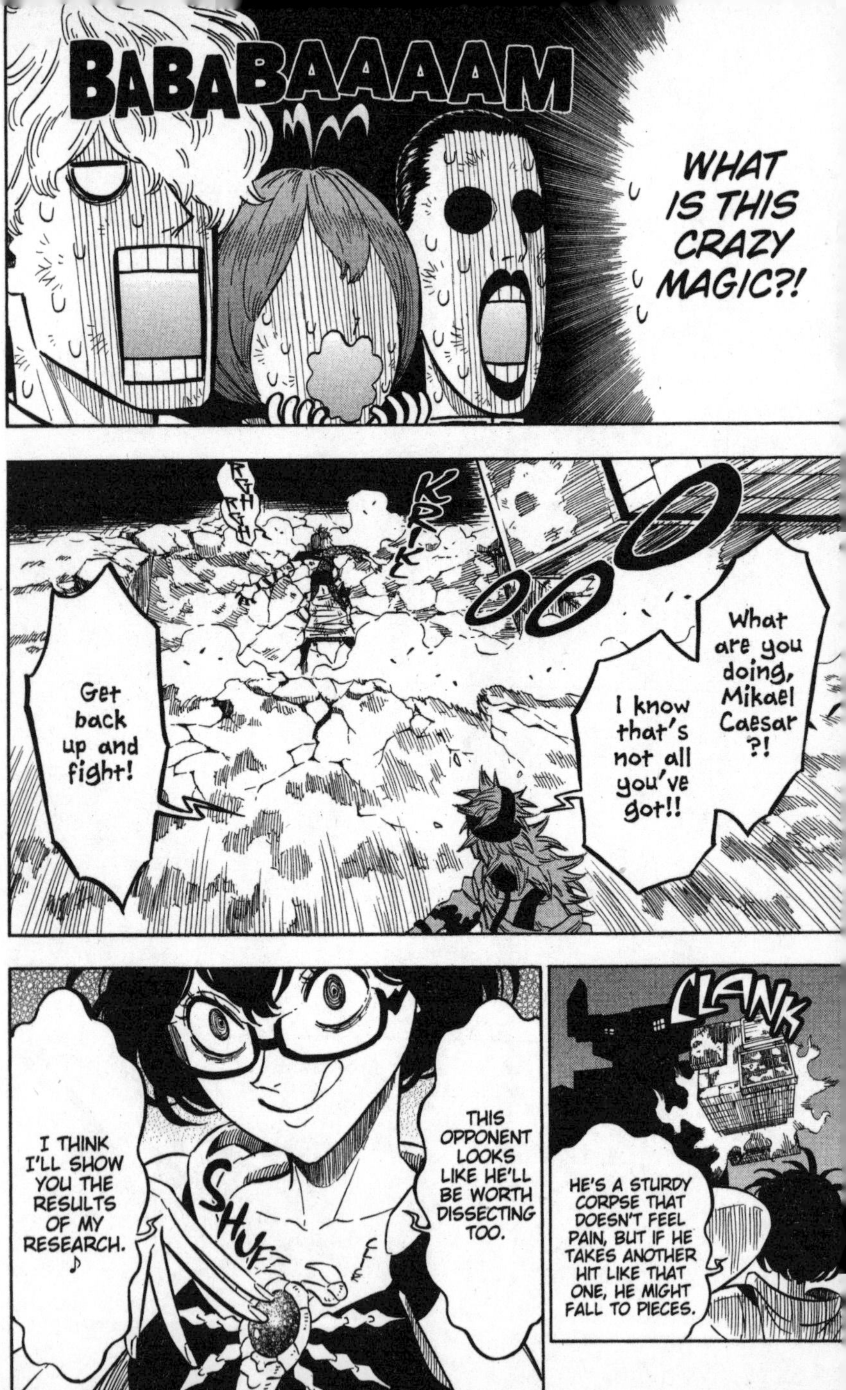
BABABAAAAAM
WHAT IS THIS CRAZY MAGIC?!
KRIK
RGH RGH RGH
What are you doing, Mikael Caesar?!
I know that's not all you've got!!
Get back up and fight!
CLANK
HE'S A STURDY CORPSE THAT DOESN'T FEEL PAIN, BUT IF HE TAKES ANOTHER HIT LIKE THAT ONE, HE MIGHT FALL TO PIECES.
THIS OPPONENT LOOKS LIKE HE'LL BE WORTH DISSECTING TOO.
SHUF
I THINK I'LL SHOW YOU THE RESULTS OF MY RESEARCH. ♪

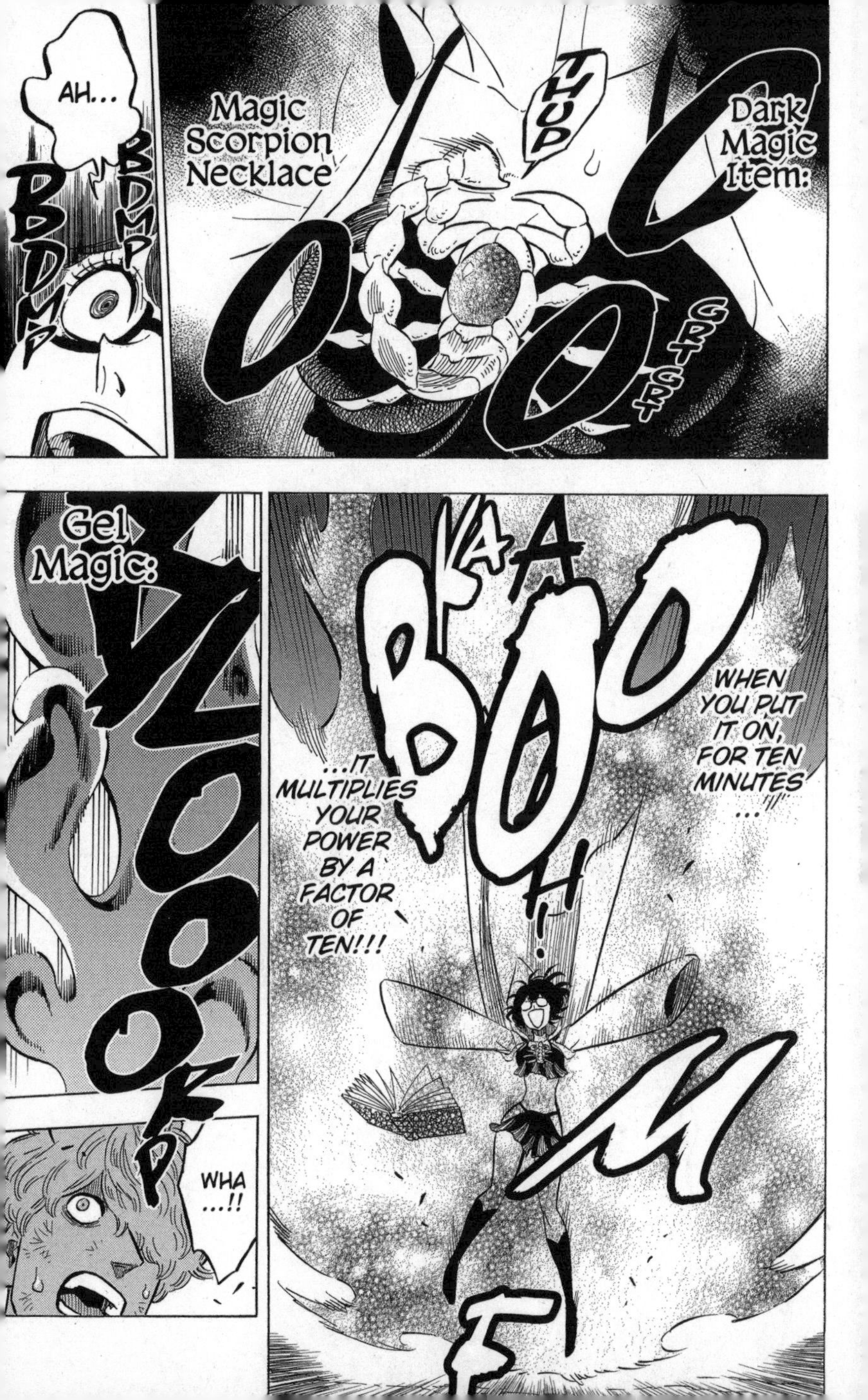

Dark Magic Item:
THUD
GRTGRT
Magic Scorpion Necklace
AH...
BDMP BDMP
WHEN YOU PUT IT ON, FOR TEN MINUTES...
...IT MULTIPLIES YOUR POWER BY A FACTOR OF TEN!!!
Gel Magic:
WHA ...!!

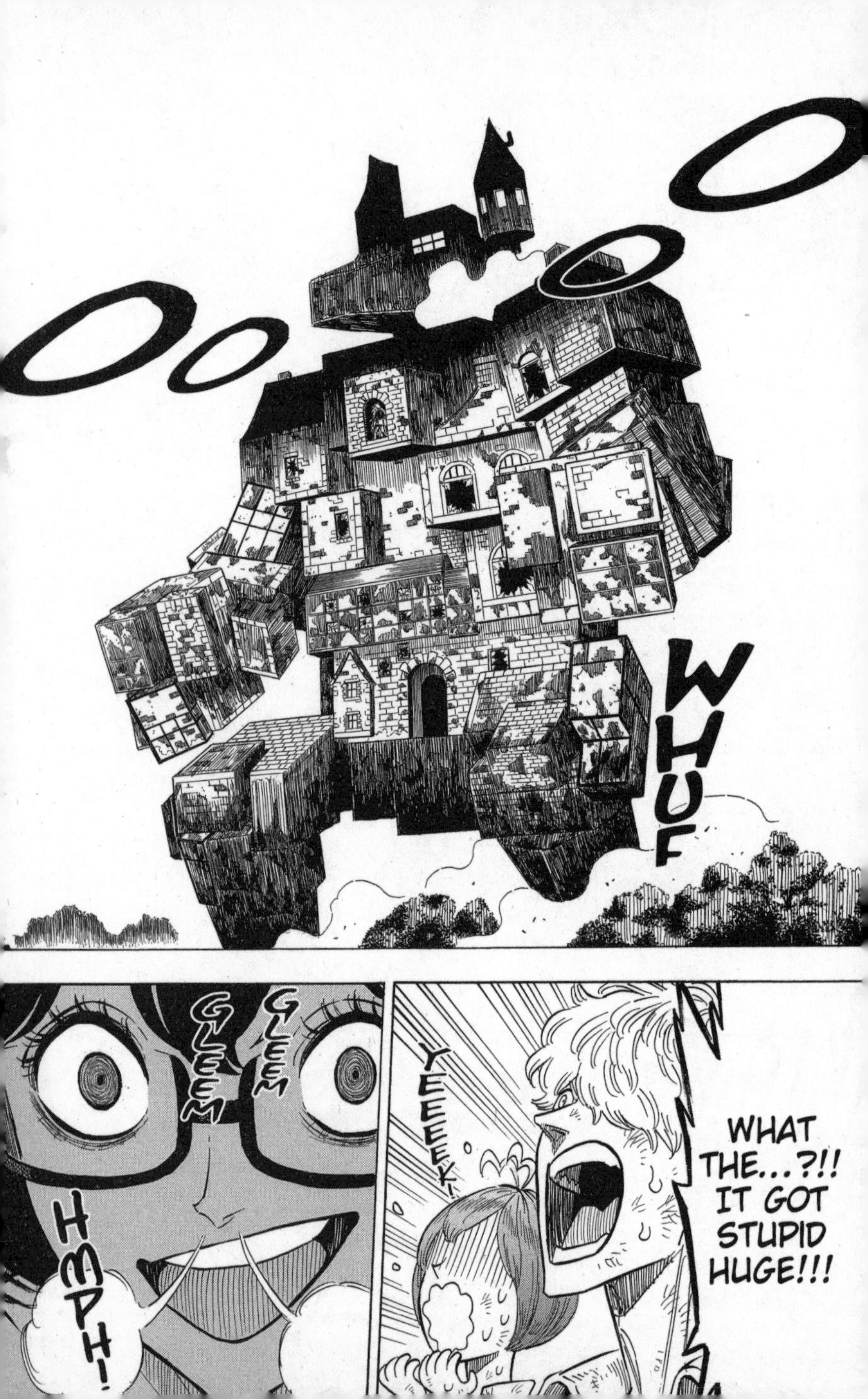
WHUF
WHAT THE...?!! IT GOT STUPID HUGE!!!
YEEEEK!
GLEEM GLEEM
HMPH!

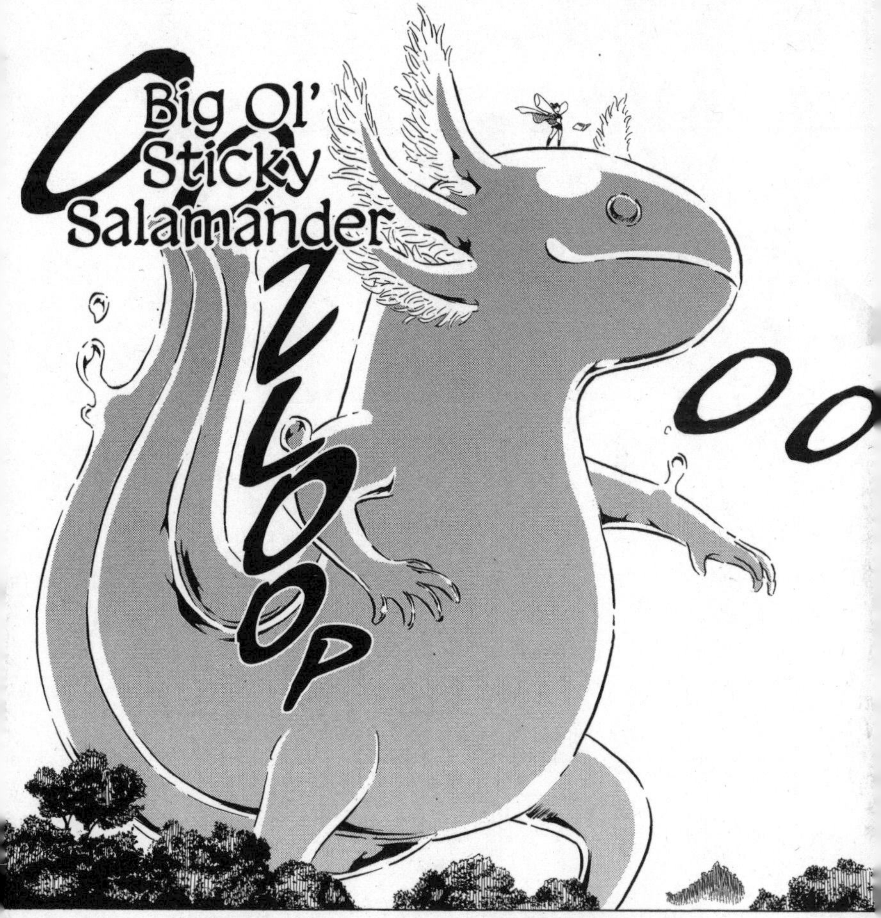
Big Ol' Sticky Salamander
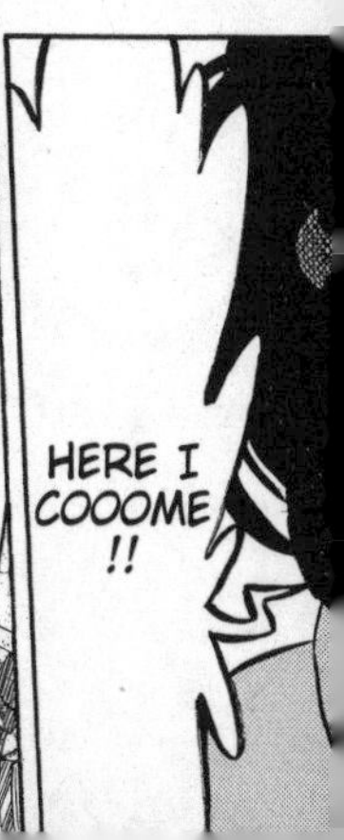
HERE I COOOME!!
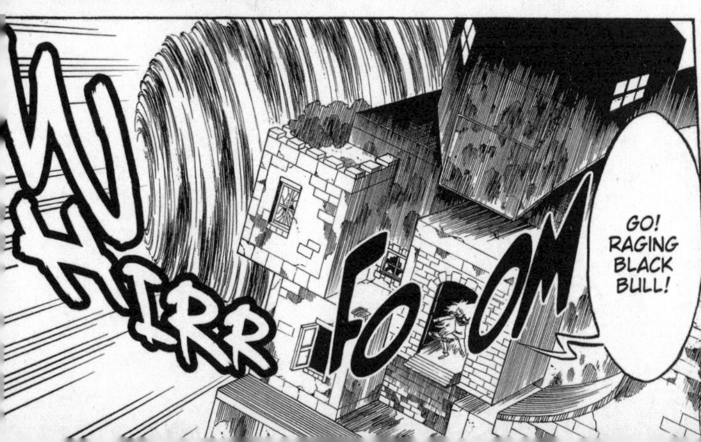
GO! RAGING BLACK BULL!

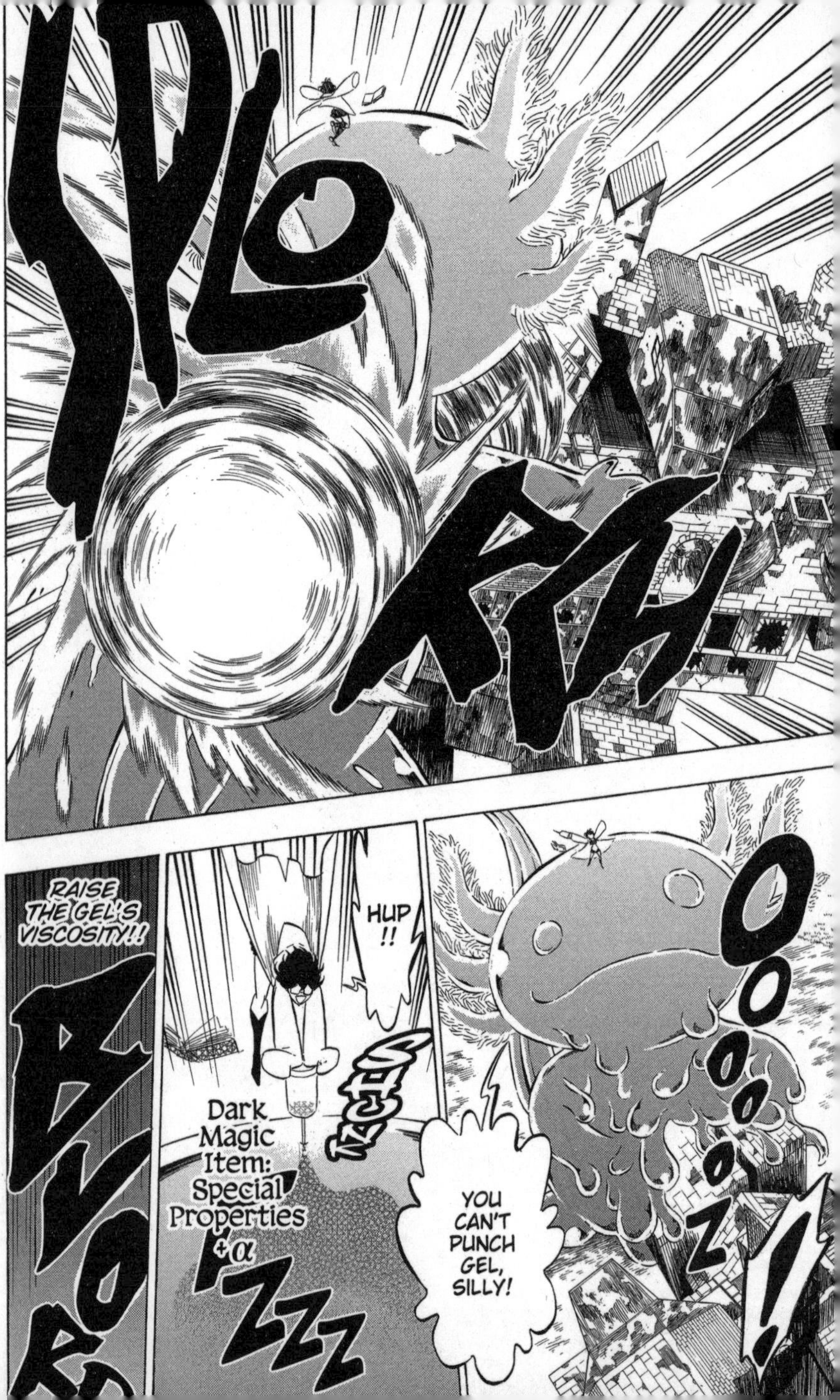
YOU CAN'T PUNCH GEL, SILLY!
HUP !!
Dark Magic Item: Special Properties +α
RAISE THE GEL'S VISCOSITY!!

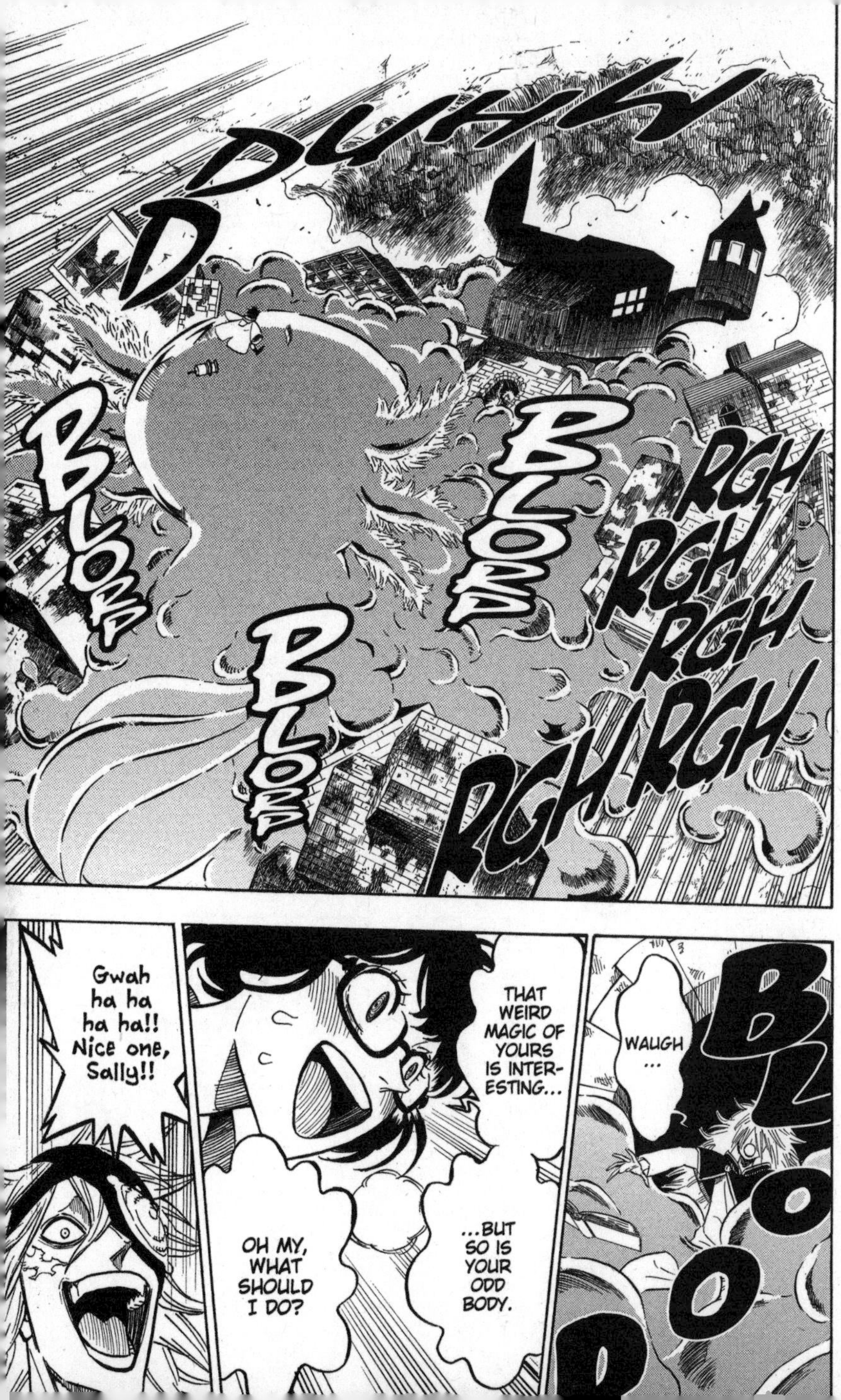
RGH RGH RGH RGH RGH RGH
BLORP
BLORP
BLORP
WAUGH…
THAT WEIRD MAGIC OF YOURS IS INTERESTING…
…BUT SO IS YOUR ODD BODY.
OH MY, WHAT SHOULD I DO?
Gwah ha ha ha ha!! Nice one, Sally!!

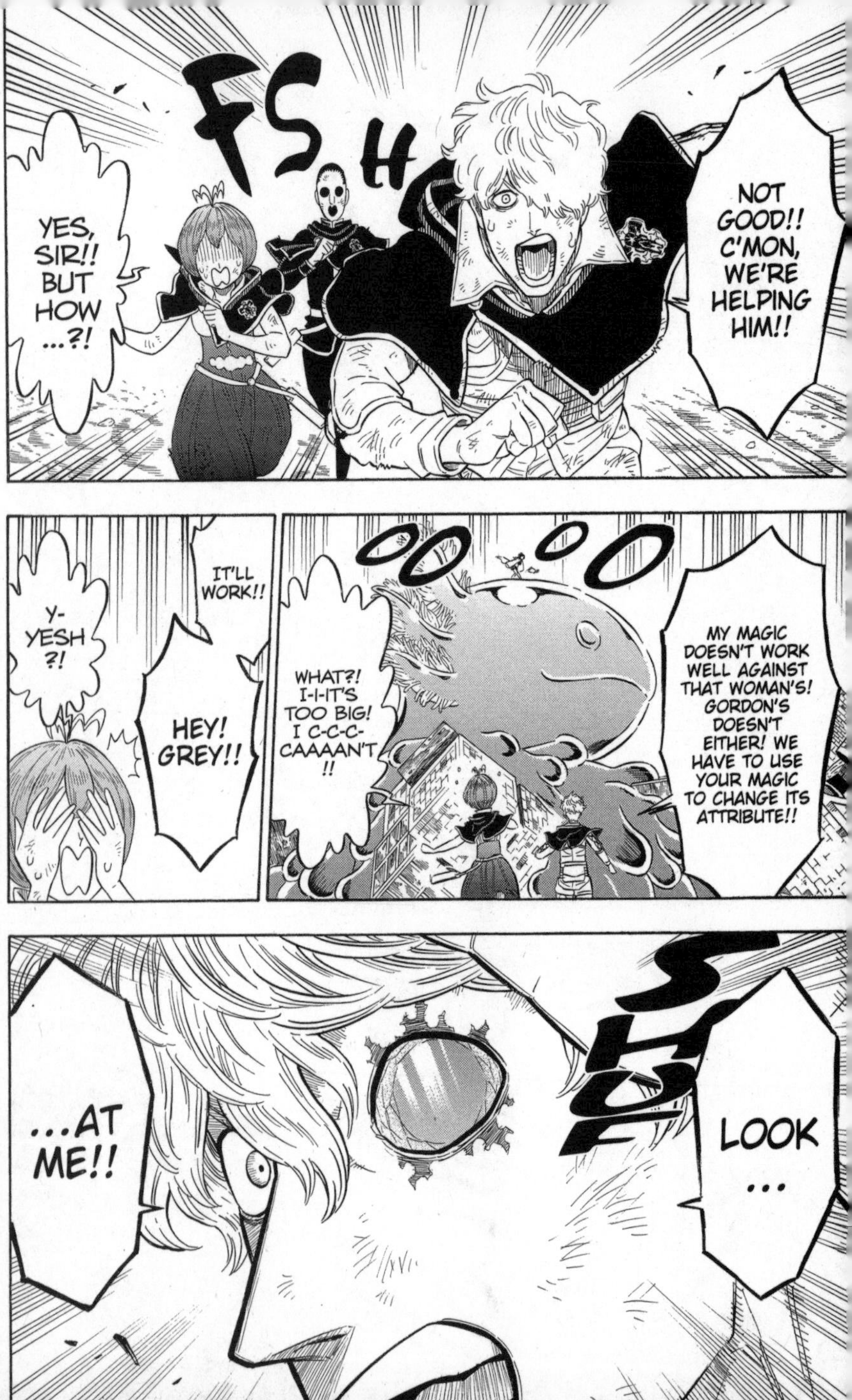
FSH
NOT GOOD!! C'MON, WE'RE HELPING HIM!!
YES, SIR!! BUT HOW...?!
OOOO
MY MAGIC DOESN'T WORK WELL AGAINST THAT WOMAN'S! GORDON'S DOESN'T EITHER! WE HAVE TO USE YOUR MAGIC TO CHANGE ITS ATTRIBUTE!!
WHAT?! I-I-IT'S TOO BIG! I C-C-C-CAAAAN'T!!
IT'LL WORK!!
HEY! GREY!!
Y-YESH?!
SHF
LOOK...
...AT ME!!

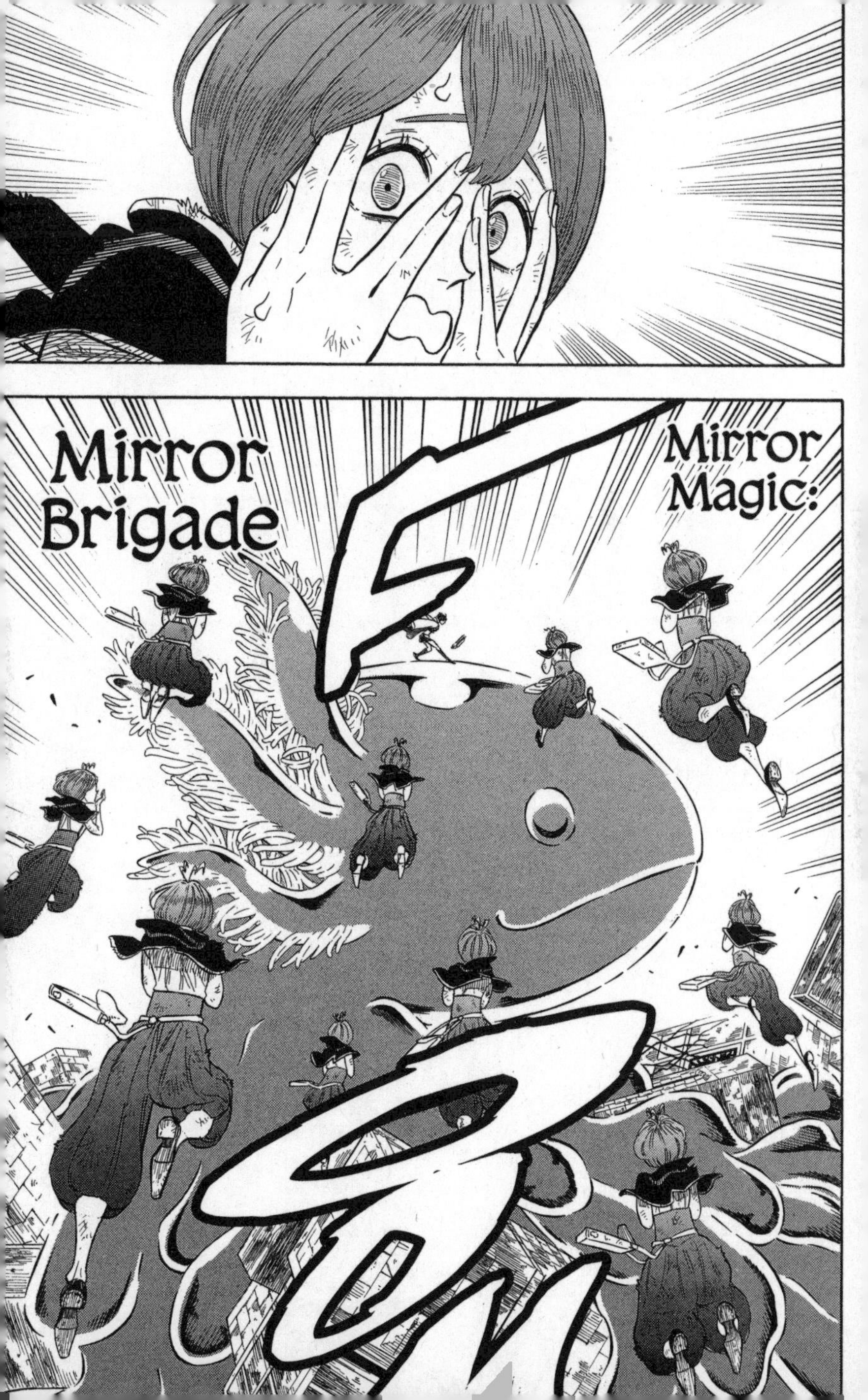
Mirror Magic:
Mirror Brigade

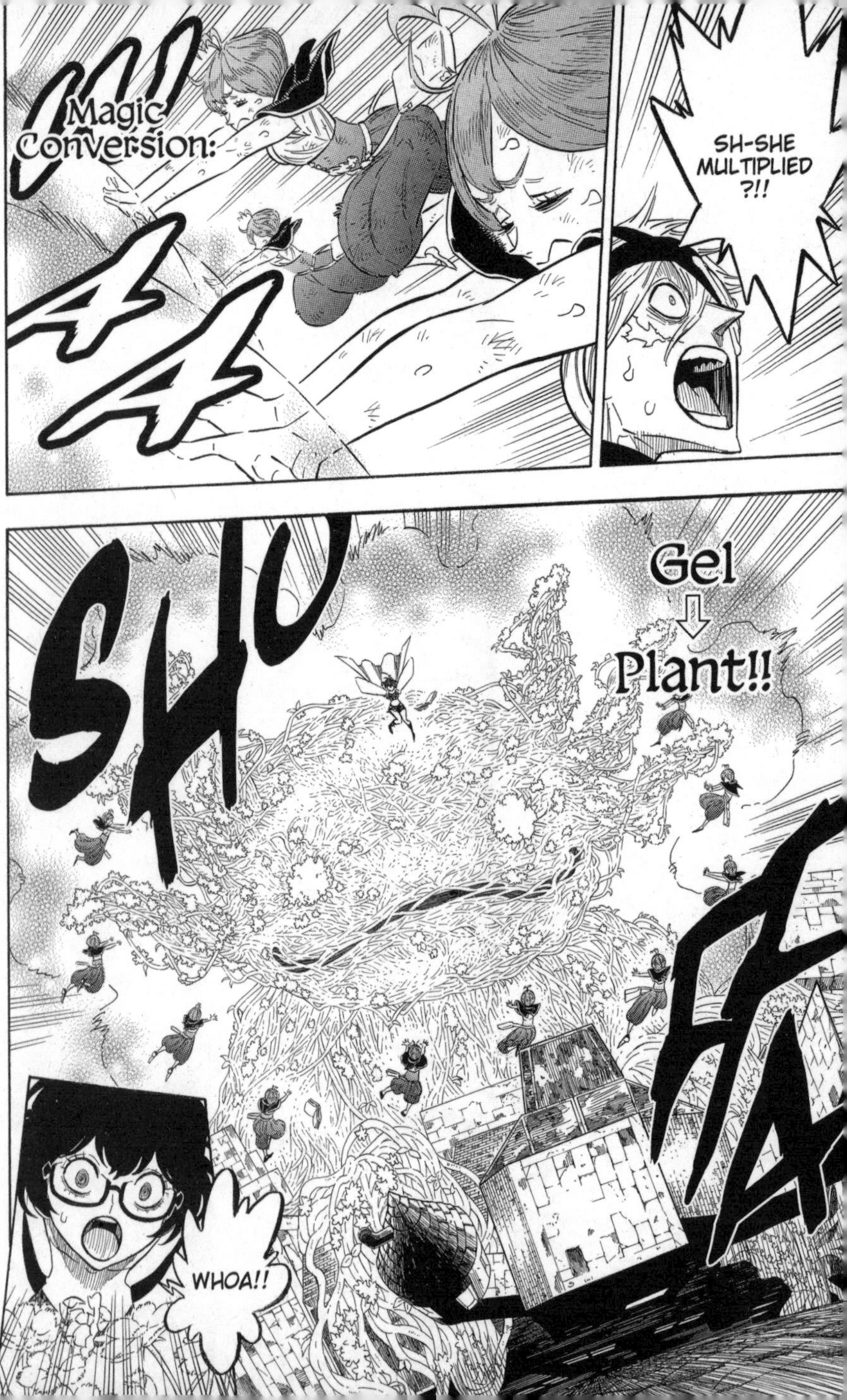
SH-SHE MULTIPLIED ?!!
Magic Conversion:
Gel ⇩ Plant!!
WHOA!!

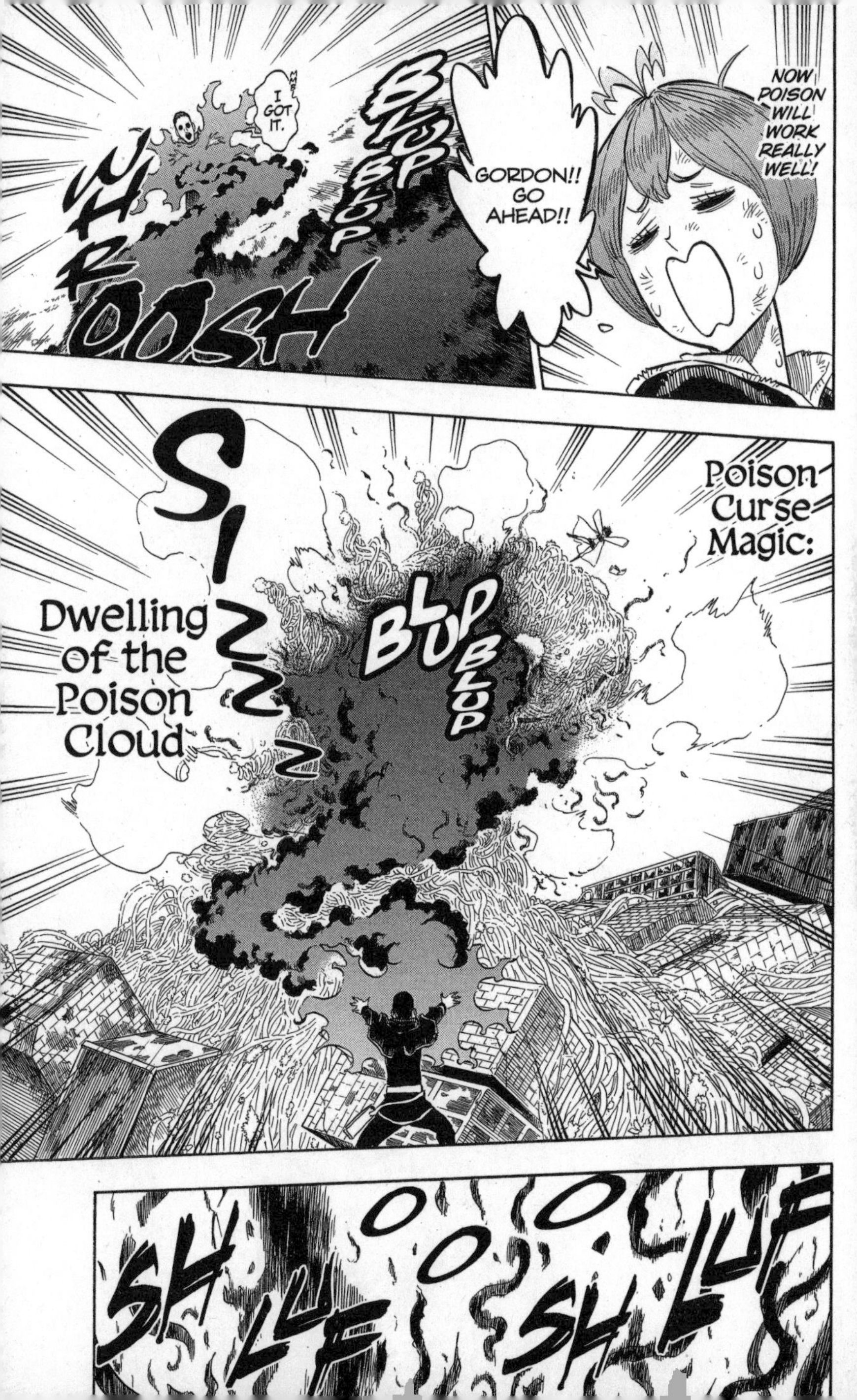
NOW POISON WILL WORK REALLY WELL!
GORDON!! GO AHEAD!!
BLUP BLUP
I GOT IT.
WHROOSH
Poison Curse Magic:
SIZZZZ
BLUP BLUP
Dwelling of the Poison Cloud
SHLUF
SHLUF

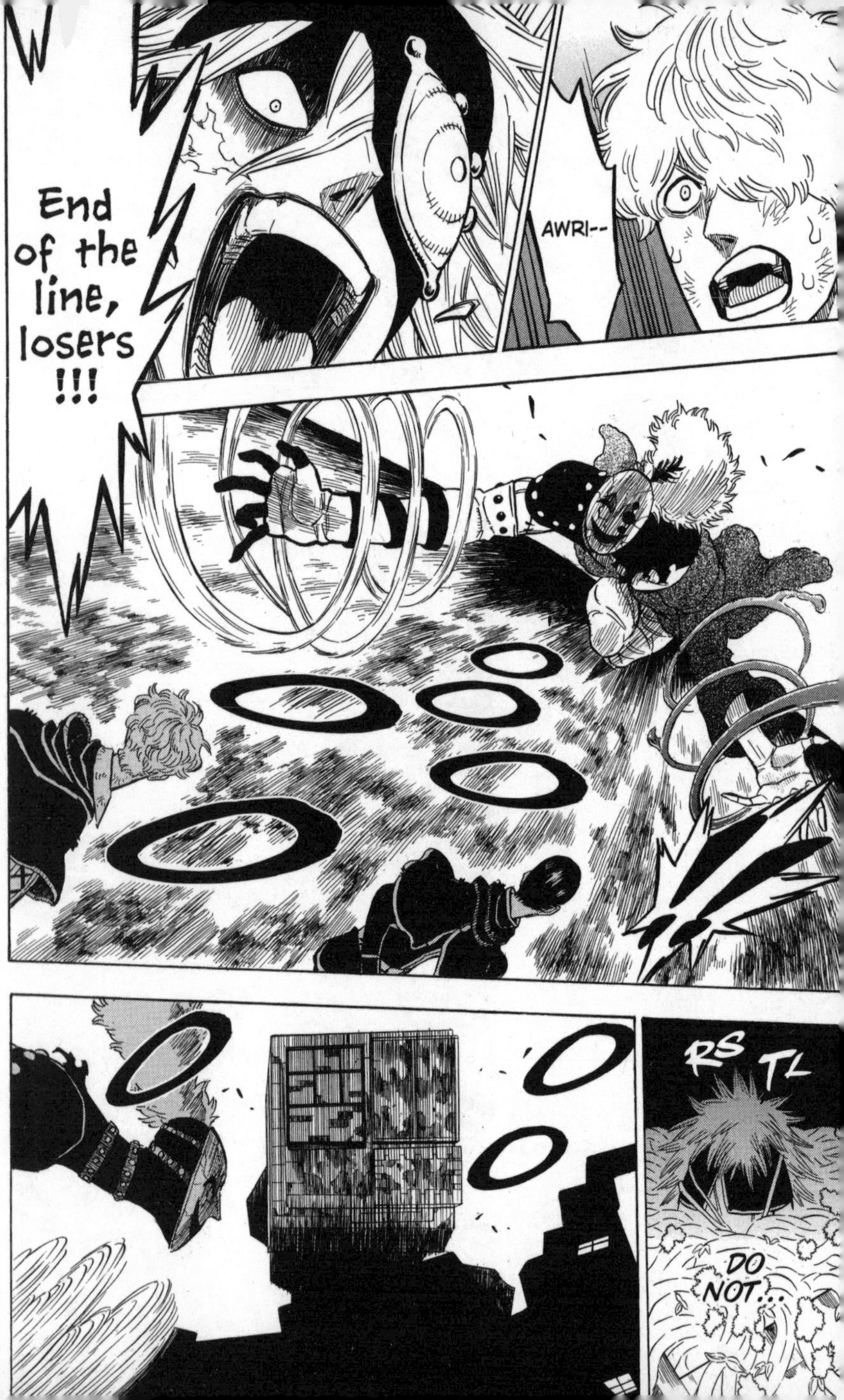
AWRI--
End of the line, losers!!!
RS TL
DO NOT...

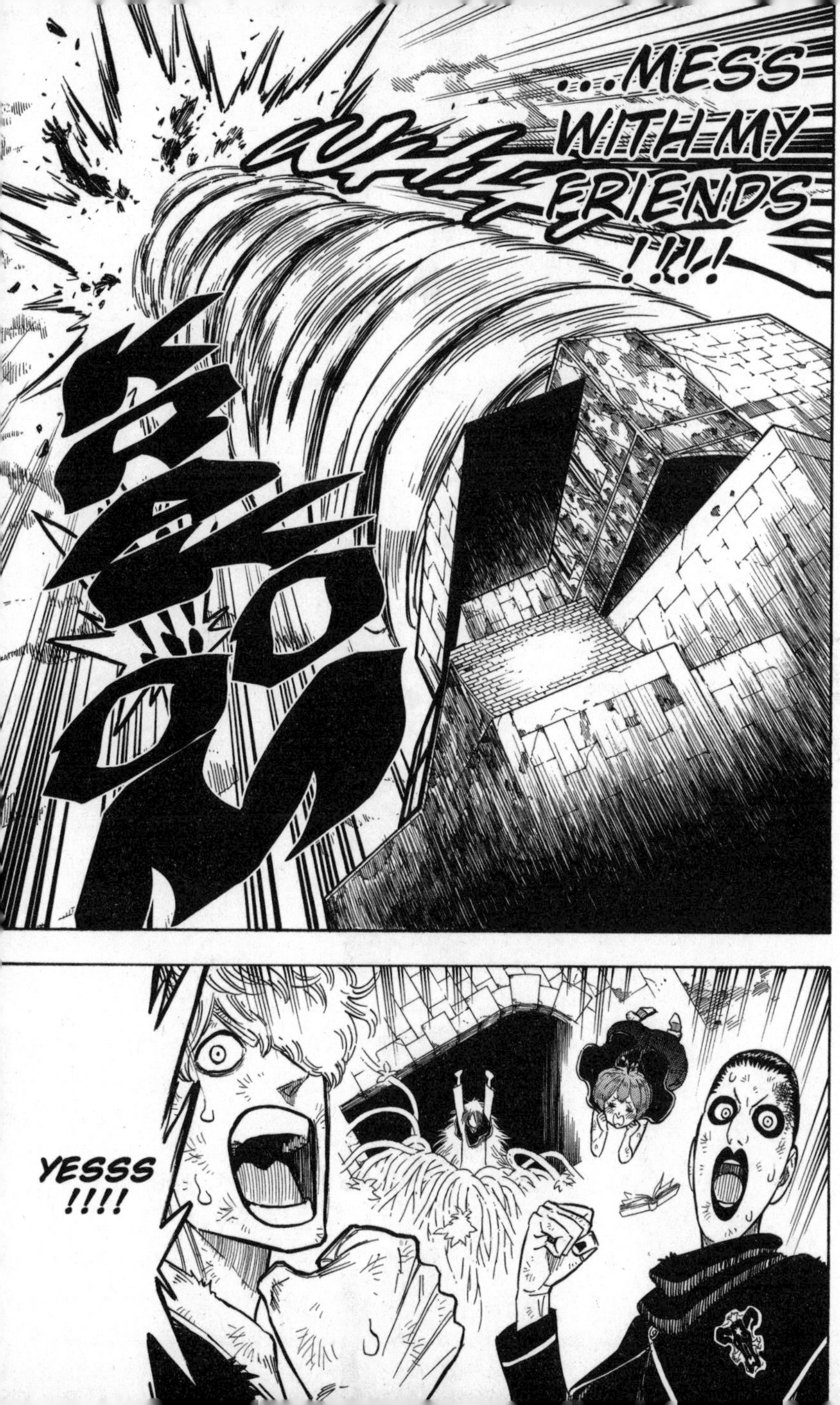
...MESS WITH MY FRIENDS !!?!!
YESSS !!!!

Henry Legolant

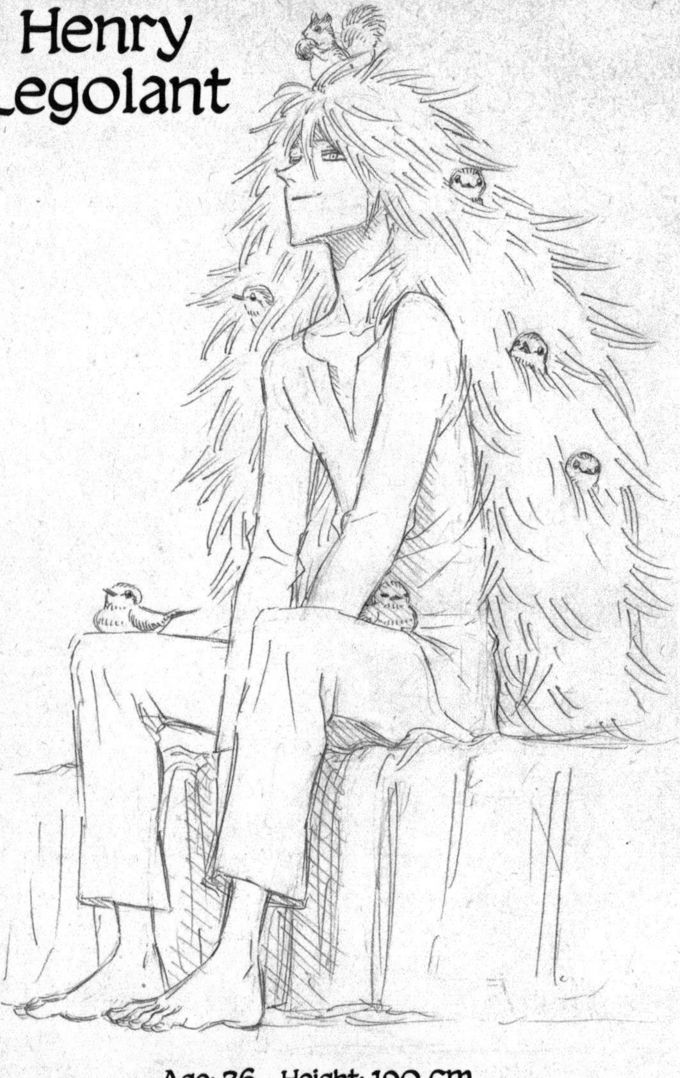

Age: 26 Height: 190 cm
Birthday: February 12 Sign: Aquarius Blood Type: AB
Likes: Small animals, and when the Black Bulls are all together and having fun

Character Profile

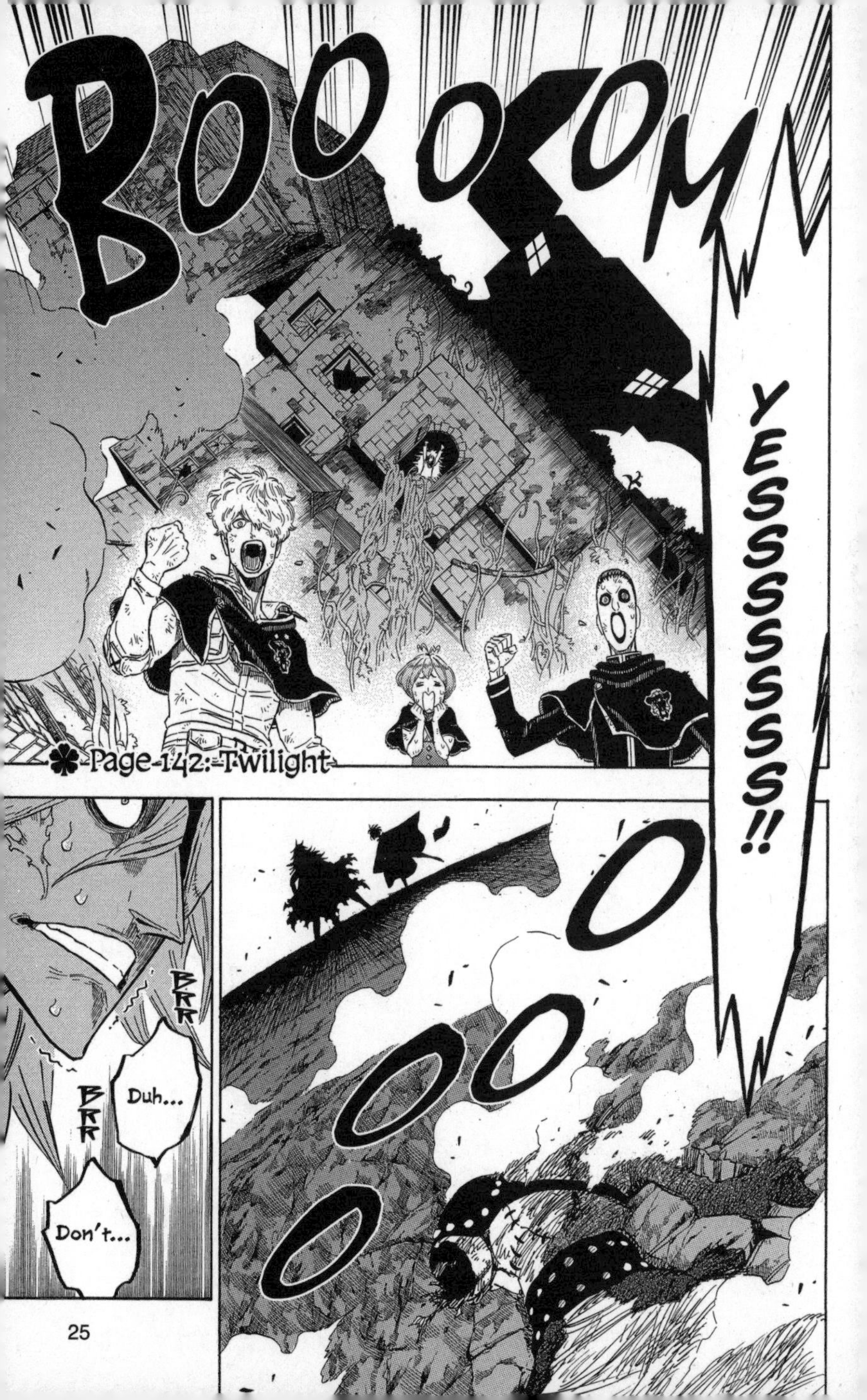
BOOOOM
YESSSSSSSS!!
Page 142: Twilight
OOOOOO
BRR
BRR
Duh...
Don't...

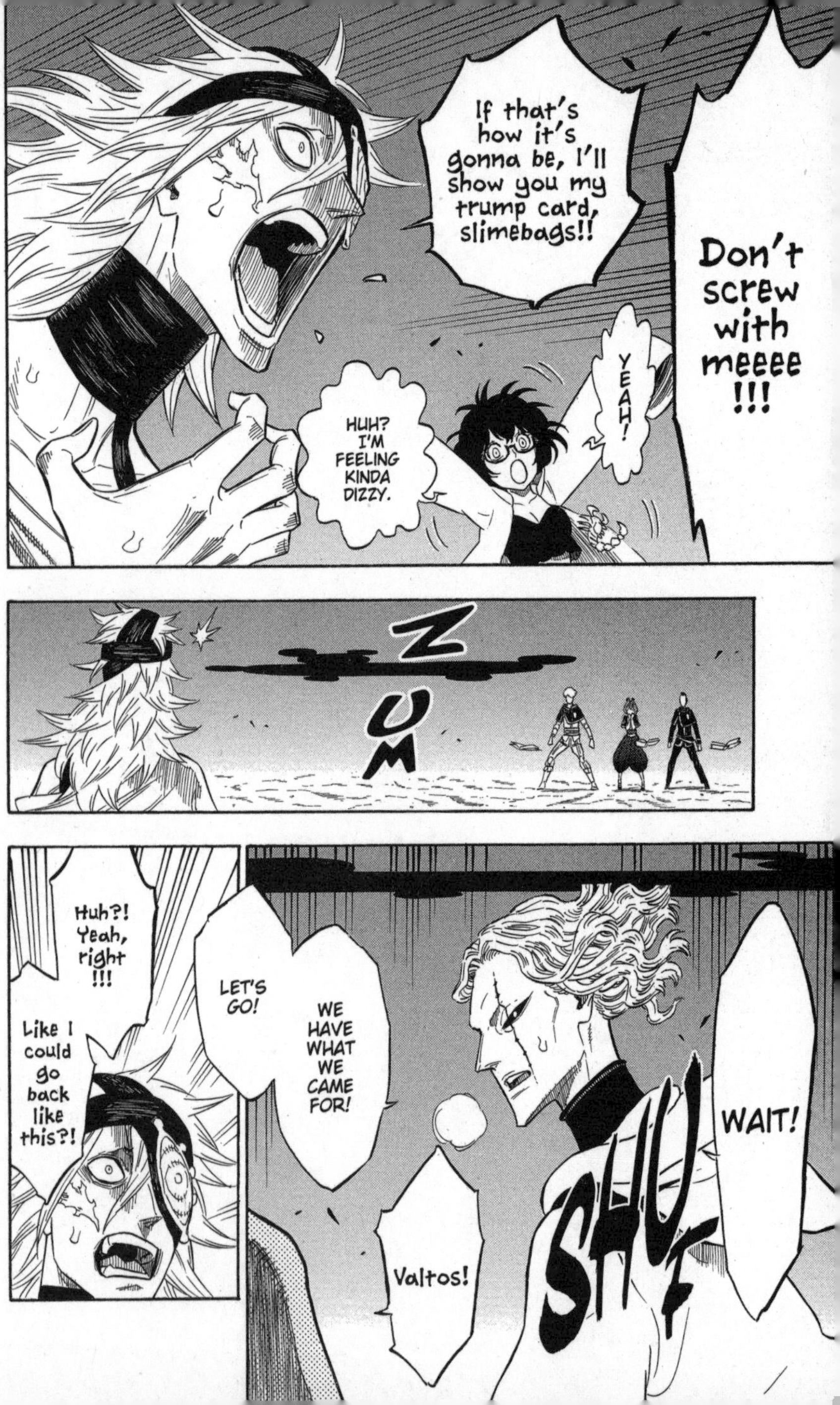
Don't screw with meeee!!!
If that's how it's gonna be, I'll show you my trump card, slimebags!!
YEAH!
HUH? I'M FEELING KINDA DIZZY.
ZUM
WAIT!
LET'S GO!
WE HAVE WHAT WE CAME FOR!
SHU
Valtos!
Huh?! Yeah, right!!!
Like I could go back like this?!

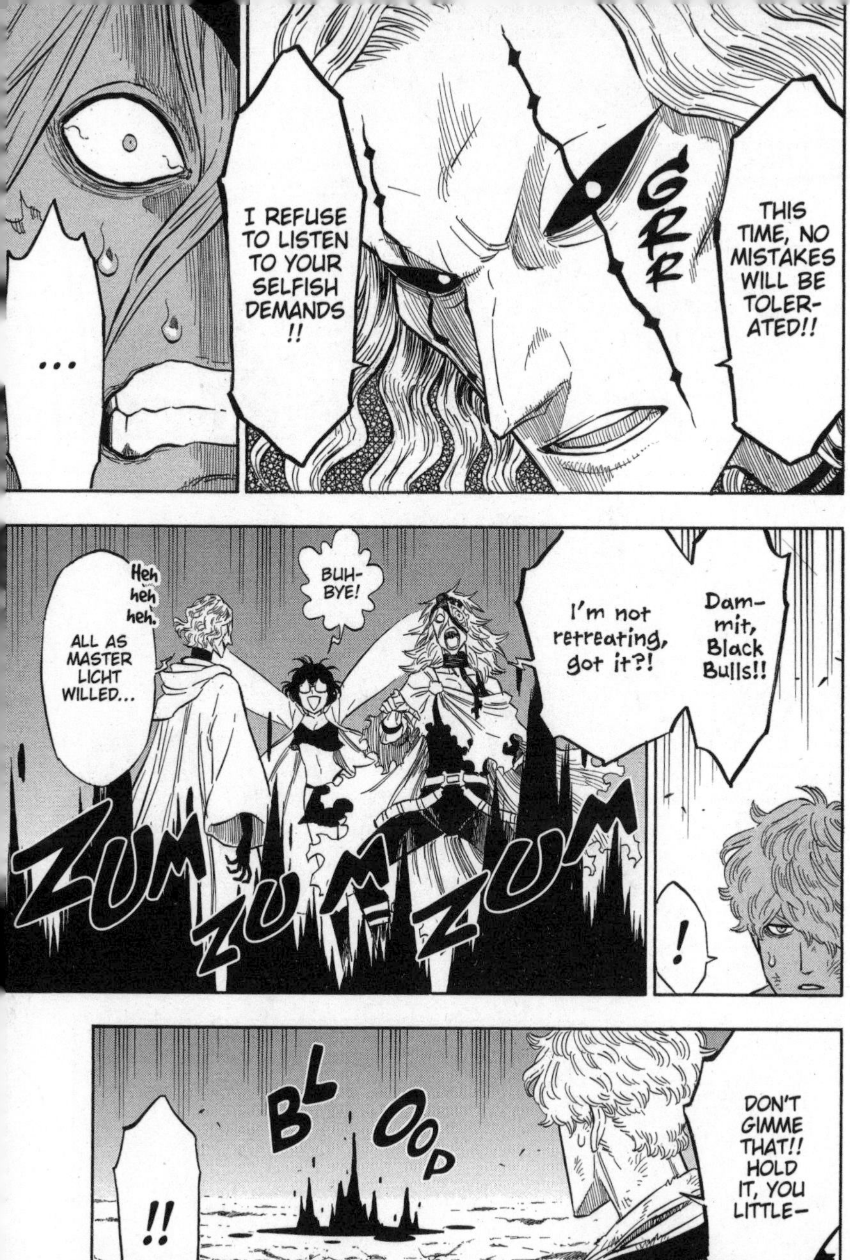
GRR
THIS TIME, NO MISTAKES WILL BE TOLERATED!!
I REFUSE TO LISTEN TO YOUR SELFISH DEMANDS!!
...
!
Dammit, Black Bulls!!
I'm not retreating, got it?!
BUH-BYE!
Heh heh heh.
ALL AS MASTER LICHT WILLED...
ZUM ZUM ZUM
DON'T GIMME THAT!! HOLD IT, YOU LITTLE—
BLOOP
!!

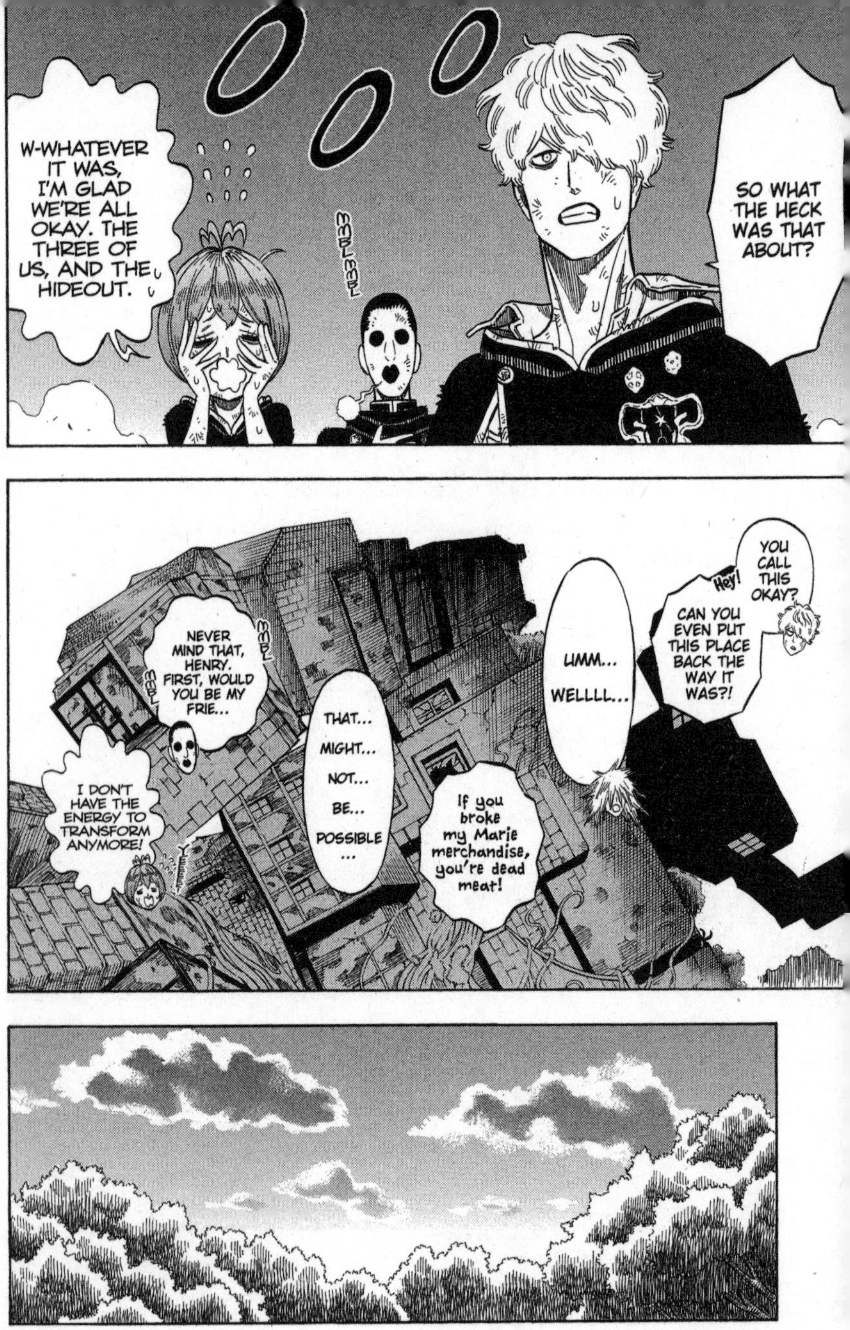
SO WHAT THE HECK WAS THAT ABOUT?
MMBL MMBL
W-WHATEVER IT WAS, I'M GLAD WE'RE ALL OKAY. THE THREE OF US, AND THE HIDEOUT.
YOU CALL THIS OKAY?
Hey!
CAN YOU EVEN PUT THIS PLACE BACK THE WAY IT WAS?!
UMM... WELLLL...
If you broke my Marie merchandise, you're dead meat!
THAT... MIGHT... NOT... BE... POSSIBLE...
NEVER MIND THAT, HENRY. FIRST, WOULD YOU BE MY FRIE...
MMBL MMBL
I DON'T HAVE THE ENERGY TO TRANSFORM ANYMORE!

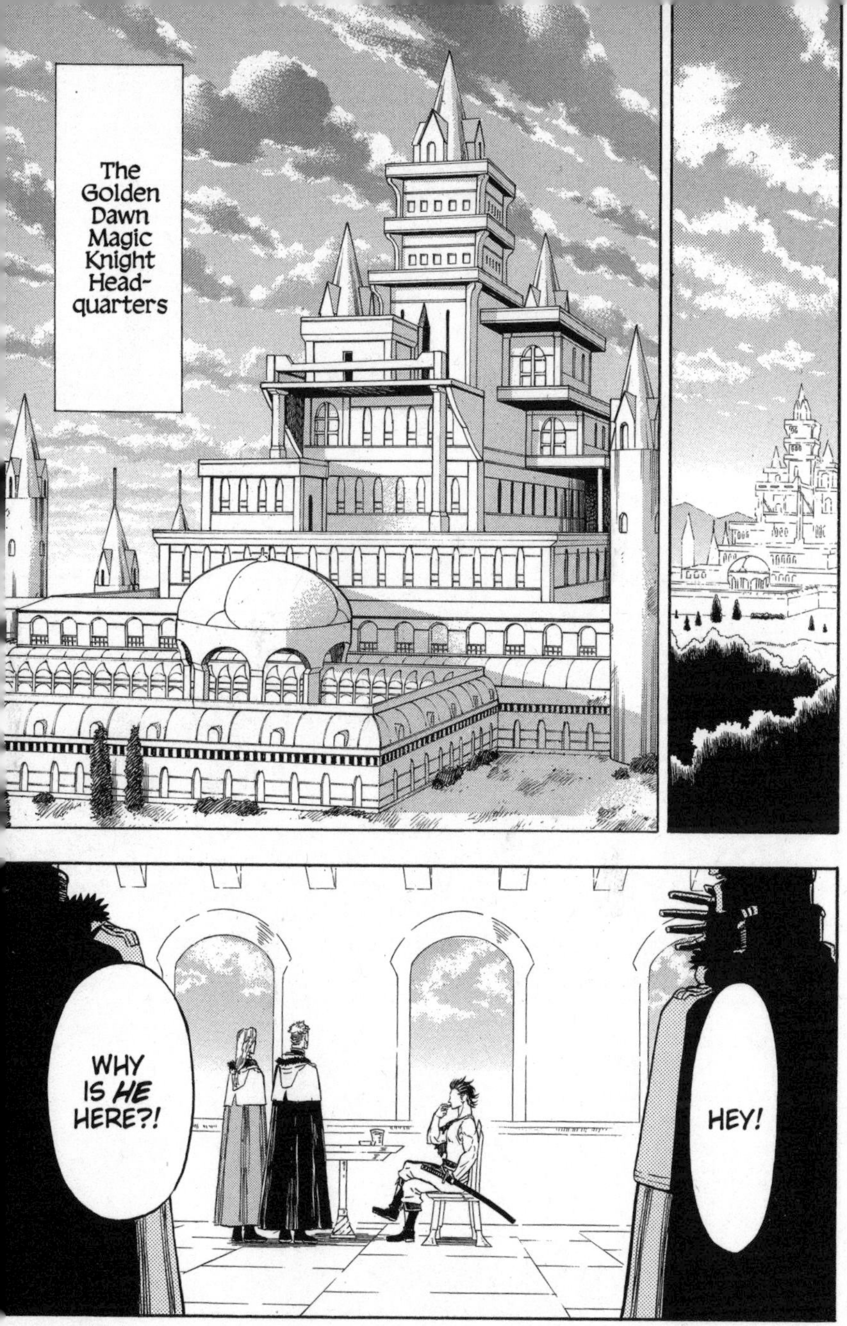
The Golden Dawn Magic Knight Head-quarters
HEY!
WHY IS *HE* HERE?!

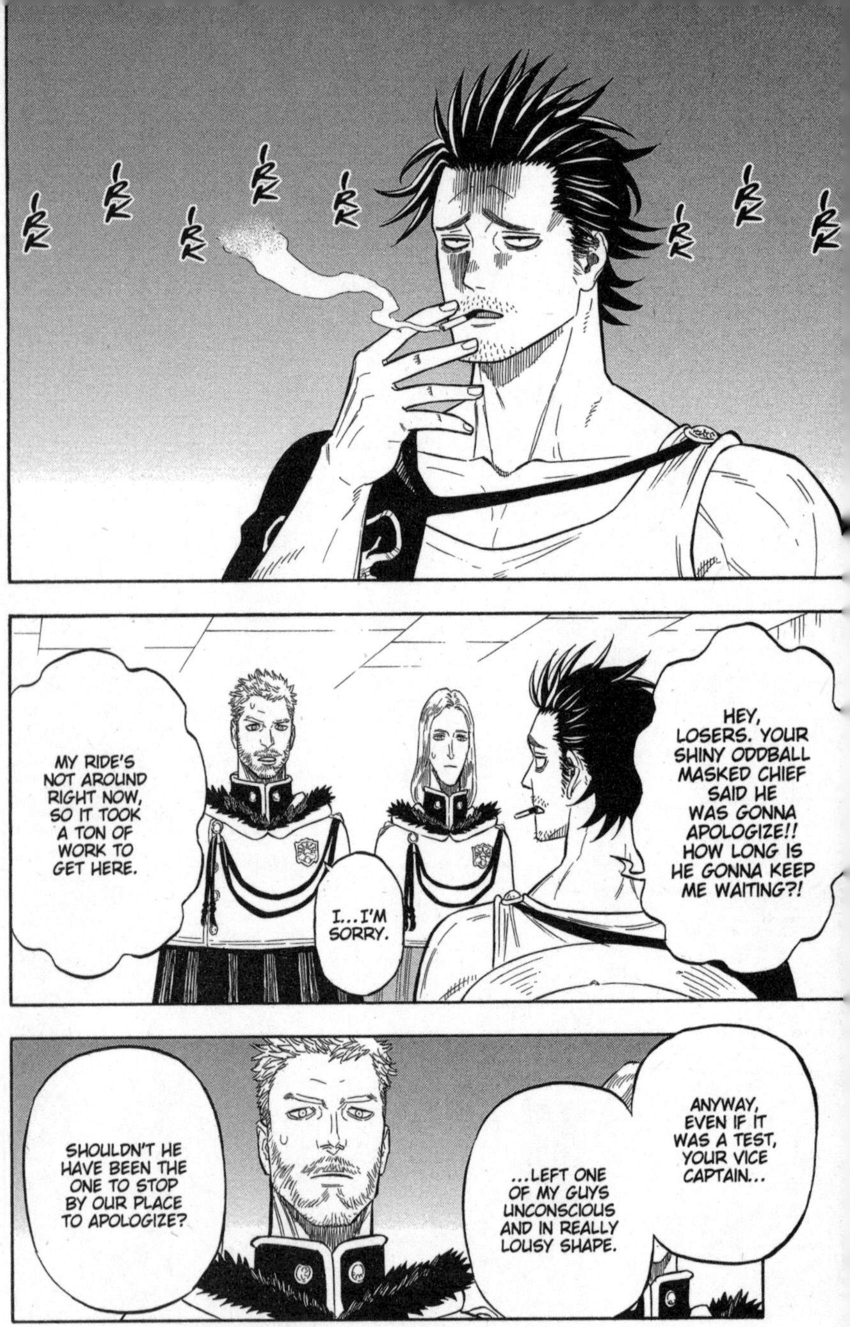
IRK
IRK
IRK
IRK
IRK
IRK
IRK
IRK
HEY, LOSERS. YOUR SHINY ODDBALL MASKED CHIEF SAID HE WAS GONNA APOLOGIZE!! HOW LONG IS HE GONNA KEEP ME WAITING?!
I...I'M SORRY.
MY RIDE'S NOT AROUND RIGHT NOW, SO IT TOOK A TON OF WORK TO GET HERE.
ANYWAY, EVEN IF IT WAS A TEST, YOUR VICE CAPTAIN...
...LEFT ONE OF MY GUYS UNCONSCIOUS AND IN REALLY LOUSY SHAPE.
SHOULDN'T HE HAVE BEEN THE ONE TO STOP BY OUR PLACE TO APOLOGIZE?

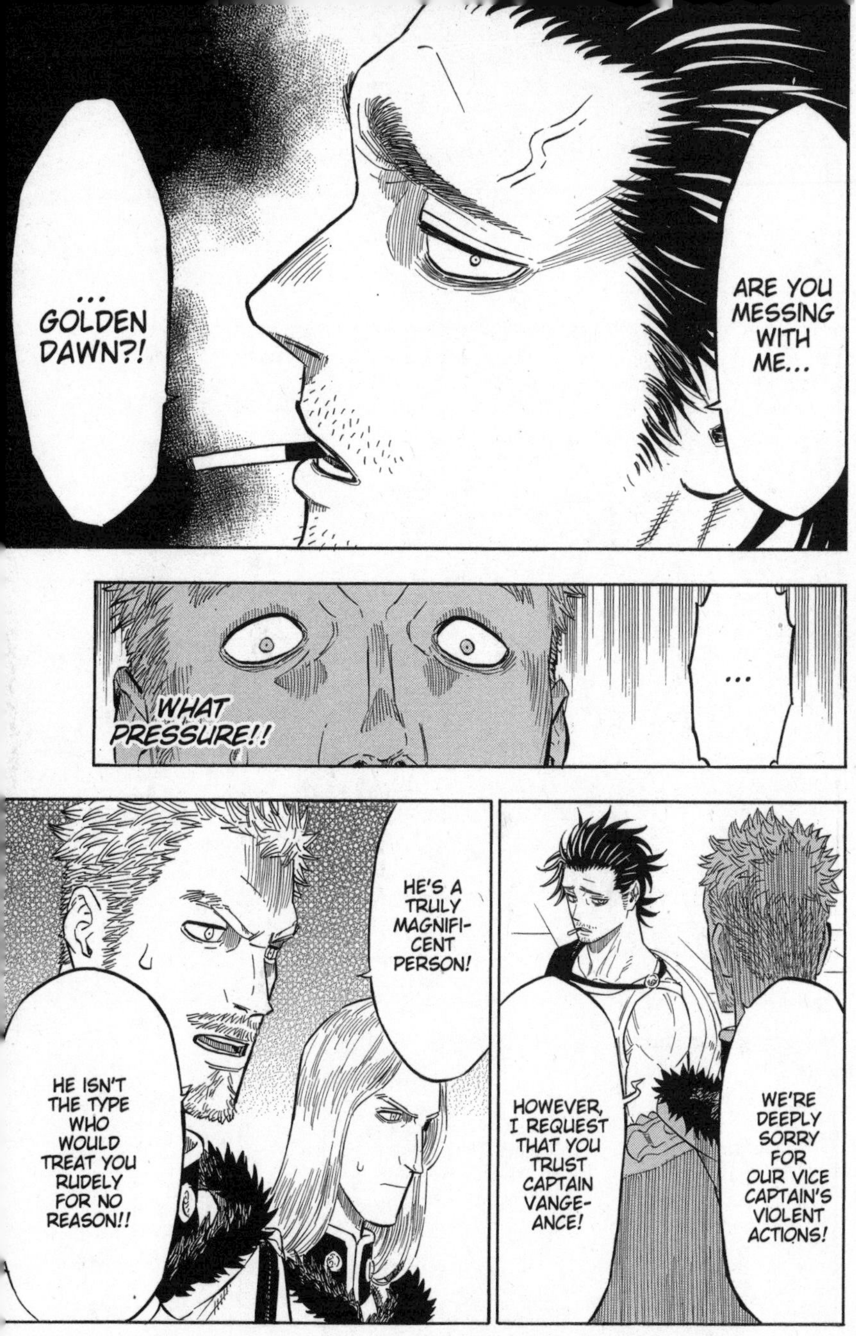
ARE YOU MESSING WITH ME...
... GOLDEN DAWN?!
...
WHAT PRESSURE!!
WE'RE DEEPLY SORRY FOR OUR VICE CAPTAIN'S VIOLENT ACTIONS!
HOWEVER, I REQUEST THAT YOU TRUST CAPTAIN VANGE-ANCE!
HE'S A TRULY MAGNIFI-CENT PERSON!
HE ISN'T THE TYPE WHO WOULD TREAT YOU RUDELY FOR NO REASON!!

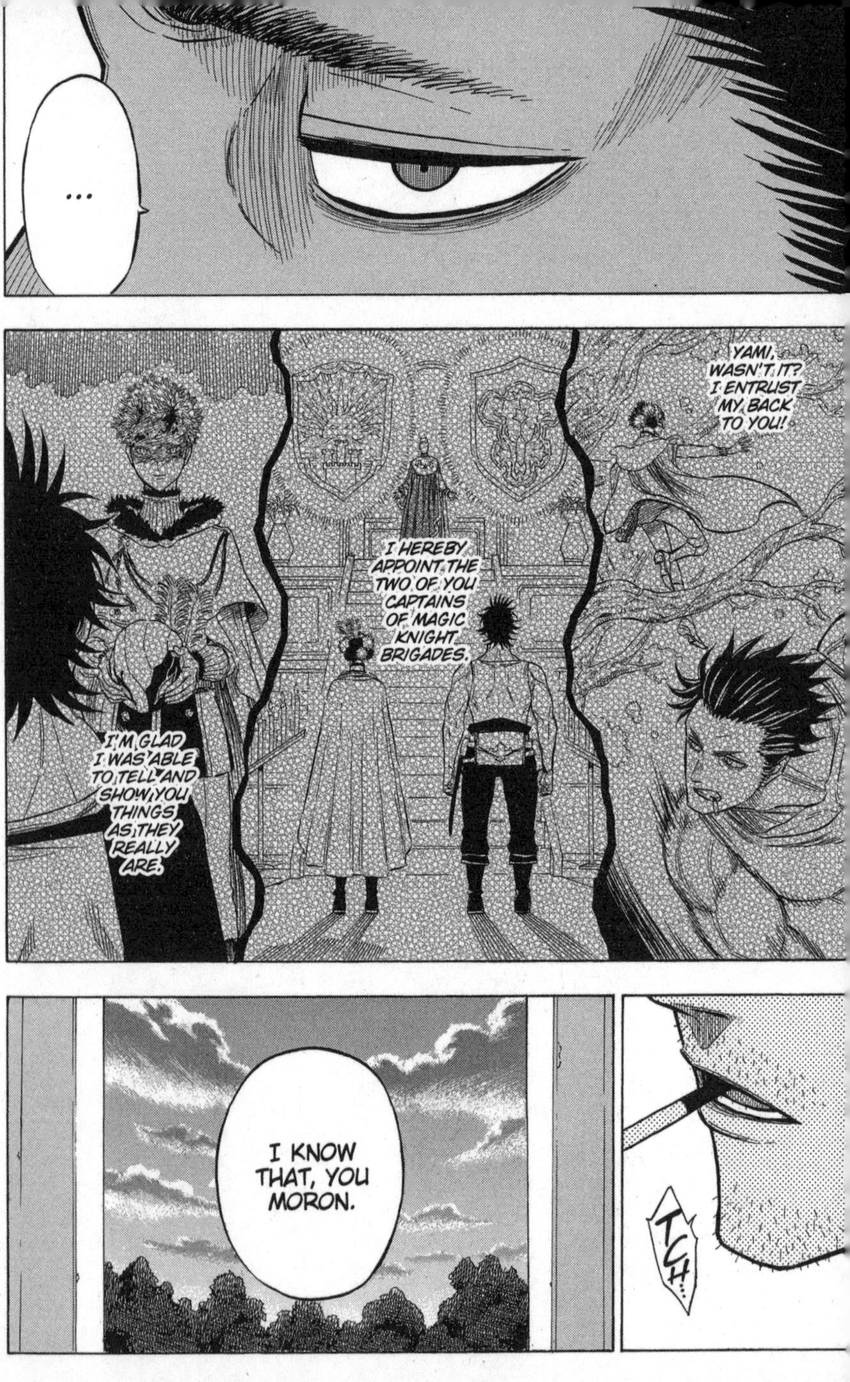
...
YAMI, WASN'T IT? I ENTRUST MY BACK TO YOU!
I HEREBY APPOINT THE TWO OF YOU CAPTAINS OF MAGIC KNIGHT BRIGADES.
I'M GLAD I WAS ABLE TO TELL AND SHOW YOU THINGS AS THEY REALLY ARE.
TCH...
I KNOW THAT, YOU MORON.

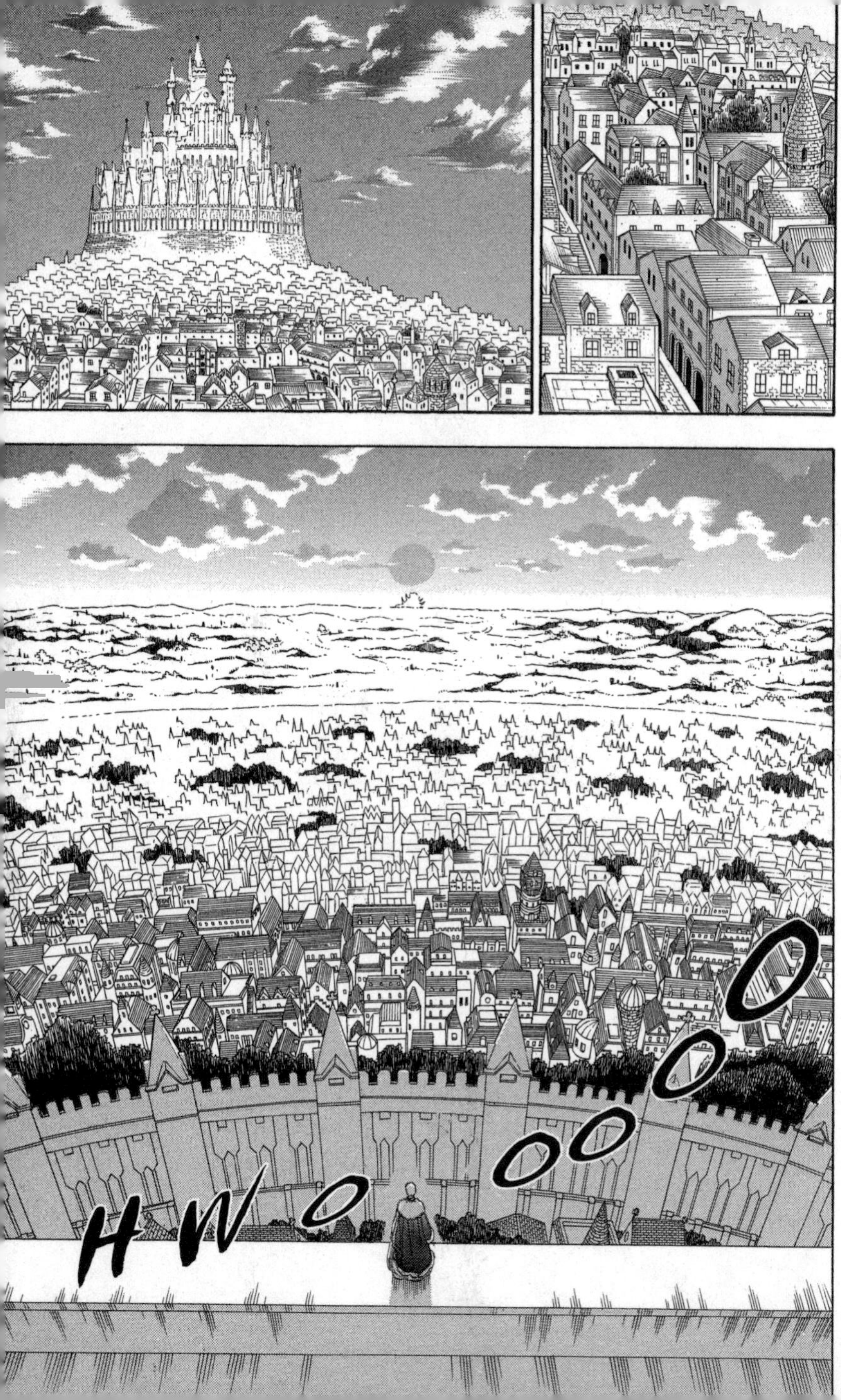
HWOOOOO

HWOO OC

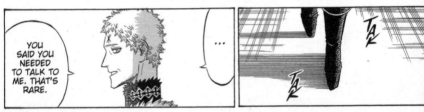

YOU SAID YOU NEEDED TO TALK TO ME. THAT'S RARE.

...

WHAT IS IT...

HWOO OOO

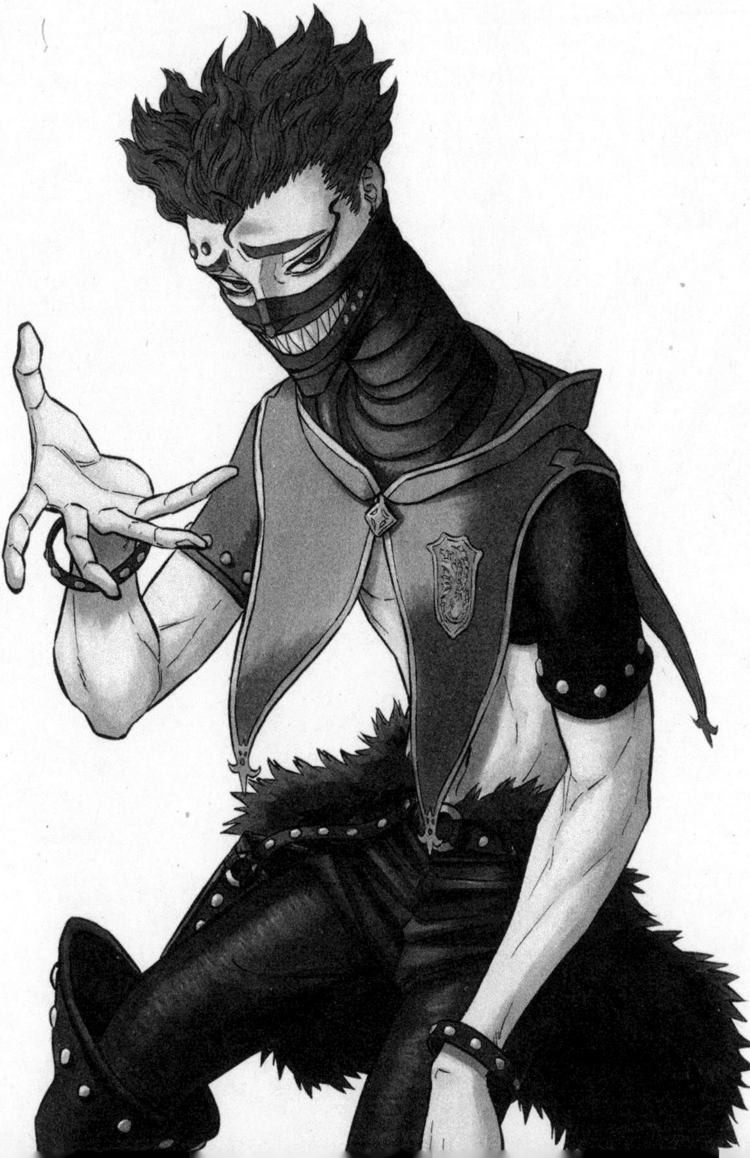

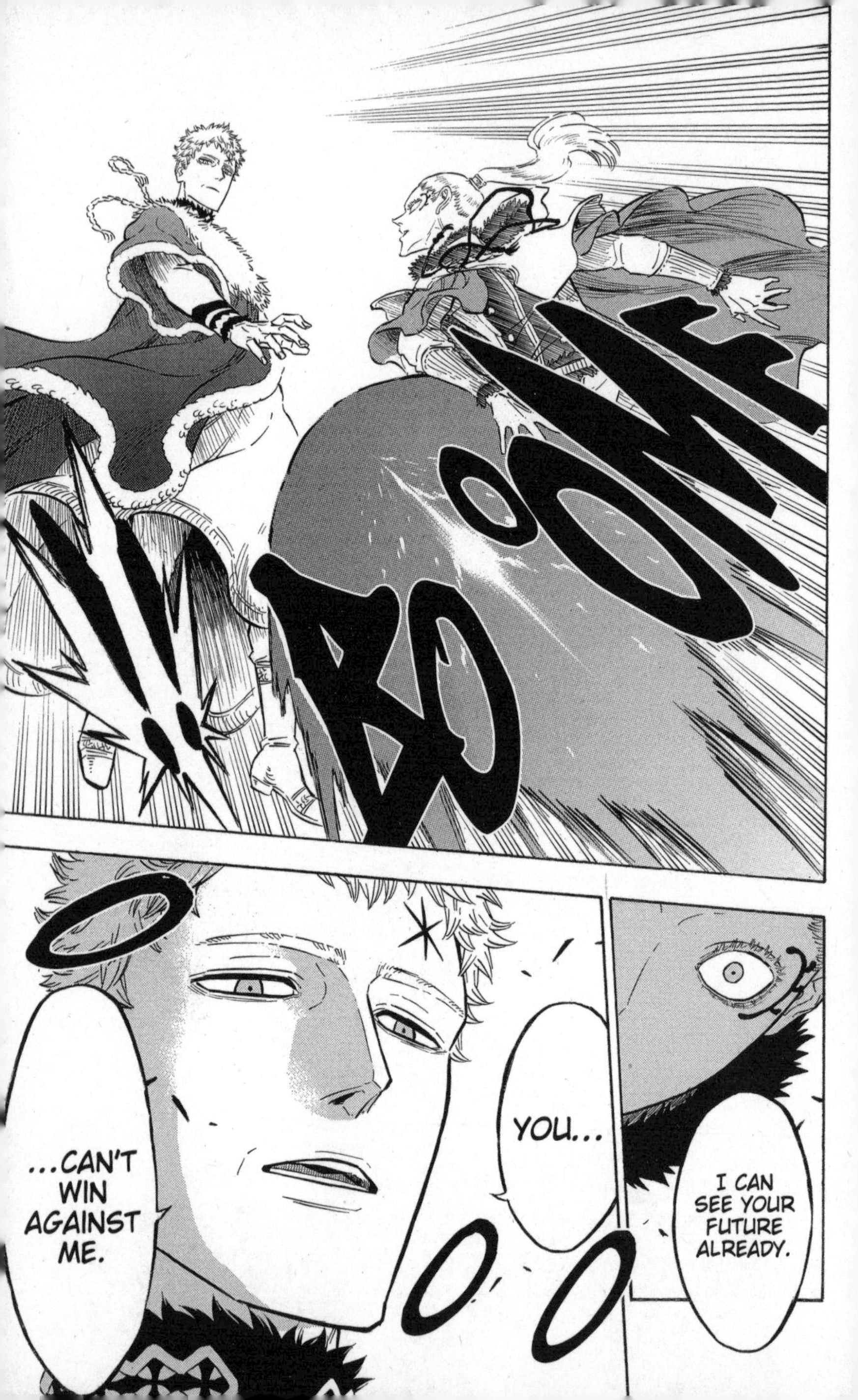
BOOOM
I CAN SEE YOUR FUTURE ALREADY.
YOU...
...CAN'T WIN AGAINST ME.

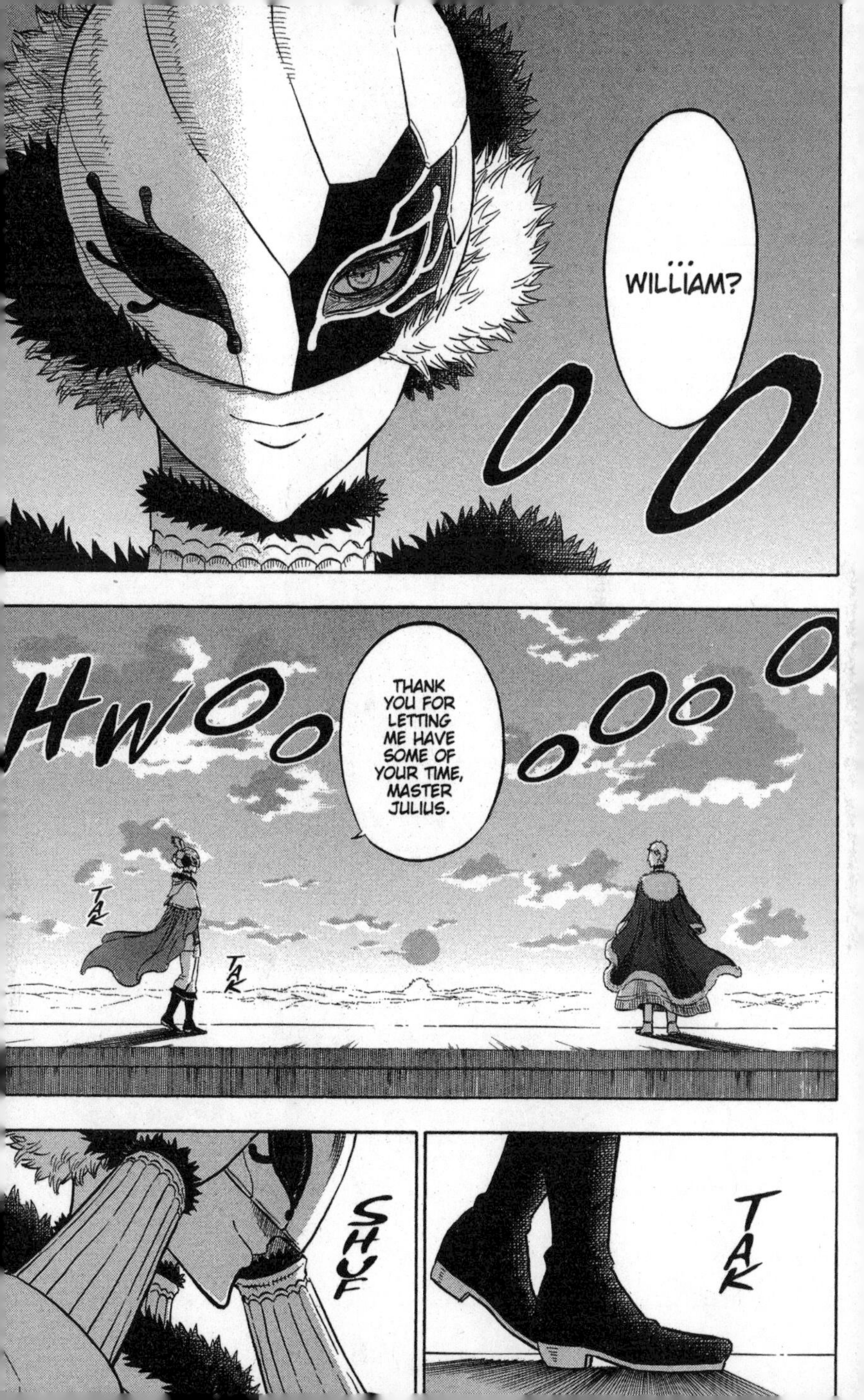

...WILLIAM?
HWOOOOOOO
THANK YOU FOR LETTING ME HAVE SOME OF YOUR TIME, MASTER JULIUS.
TAK
TAK
TAK
SHUF

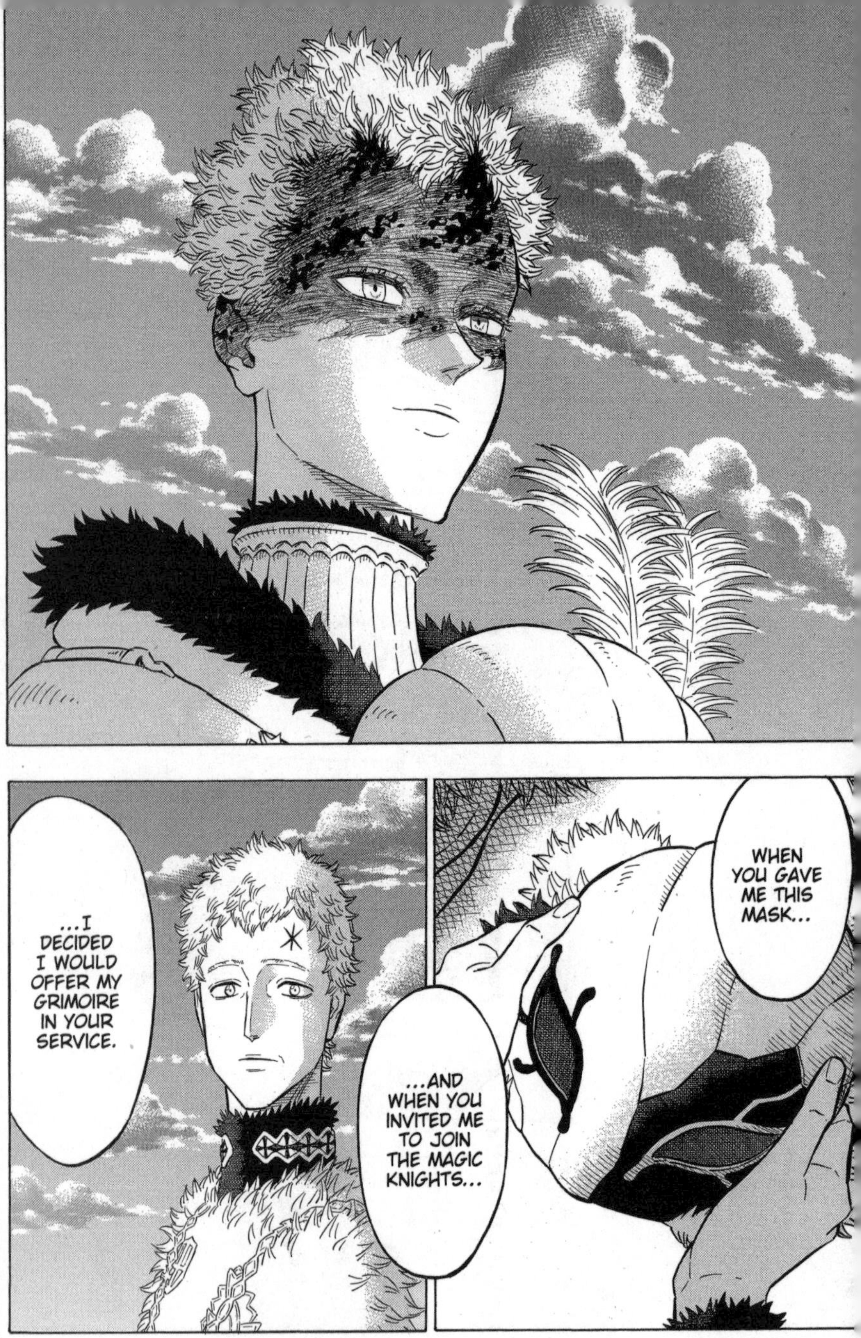
WHEN YOU GAVE ME THIS MASK...
...AND WHEN YOU INVITED ME TO JOIN THE MAGIC KNIGHTS...
...I DECIDED I WOULD OFFER MY GRIMOIRE IN YOUR SERVICE.

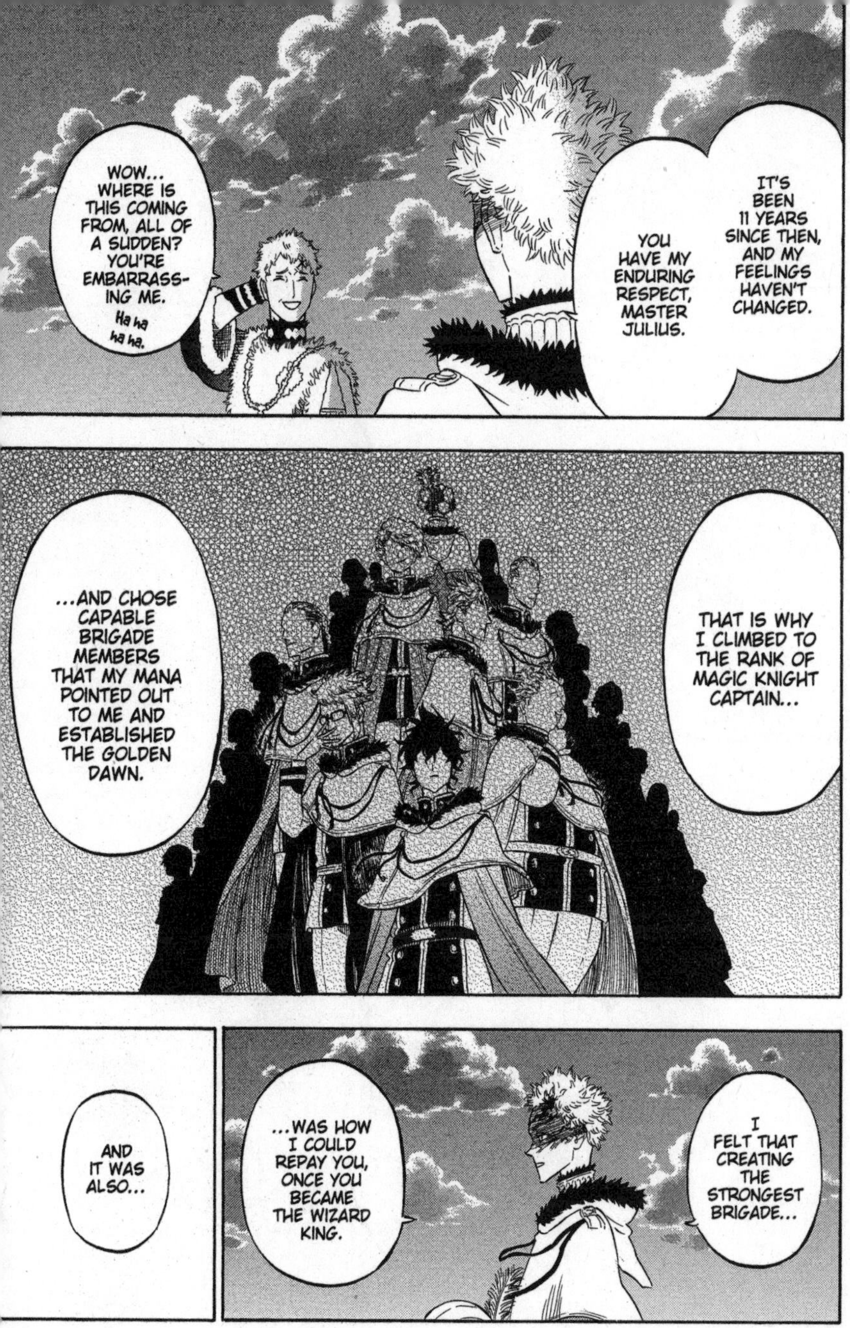
IT'S BEEN 11 YEARS SINCE THEN, AND MY FEELINGS HAVEN'T CHANGED.
YOU HAVE MY ENDURING RESPECT, MASTER JULIUS.
WOW... WHERE IS THIS COMING FROM, ALL OF A SUDDEN? YOU'RE EMBARRASS-ING ME.
Ha ha ha ha.
THAT IS WHY I CLIMBED TO THE RANK OF MAGIC KNIGHT CAPTAIN...
...AND CHOSE CAPABLE BRIGADE MEMBERS THAT MY MANA POINTED OUT TO ME AND ESTABLISHED THE GOLDEN DAWN.
I FELT THAT CREATING THE STRONGEST BRIGADE...
...WAS HOW I COULD REPAY YOU, ONCE YOU BECAME THE WIZARD KING.
AND IT WAS ALSO...

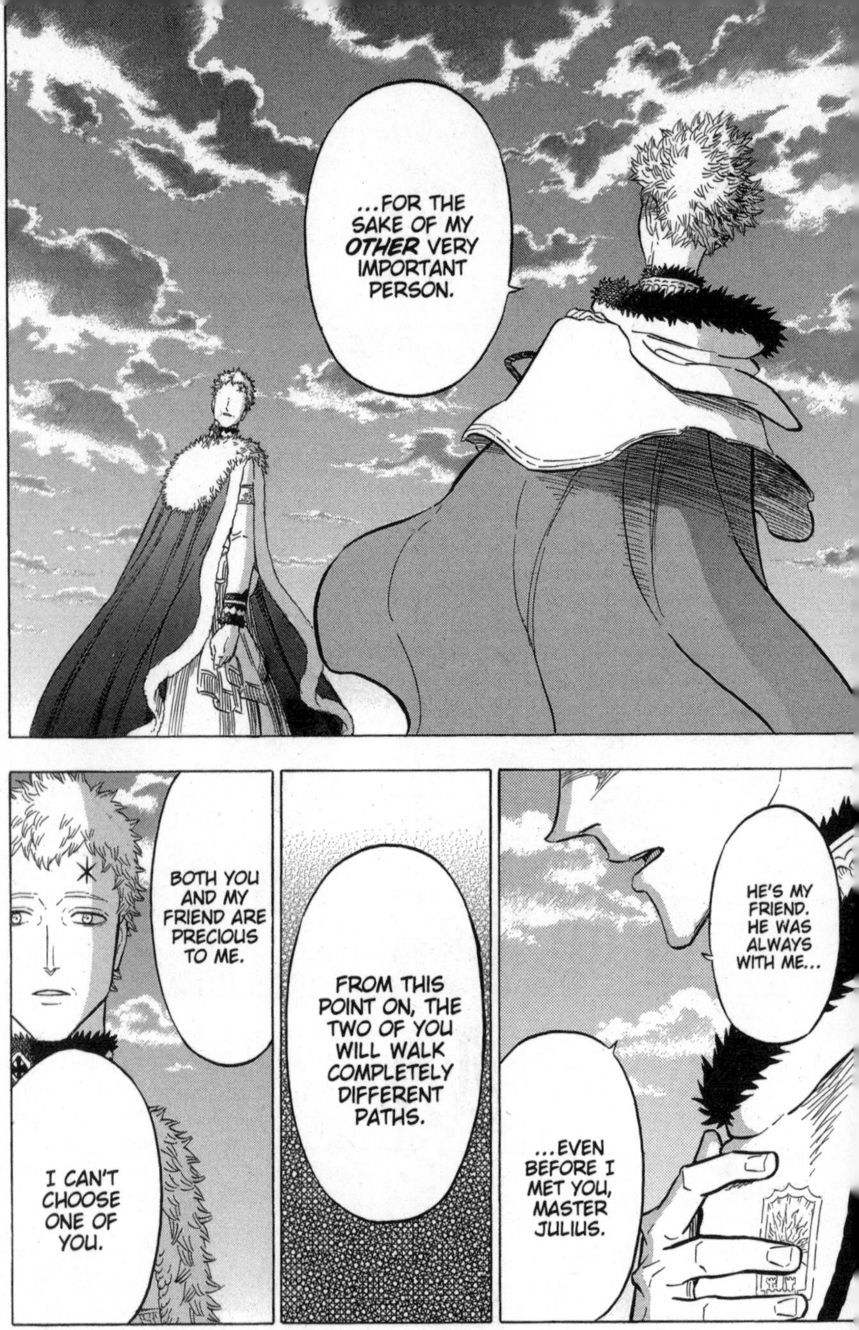
...FOR THE SAKE OF MY *OTHER* VERY IMPORTANT PERSON.
HE'S MY FRIEND. HE WAS ALWAYS WITH ME...
...EVEN BEFORE I MET YOU, MASTER JULIUS.
FROM THIS POINT ON, THE TWO OF YOU WILL WALK COMPLETELY DIFFERENT PATHS.
BOTH YOU AND MY FRIEND ARE PRECIOUS TO ME.
I CAN'T CHOOSE ONE OF YOU.

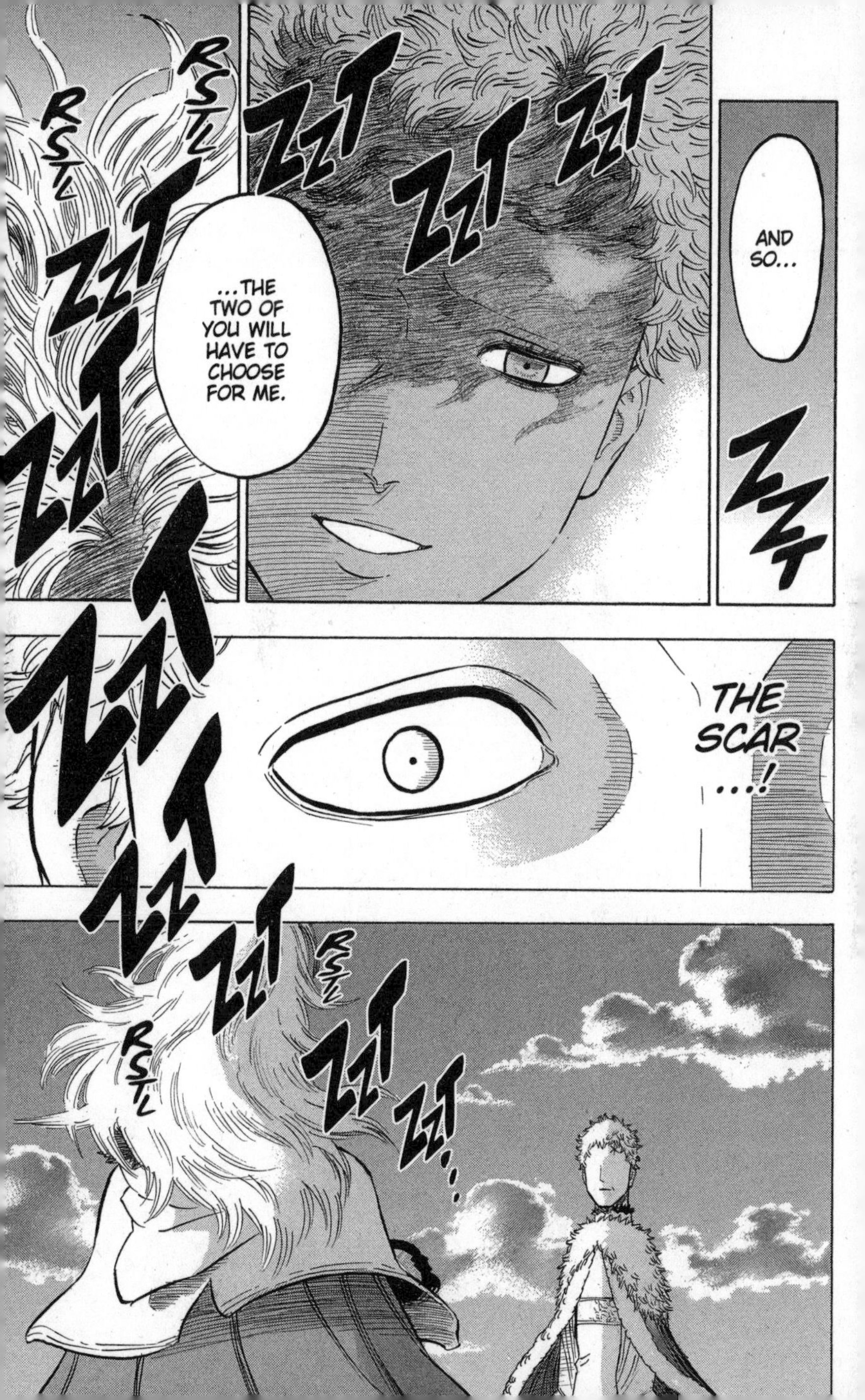
AND SO...
ZZT
...THE TWO OF YOU WILL HAVE TO CHOOSE FOR ME.
ZZT
ZZT
ZZT
RSTL
RSTL
ZZT
ZZT
ZZT
THE SCAR ...!
ZZT
RSTL
RSTL
ZZT
ZZT...

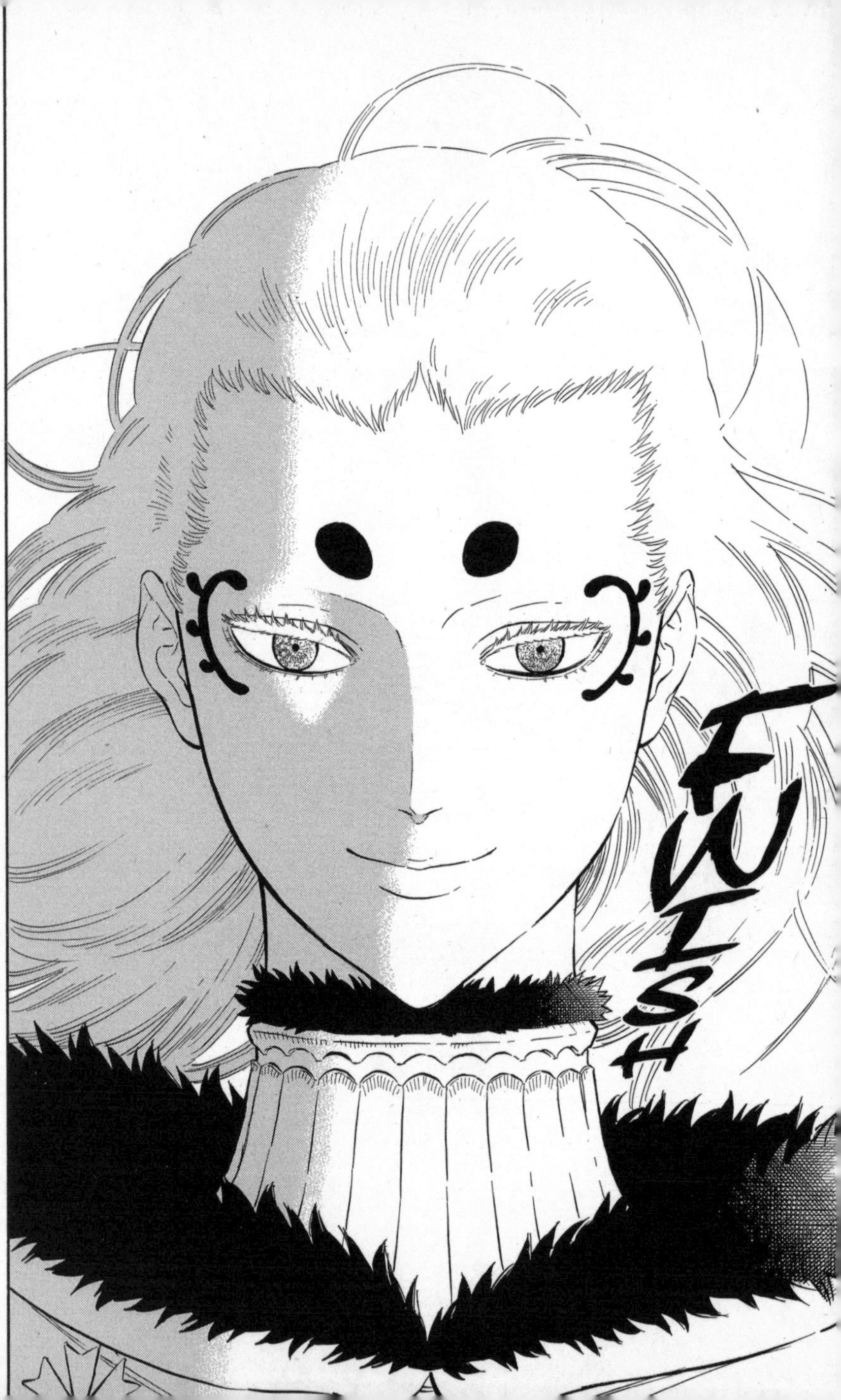
FWISH

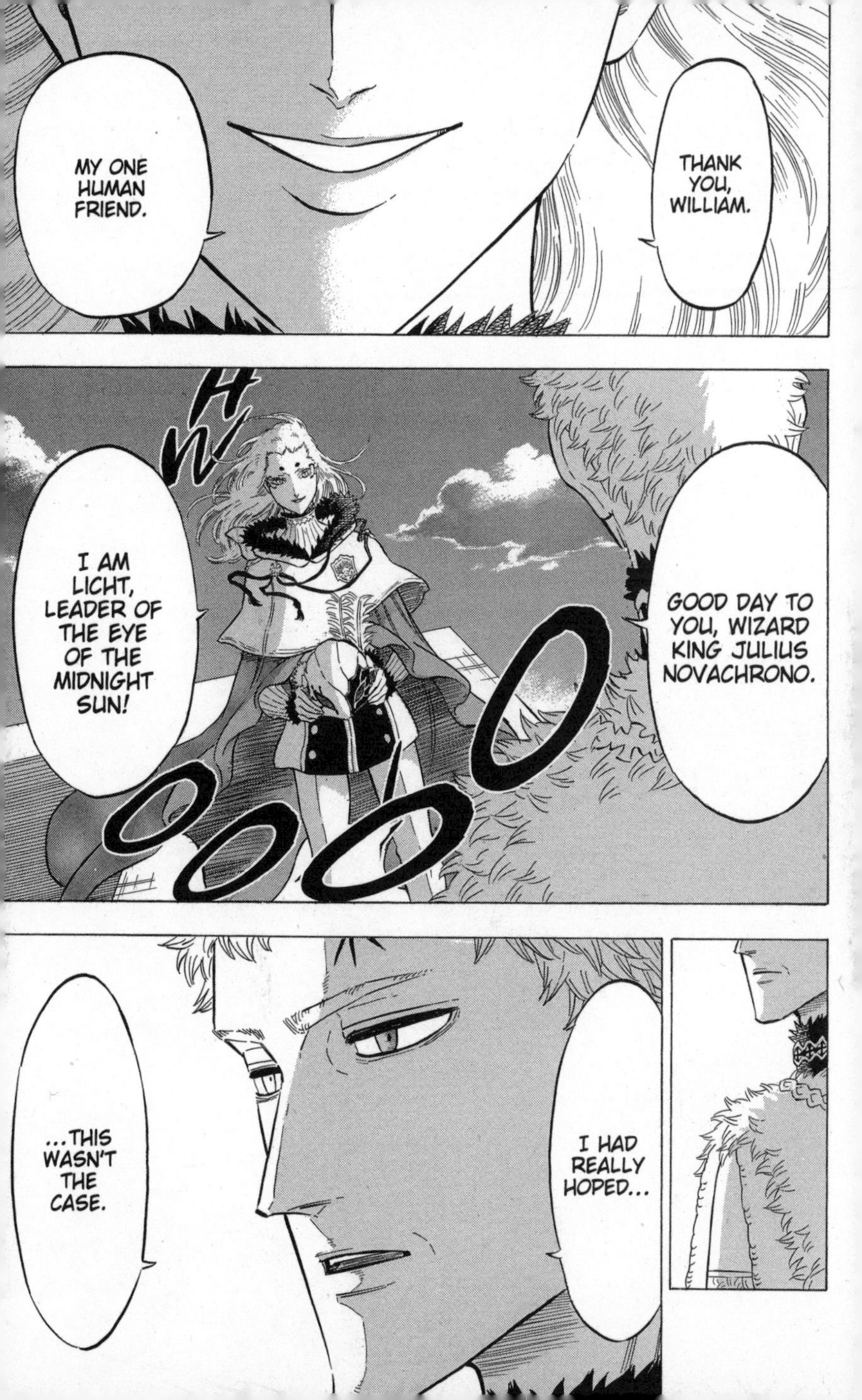
THANK YOU, WILLIAM.
MY ONE HUMAN FRIEND.
GOOD DAY TO YOU, WIZARD KING JULIUS NOVACHRONO.
I AM LICHT, LEADER OF THE EYE OF THE MIDNIGHT SUN!
I HAD REALLY HOPED...
...THIS WASN'T THE CASE.

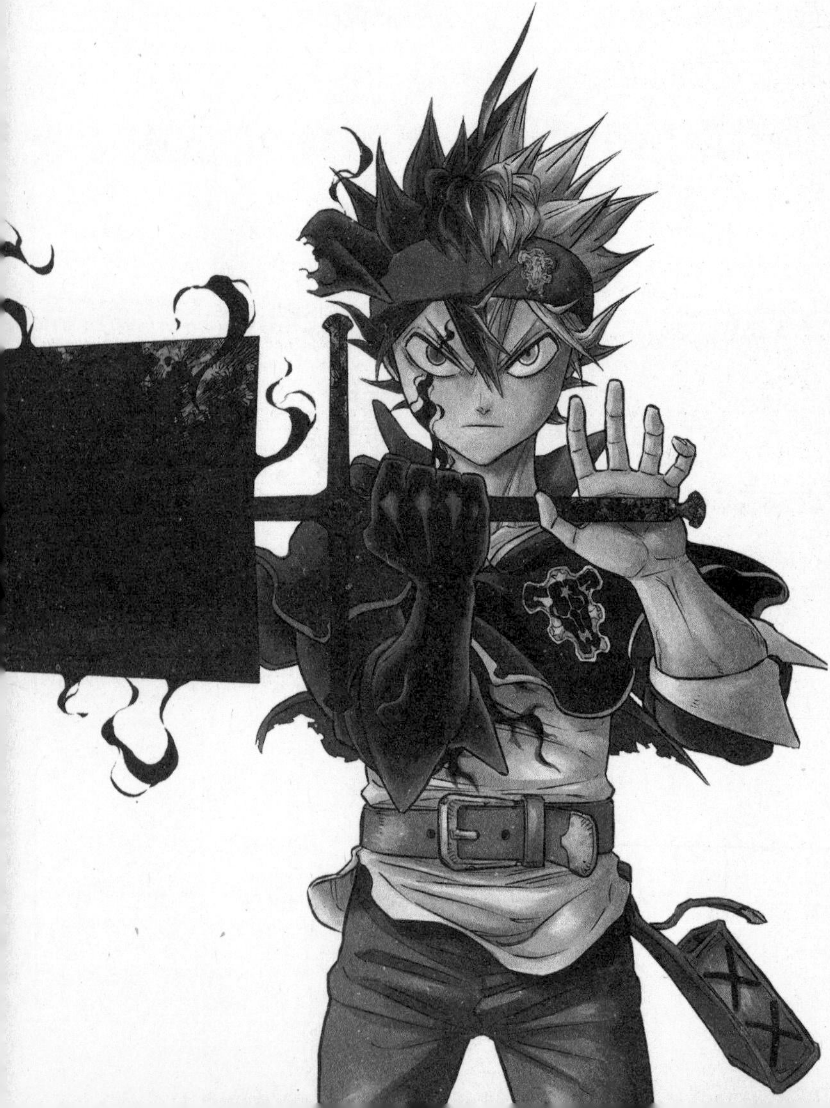

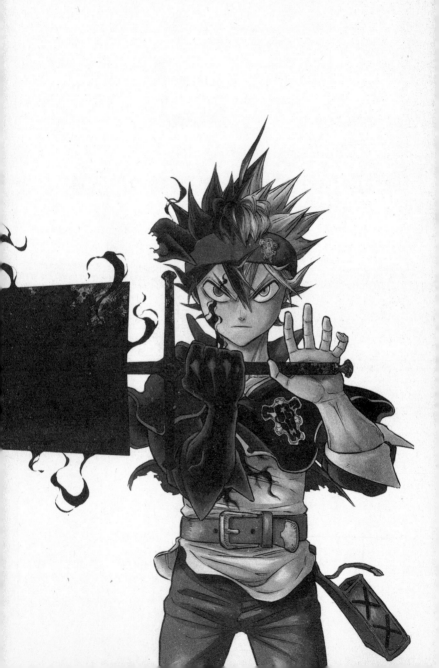

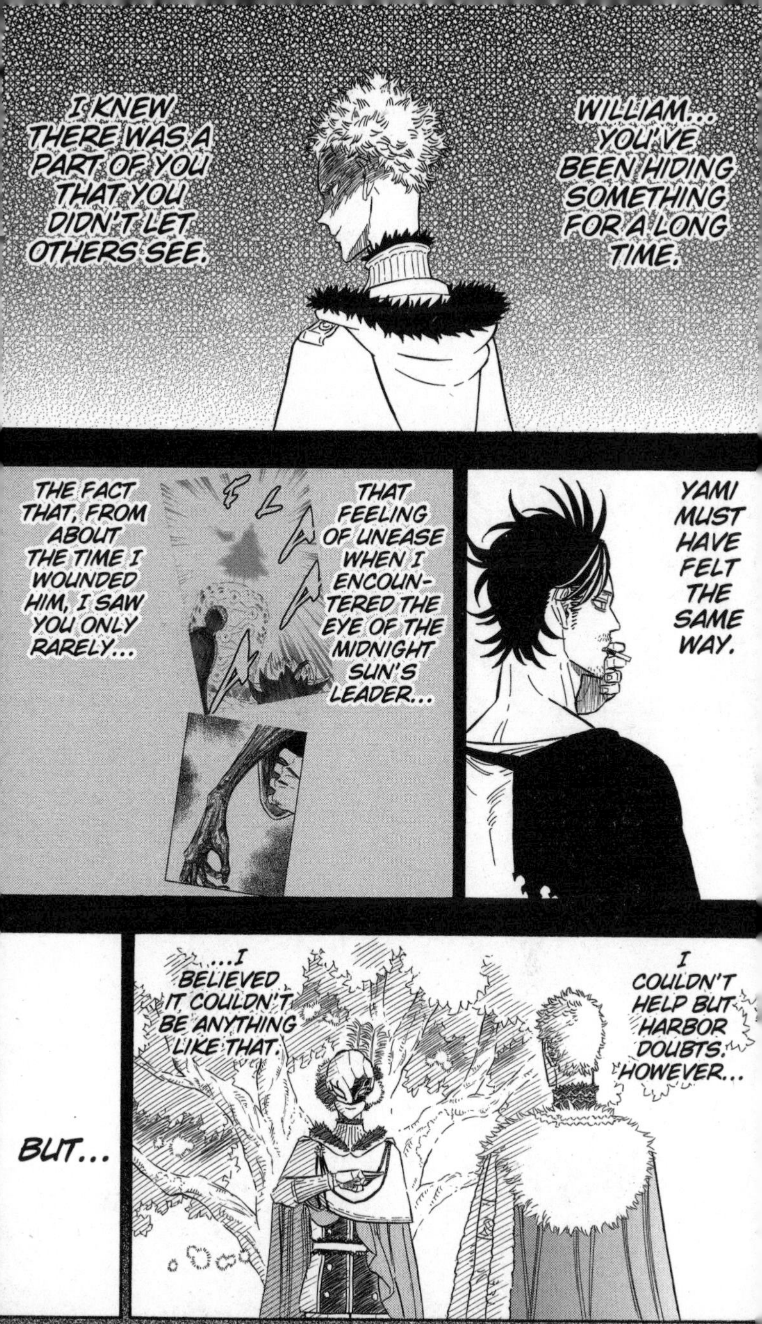
WILLIAM... YOU'VE BEEN HIDING SOMETHING FOR A LONG TIME.
I KNEW THERE WAS A PART OF YOU THAT YOU DIDN'T LET OTHERS SEE.
YAMI MUST HAVE FELT THE SAME WAY.
THAT FEELING OF UNEASE WHEN I ENCOUNTERED THE EYE OF THE MIDNIGHT SUN'S LEADER...
THE FACT THAT, FROM ABOUT THE TIME I WOUNDED HIM, I SAW YOU ONLY RARELY...
I COULDN'T HELP BUT HARBOR DOUBTS. HOWEVER...
...I BELIEVED IT COULDN'T BE ANYTHING LIKE THAT.
BUT...

Page 143: The Wizard King vs. the Leader of the Eye of the Midnight Sun

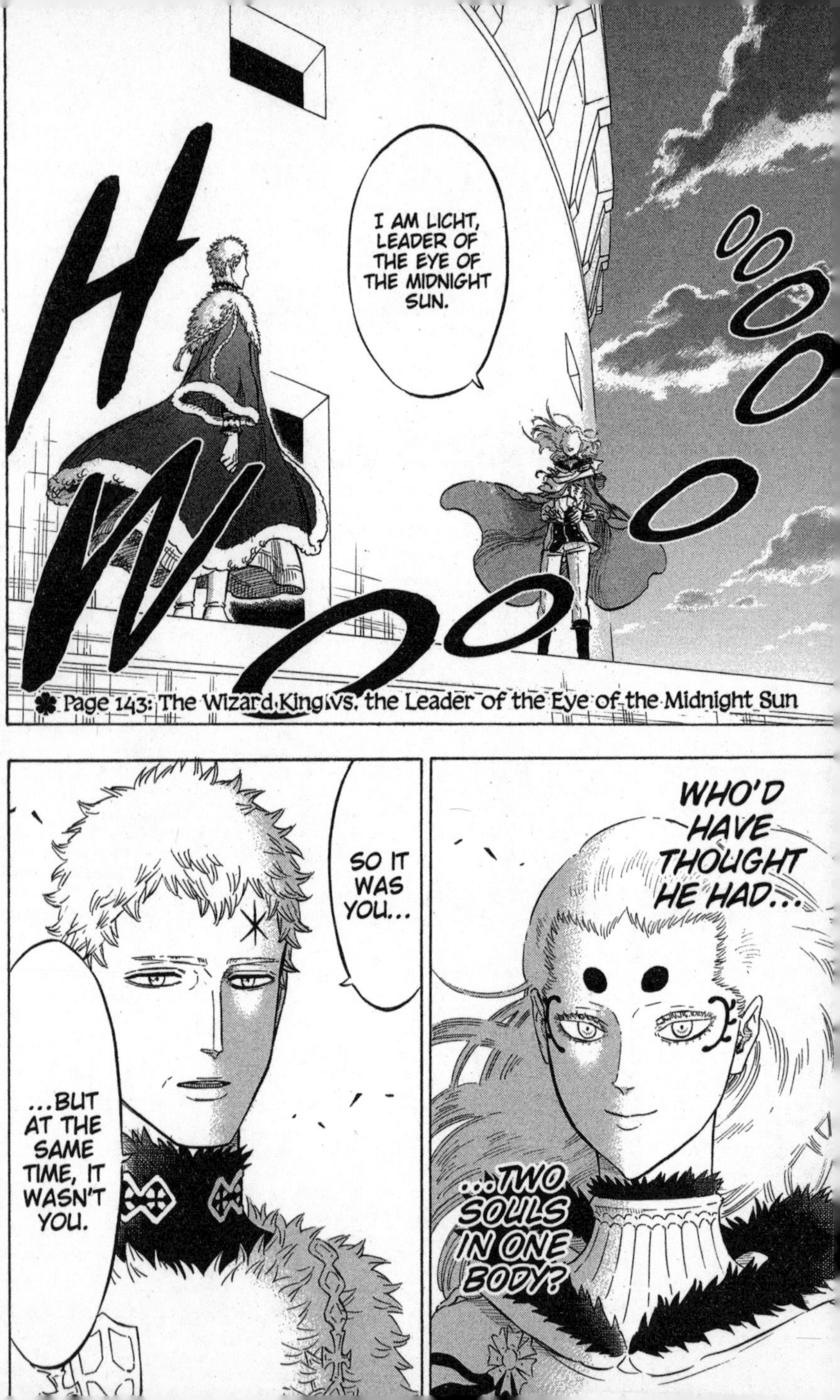
HWOOOOOOOOO
I AM LICHT, LEADER OF THE EYE OF THE MIDNIGHT SUN.
Page 143: The Wizard King vs. the Leader of the Eye of the Midnight Sun
WHO'D HAVE THOUGHT HE HAD...
...TWO SOULS IN ONE BODY?
SO IT WAS YOU...
...BUT AT THE SAME TIME, IT WASN'T YOU.

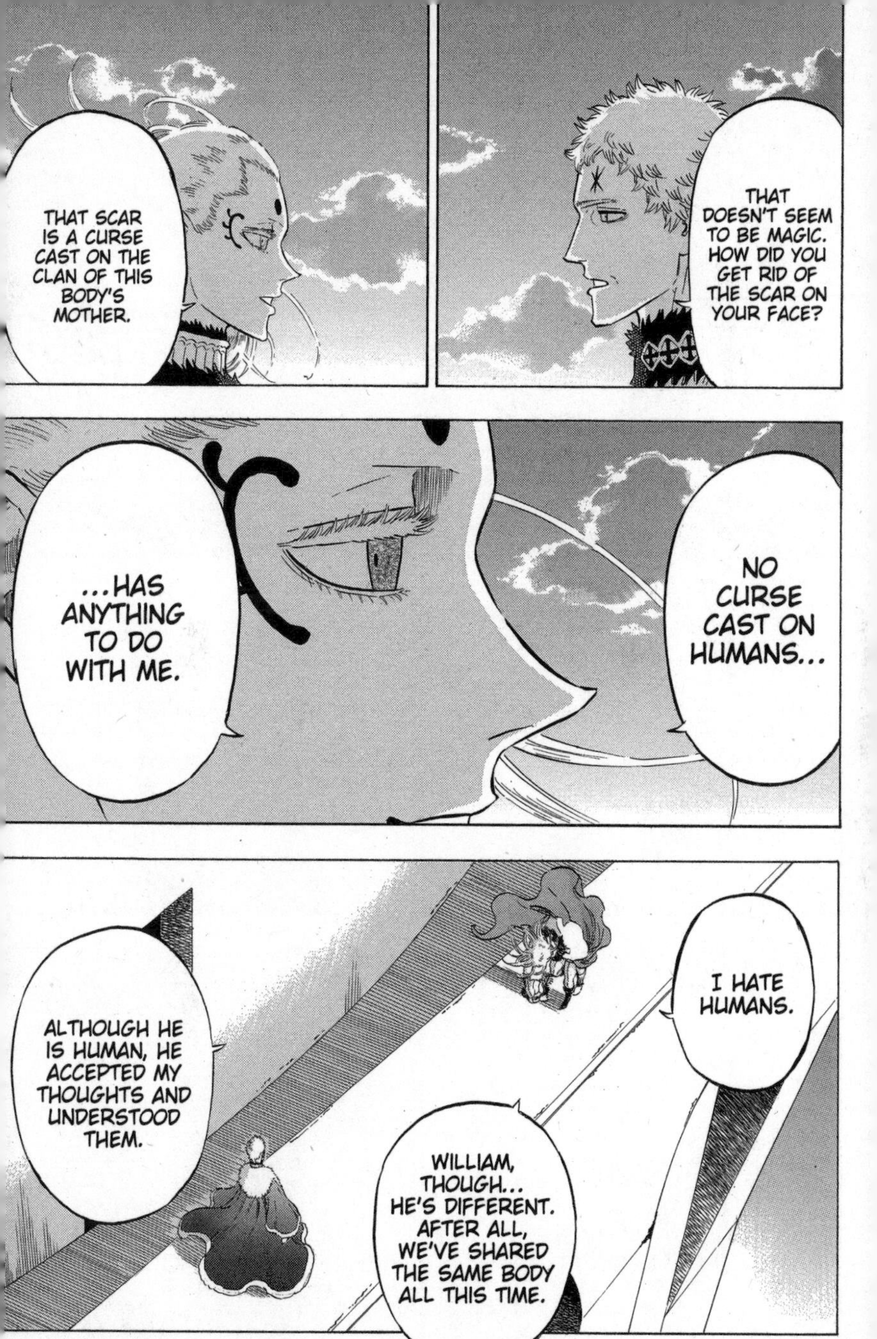
THAT DOESN'T SEEM TO BE MAGIC. HOW DID YOU GET RID OF THE SCAR ON YOUR FACE?
THAT SCAR IS A CURSE CAST ON THE CLAN OF THIS BODY'S MOTHER.
NO CURSE CAST ON HUMANS...
...HAS ANYTHING TO DO WITH ME.
I HATE HUMANS.
WILLIAM, THOUGH... HE'S DIFFERENT. AFTER ALL, WE'VE SHARED THE SAME BODY ALL THIS TIME.
ALTHOUGH HE IS HUMAN, HE ACCEPTED MY THOUGHTS AND UNDERSTOOD THEM.

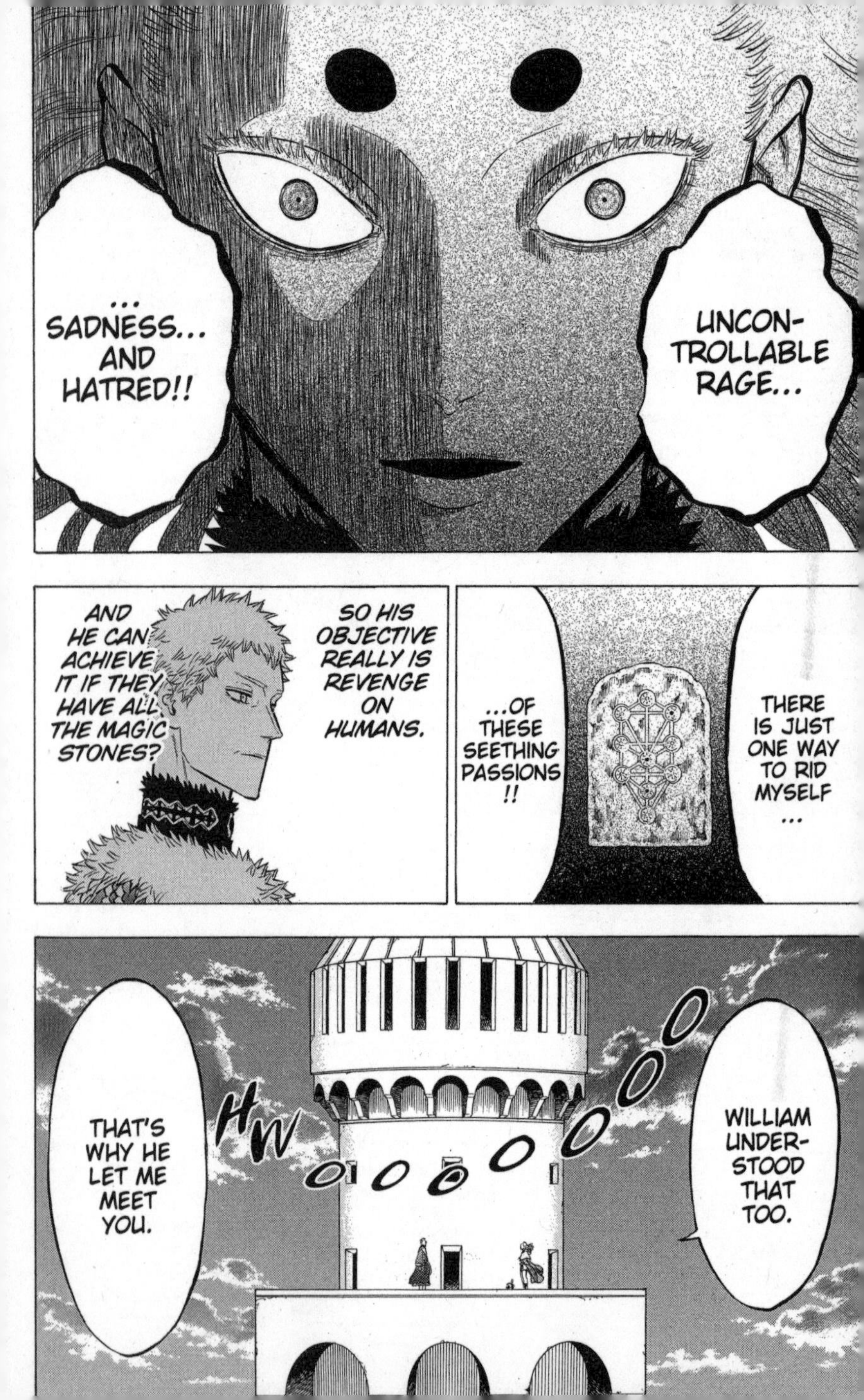
UNCON-TROLLABLE RAGE...
...SADNESS... AND HATRED!!
THERE IS JUST ONE WAY TO RID MYSELF...
...OF THESE SEETHING PASSIONS!!
SO HIS OBJECTIVE REALLY IS REVENGE ON HUMANS.
AND HE CAN ACHIEVE IT IF THEY HAVE ALL THE MAGIC STONES?
WILLIAM UNDER-STOOD THAT TOO.
HWOOOOOOOOOO
THAT'S WHY HE LET ME MEET YOU.

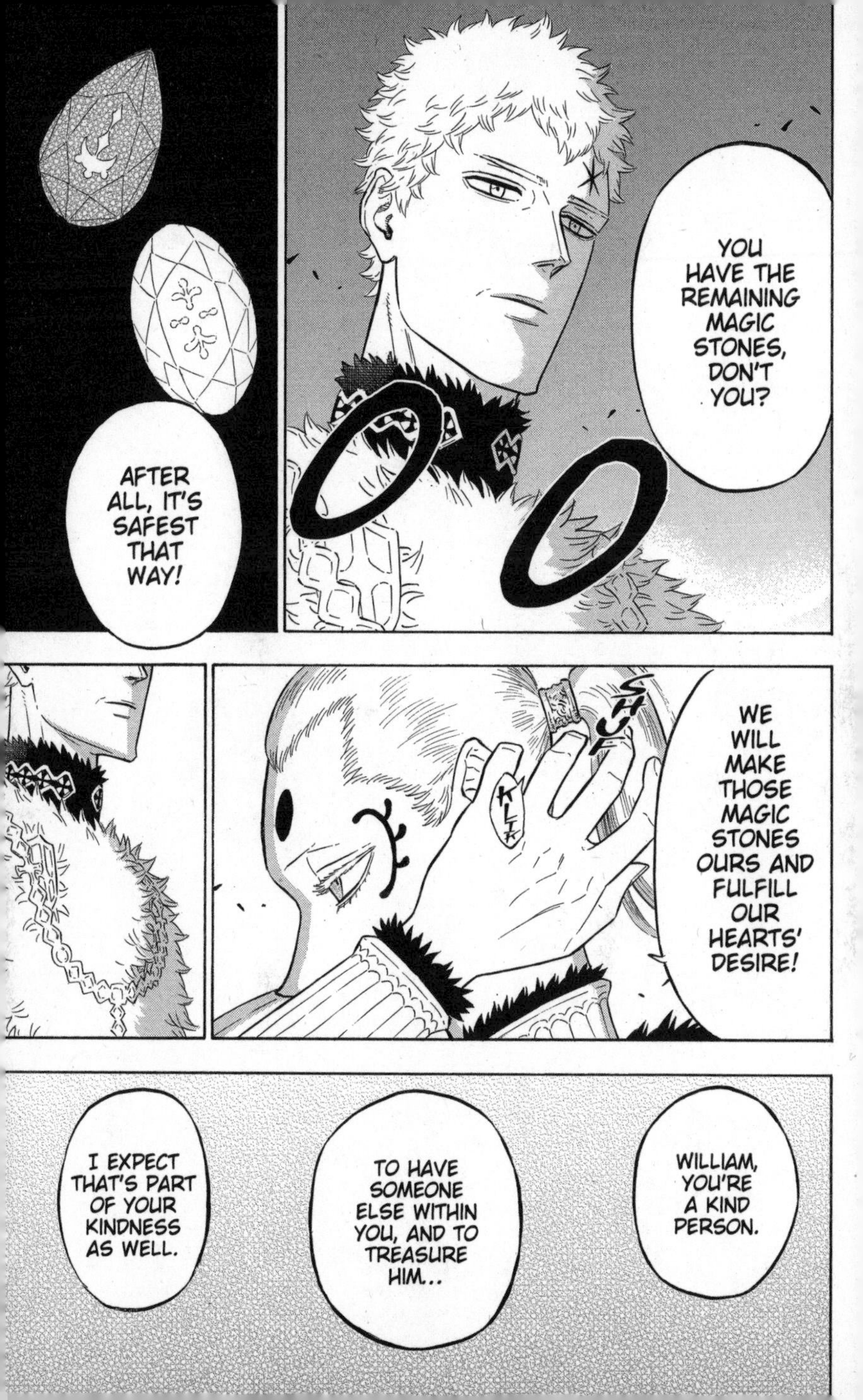
YOU HAVE THE REMAINING MAGIC STONES, DON'T YOU?
AFTER ALL, IT'S SAFEST THAT WAY!
WE WILL MAKE THOSE MAGIC STONES OURS AND FULFILL OUR HEARTS' DESIRE!
SHUF
KLIK
WILLIAM, YOU'RE A KIND PERSON.
TO HAVE SOMEONE ELSE WITHIN YOU, AND TO TREASURE HIM...
I EXPECT THAT'S PART OF YOUR KINDNESS AS WELL.

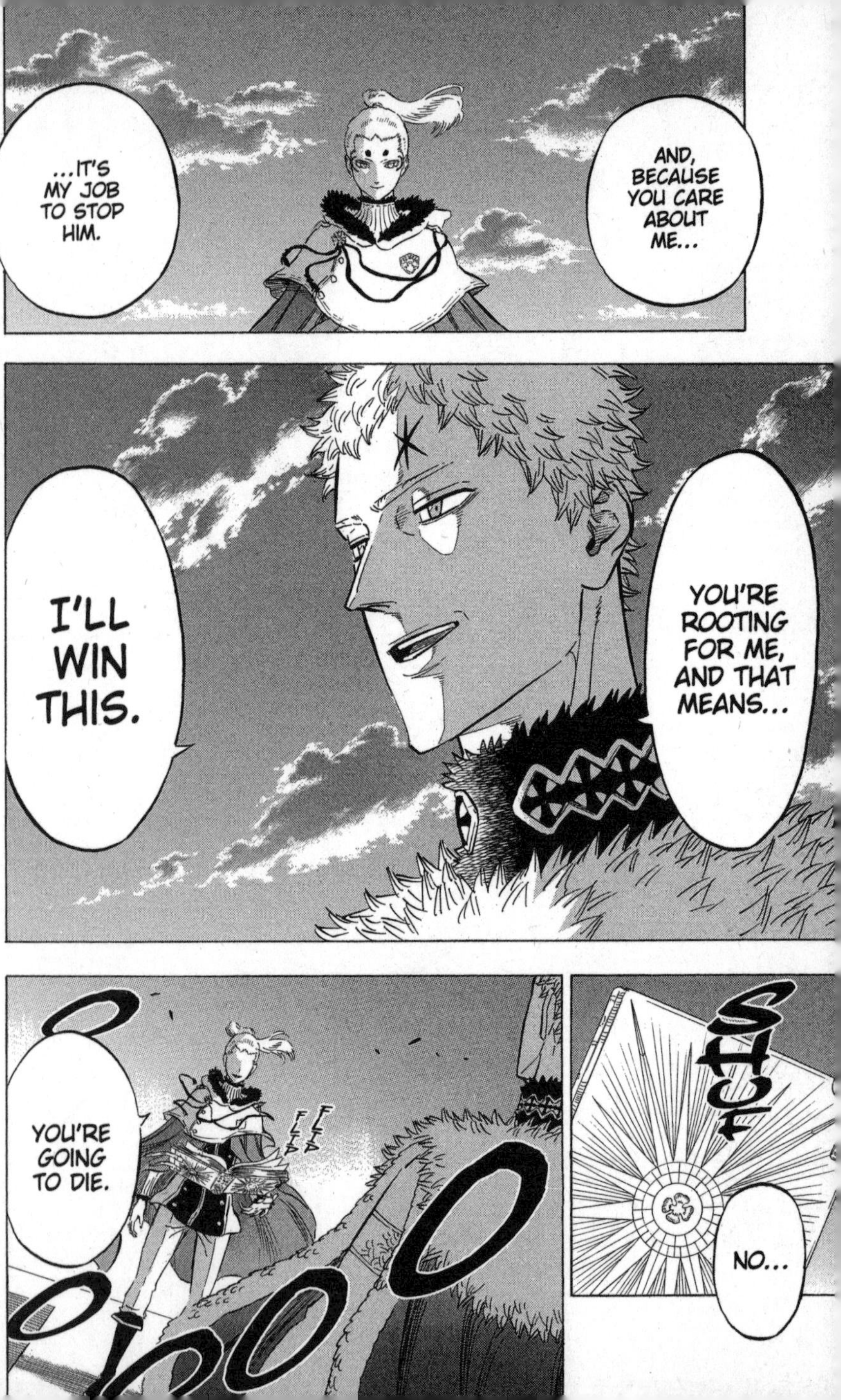
AND, BECAUSE YOU CARE ABOUT ME...
...IT'S MY JOB TO STOP HIM.
YOU'RE ROOTING FOR ME, AND THAT MEANS...
I'LL WIN THIS.
SHOF
NO...
FLIP FLIP
YOU'RE GOING TO DIE.

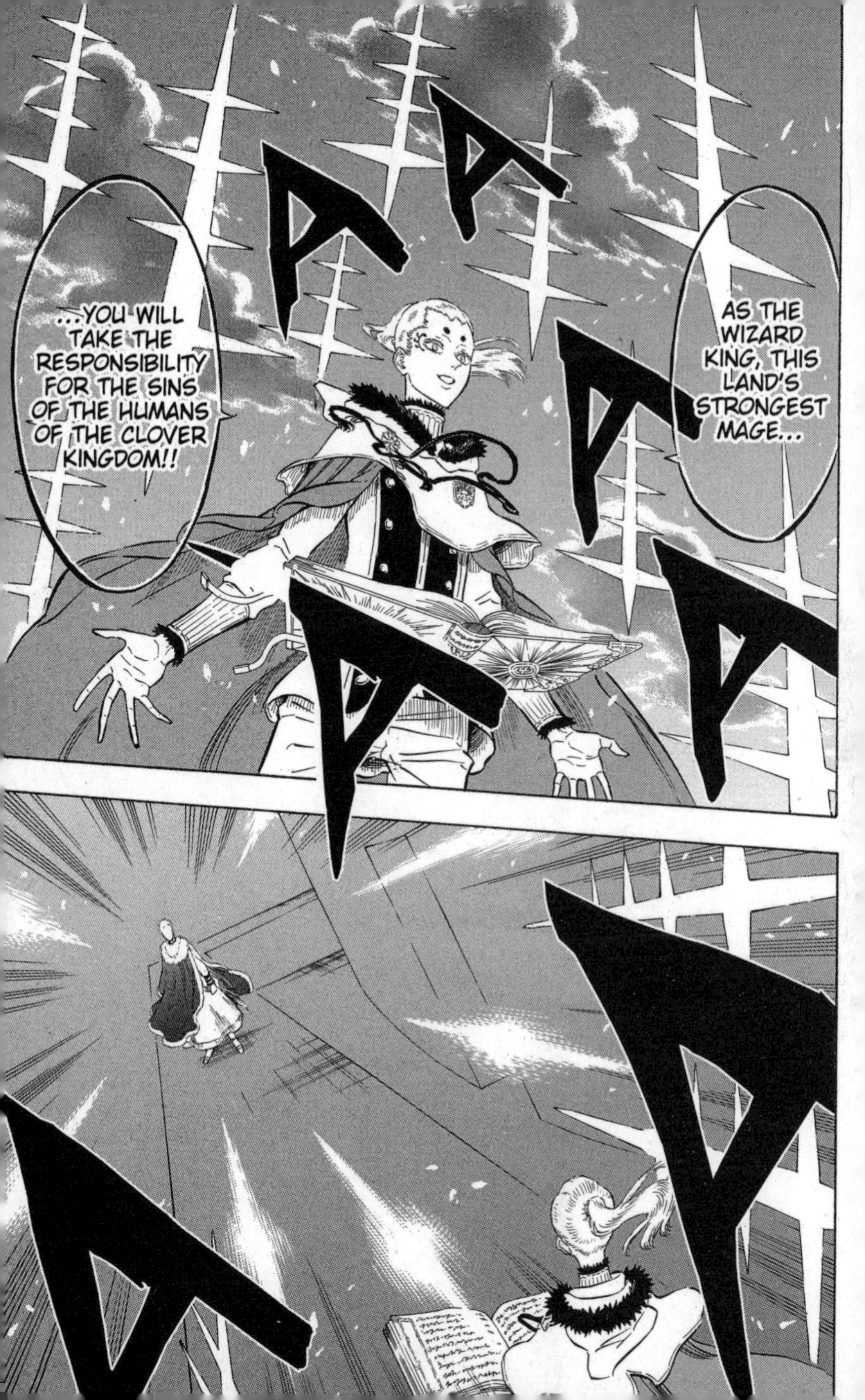
AS THE WIZARD KING, THIS LAND'S STRONGEST MAGE...
...YOU WILL TAKE THE RESPONSIBILITY FOR THE SINS OF THE HUMANS OF THE CLOVER KINGDOM!!

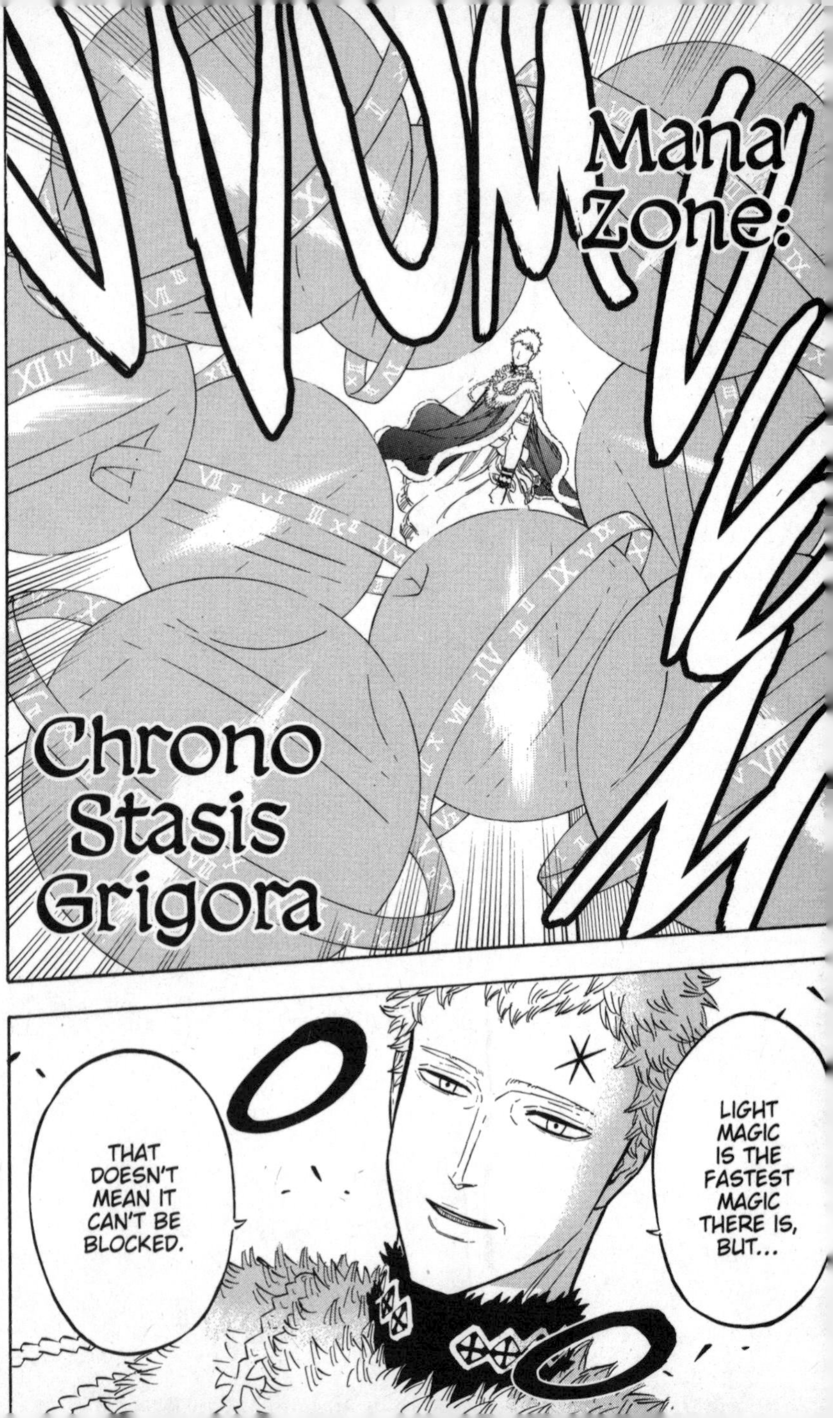
Mana Zone:
Chrono Stasis Grigora
LIGHT MAGIC IS THE FASTEST MAGIC THERE IS, BUT...
THAT DOESN'T MEAN IT CAN'T BE BLOCKED.

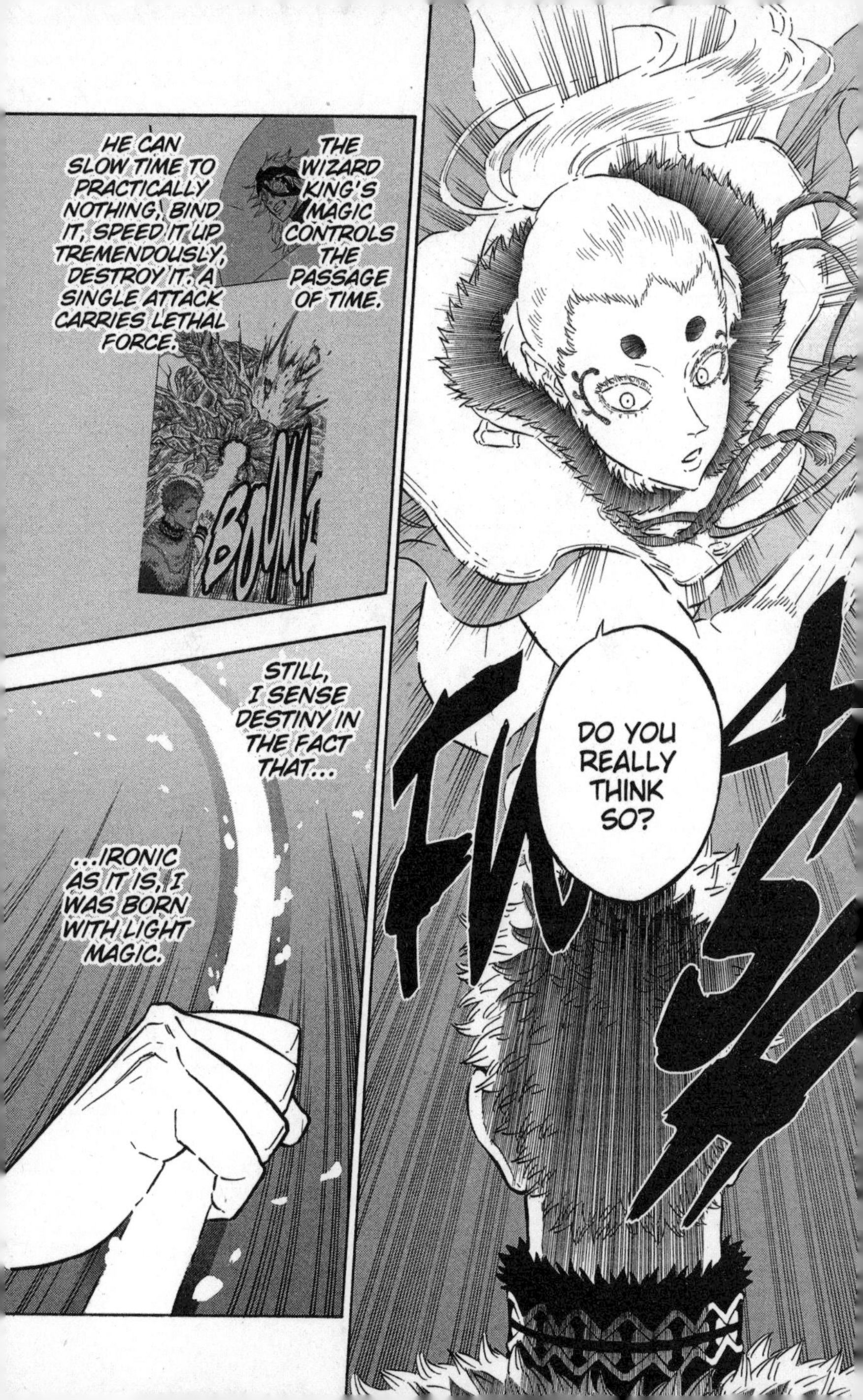

DO YOU REALLY THINK SO?
THE WIZARD KING'S MAGIC CONTROLS THE PASSAGE OF TIME.
HE CAN SLOW TIME TO PRACTICALLY NOTHING, BIND IT, SPEED IT UP TREMENDOUSLY, DESTROY IT. A SINGLE ATTACK CARRIES LETHAL FORCE.
STILL, I SENSE DESTINY IN THE FACT THAT...
...IRONIC AS IT IS, I WAS BORN WITH LIGHT MAGIC.

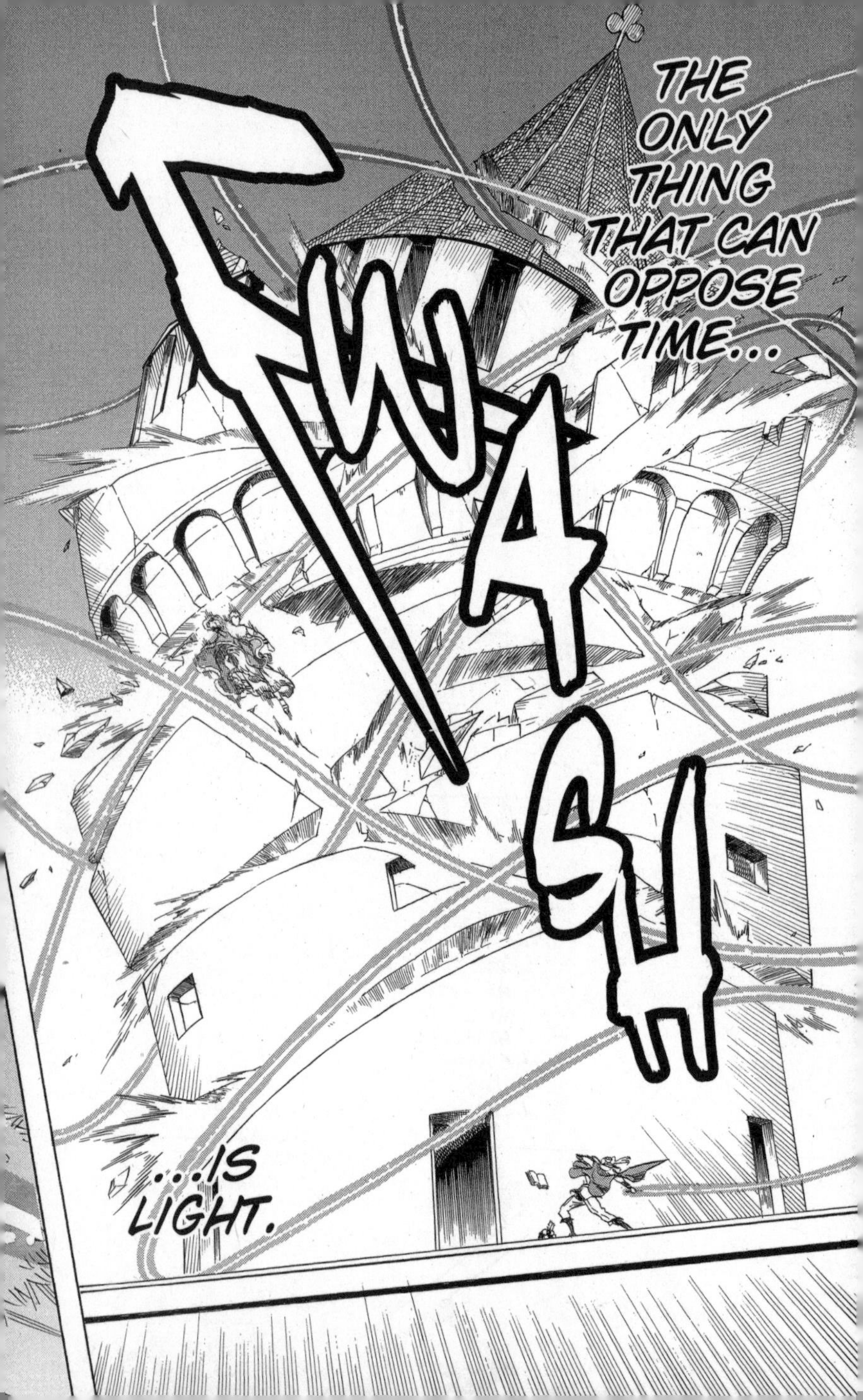
THE ONLY THING THAT CAN OPPOSE TIME...
FWASH
...IS LIGHT.

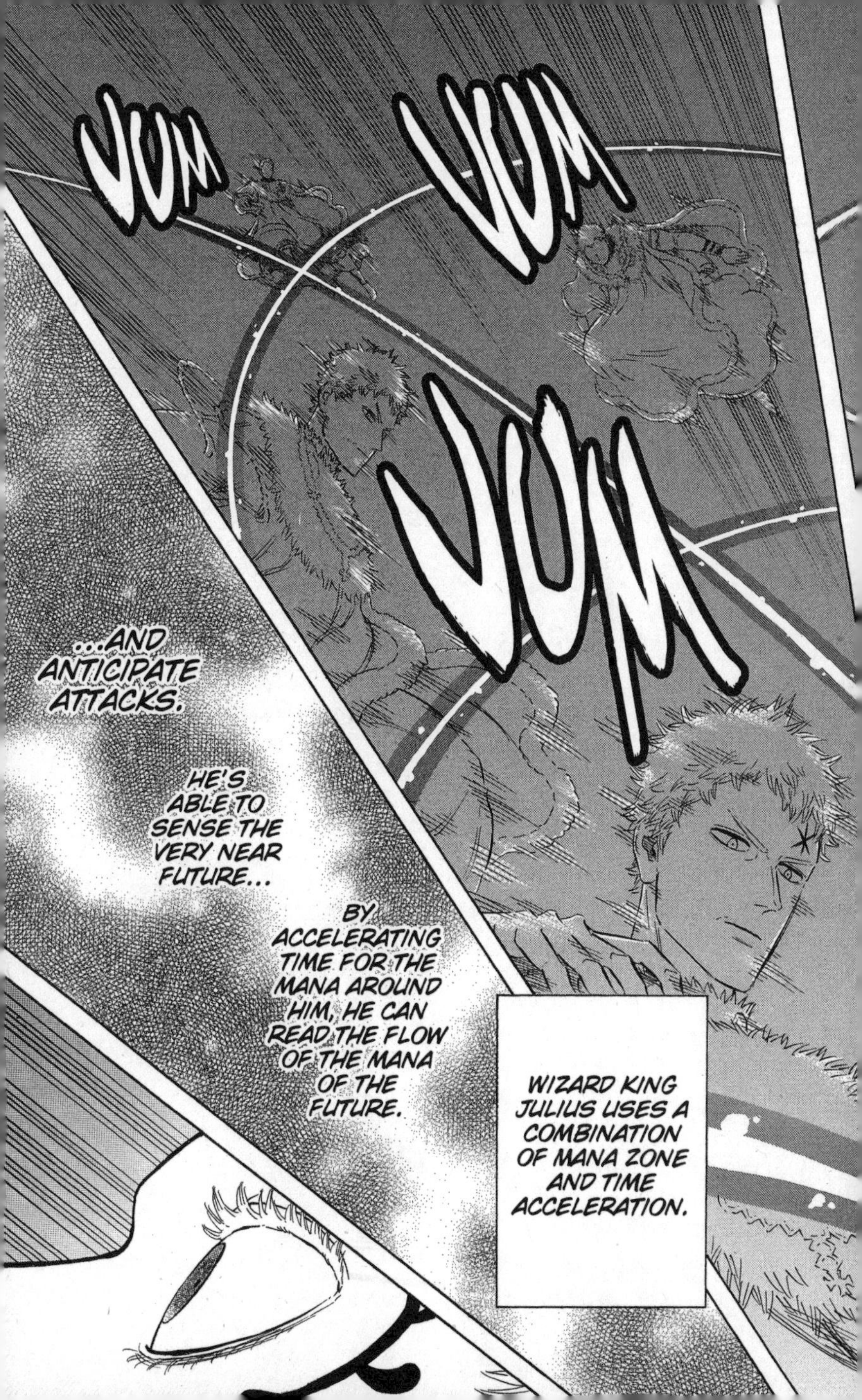
VUM
VUM
VUM
WIZARD KING JULIUS USES A COMBINATION OF MANA ZONE AND TIME ACCELERATION.
BY ACCELERATING TIME FOR THE MANA AROUND HIM, HE CAN READ THE FLOW OF THE MANA OF THE FUTURE.
HE'S ABLE TO SENSE THE VERY NEAR FUTURE...
...AND ANTICIPATE ATTACKS.

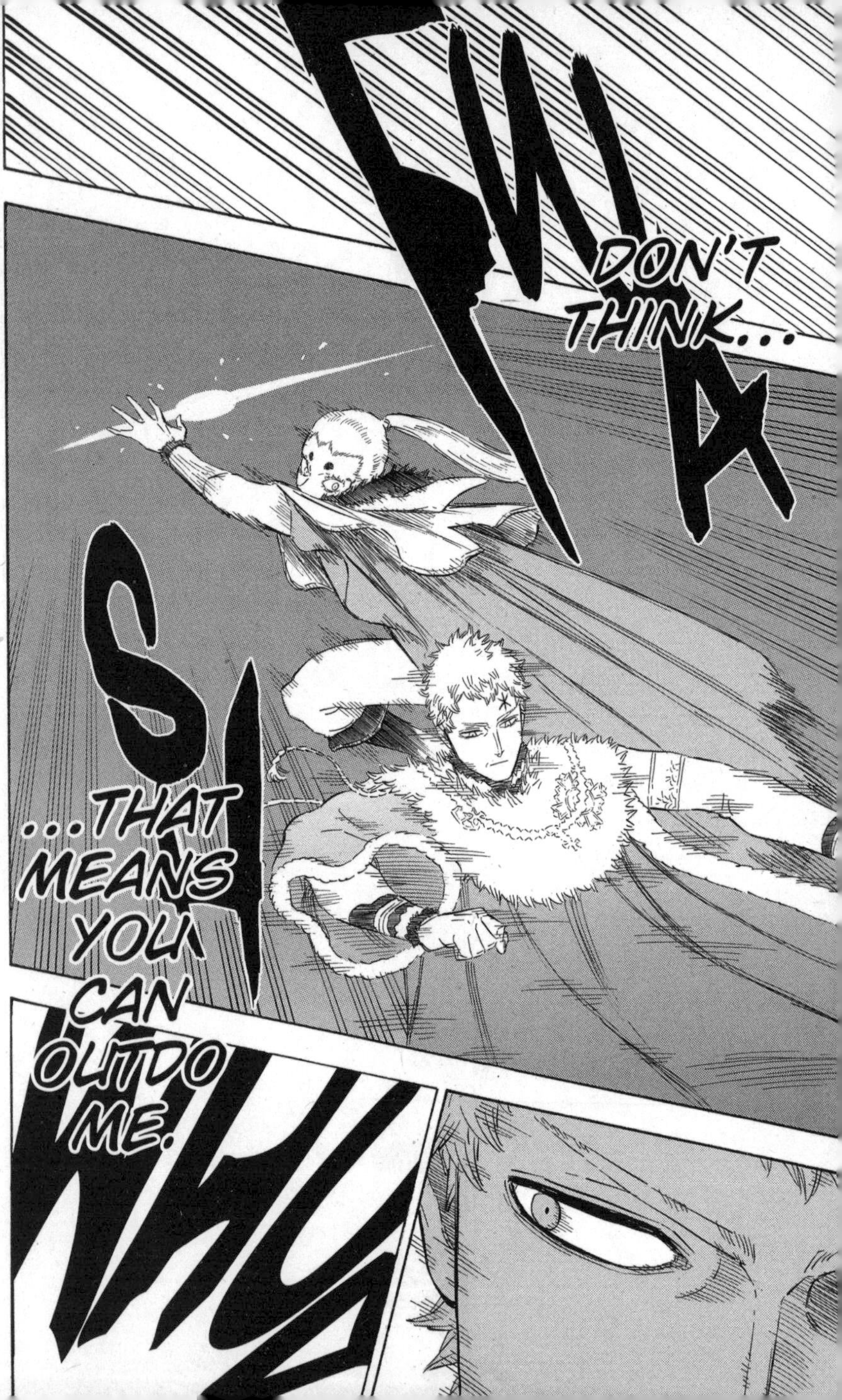
DON'T THINK...
...THAT MEANS YOU CAN OUTDO ME.

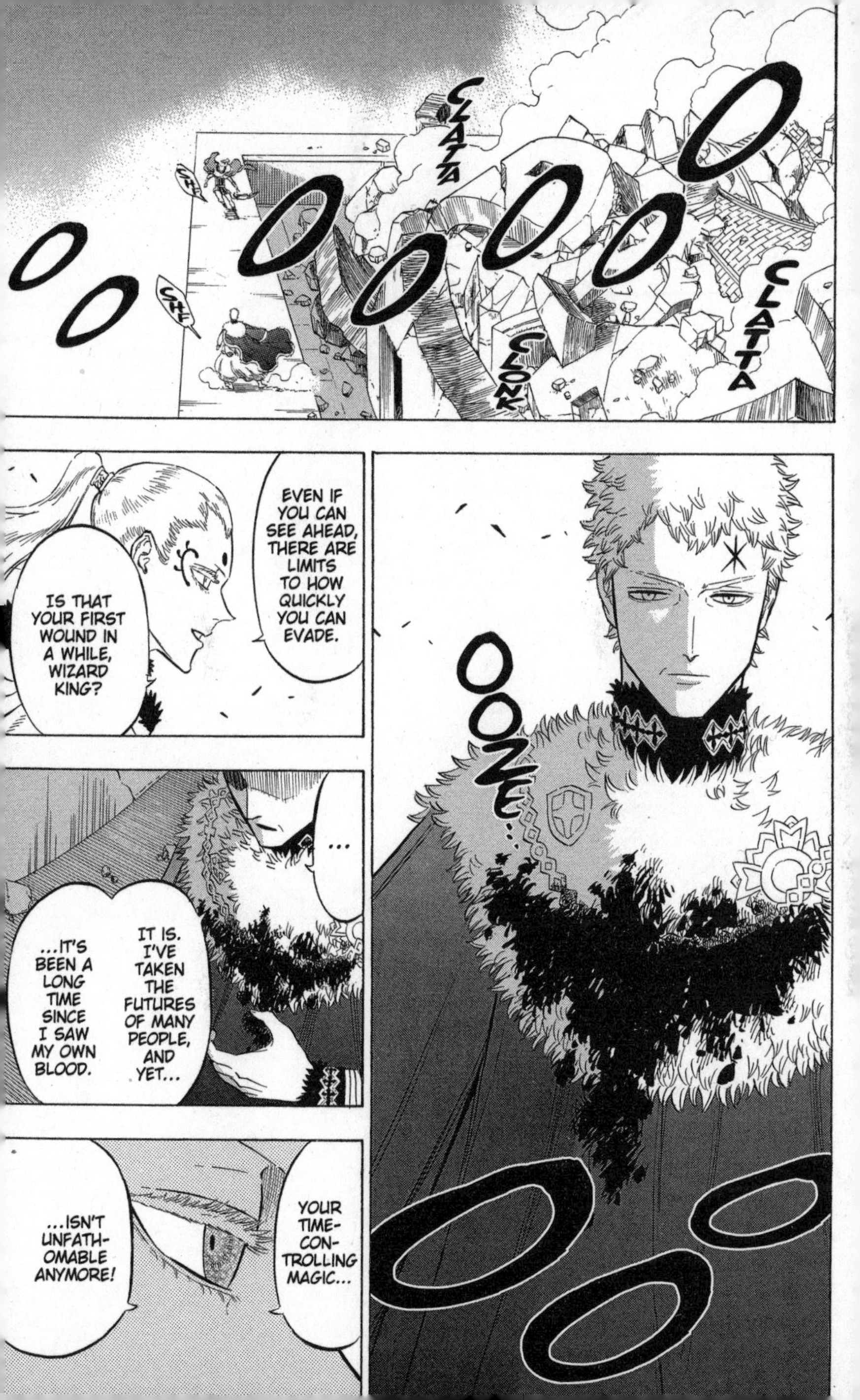
CLATTA
CLATTA
CLONK
SHF
SHF
OOZE...
EVEN IF YOU CAN SEE AHEAD, THERE ARE LIMITS TO HOW QUICKLY YOU CAN EVADE.
IS THAT YOUR FIRST WOUND IN A WHILE, WIZARD KING?
...
IT IS. I'VE TAKEN THE FUTURES OF MANY PEOPLE, AND YET...
...IT'S BEEN A LONG TIME SINCE I SAW MY OWN BLOOD.
YOUR TIME-CONTROLLING MAGIC...
...ISN'T UNFATHOMABLE ANYMORE!

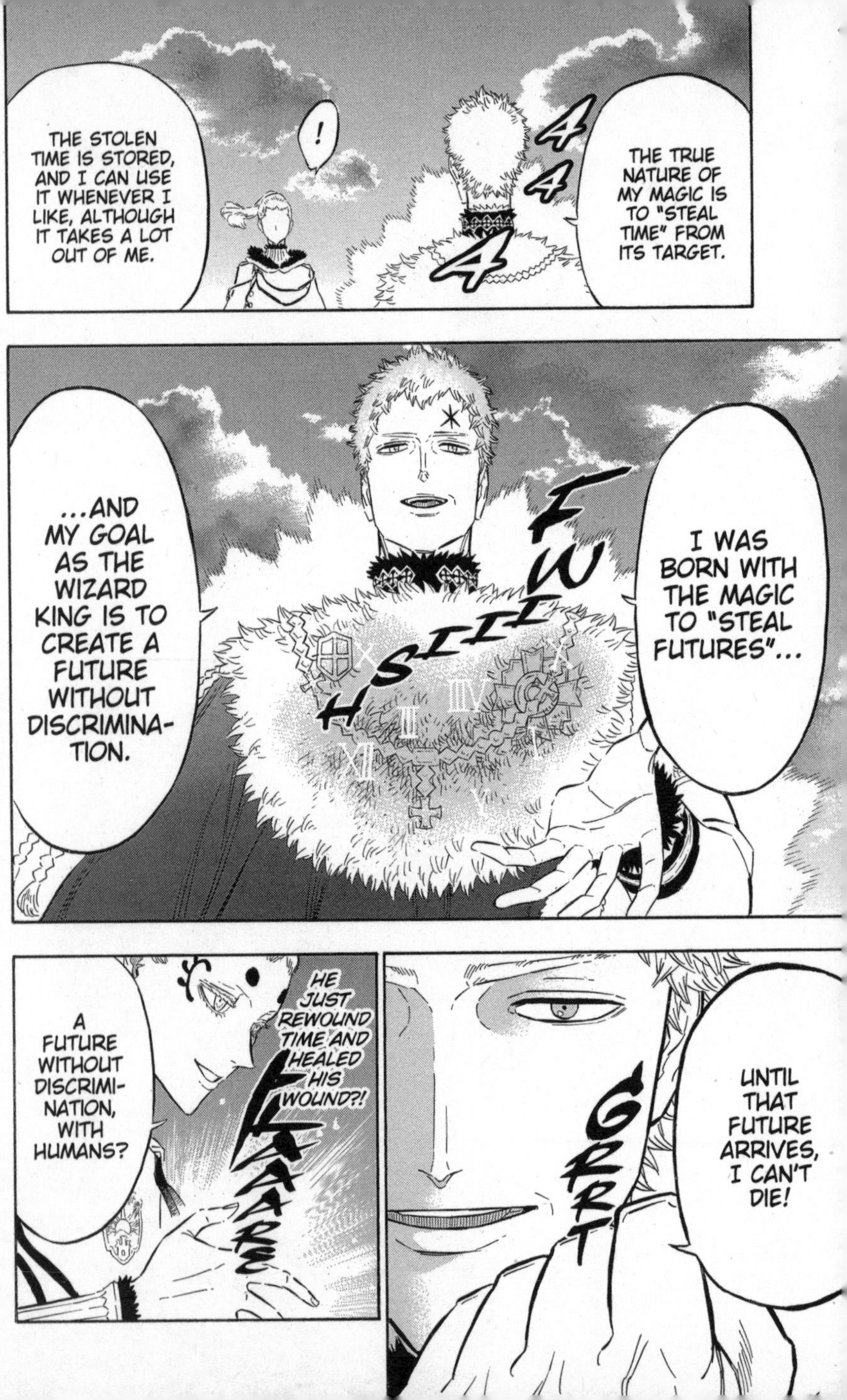
THE TRUE NATURE OF MY MAGIC IS TO "STEAL TIME" FROM ITS TARGET.
!
THE STOLEN TIME IS STORED, AND I CAN USE IT WHENEVER I LIKE, ALTHOUGH IT TAKES A LOT OUT OF ME.
I WAS BORN WITH THE MAGIC TO "STEAL FUTURES"...
...AND MY GOAL AS THE WIZARD KING IS TO CREATE A FUTURE WITHOUT DISCRIMINATION.
UNTIL THAT FUTURE ARRIVES, I CAN'T DIE!
GRRT
HE JUST REWOUND TIME AND HEALED HIS WOUND?!
A FUTURE WITHOUT DISCRIMINATION, WITH HUMANS?

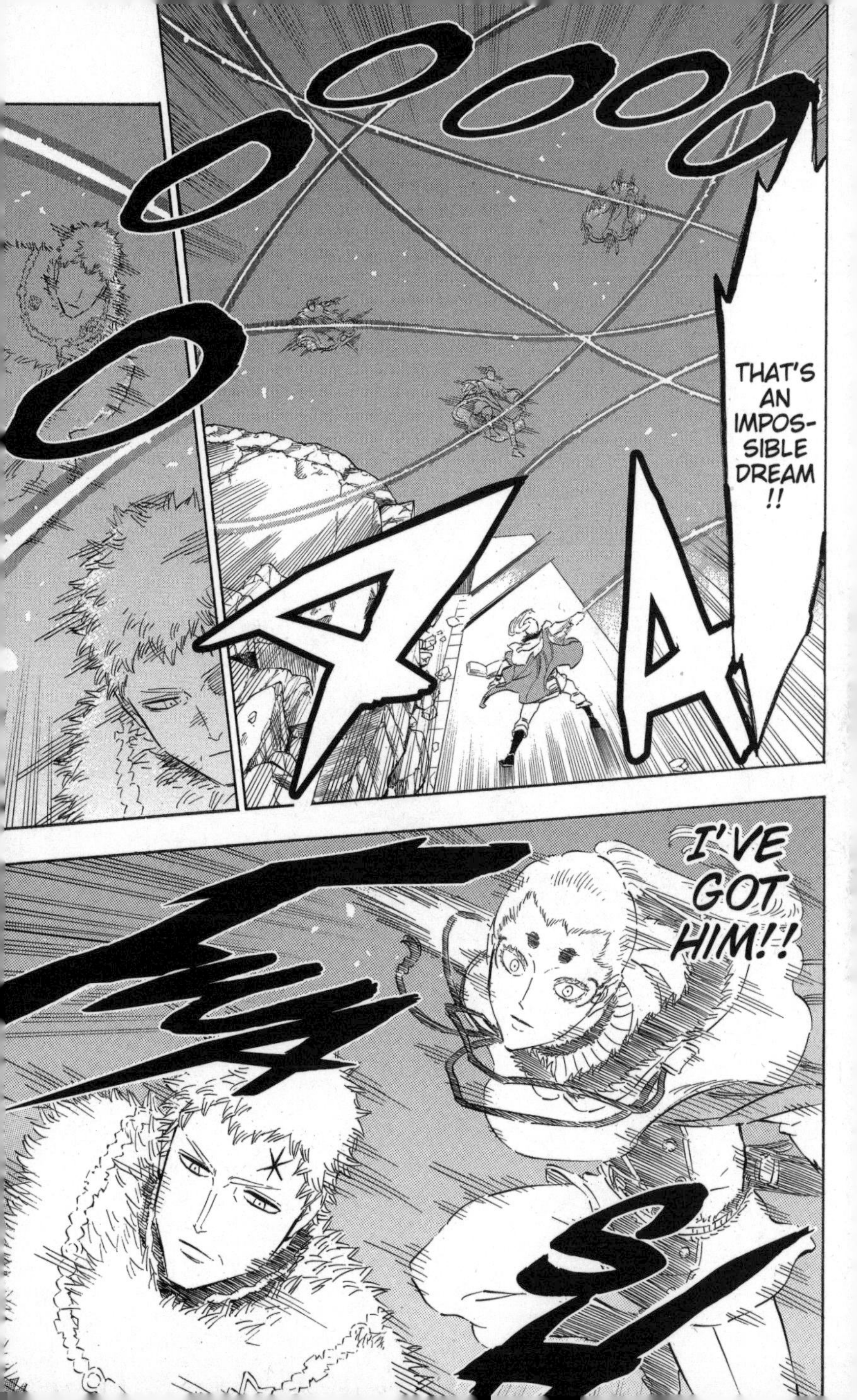
THAT'S AN IMPOSSIBLE DREAM!!
I'VE GOT HIM!!

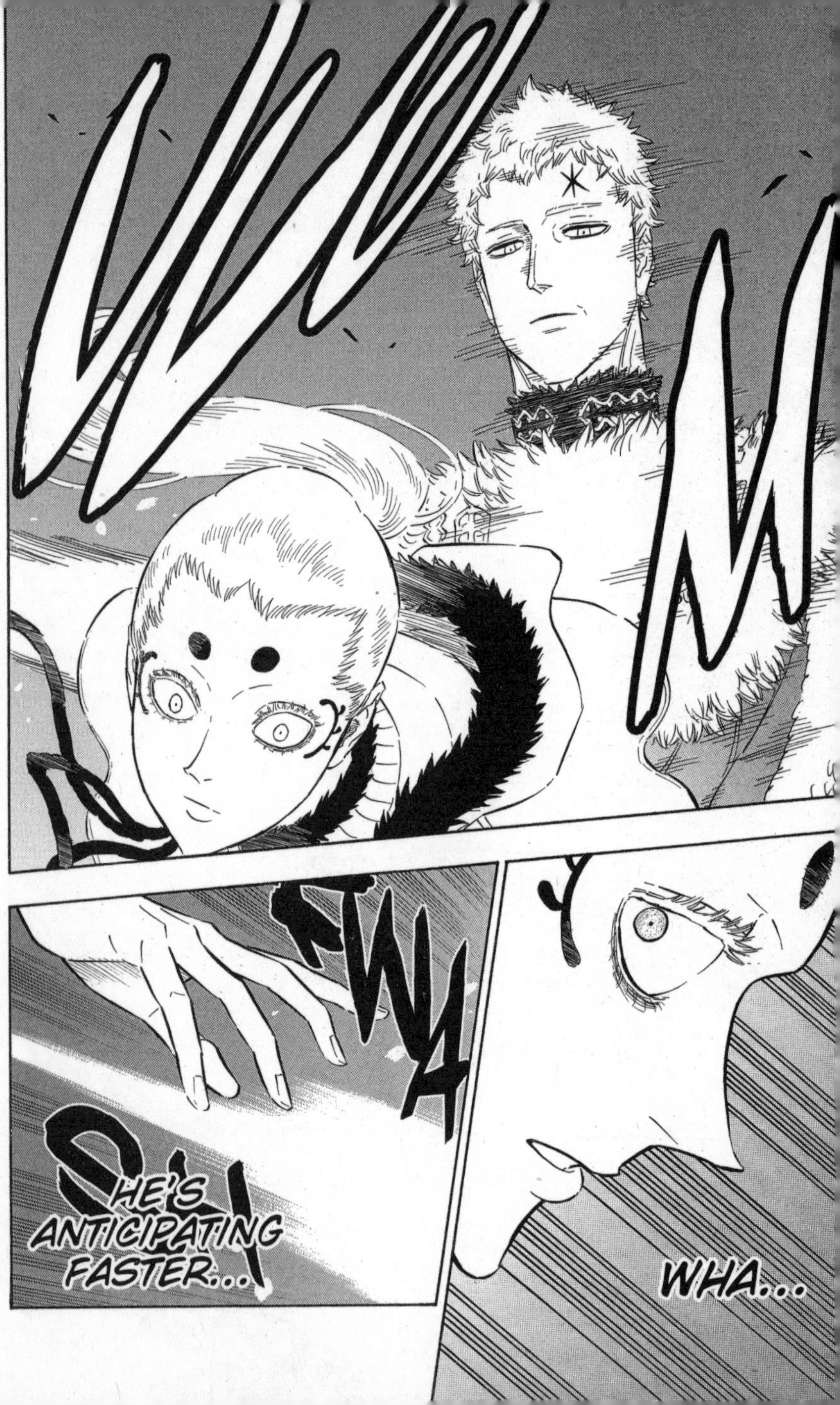
WHA...
SHE'S ANTICIPATING FASTER...!

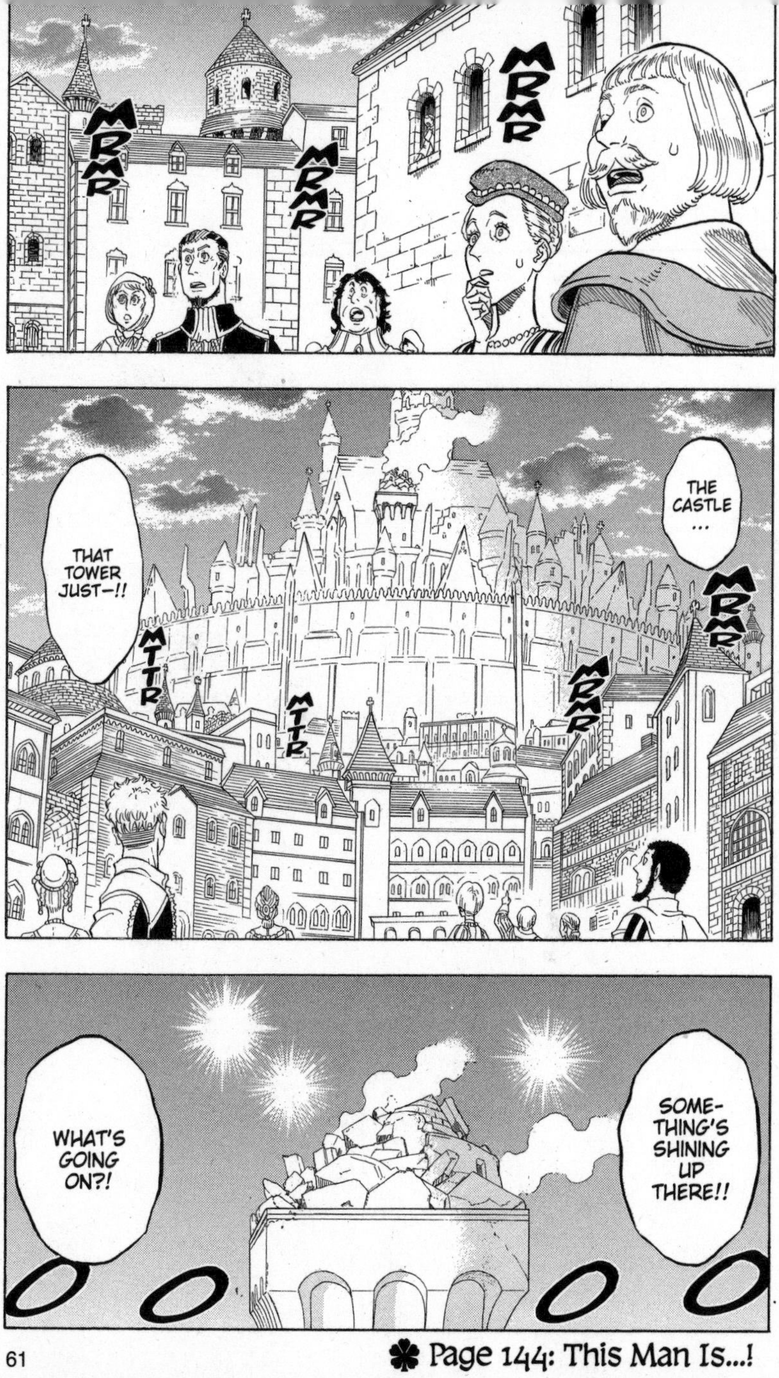
MRMR
MRMR
MRMR
THE CASTLE...
MRMR
MRMR
MTTR
THAT TOWER JUST—!!
MTTR
SOME-THING'S SHINING UP THERE!!
WHAT'S GOING ON?!
O O O O

♣ Page 144: This Man Is...!

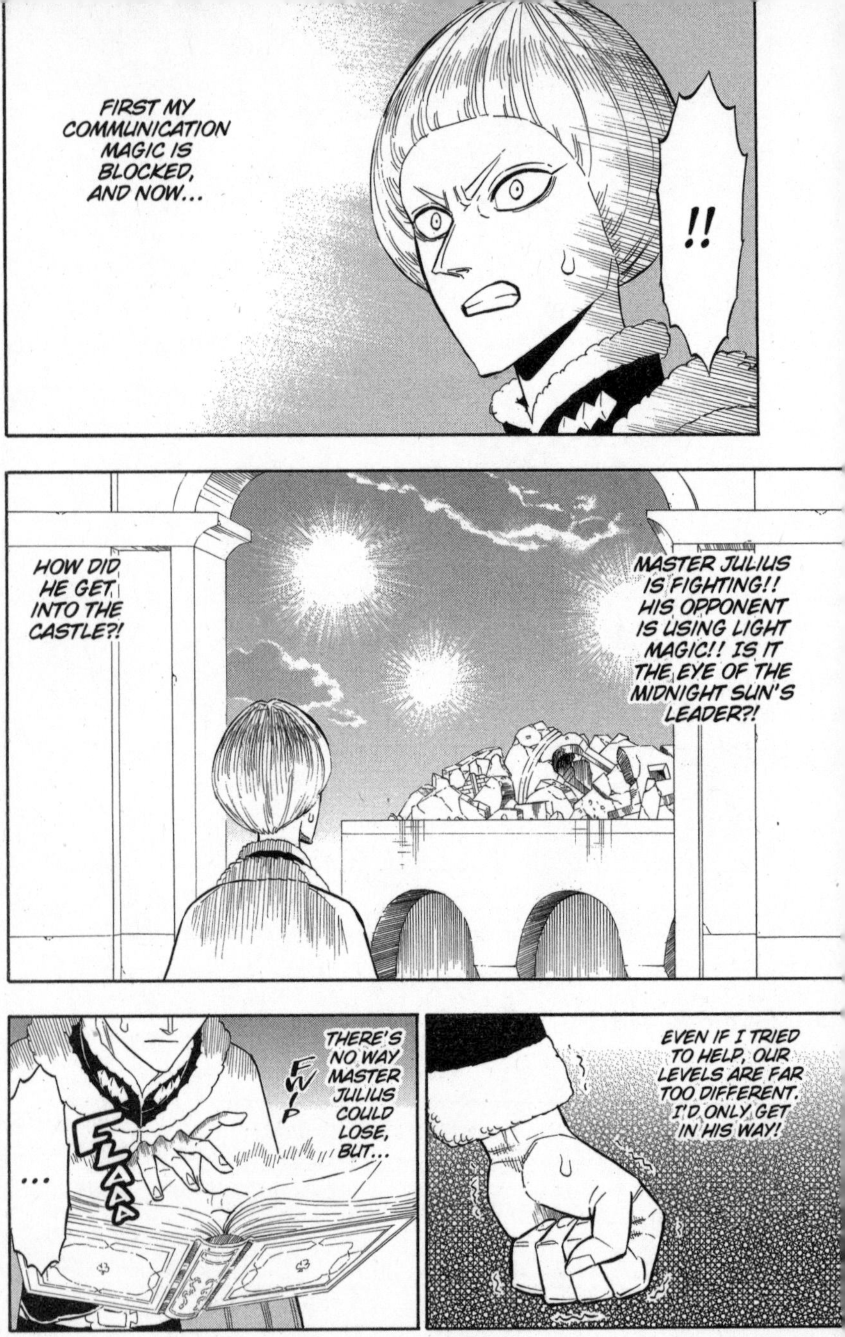
FIRST MY COMMUNICATION MAGIC IS BLOCKED, AND NOW...
!!
MASTER JULIUS IS FIGHTING!! HIS OPPONENT IS USING LIGHT MAGIC!! IS IT THE EYE OF THE MIDNIGHT SUN'S LEADER?!
HOW DID HE GET INTO THE CASTLE?!
EVEN IF I TRIED TO HELP, OUR LEVELS ARE FAR TOO DIFFERENT. I'D ONLY GET IN HIS WAY!
THERE'S NO WAY MASTER JULIUS COULD LOSE, BUT...
FWIP
FLAAAP
...

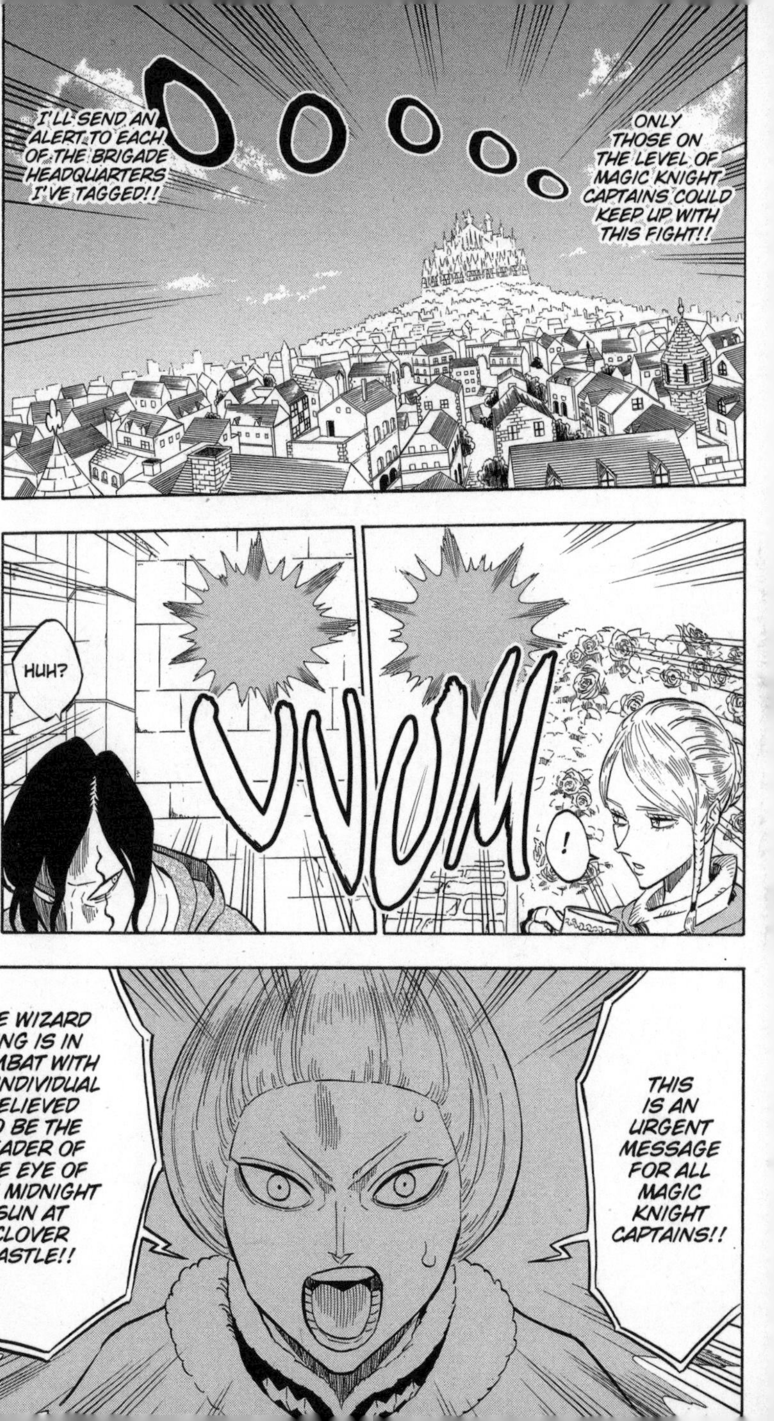
ONLY THOSE ON THE LEVEL OF MAGIC KNIGHT CAPTAINS COULD KEEP UP WITH THIS FIGHT!!
I'LL SEND AN ALERT TO EACH OF THE BRIGADE HEADQUARTERS I'VE TAGGED!!
OOOOO
!
VVOM
HUH?
THIS IS AN URGENT MESSAGE FOR ALL MAGIC KNIGHT CAPTAINS!!
THE WIZARD KING IS IN COMBAT WITH AN INDIVIDUAL BELIEVED TO BE THE LEADER OF THE EYE OF THE MIDNIGHT SUN AT CLOVER CASTLE!!

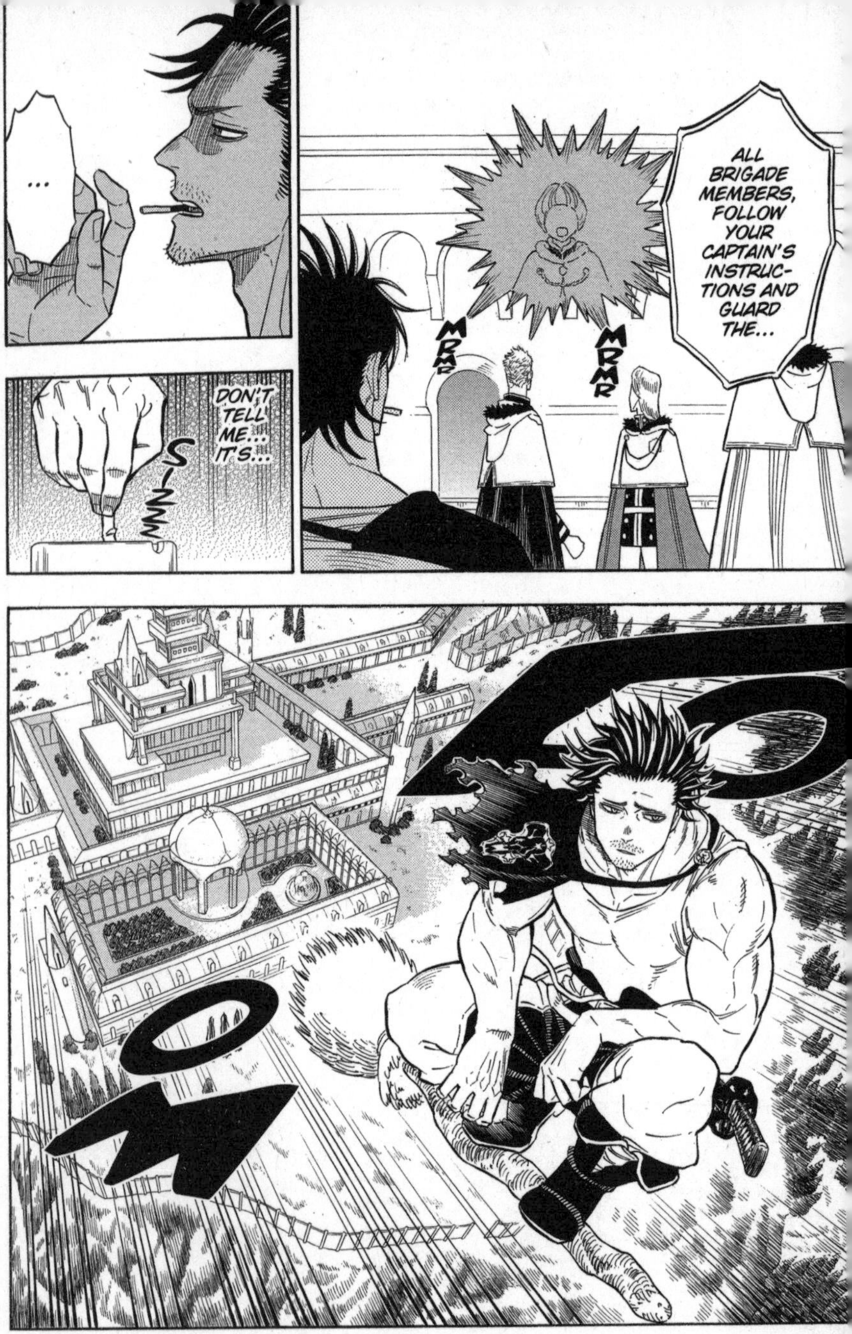

ALL BRIGADE MEMBERS, FOLLOW YOUR CAPTAIN'S INSTRUCTIONS AND GUARD THE...
MRMR
MRMR
...
DON'T TELL ME... IT'S...
S-ZZZ

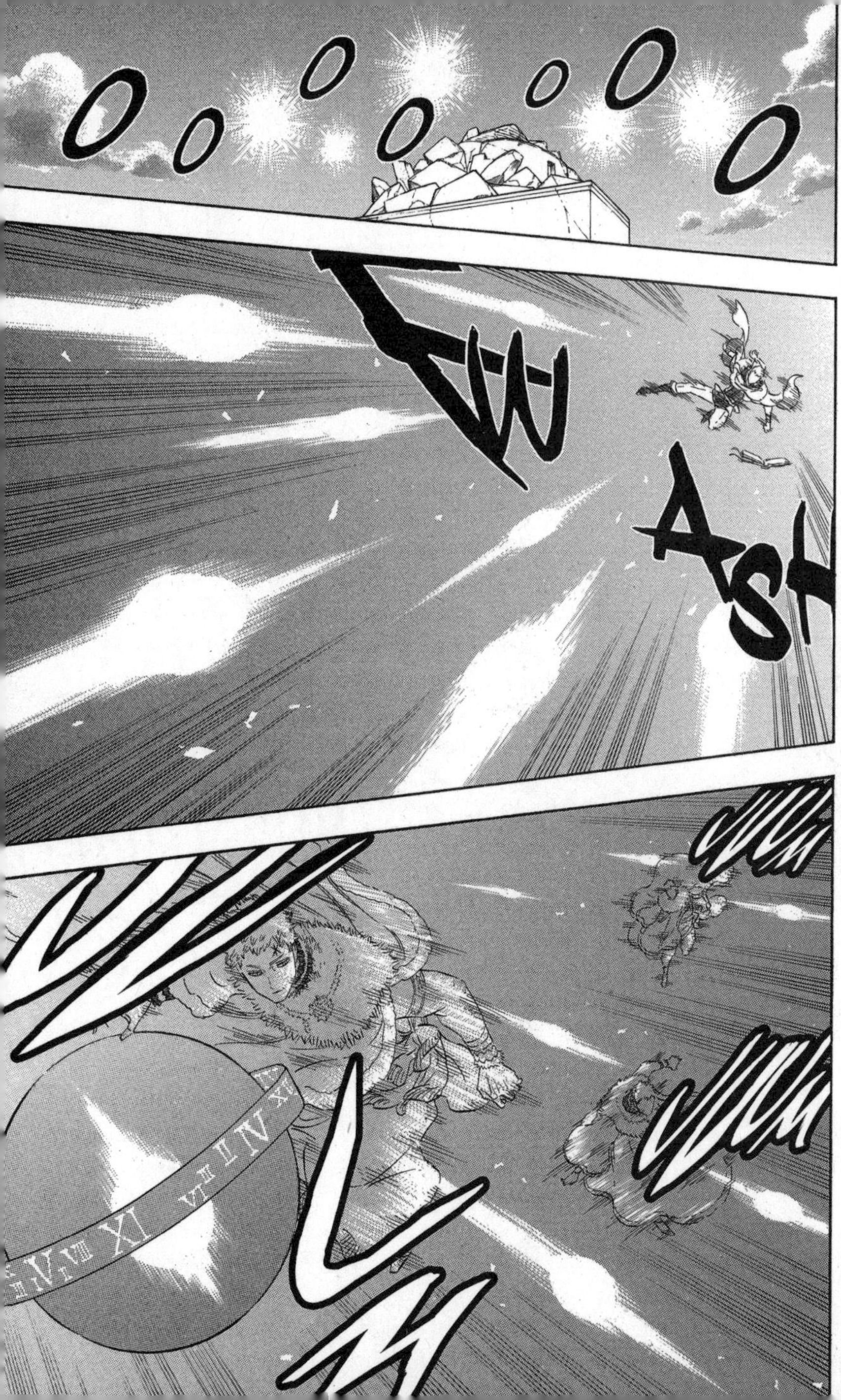
OOOOOOO
FWASH

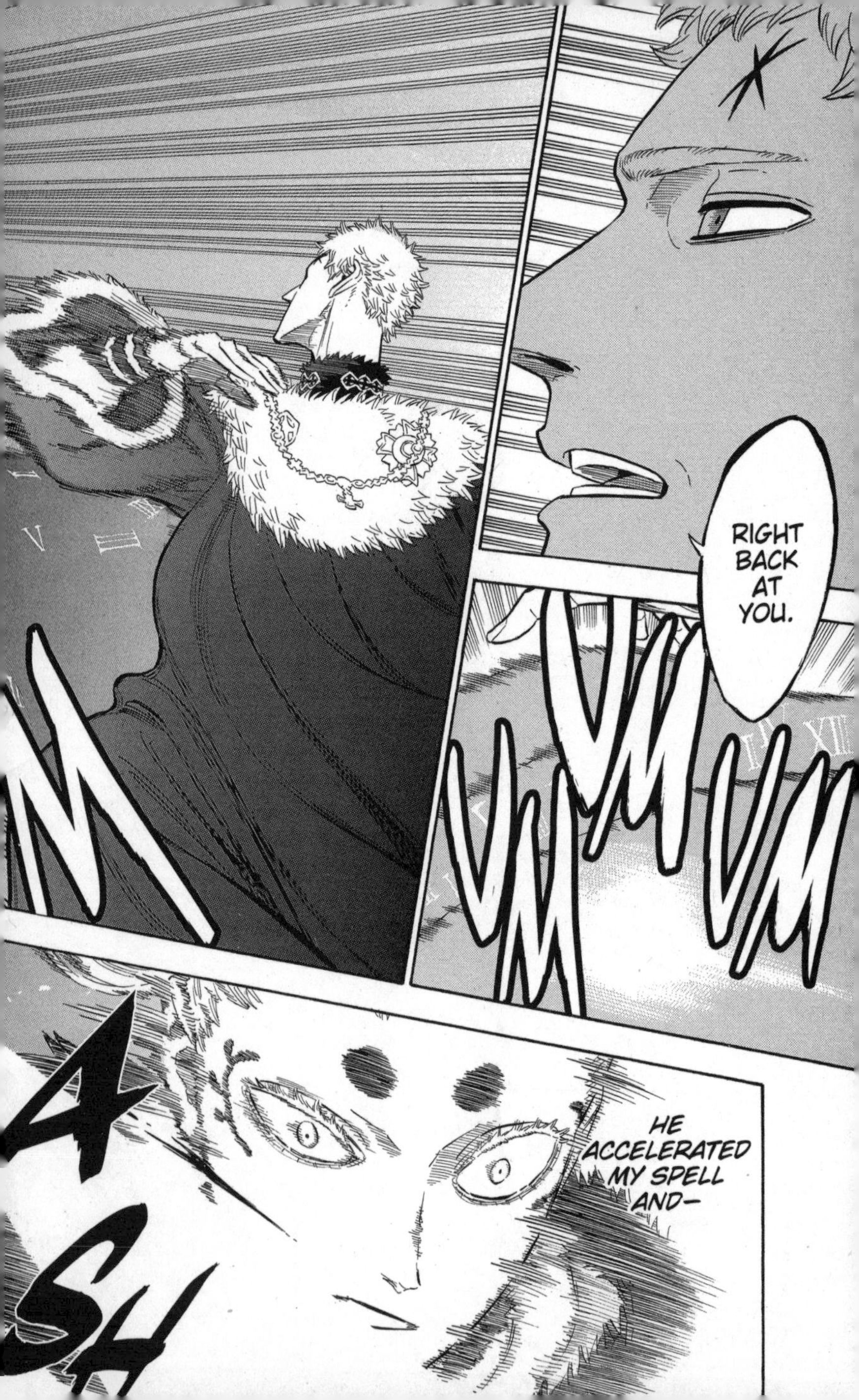
RIGHT BACK AT YOU.
HE ACCELERATED MY SPELL AND—

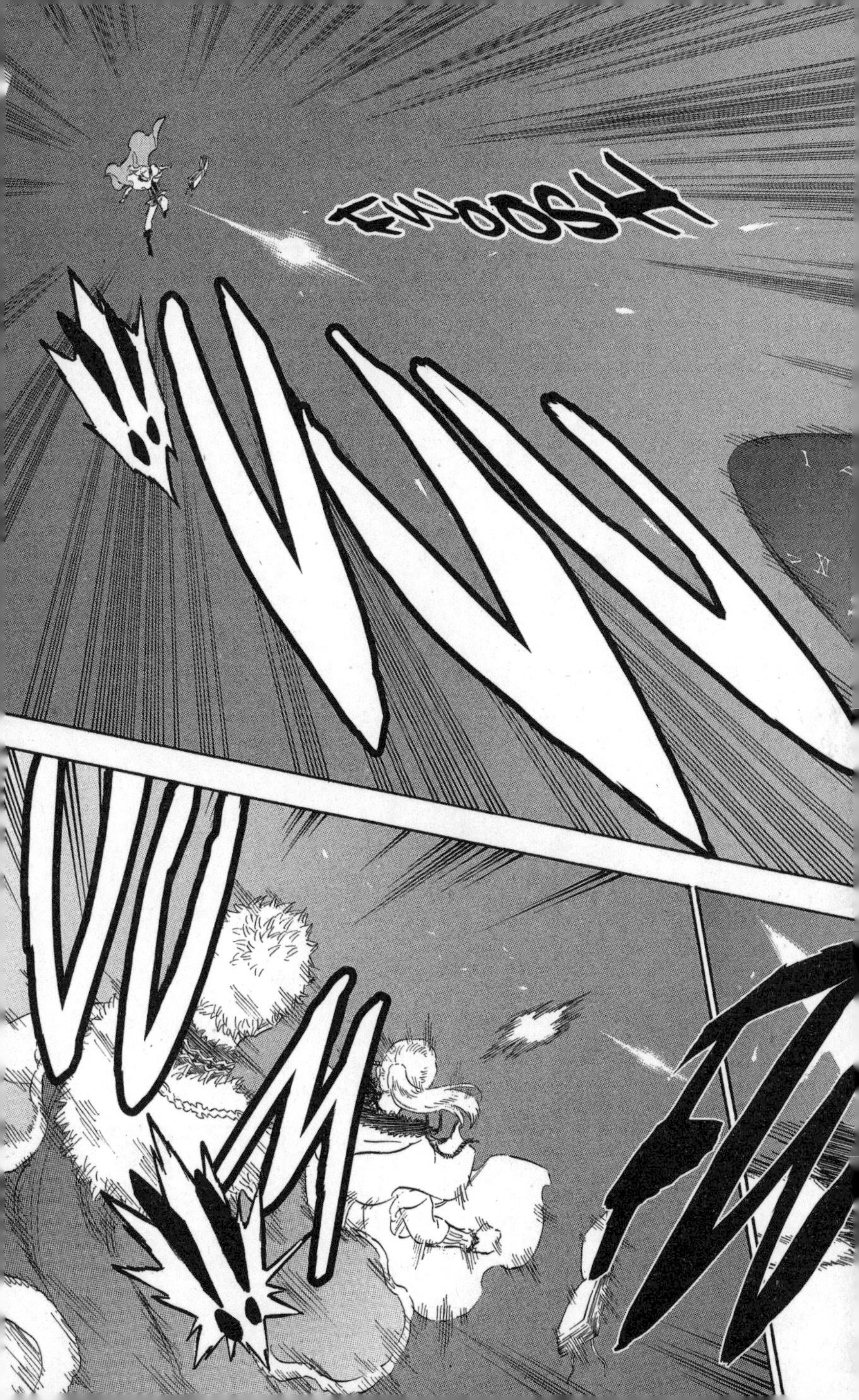
FWOOSH

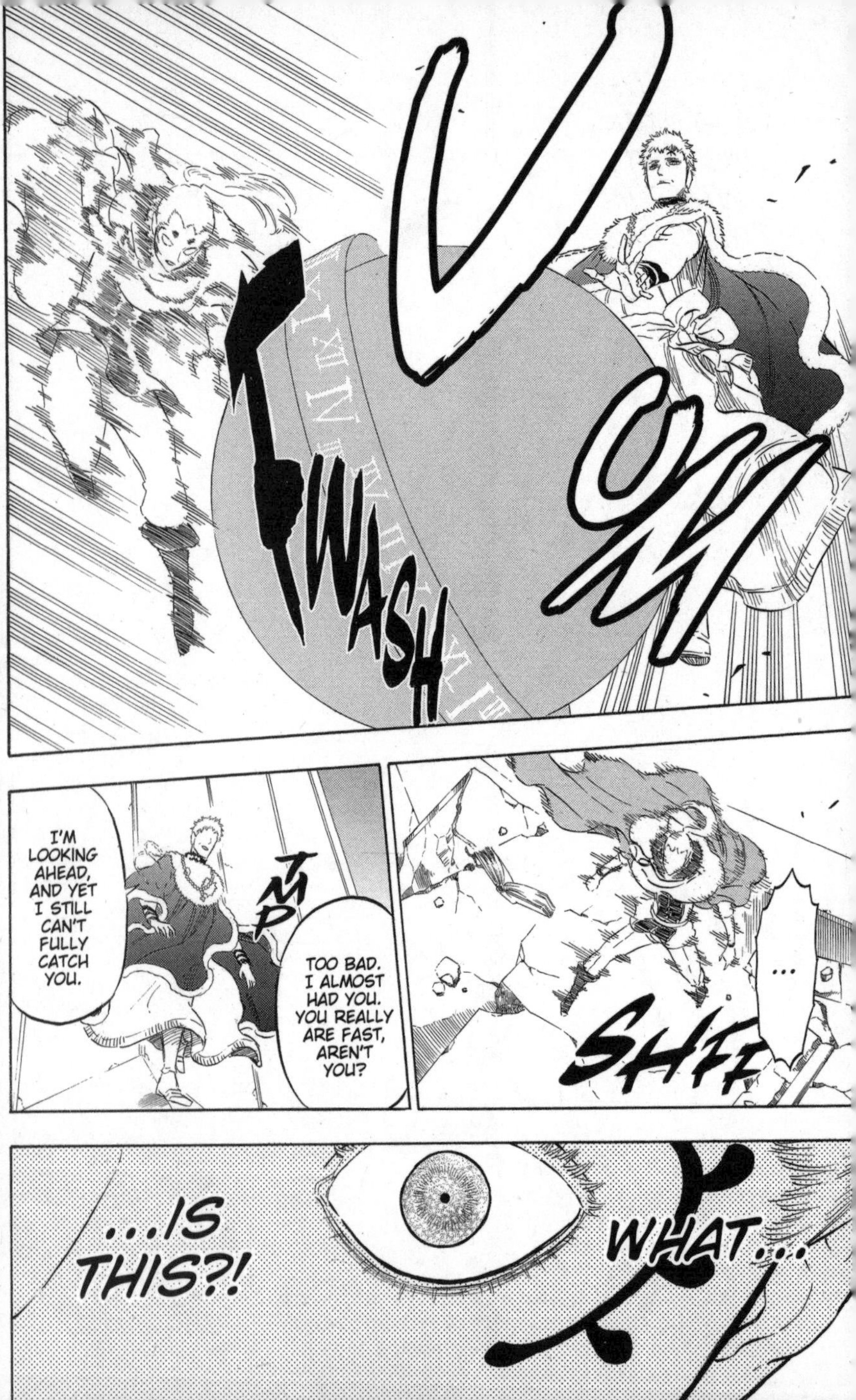
VOOM
FWASH
...
SHFF
TMP
TOO BAD. I ALMOST HAD YOU. YOU REALLY ARE FAST, AREN'T YOU?
I'M LOOKING AHEAD, AND YET I STILL CAN'T FULLY CATCH YOU.
WHAT...
...IS THIS?!

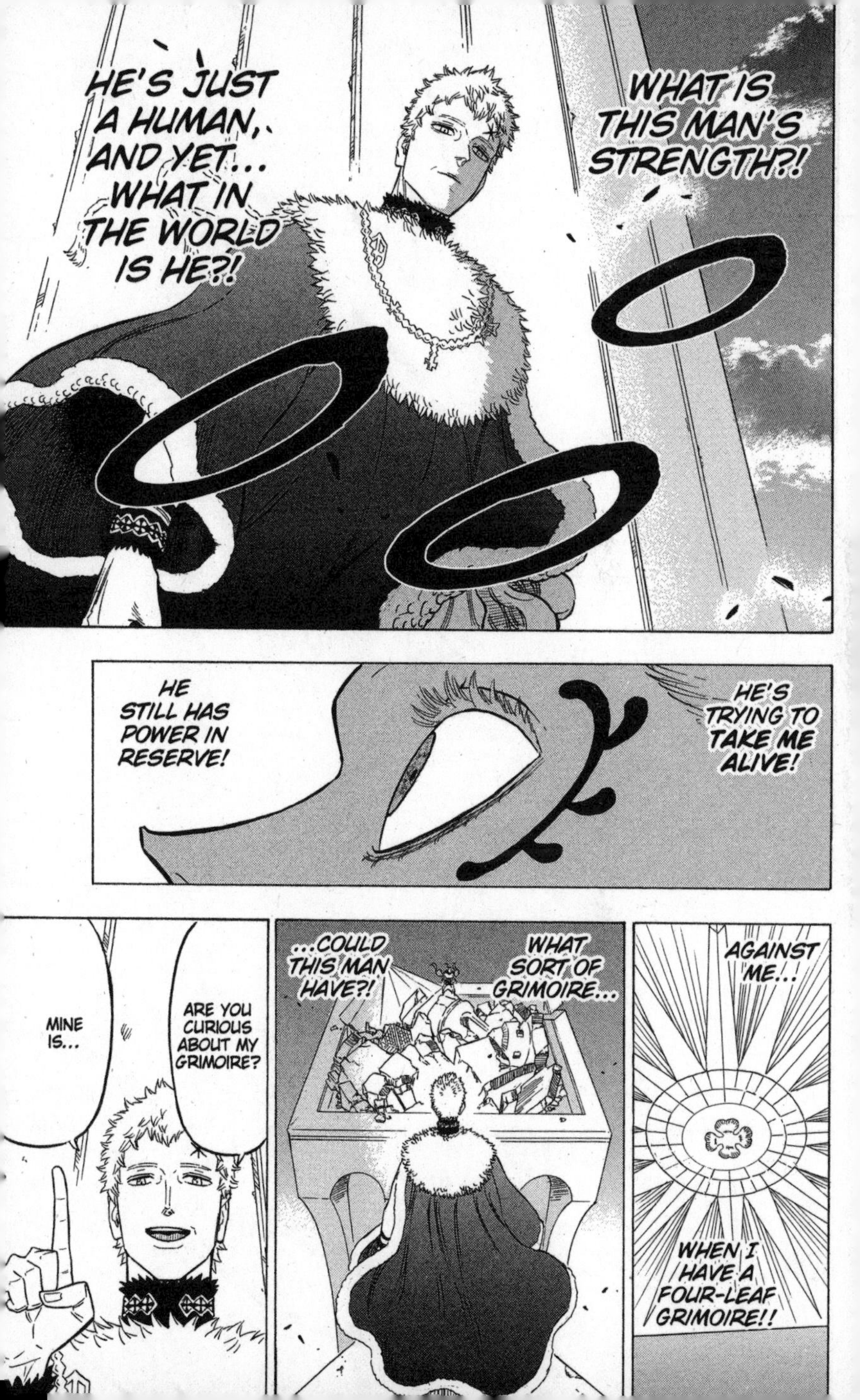
WHAT IS THIS MAN'S STRENGTH?!
HE'S JUST A HUMAN, AND YET... WHAT IN THE WORLD IS HE?!
HE'S TRYING TO TAKE ME ALIVE!
HE STILL HAS POWER IN RESERVE!
AGAINST ME...
WHEN I HAVE A FOUR-LEAF GRIMOIRE!!
WHAT SORT OF GRIMOIRE...
...COULD THIS MAN HAVE?!
ARE YOU CURIOUS ABOUT MY GRIMOIRE?
MINE IS...

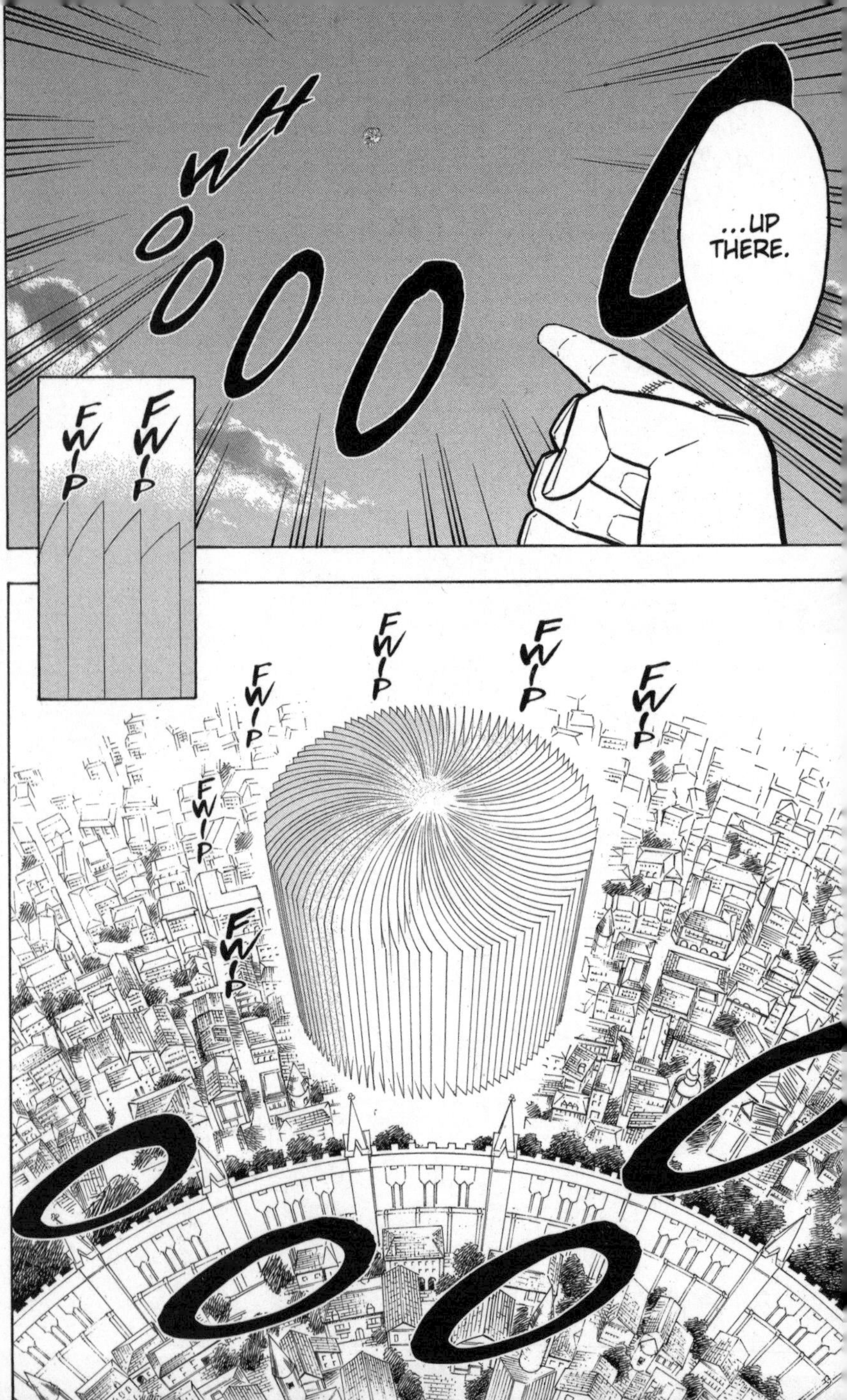
...UP THERE.
FWIP
FWIP
FWIP
FWIP
FWIP
FWIP
FWIP
FWIP

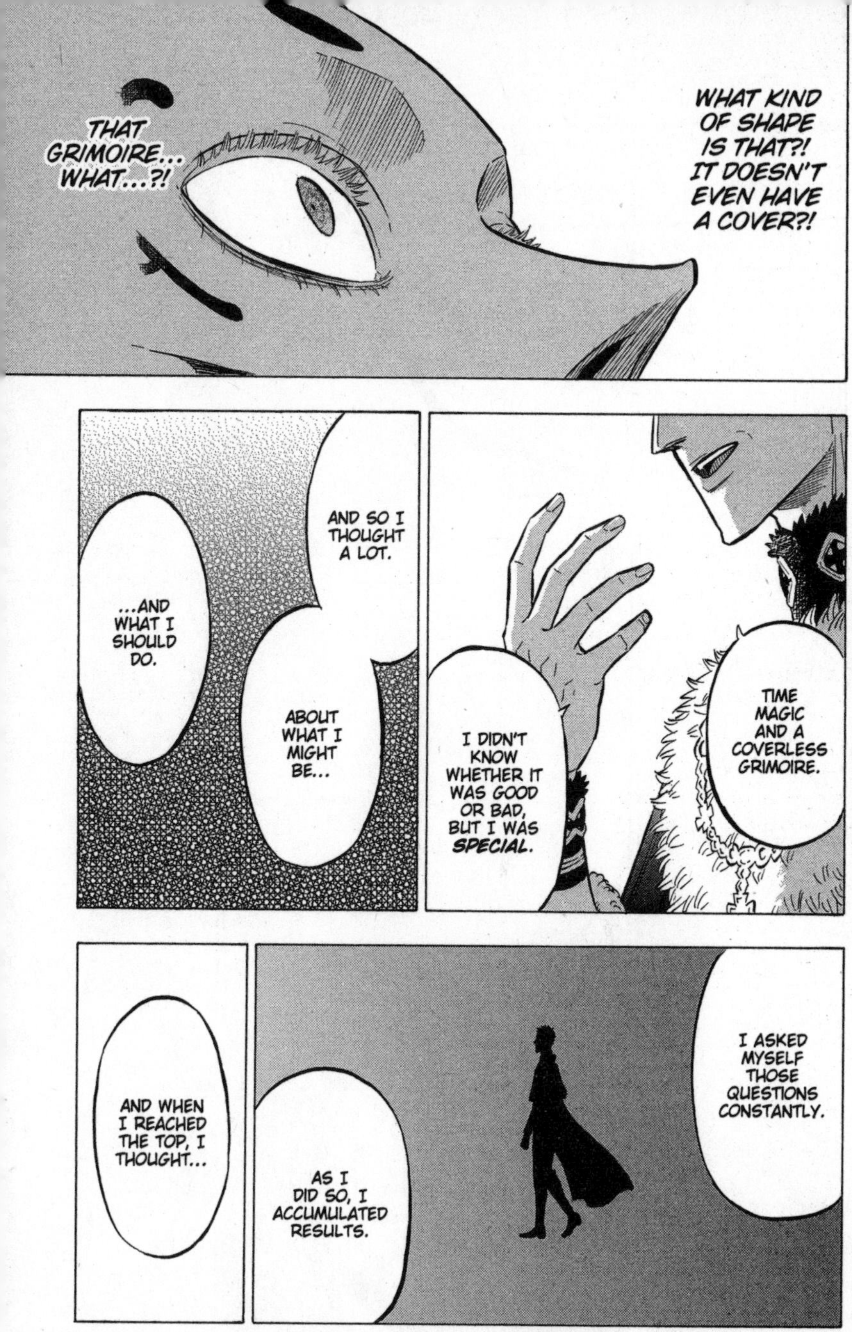
WHAT KIND OF SHAPE IS THAT?! IT DOESN'T EVEN HAVE A COVER?!
THAT GRIMOIRE... WHAT...?!
TIME MAGIC AND A COVERLESS GRIMOIRE.
I DIDN'T KNOW WHETHER IT WAS GOOD OR BAD, BUT I WAS *SPECIAL*.
AND SO I THOUGHT A LOT.
ABOUT WHAT I MIGHT BE...
...AND WHAT I SHOULD DO.
I ASKED MYSELF THOSE QUESTIONS CONSTANTLY.
AS I DID SO, I ACCUMULATED RESULTS.
AND WHEN I REACHED THE TOP, I THOUGHT...

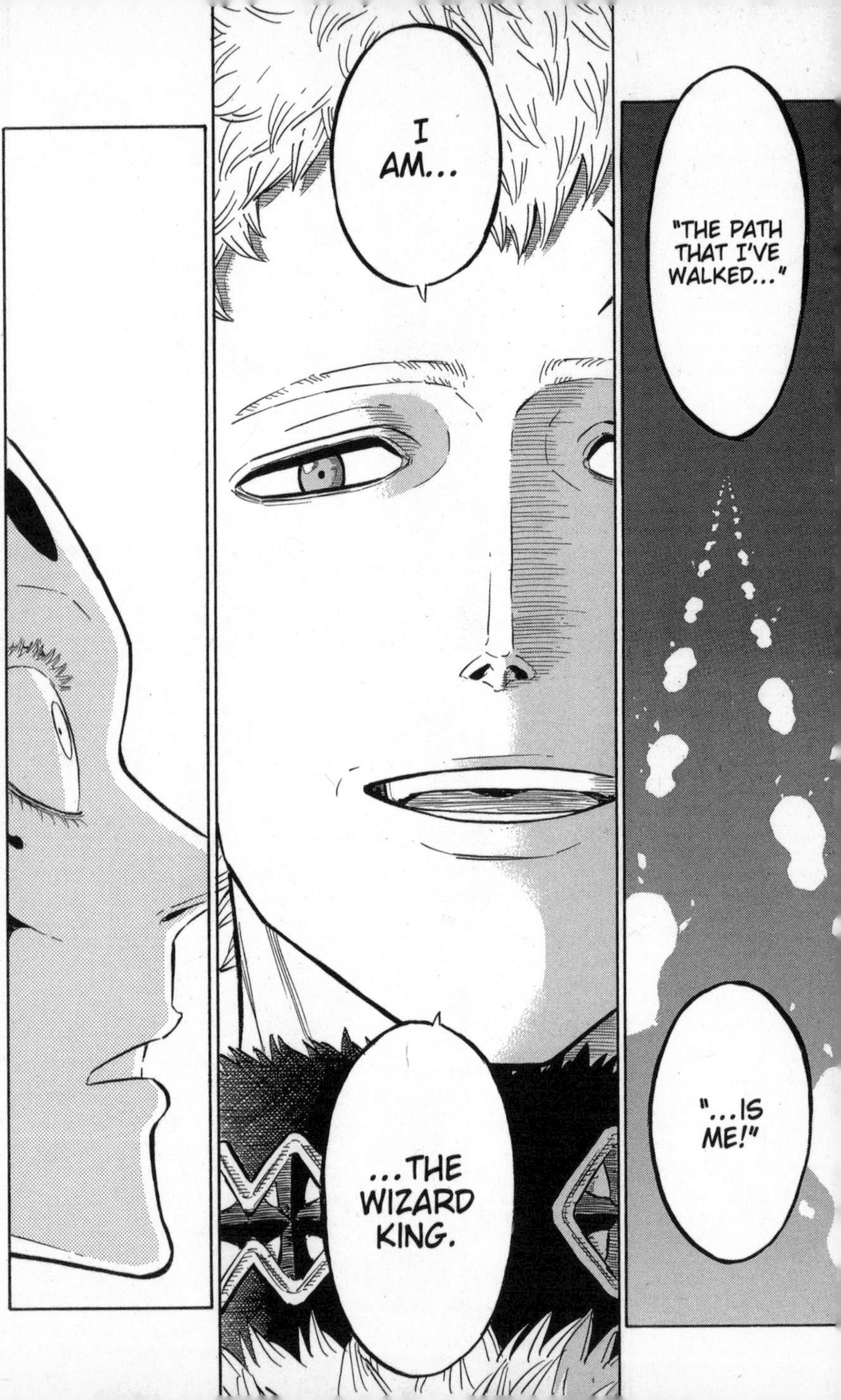
"THE PATH THAT I'VE WALKED..."
"...IS ME!"
I AM...
...THE WIZARD KING.

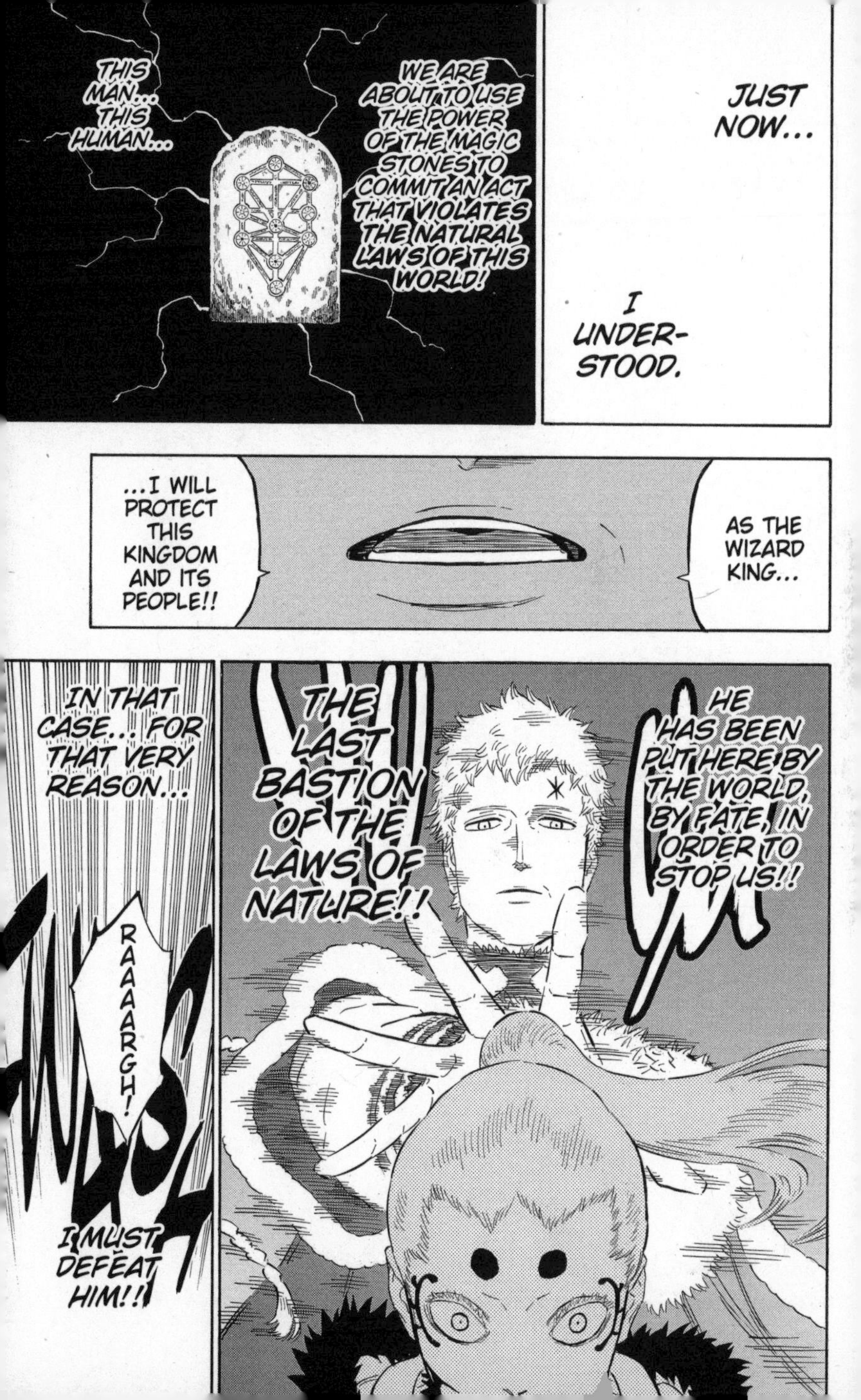
JUST NOW...
I UNDERSTOOD.
WE ARE ABOUT TO USE THE POWER OF THE MAGIC STONES TO COMMIT AN ACT THAT VIOLATES THE NATURAL LAWS OF THIS WORLD!
THIS MAN... THIS HUMAN...
AS THE WIZARD KING...
...I WILL PROTECT THIS KINGDOM AND ITS PEOPLE!!
HE HAS BEEN PUT HERE BY THE WORLD, BY FATE, IN ORDER TO STOP US!!
THE LAST BASTION OF THE LAWS OF NATURE!!
IN THAT CASE... FOR THAT VERY REASON...
RAAAAARGH!
I MUST DEFEAT HIM!!

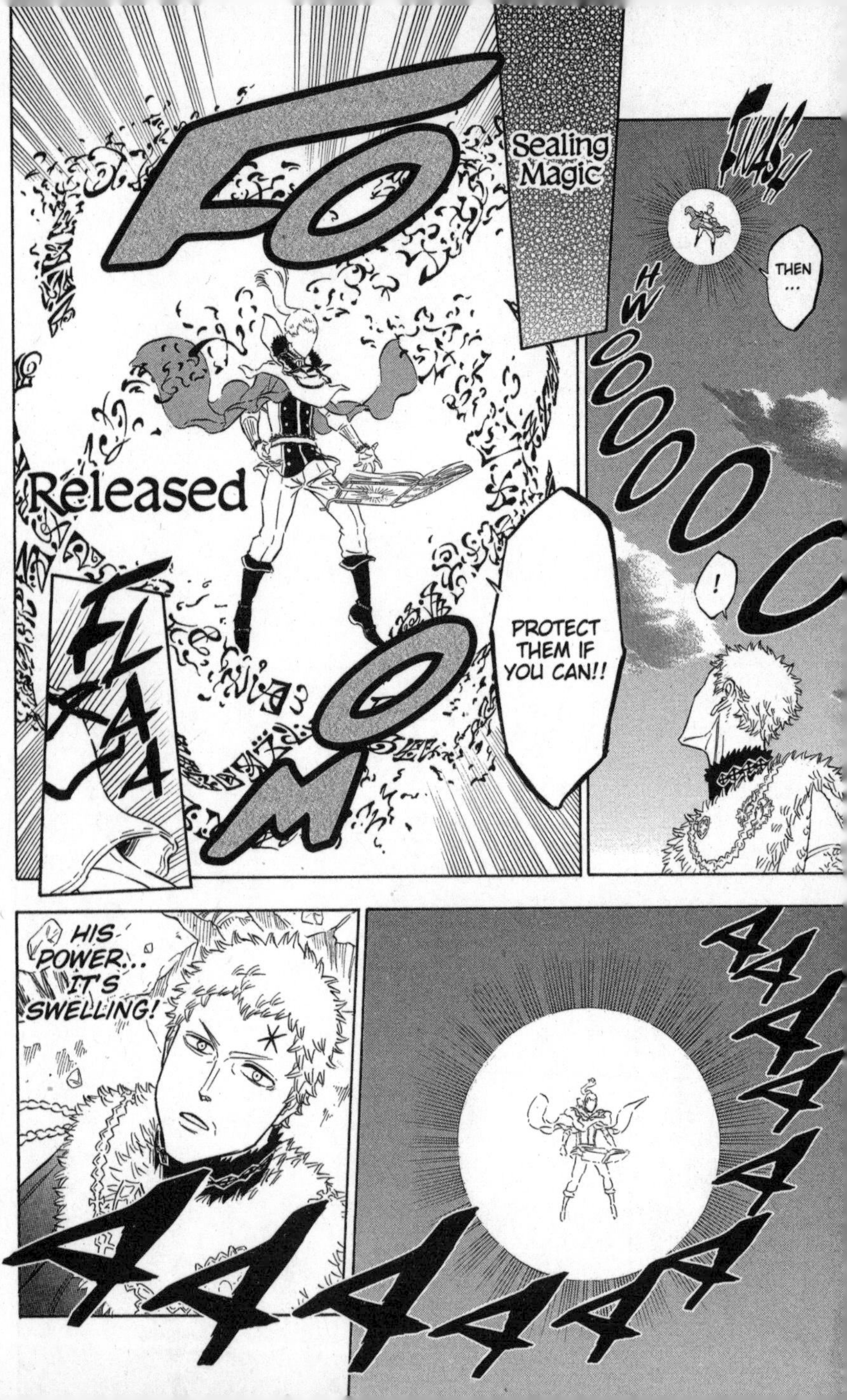
THEN...
HWOOOOOO
!
Sealing Magic
FOOM
Released
FLAAA
PROTECT THEM IF YOU CAN!!
AAAAAAAAAAA
HIS POWER... IT'S SWELLING!

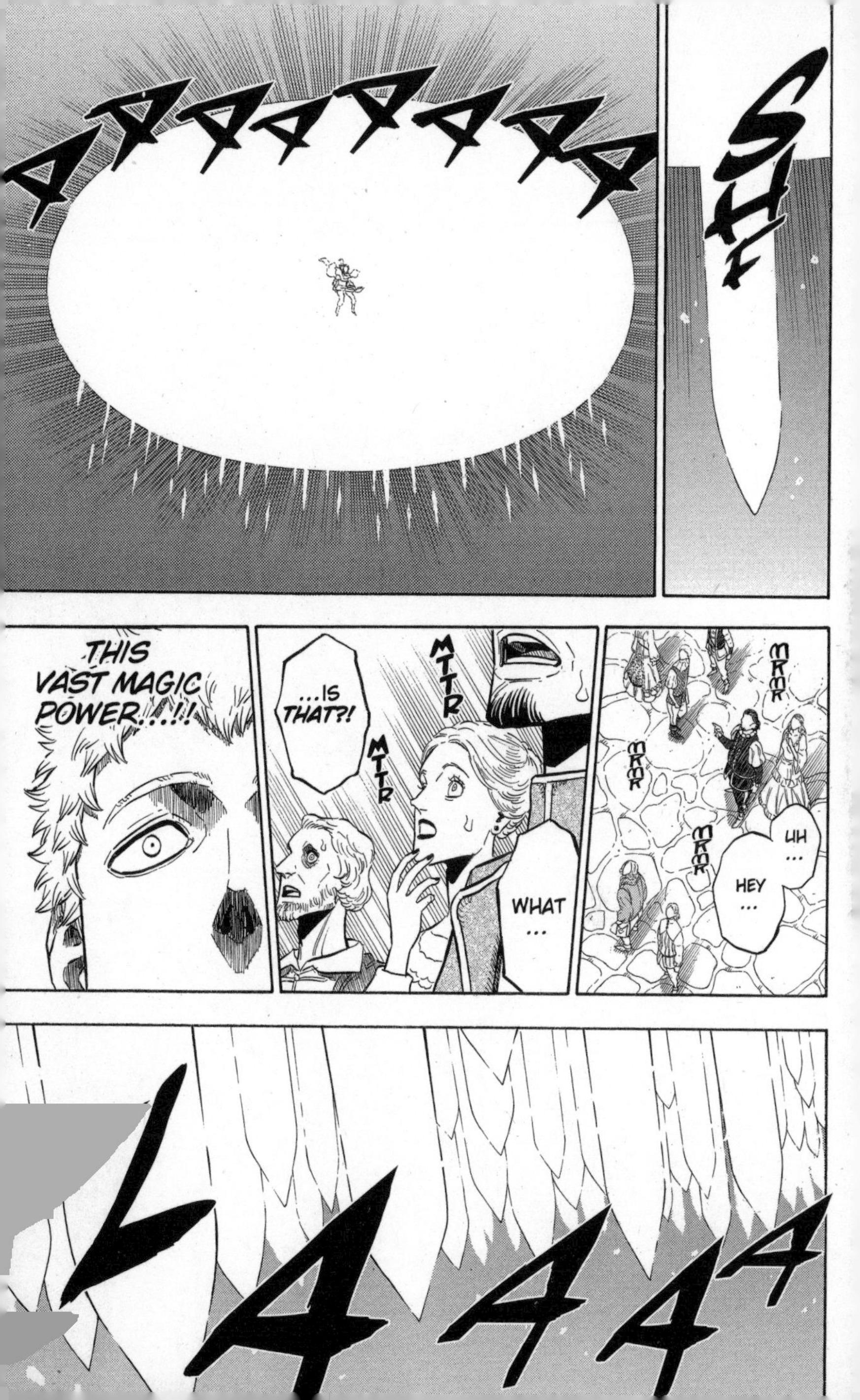
SHF
MRMR
MRMR
MRMR
UH ...
HEY ...
MTTR
MTTR
WHAT ...
...IS THAT?!
THIS VAST MAGIC POWER...!!

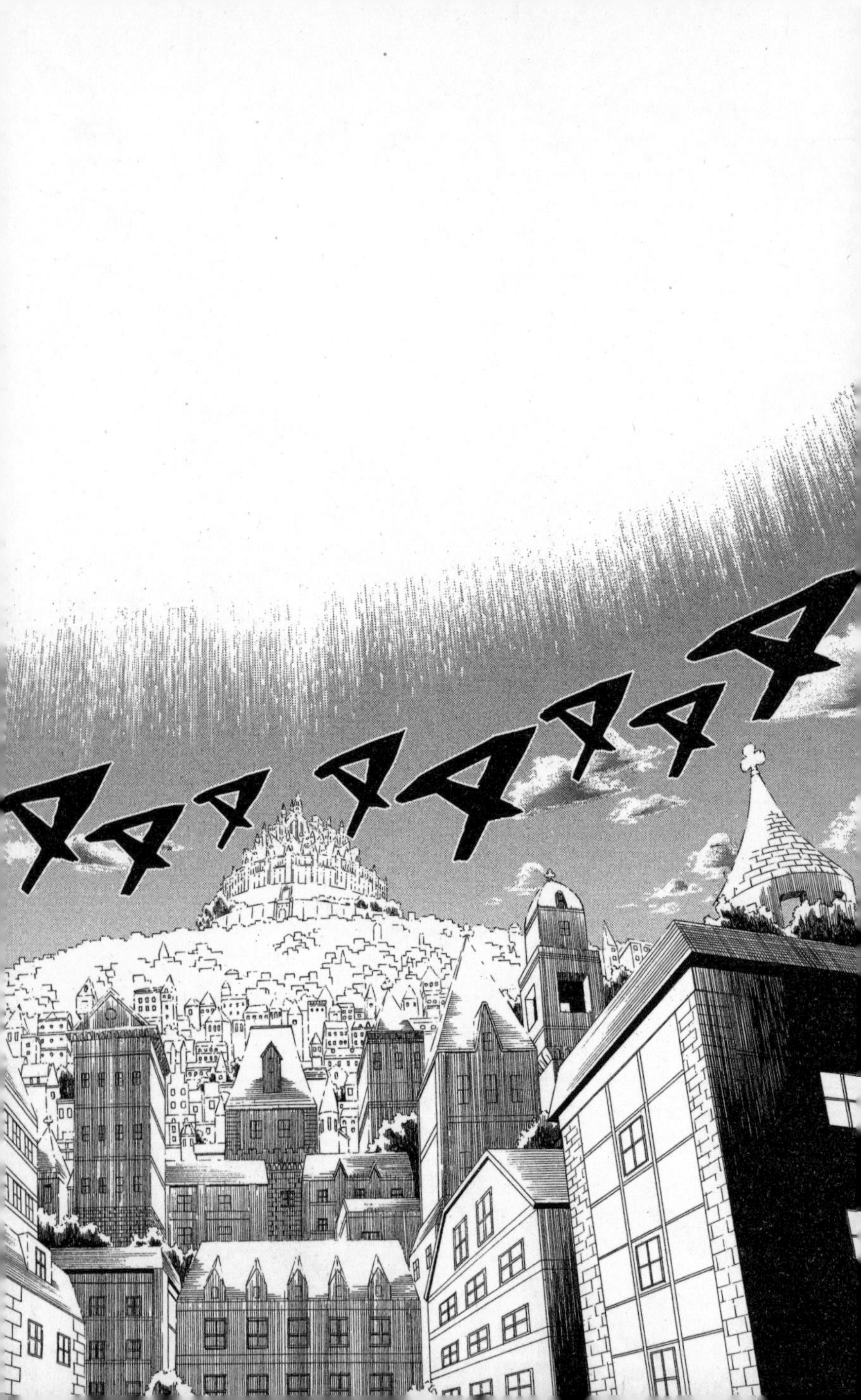

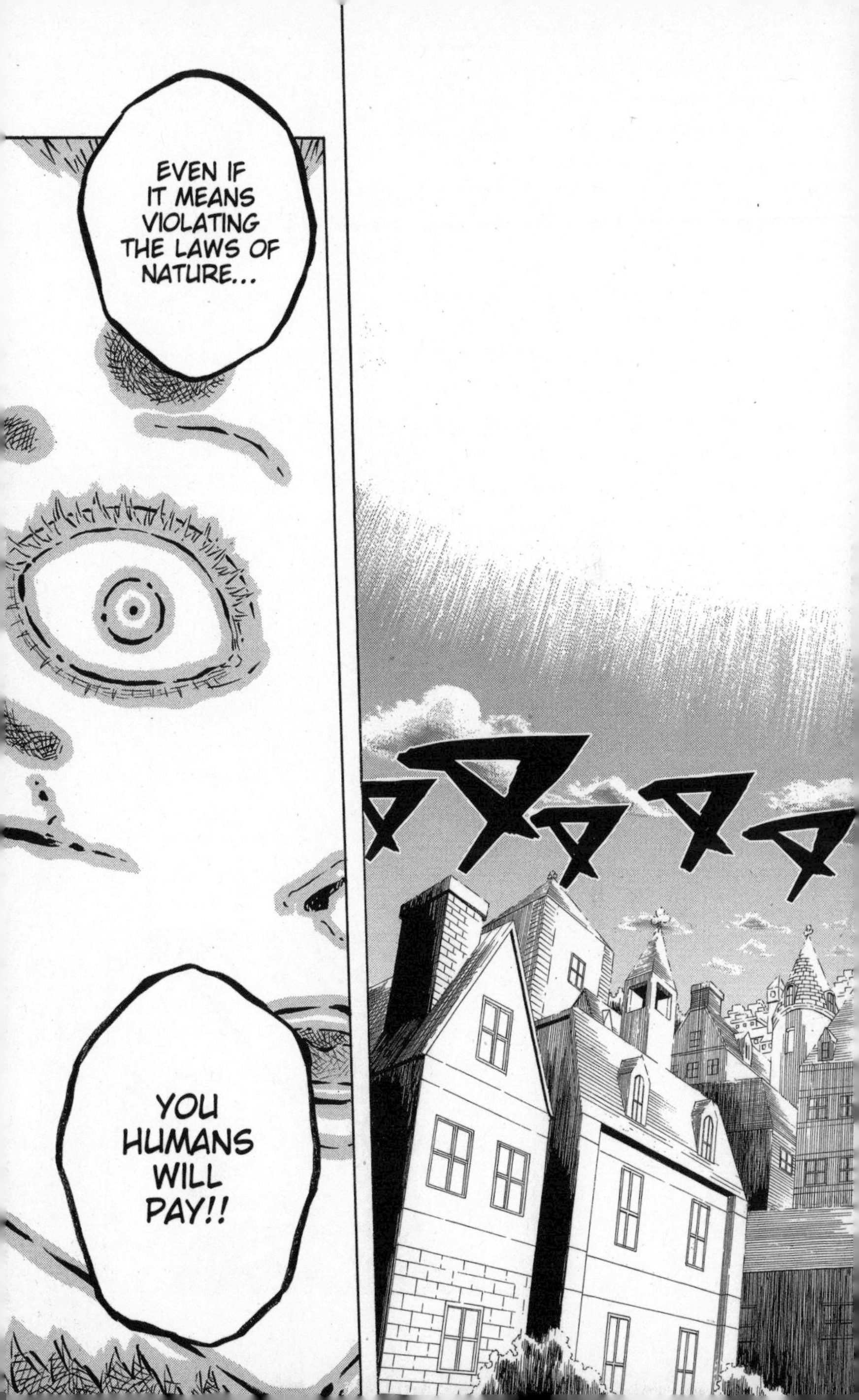
EVEN IF IT MEANS VIOLATING THE LAWS OF NATURE...
YOU HUMANS WILL PAY!!

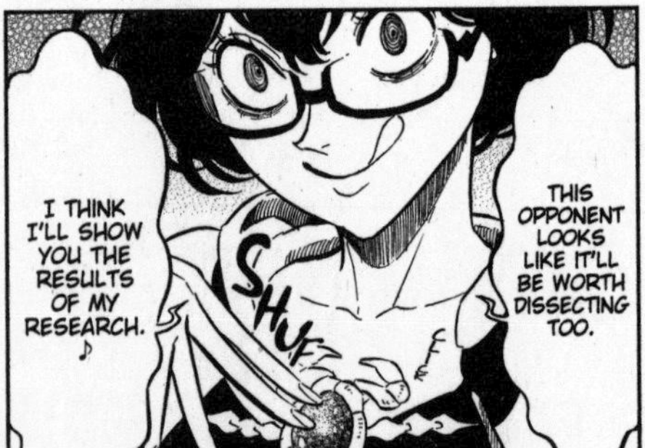
THIS OPPONENT LOOKS LIKE IT'LL BE WORTH DISSECTING TOO.
SHUK
I THINK I'LL SHOW YOU THE RESULTS OF MY RESEARCH. ♪

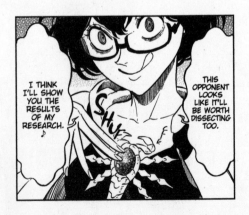

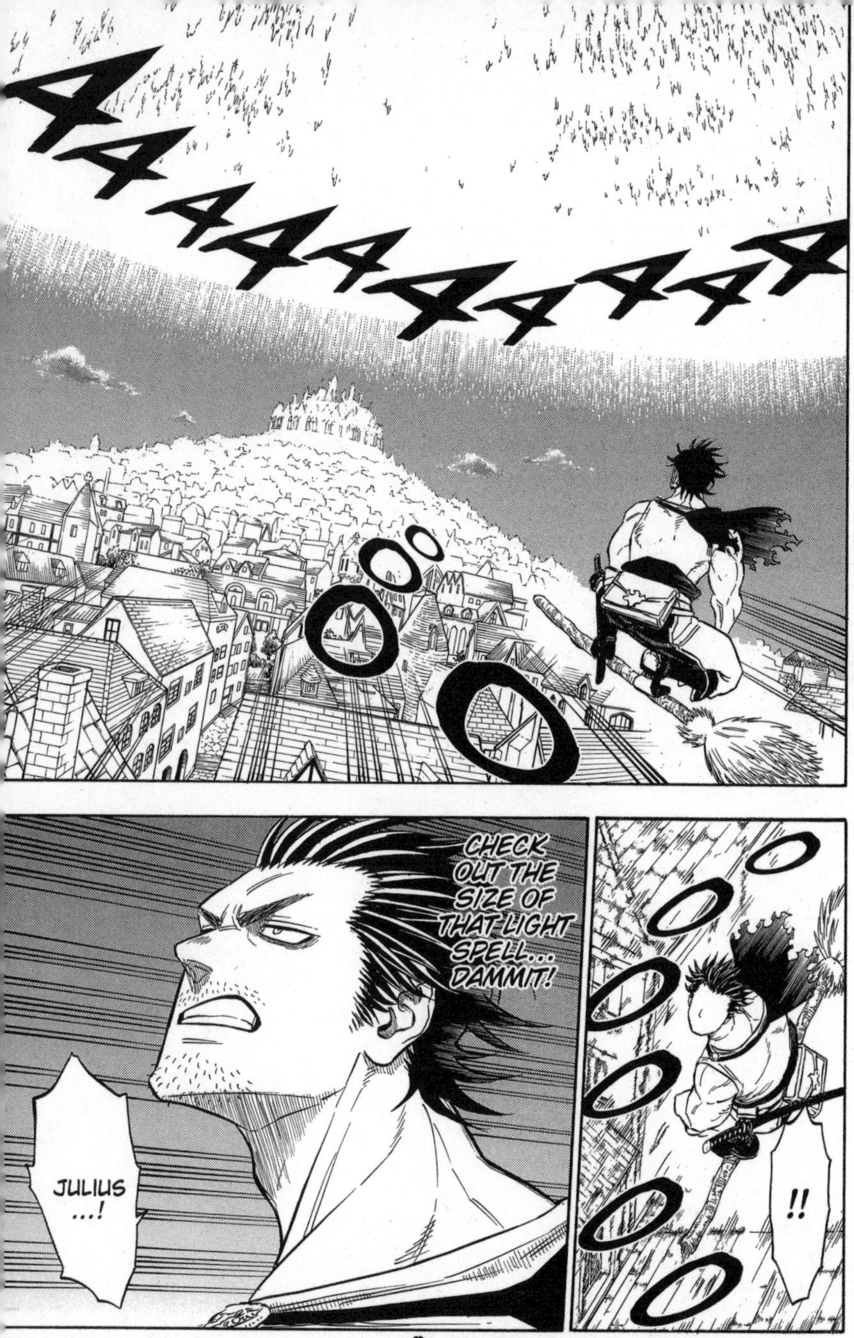
!!
CHECK OUT THE SIZE OF THAT LIGHT SPELL... DAMMIT!
JULIUS ...!

Page 145: Julius Novachrono

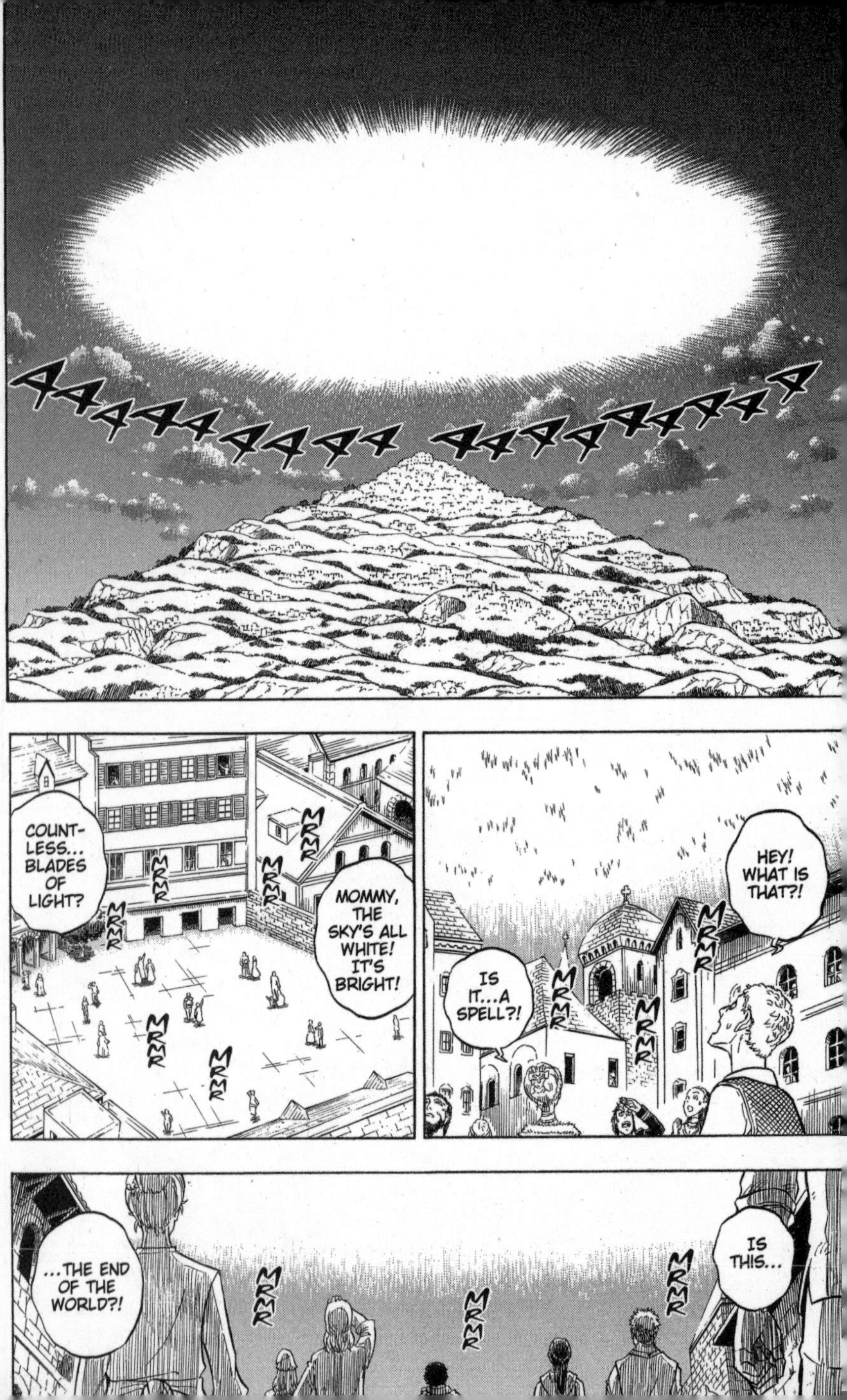
HEY! WHAT IS THAT?!
MRMR
IS IT...A SPELL?!
MRMR
MRMR
MOMMY, THE SKY'S ALL WHITE! IT'S BRIGHT!
MRMR
MRMR
COUNT-LESS... BLADES OF LIGHT?
MRMR
MRMR
MRMR
MRMR
IS THIS...
MRMR
MRMR
MRMR
...THE END OF THE WORLD?!

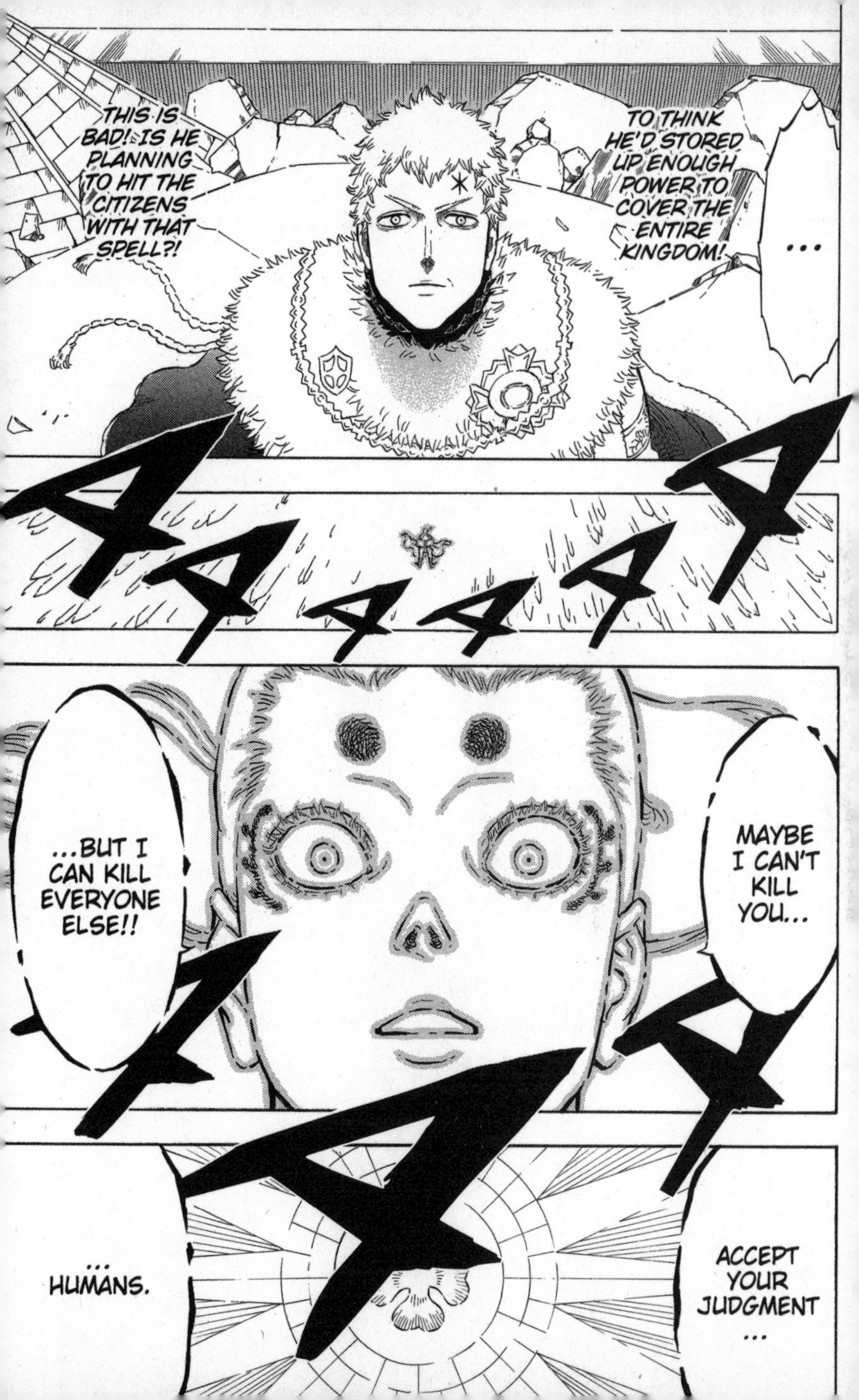
...
TO THINK HE'D STORED UP ENOUGH POWER TO COVER THE ENTIRE KINGDOM!
THIS IS BAD! IS HE PLANNING TO HIT THE CITIZENS WITH THAT SPELL?!
MAYBE I CAN'T KILL YOU...
...BUT I CAN KILL EVERYONE ELSE!!
ACCEPT YOUR JUDGMENT...
...HUMANS.

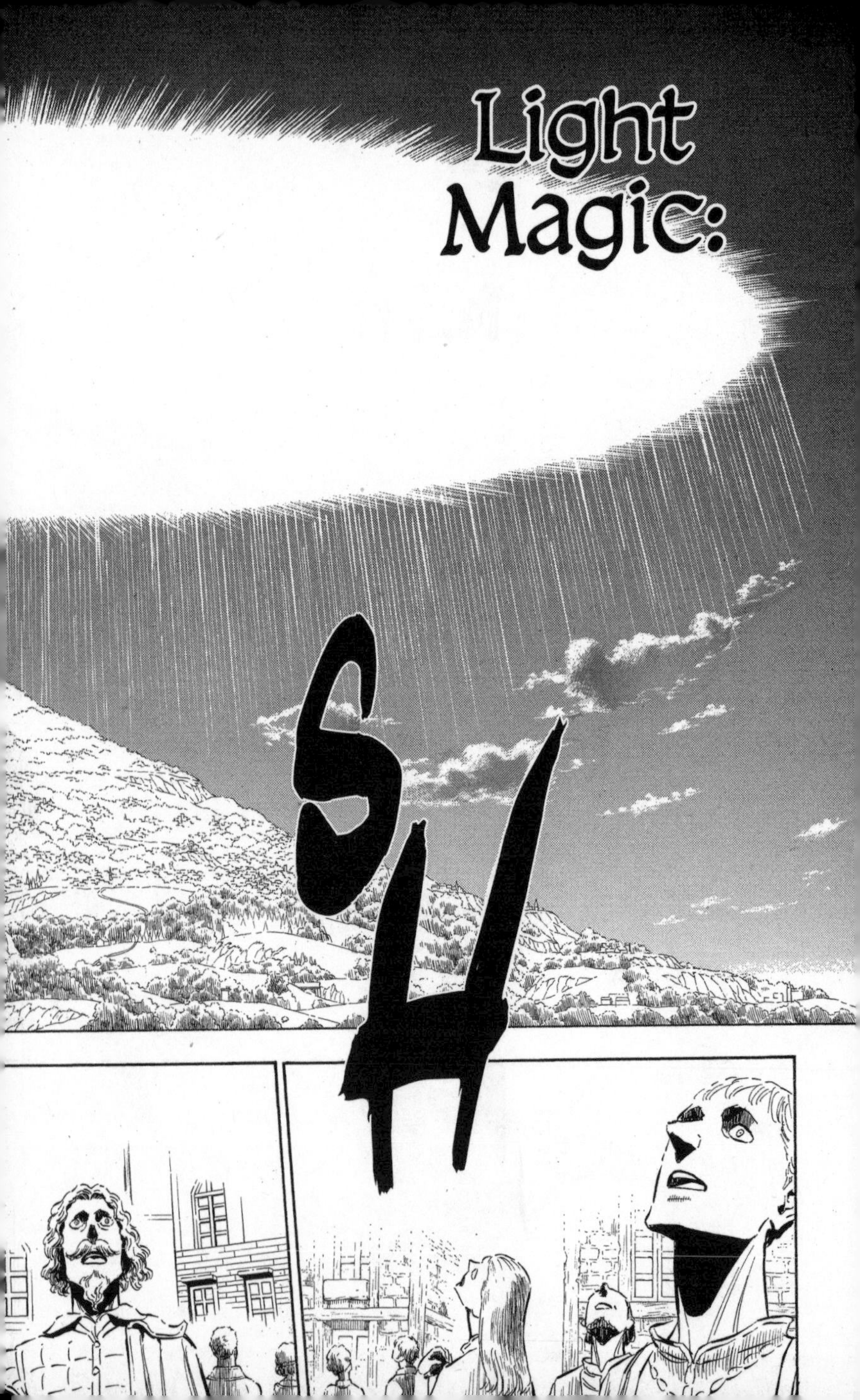
Light Magic:
SH

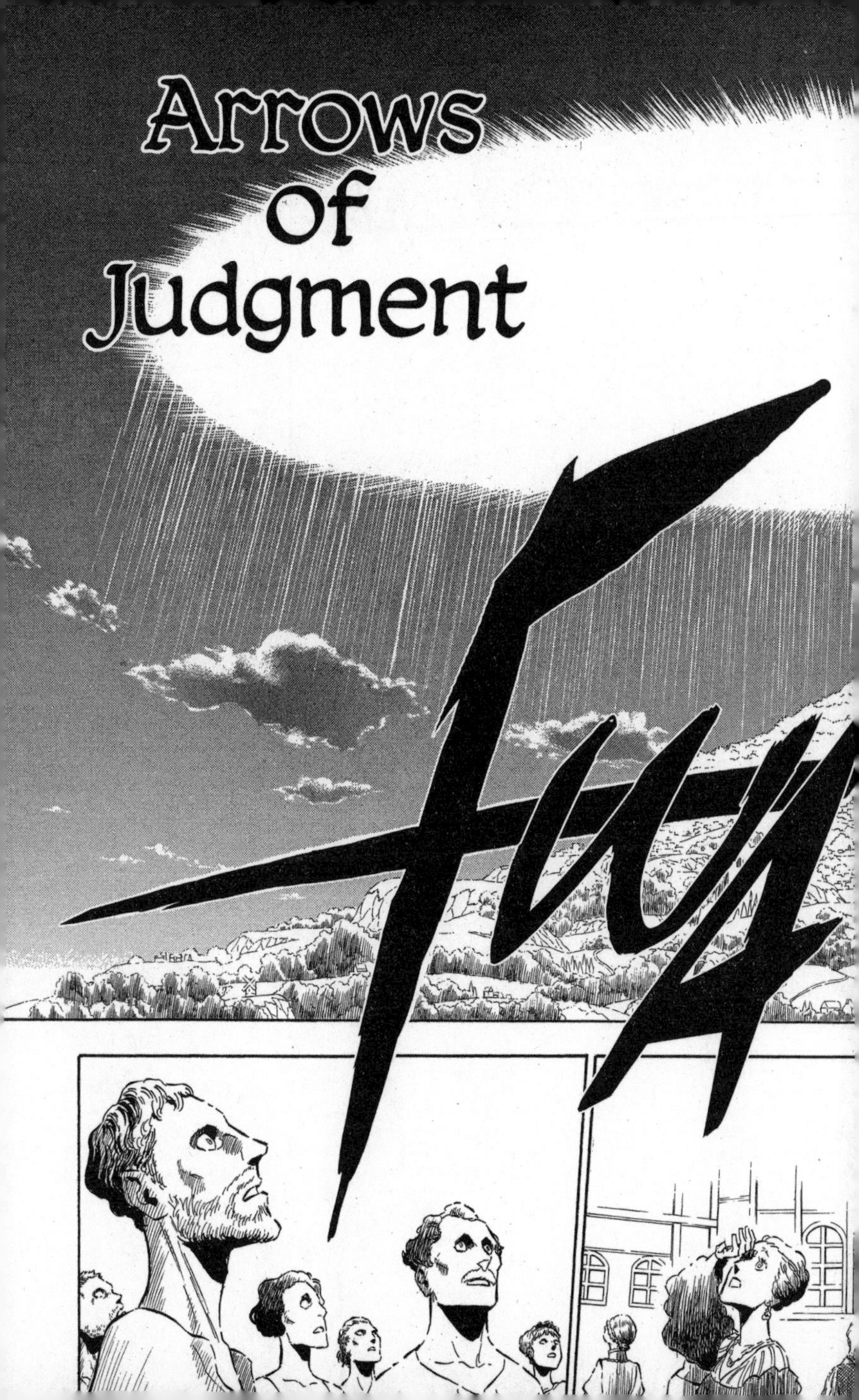
Arrows of Judgment

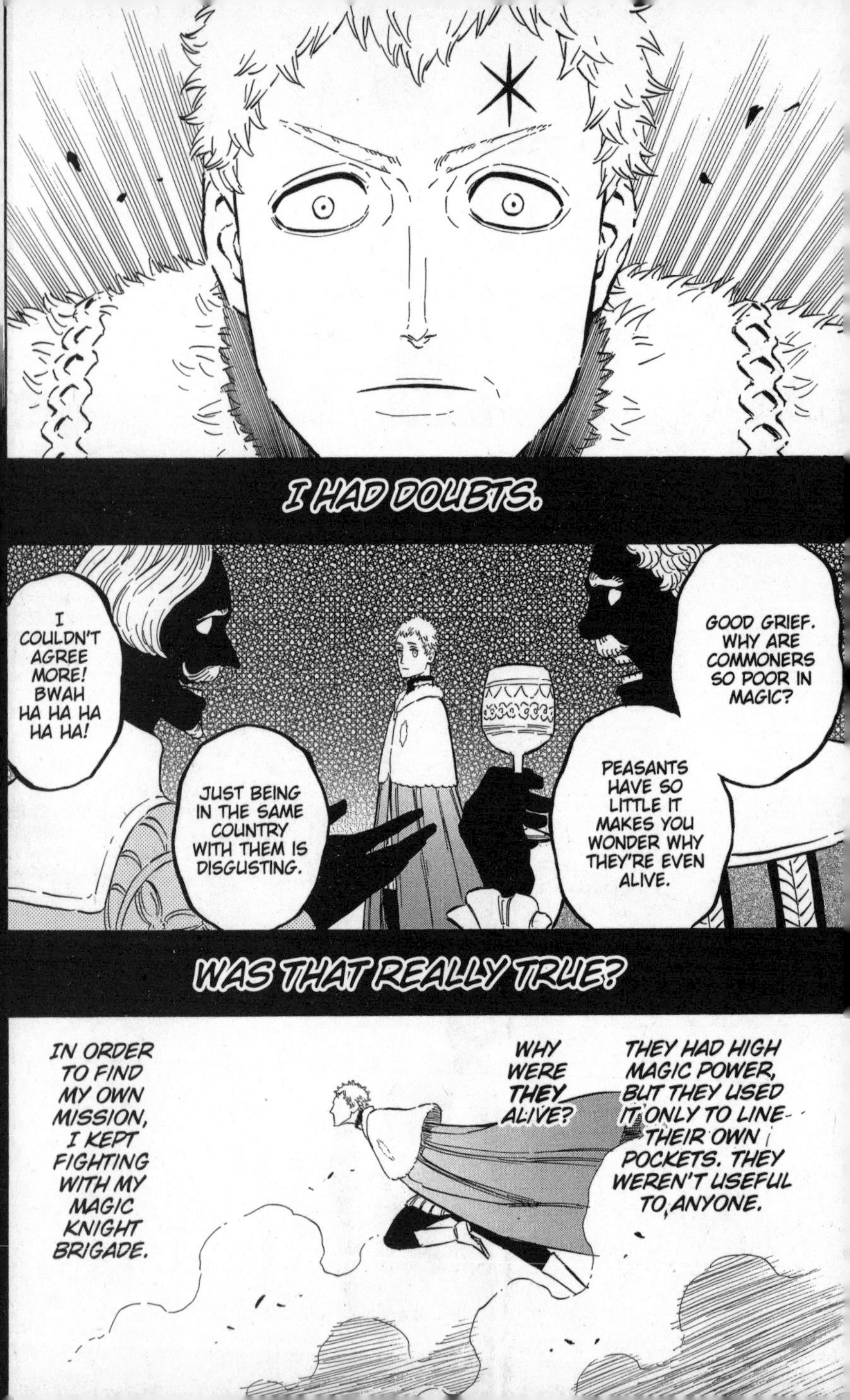
I HAD DOUBTS.
GOOD GRIEF. WHY ARE COMMONERS SO POOR IN MAGIC?
PEASANTS HAVE SO LITTLE IT MAKES YOU WONDER WHY THEY'RE EVEN ALIVE.
I COULDN'T AGREE MORE! BWAH HA HA HA HA HA!
JUST BEING IN THE SAME COUNTRY WITH THEM IS DISGUSTING.
WAS THAT REALLY TRUE?
THEY HAD HIGH MAGIC POWER, BUT THEY USED IT ONLY TO LINE THEIR OWN POCKETS. THEY WEREN'T USEFUL TO ANYONE.
WHY WERE THEY ALIVE?
IN ORDER TO FIND MY OWN MISSION, I KEPT FIGHTING WITH MY MAGIC KNIGHT BRIGADE.

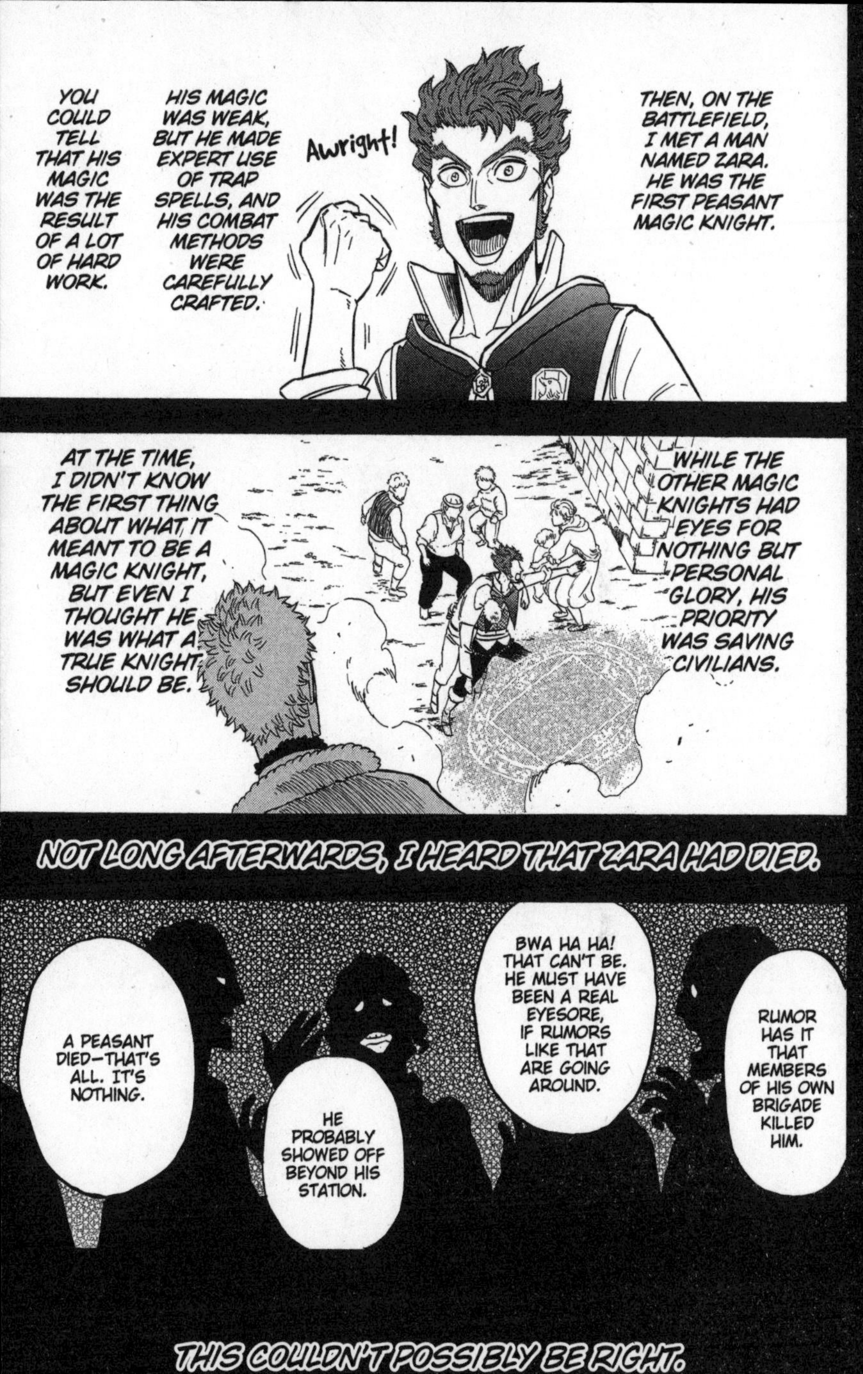
THEN, ON THE BATTLEFIELD, I MET A MAN NAMED ZARA. HE WAS THE FIRST PEASANT MAGIC KNIGHT.
Awright!
HIS MAGIC WAS WEAK, BUT HE MADE EXPERT USE OF TRAP SPELLS, AND HIS COMBAT METHODS WERE CAREFULLY CRAFTED.
YOU COULD TELL THAT HIS MAGIC WAS THE RESULT OF A LOT OF HARD WORK.
WHILE THE OTHER MAGIC KNIGHTS HAD EYES FOR NOTHING BUT PERSONAL GLORY, HIS PRIORITY WAS SAVING CIVILIANS.
AT THE TIME, I DIDN'T KNOW THE FIRST THING ABOUT WHAT IT MEANT TO BE A MAGIC KNIGHT, BUT EVEN I THOUGHT HE WAS WHAT A TRUE KNIGHT SHOULD BE.
NOT LONG AFTERWARDS, I HEARD THAT ZARA HAD DIED.
RUMOR HAS IT THAT MEMBERS OF HIS OWN BRIGADE KILLED HIM.
BWA HA HA! THAT CAN'T BE. HE MUST HAVE BEEN A REAL EYESORE, IF RUMORS LIKE THAT ARE GOING AROUND.
HE PROBABLY SHOWED OFF BEYOND HIS STATION.
A PEASANT DIED—THAT'S ALL. IT'S NOTHING.
THIS COULDN'T POSSIBLY BE RIGHT.

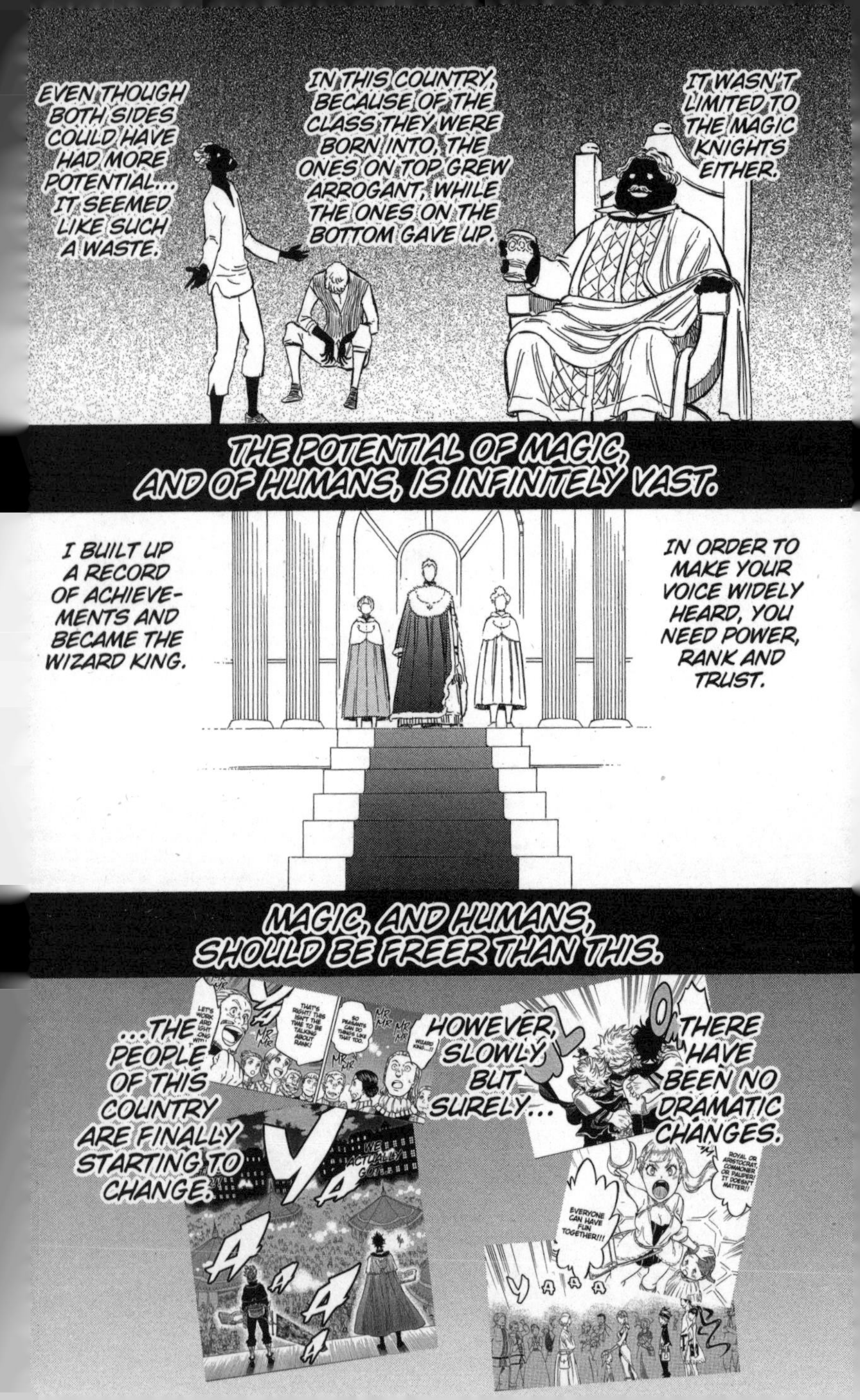
IT WASN'T LIMITED TO THE MAGIC KNIGHTS EITHER.
IN THIS COUNTRY, BECAUSE OF THE CLASS THEY WERE BORN INTO, THE ONES ON TOP GREW ARROGANT, WHILE THE ONES ON THE BOTTOM GAVE UP.
EVEN THOUGH BOTH SIDES COULD HAVE HAD MORE POTENTIAL... IT SEEMED LIKE SUCH A WASTE.
THE POTENTIAL OF MAGIC, AND OF HUMANS, IS INFINITELY VAST.
IN ORDER TO MAKE YOUR VOICE WIDELY HEARD, YOU NEED POWER, RANK AND TRUST.
I BUILT UP A RECORD OF ACHIEVEMENTS AND BECAME THE WIZARD KING.
MAGIC, AND HUMANS, SHOULD BE FREER THAN THIS.
THERE HAVE BEEN NO DRAMATIC CHANGES.
ROYAL OR ARISTOCRAT, COMMONER OR PAUPER! IT DOESN'T MATTER!!
EVERYONE CAN HAVE FUN TOGETHER!!!
HOWEVER, SLOWLY BUT SURELY...
WIZARD KING...!!
SO PEASANTS CAN DO THINGS LIKE THAT TOO.
THAT'S RIGHT! THIS ISN'T THE TIME TO BE TALKING ABOUT RANK!
...THE PEOPLE OF THIS COUNTRY ARE FINALLY STARTING TO CHANGE.

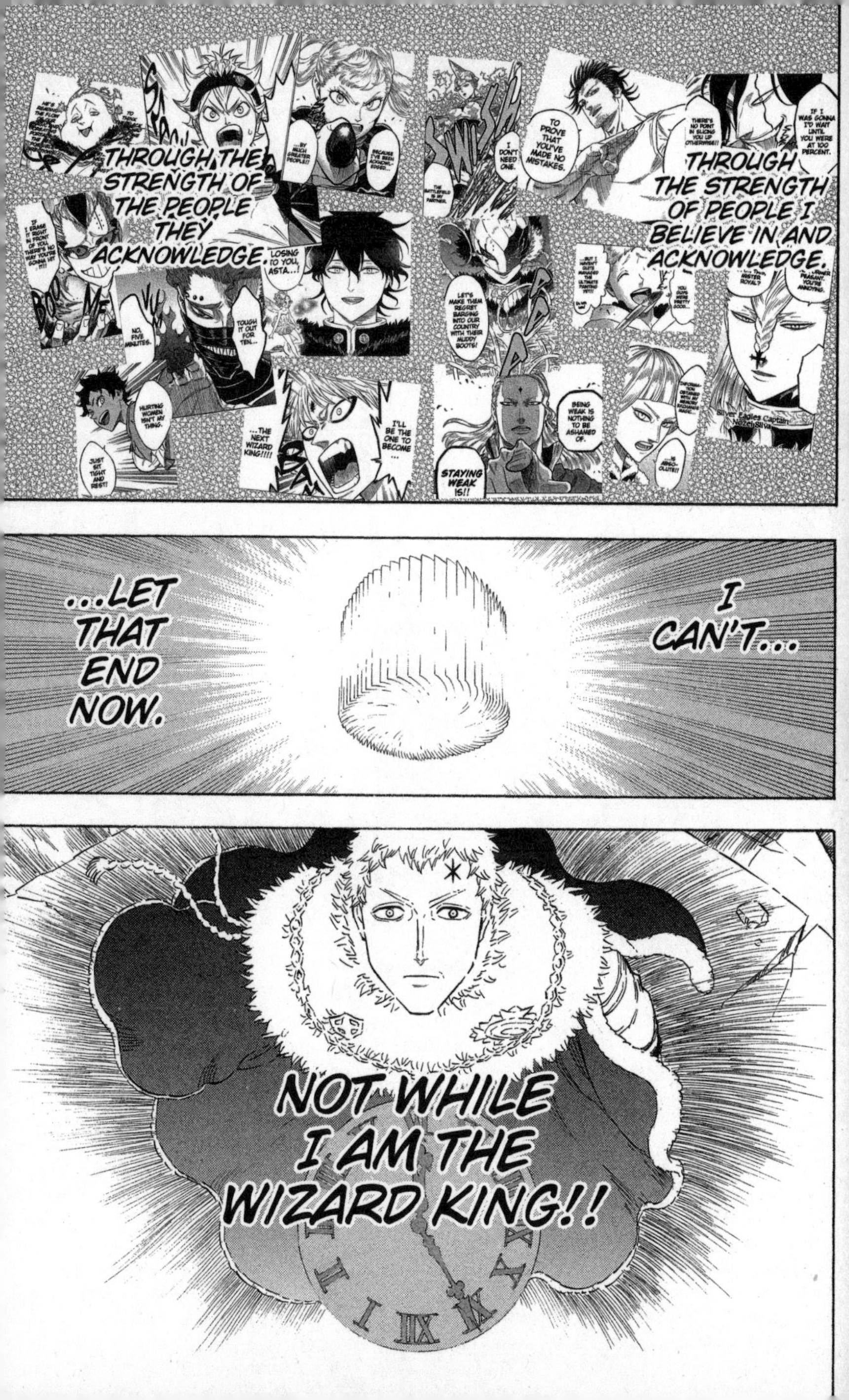
IF I WAS GONNA I'D WAIT UNTIL YOU WERE AT 100 PERCENT.
THERE'S NO POINT IN SLICING YOU UP OTHERWISE!!
TO PROVE THAT YOU'VE MADE NO MISTAKES.
I DON'T NEED ONE.
THE BATTLEFIELD IS MY PARTNER.
SWISH
THROUGH THE STRENGTH OF PEOPLE I BELIEVE IN AND ACKNOWLEDGE.
PEASANT. YOU'RE ANNOYING.
MISTER ROYAL?
YOU GUYS WERE PRETTY GOOD...
...BUT I HAVEN'T QUITE MANAGED THE ULTIMATE PAINTING YET!!
LET'S MAKE THEM REGRET BARGING INTO OUR COUNTRY WITH THEIR MUDDY BOOTS!
Silver Eagles Captain Nozel Silva
INFORMATION OBTAINED WITH MY MEMORY EXCHANGE MAGIC...
...IS ABSOLUTE!!
BEING WEAK IS NOTHING TO BE ASHAMED OF.
STAYING WEAK IS!!
BECAUSE I'VE BEEN ACKNOWLEDGED...
...BY MUCH GREATER PEOPLE!!
THROUGH THE STRENGTH OF THE PEOPLE THEY ACKNOWLEDGE.
LOSING TO YOU, ASTA...!
TOUGH IT OUT FOR TEN...
NO. FIVE MINUTES.
IF I ERASE IT RIGHT IN FRONT OF YOU, THERE'S NO WAY YOU'RE GONNA HIT IT!!
I'LL BE THE ONE TO BECOME...
...THE NEXT WIZARD KING!!!!
HURTING WOMEN ISN'T MY THING.
JUST SIT TIGHT AND REST!
I CAN'T...
...LET THAT END NOW.
NOT WHILE I AM THE WIZARD KING!!

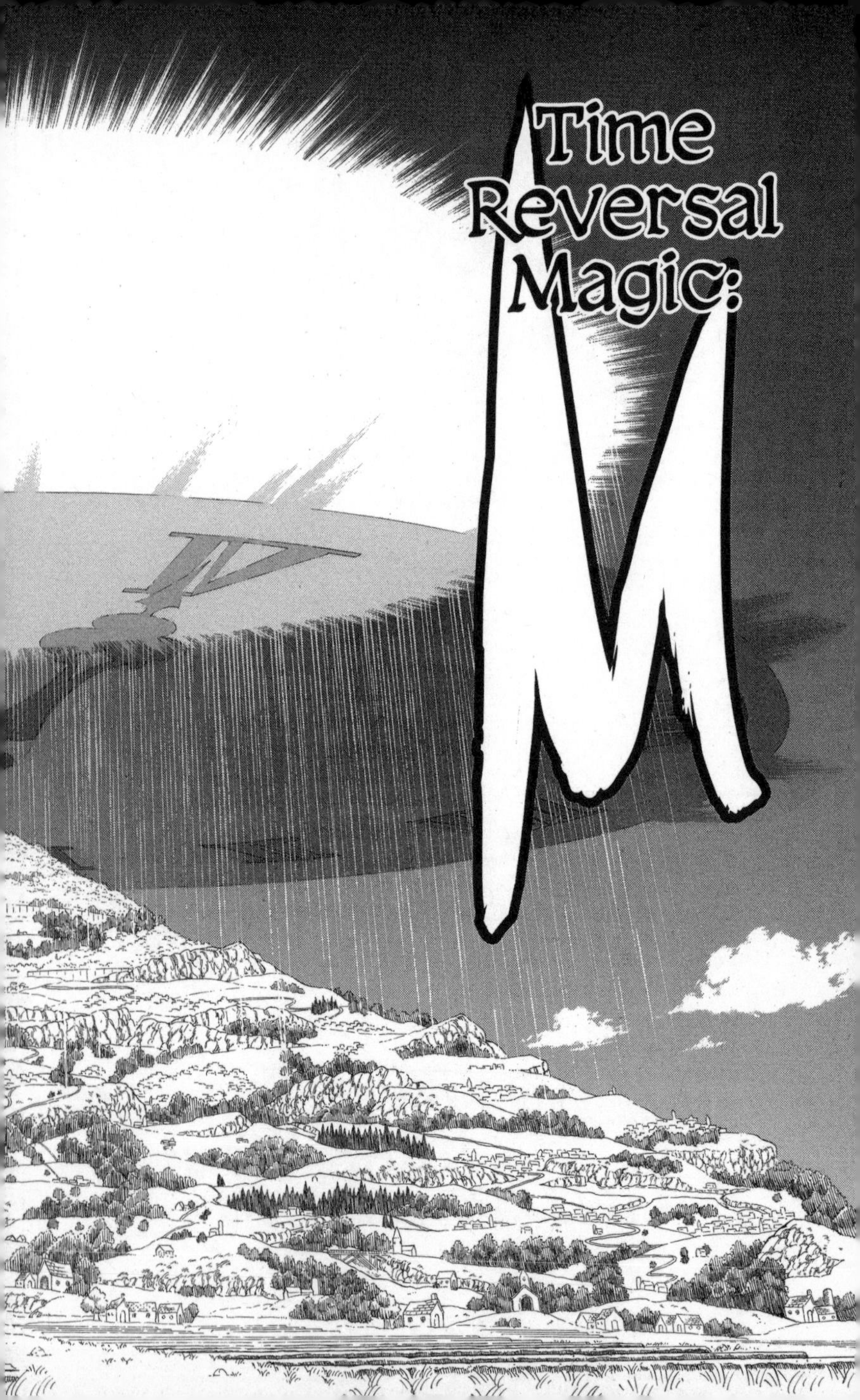
Time Reversal Magic:
M

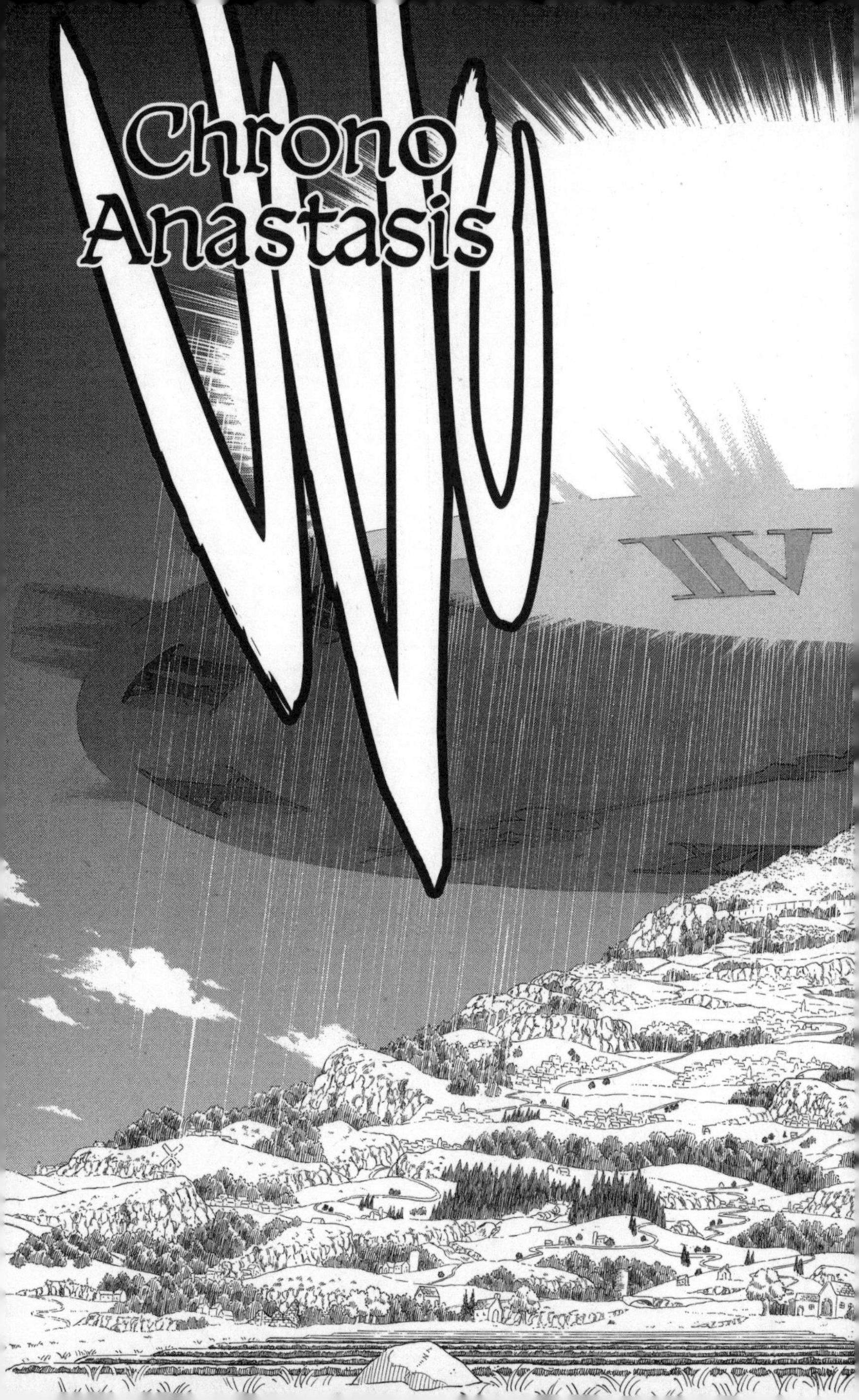
Chrono Anastasis

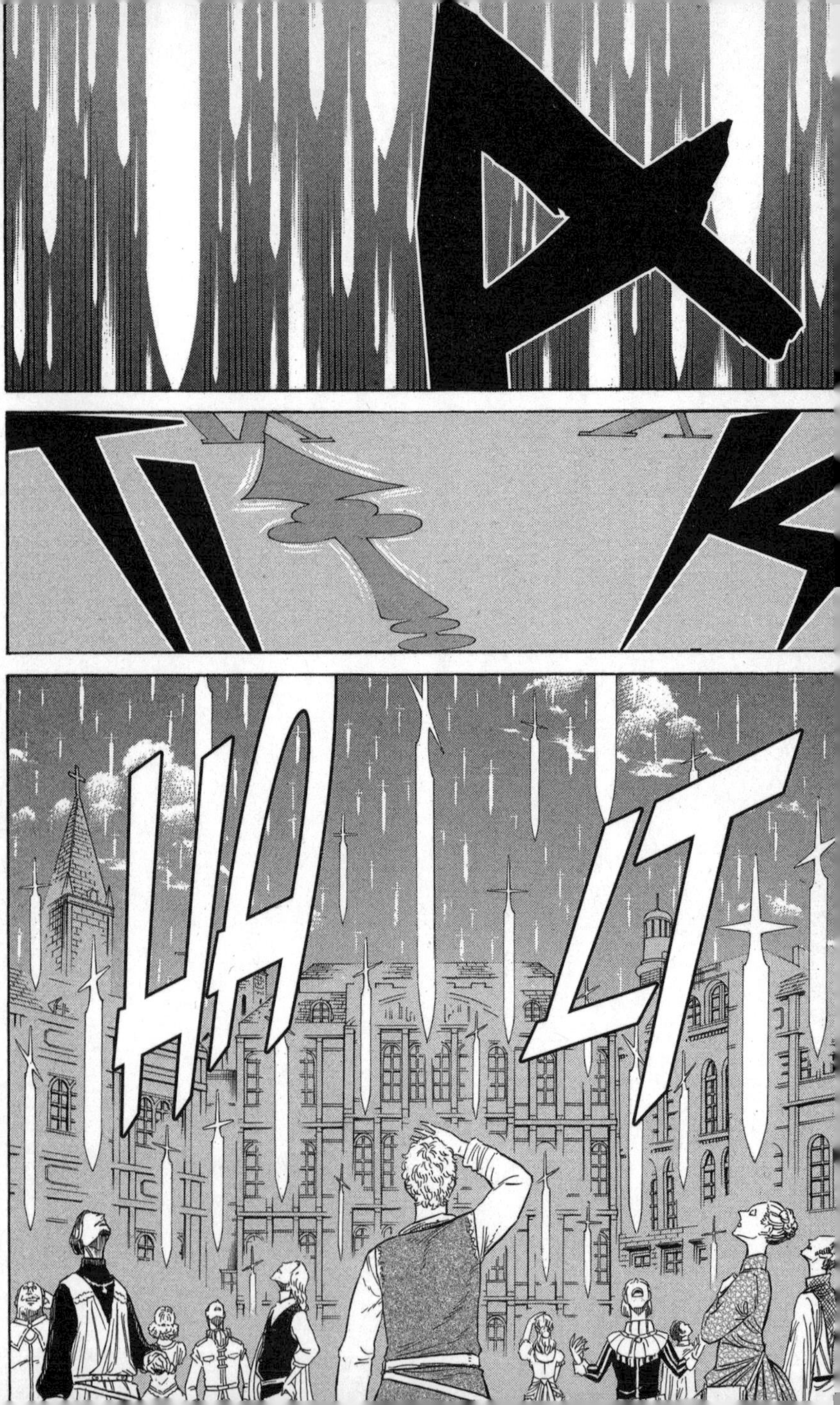

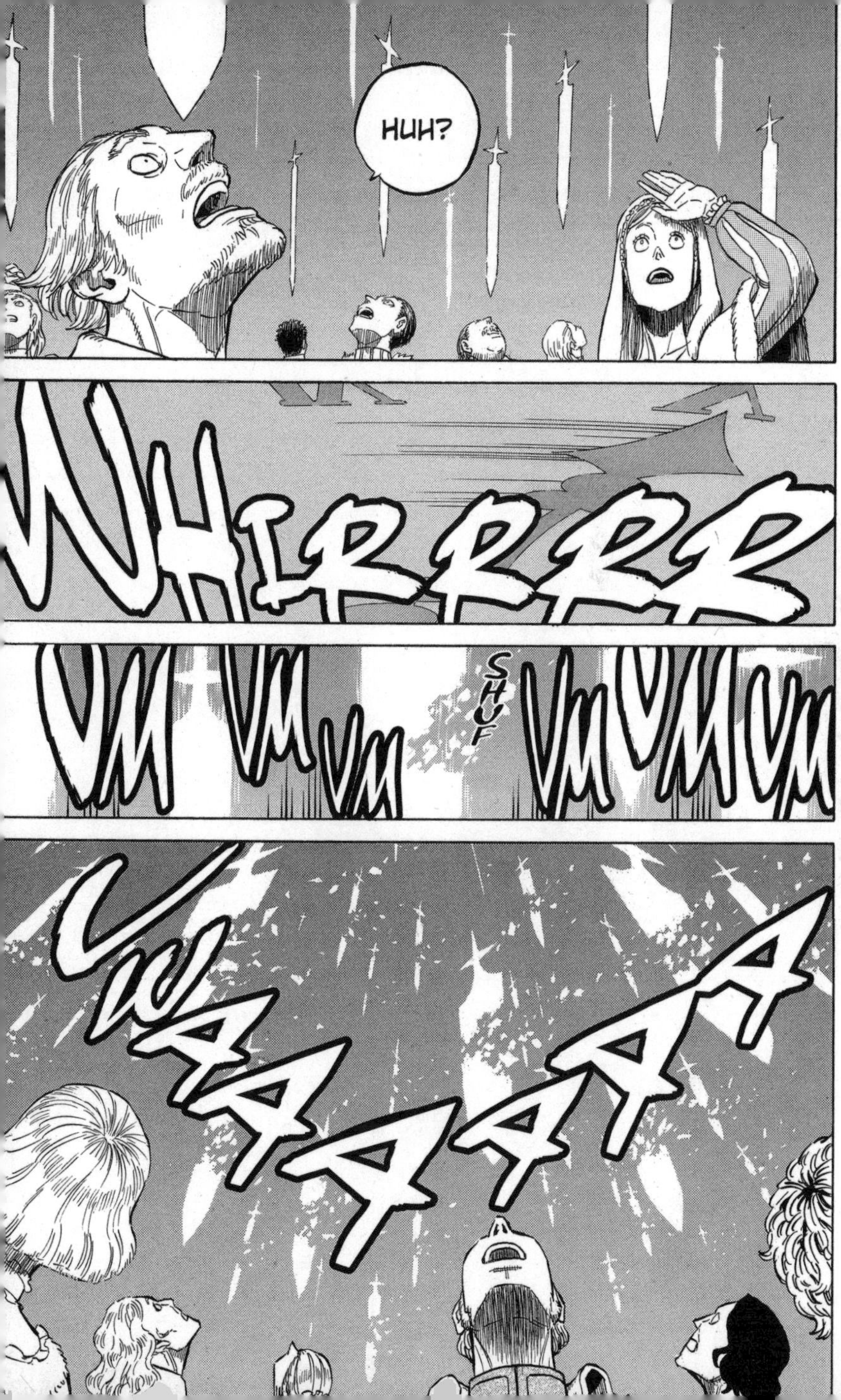
HUH?
WHIRRR
VM VM VM VM
SHUF
VMVMVM
VWAAAAA

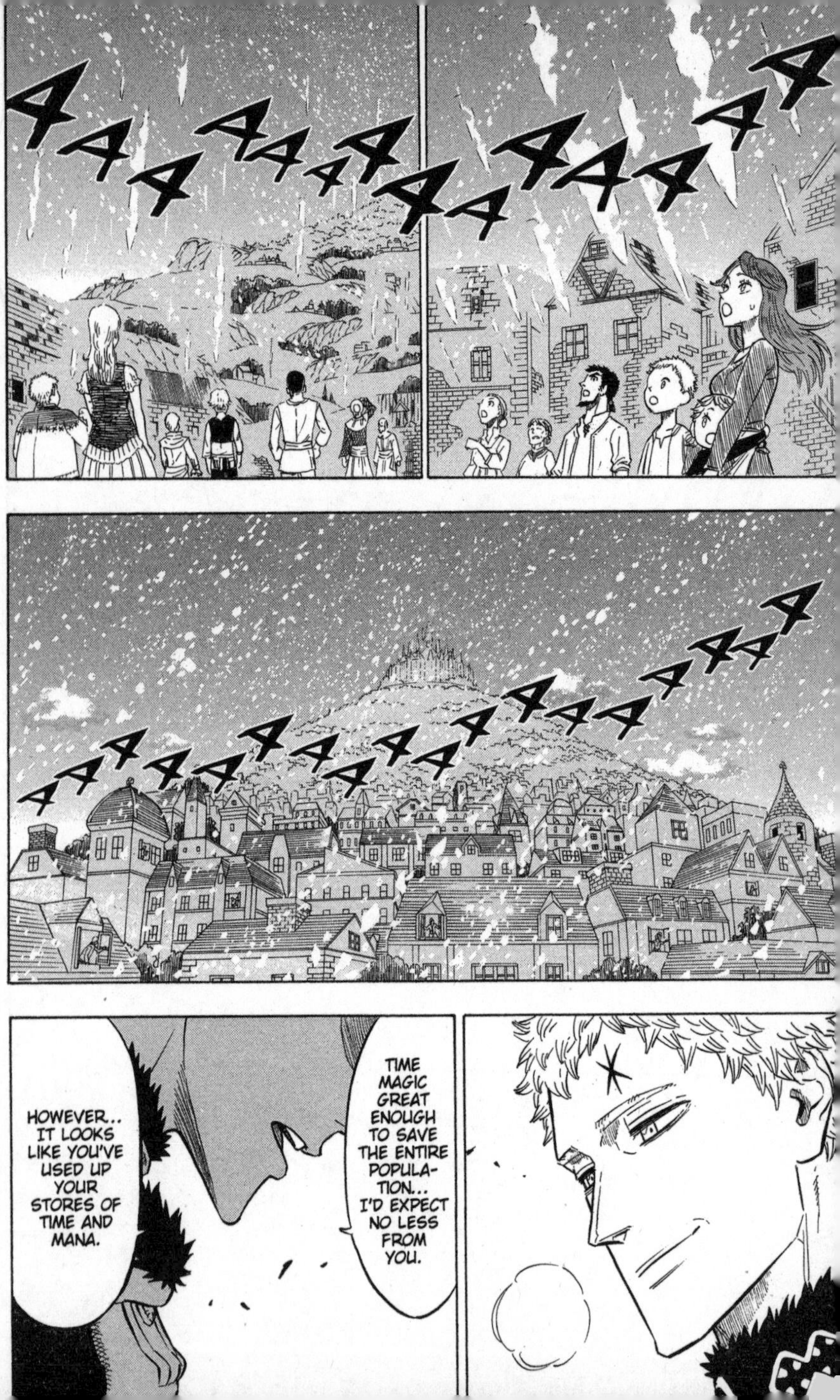
TIME MAGIC GREAT ENOUGH TO SAVE THE ENTIRE POPULATION... I'D EXPECT NO LESS FROM YOU.
HOWEVER... IT LOOKS LIKE YOU'VE USED UP YOUR STORES OF TIME AND MANA.

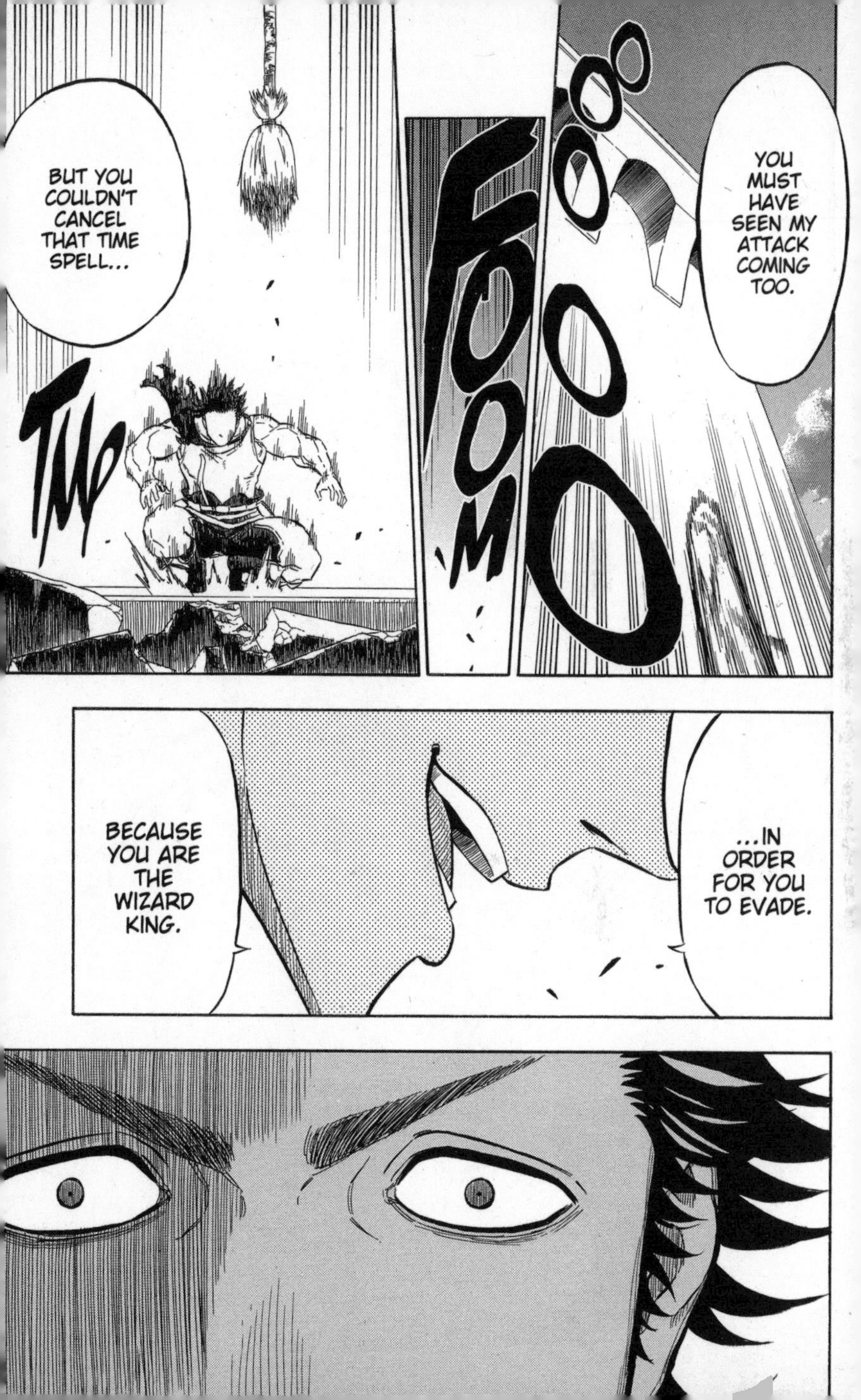
YOU MUST HAVE SEEN MY ATTACK COMING TOO.
FOOOOM
BUT YOU COULDN'T CANCEL THAT TIME SPELL...
TMP
...IN ORDER FOR YOU TO EVADE.
BECAUSE YOU ARE THE WIZARD KING.

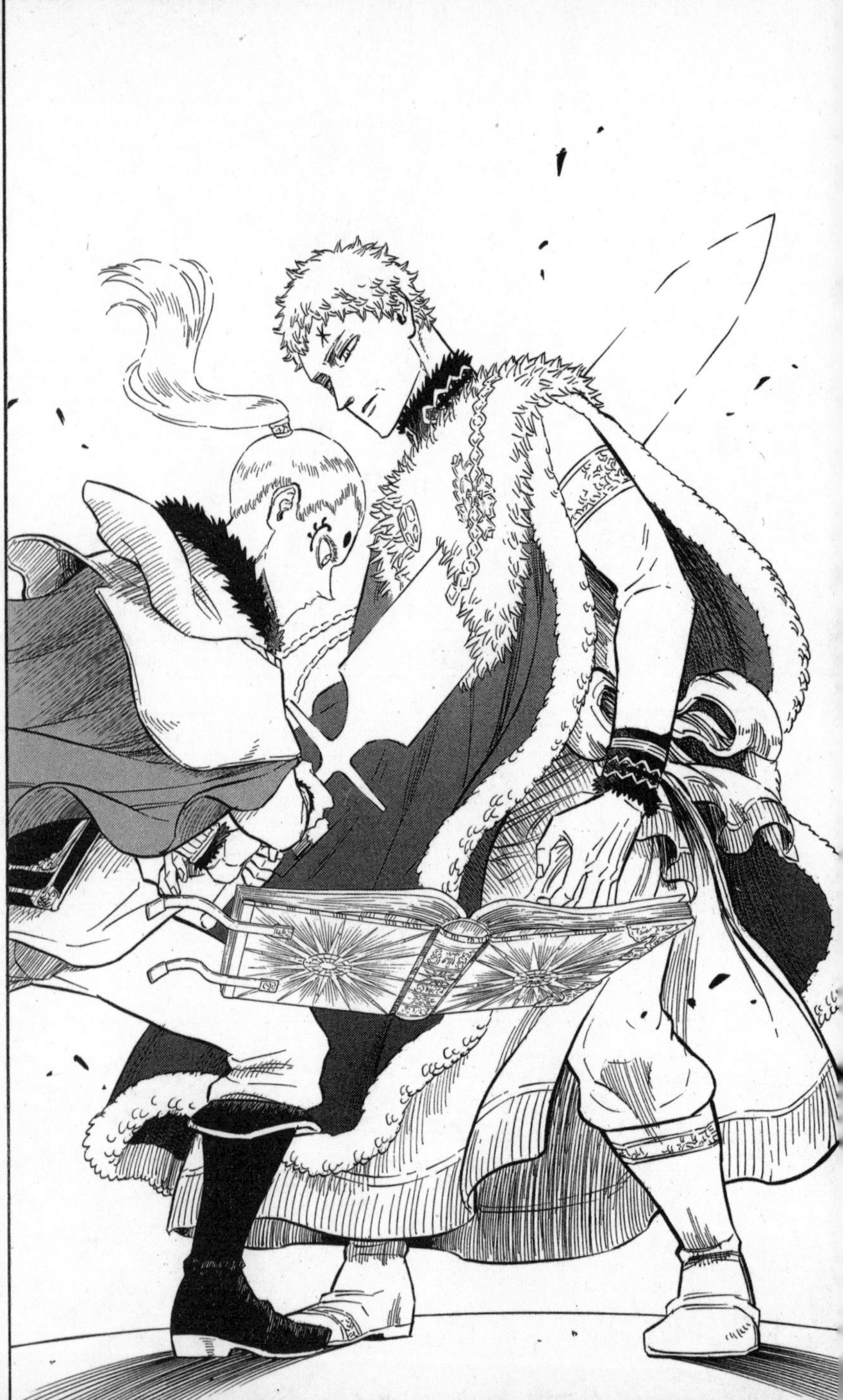

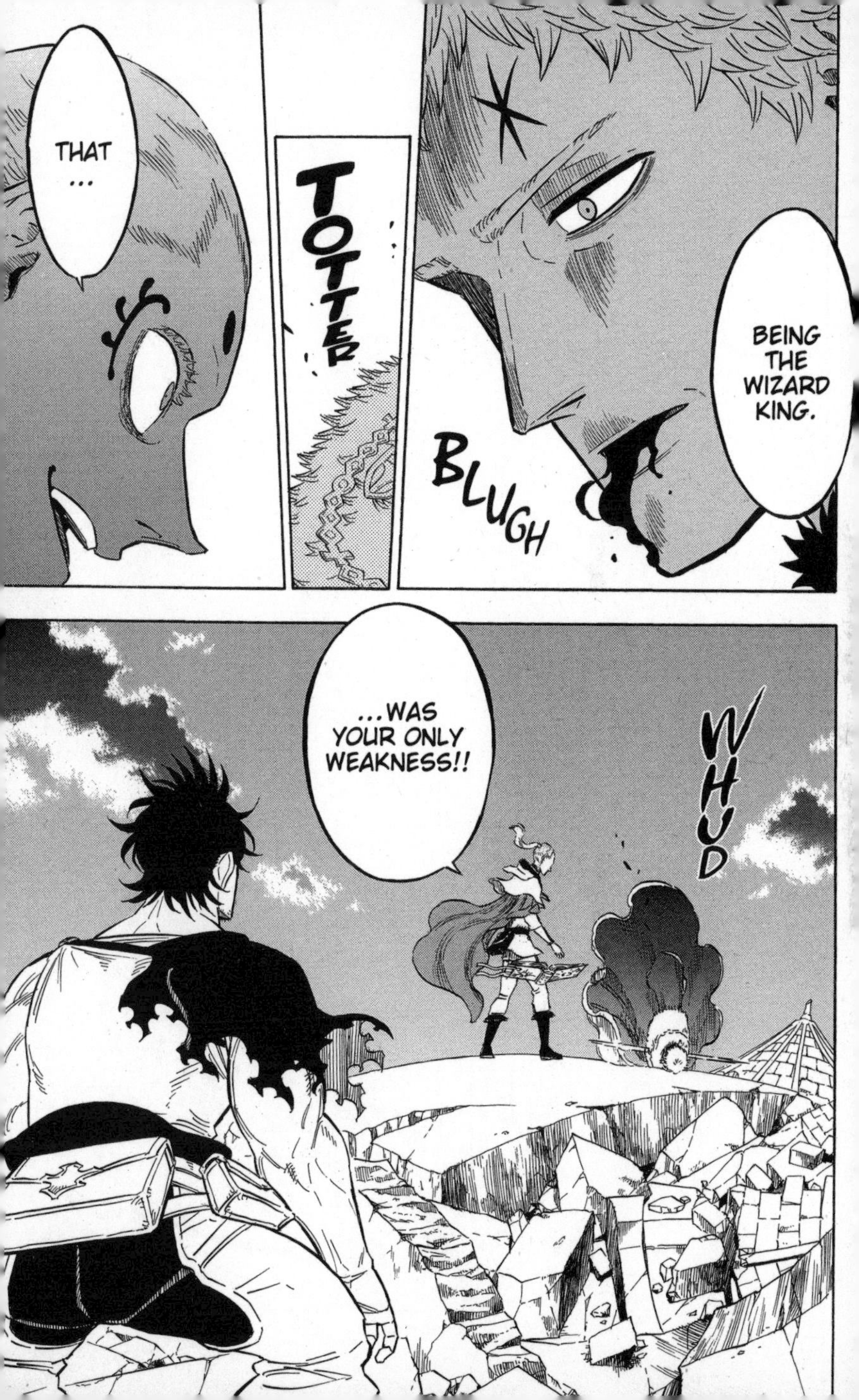
BEING THE WIZARD KING.
BLUGH
TOTTER
THAT ...
...WAS YOUR ONLY WEAKNESS!!
WHUD

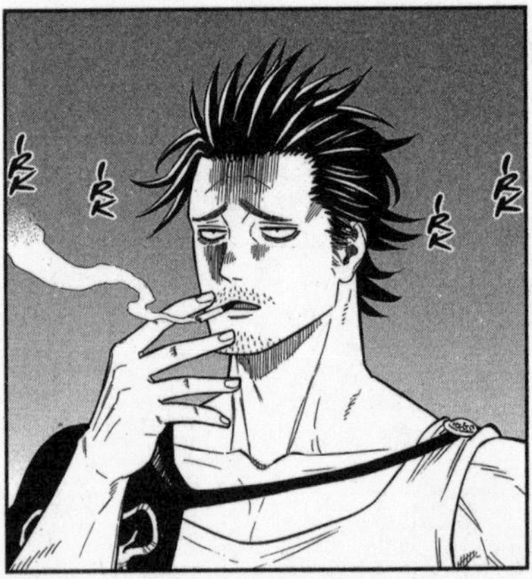
IRK
IRK
IRK
IRK

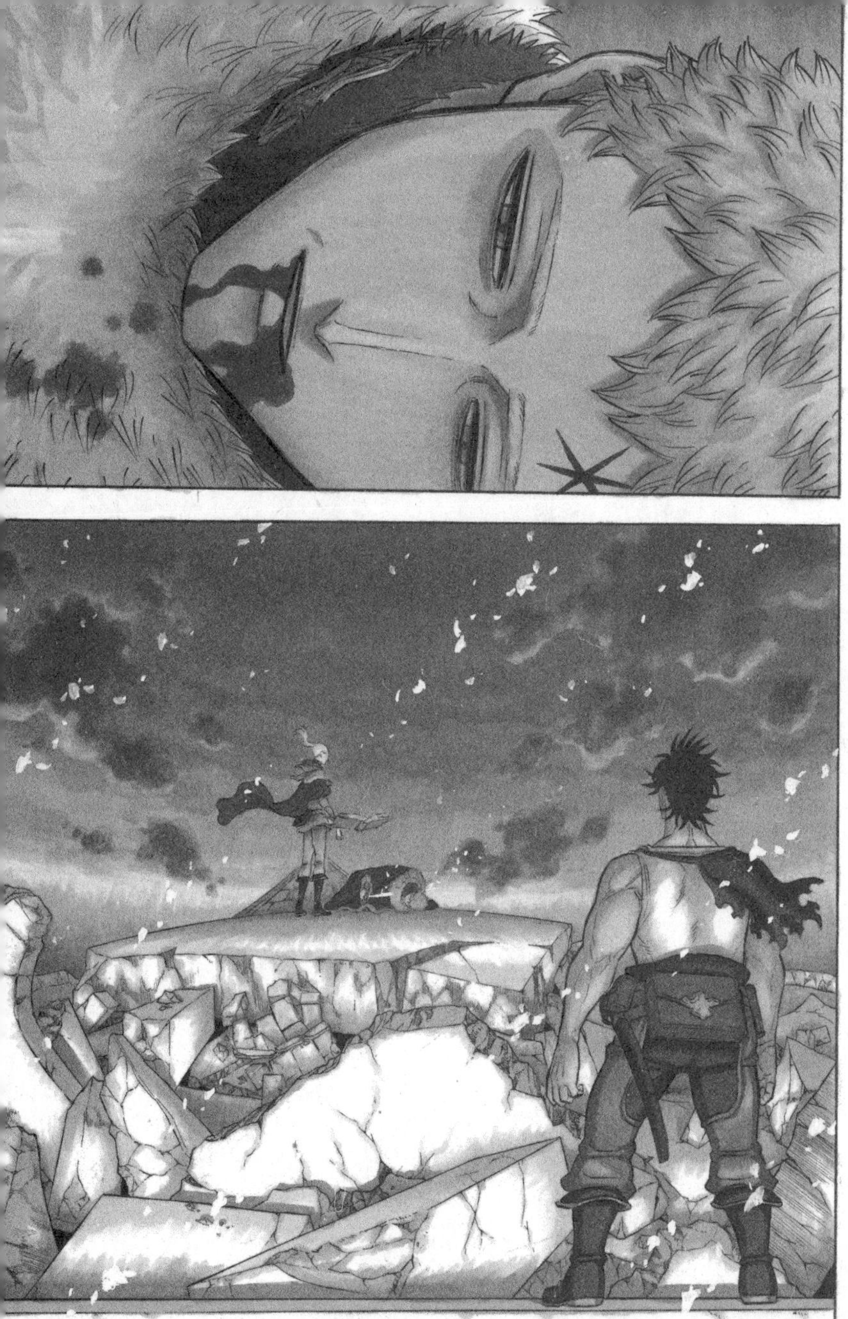

Page 146: New Future

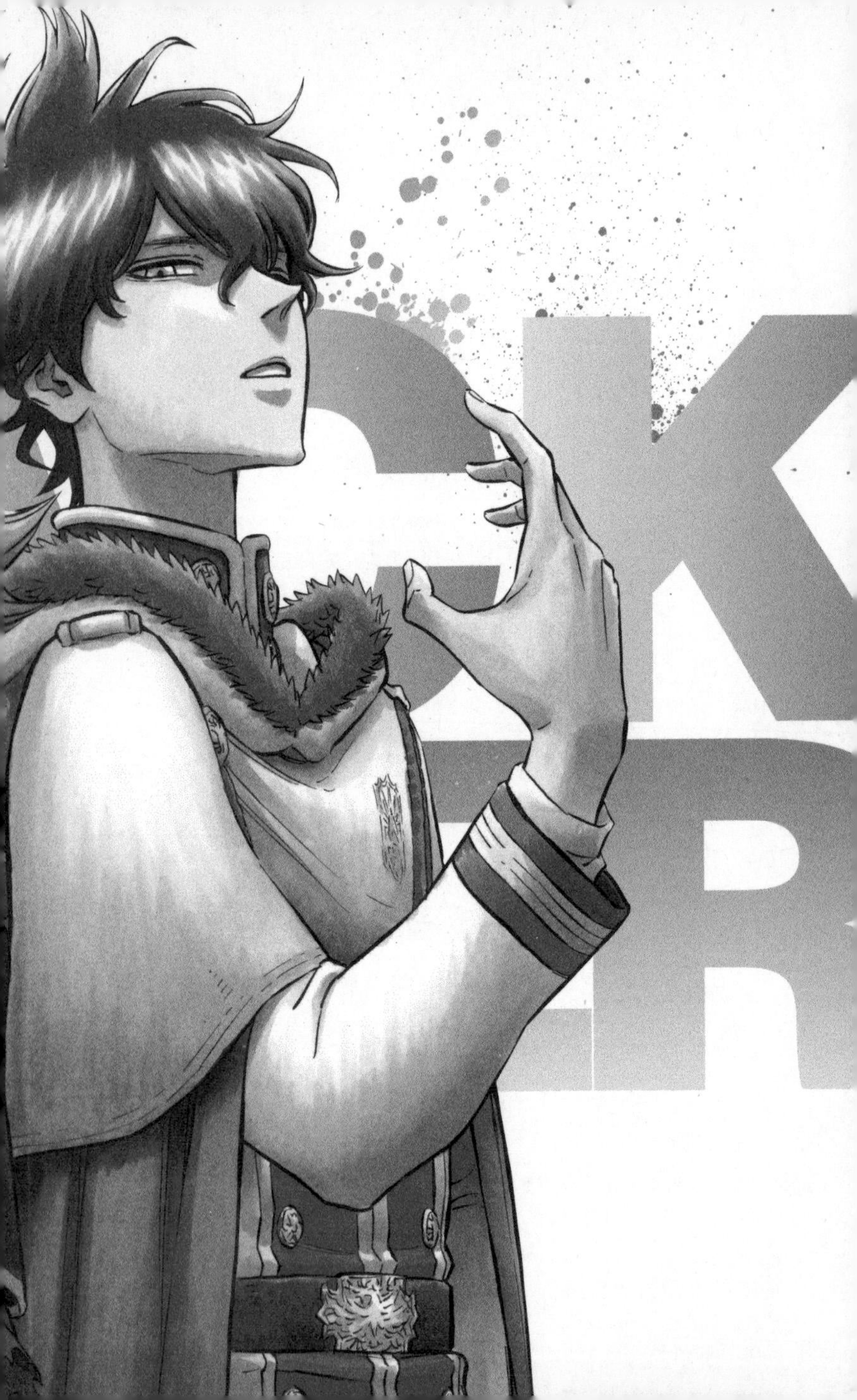

✽ Page 146: New Future

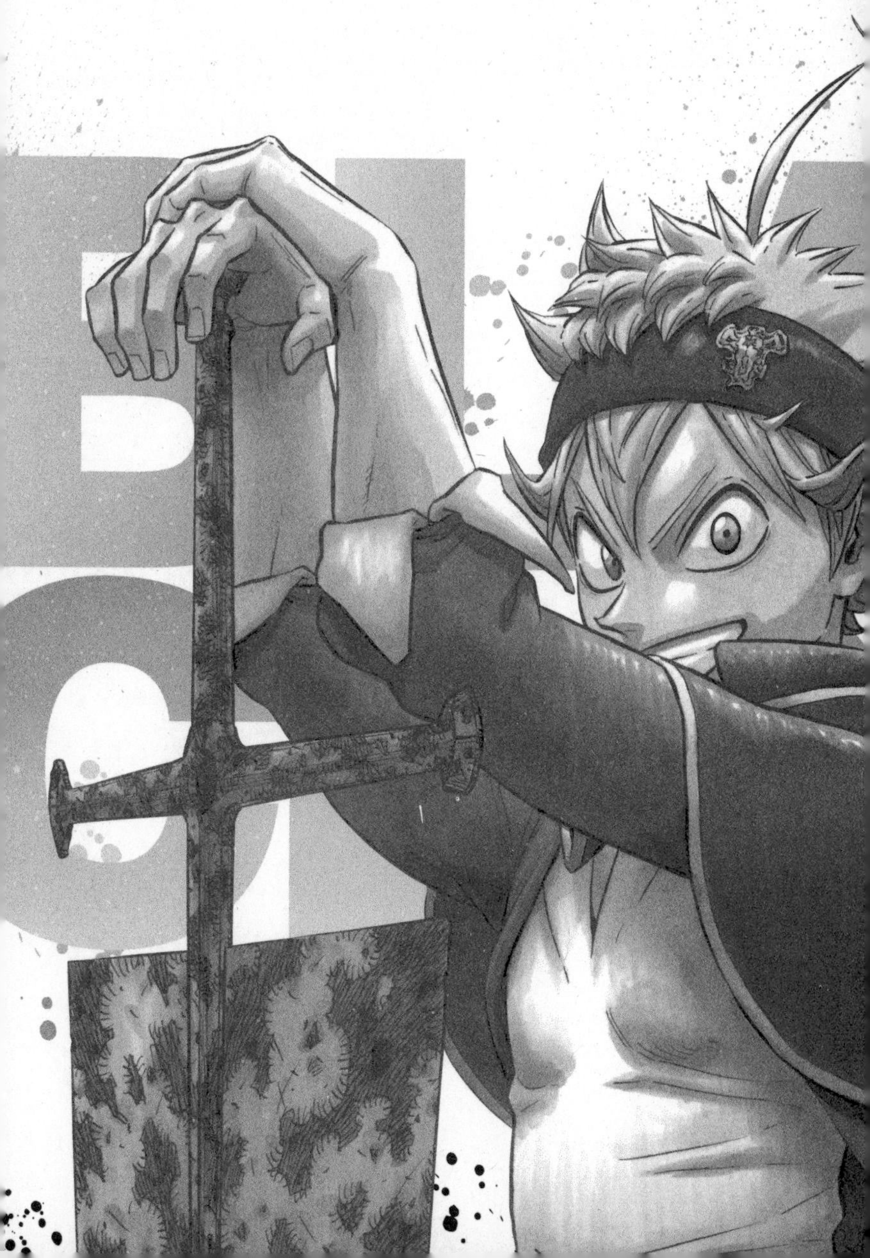

WHAT'S GOING ON HERE...?
HWOO

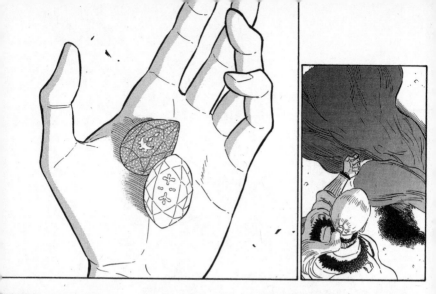

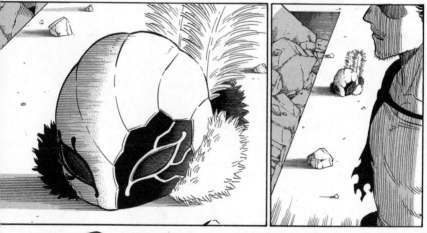

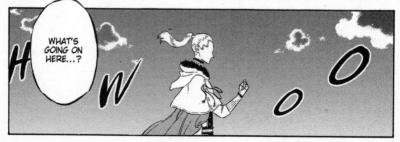

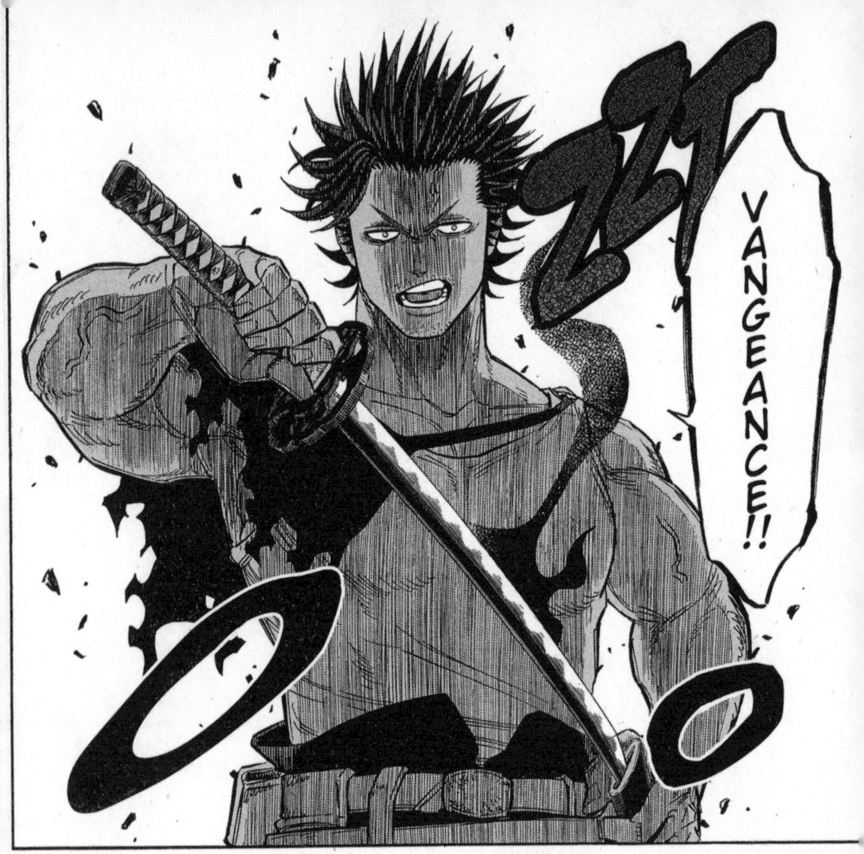
VANGEANCE!!

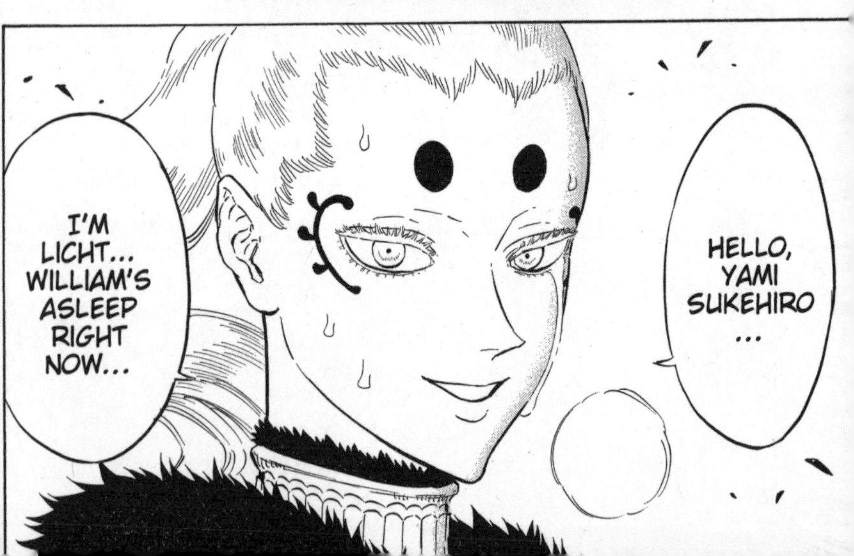
HELLO, YAMI SUKEHIRO ...
I'M LICHT... WILLIAM'S ASLEEP RIGHT NOW...

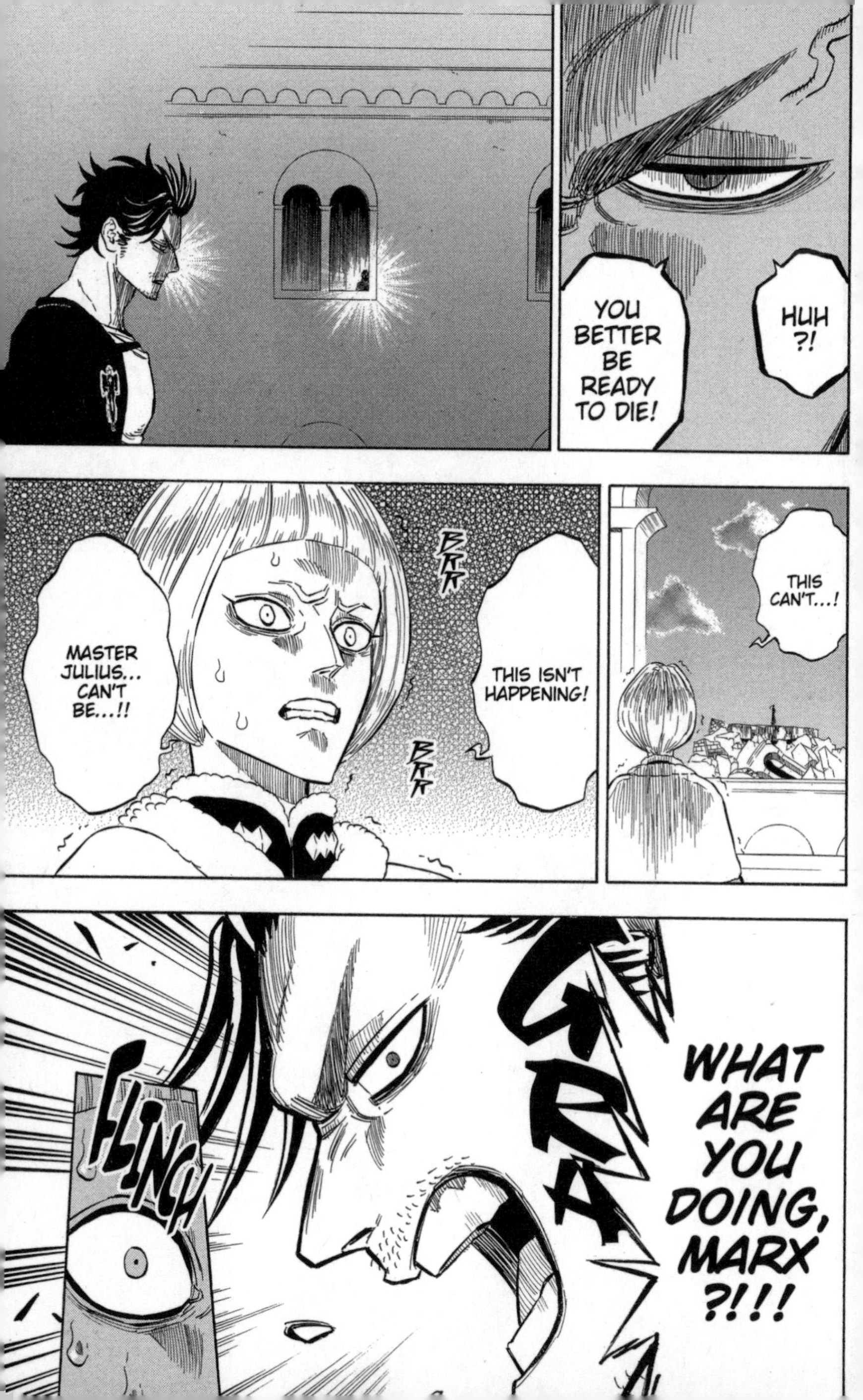
HUH?!
YOU BETTER BE READY TO DIE!
THIS CAN'T...!
THIS ISN'T HAPPENING!
BRRR
BRRR
MASTER JULIUS... CAN'T BE...!!
WHAT ARE YOU DOING, MARX?!!!
FLINCH

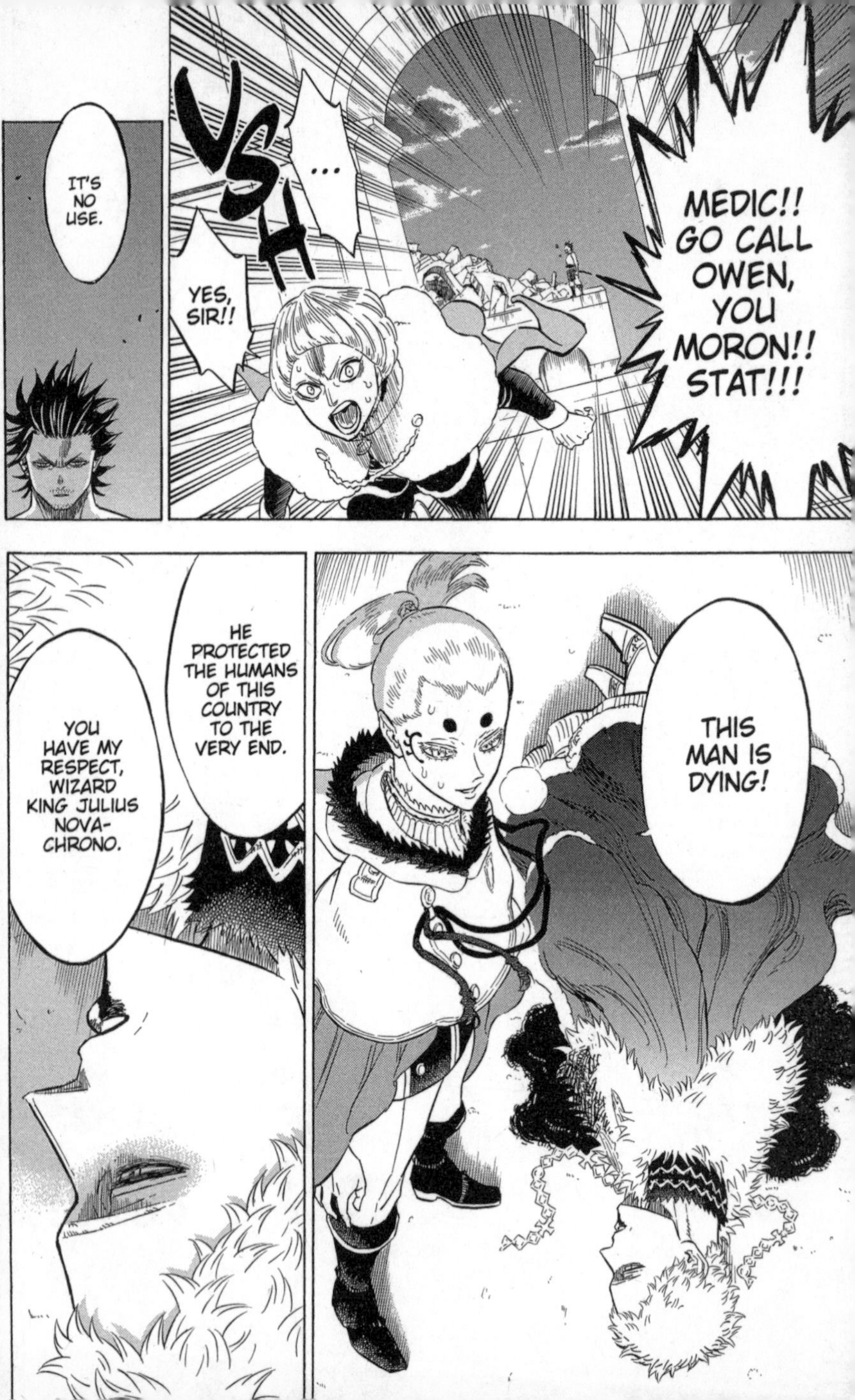
MEDIC!! GO CALL OWEN, YOU MORON!! STAT!!!
...
VSH
YES, SIR!!
IT'S NO USE.
THIS MAN IS DYING!
HE PROTECTED THE HUMANS OF THIS COUNTRY TO THE VERY END.
YOU HAVE MY RESPECT, WIZARD KING JULIUS NOVA-CHRONO.

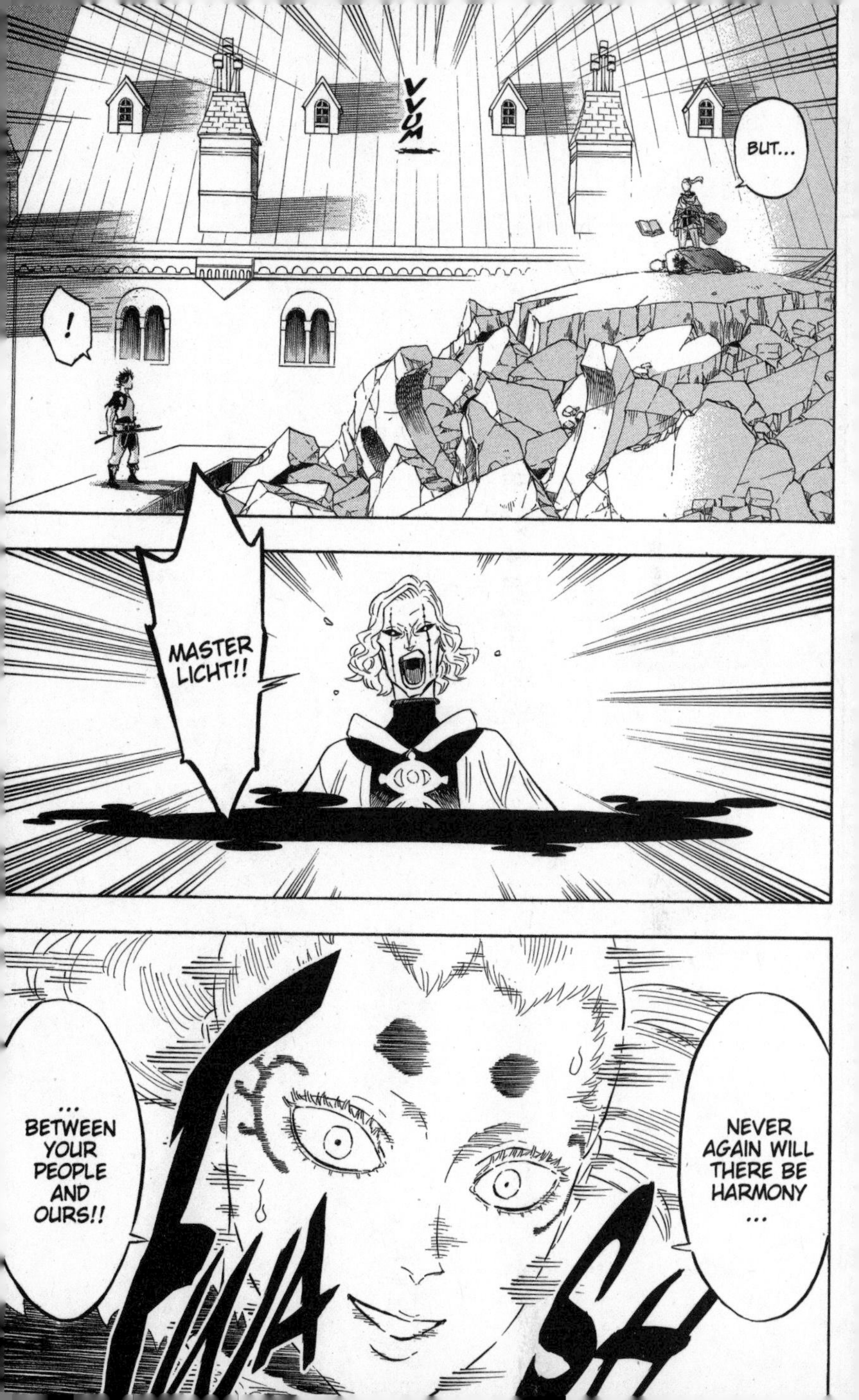
BUT...
VVUM
!
MASTER LICHT!!
NEVER AGAIN WILL THERE BE HARMONY...
...BETWEEN YOUR PEOPLE AND OURS!!
FWASH

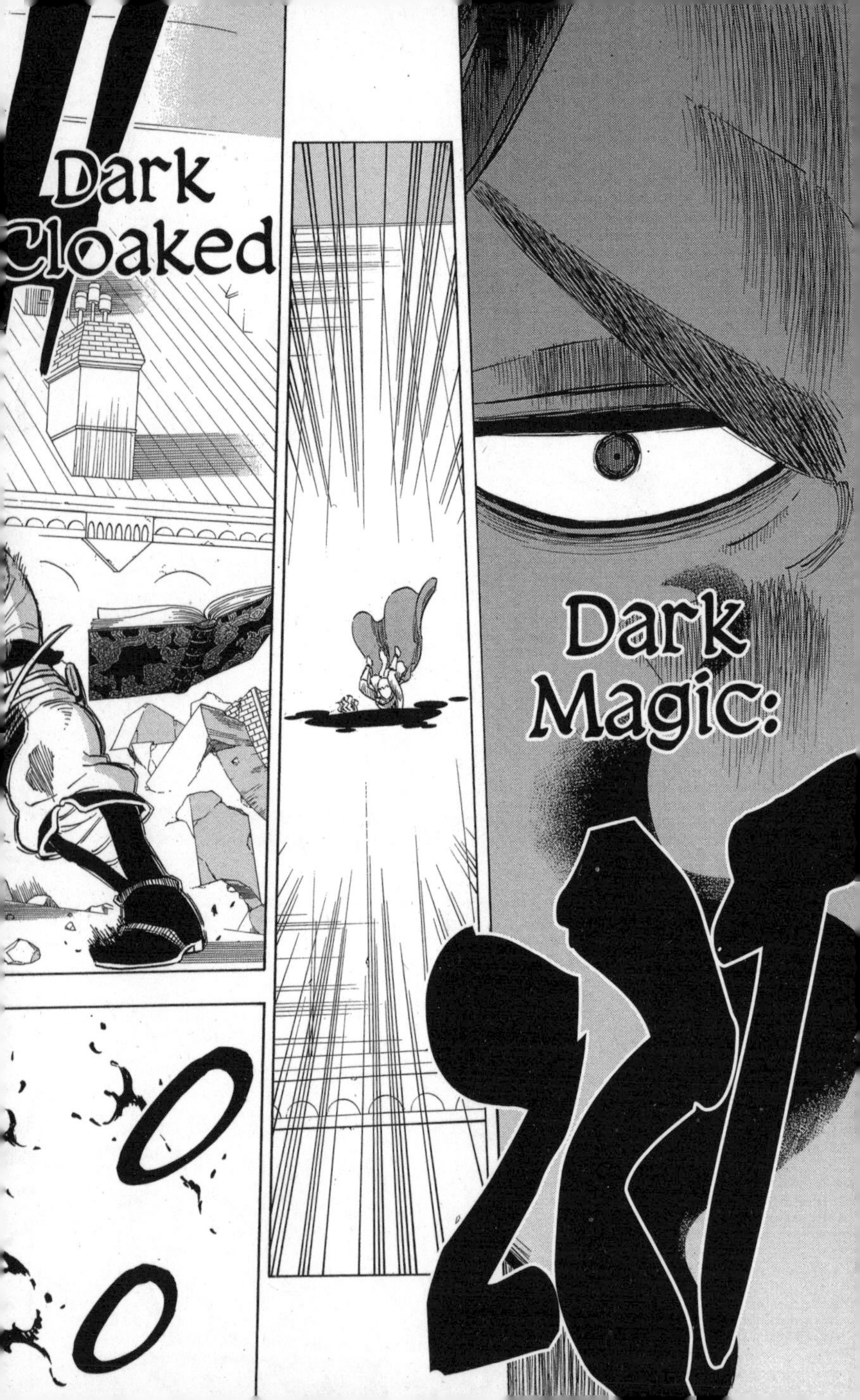
Dark
Magic:
Dark
Cloaked

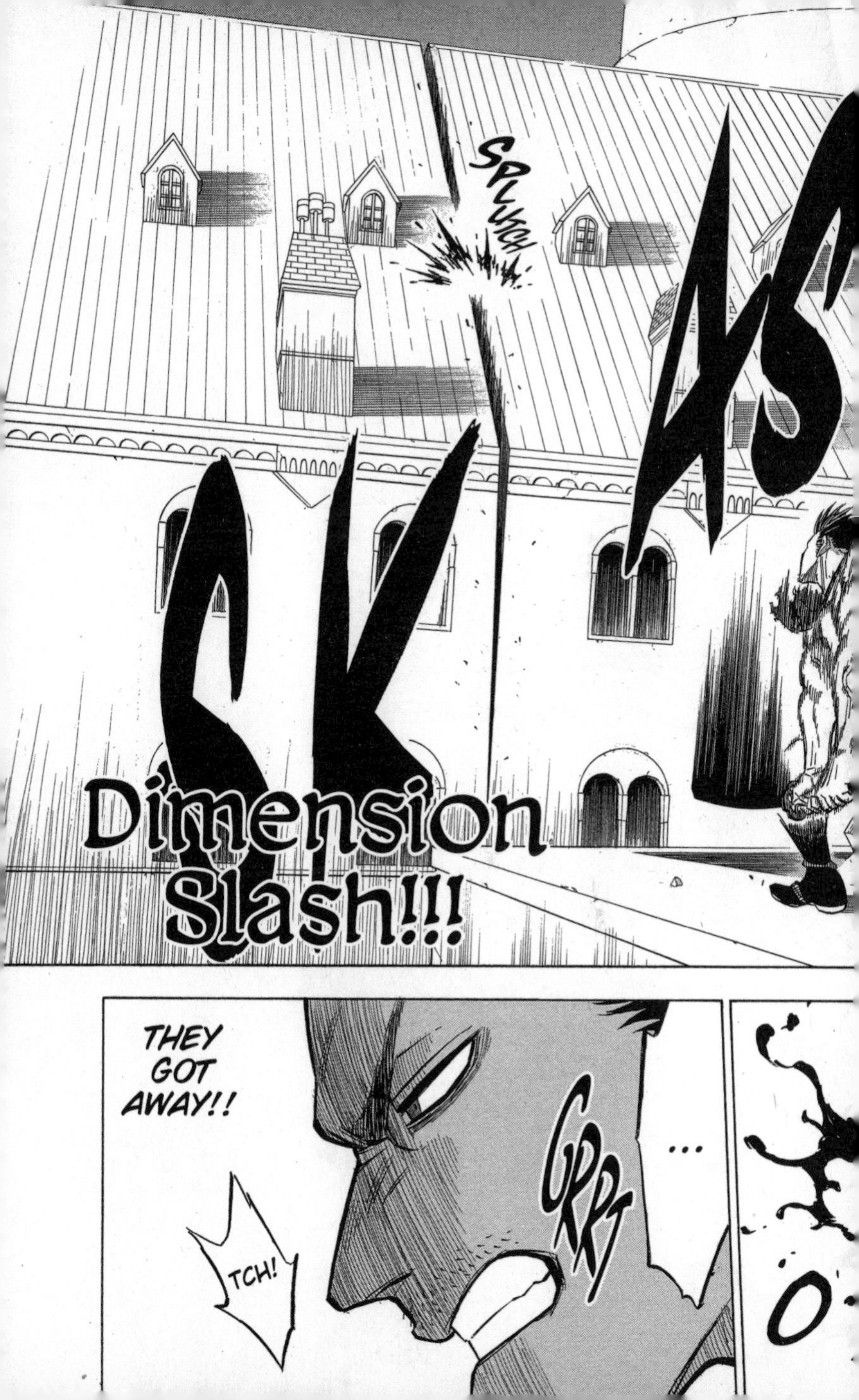
SPLUNCH
Dimension Slash!!!
...
GRRT
THEY GOT AWAY!!
TCH!

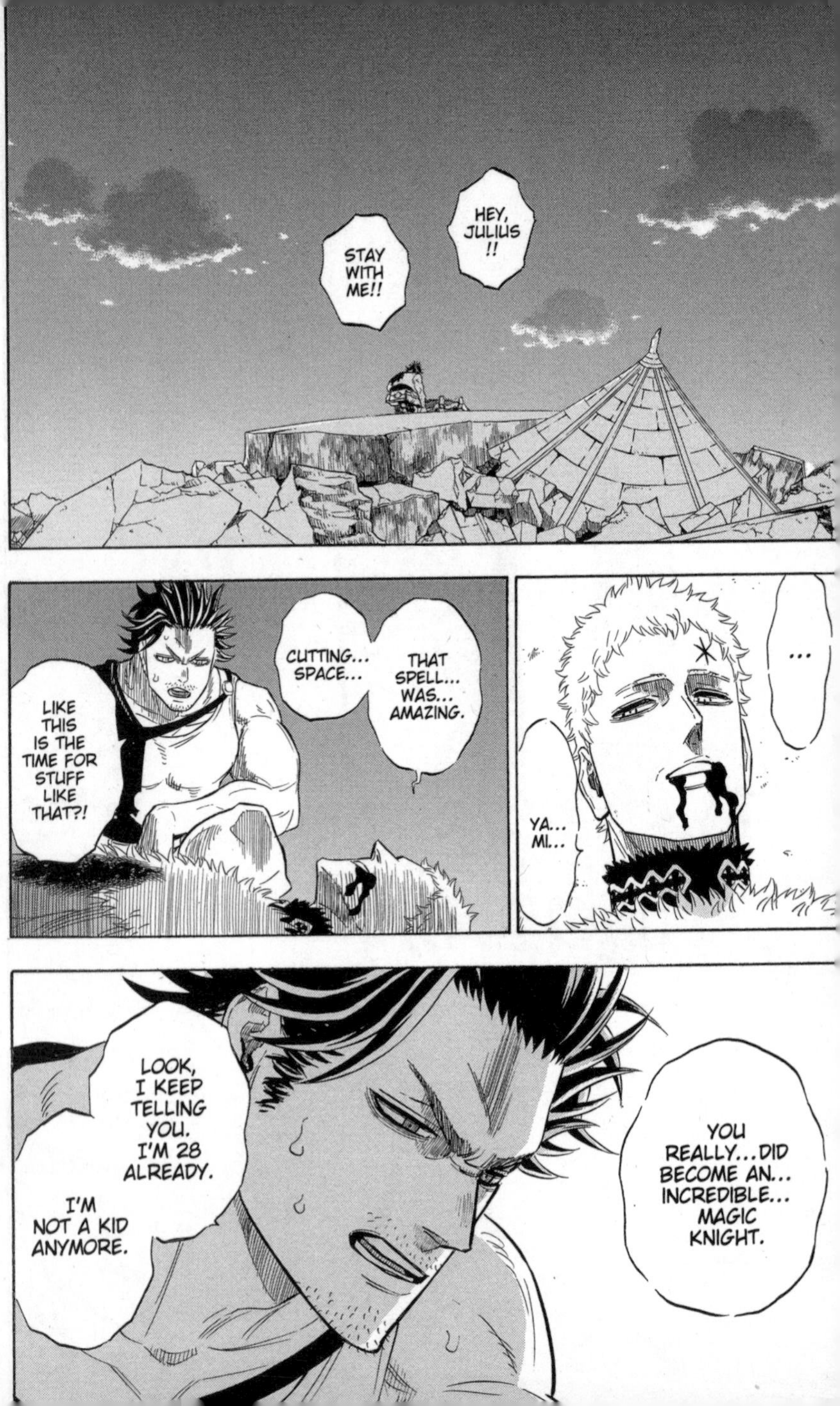
HEY, JULIUS!!
STAY WITH ME!!
...
YA... MI...
CUTTING... SPACE...
THAT SPELL... WAS... AMAZING.
LIKE THIS IS THE TIME FOR STUFF LIKE THAT?!
YOU REALLY...DID BECOME AN... INCREDIBLE... MAGIC KNIGHT.
LOOK, I KEEP TELLING YOU. I'M 28 ALREADY.
I'M NOT A KID ANYMORE.

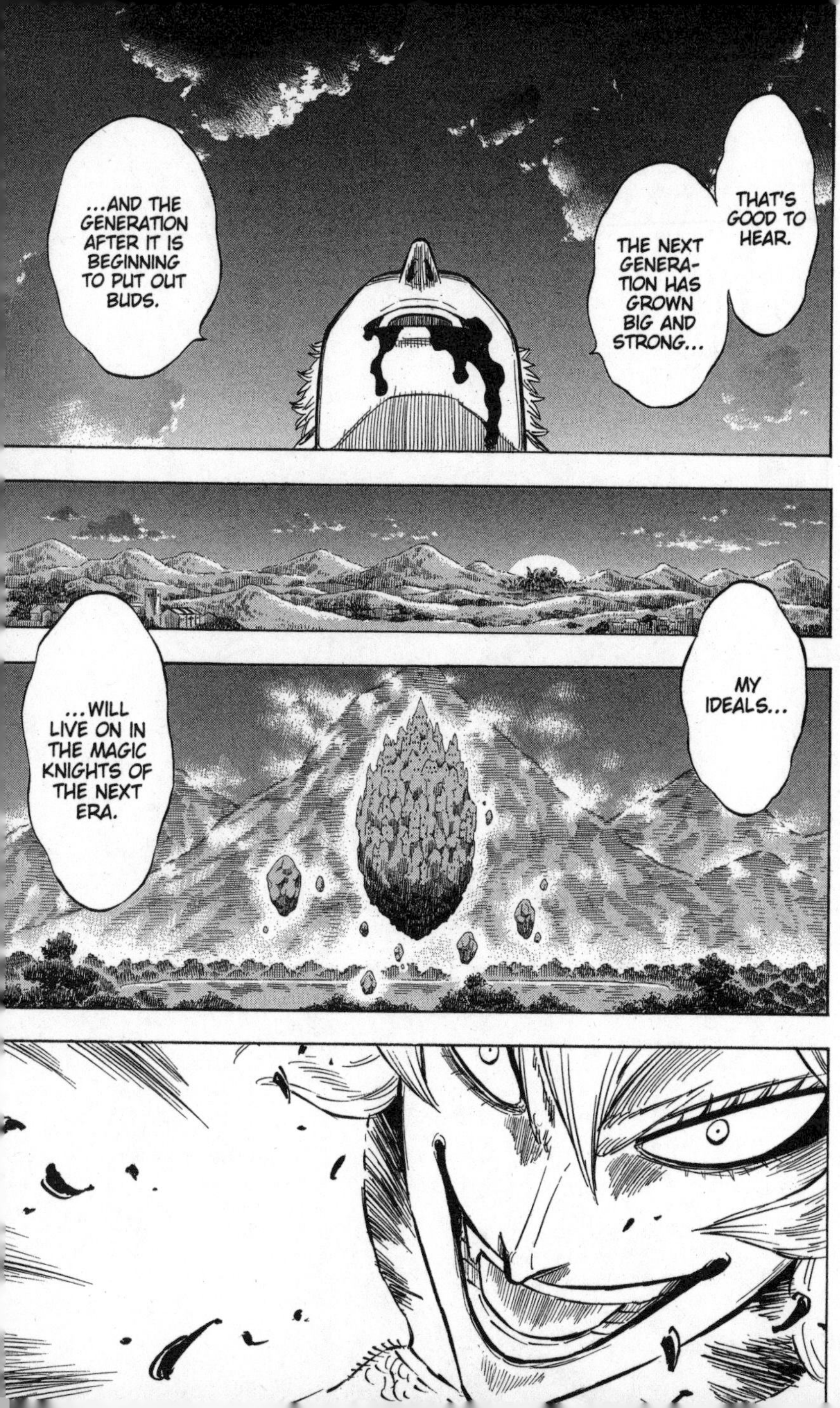
THAT'S GOOD TO HEAR.
THE NEXT GENERATION HAS GROWN BIG AND STRONG...
...AND THE GENERATION AFTER IT IS BEGINNING TO PUT OUT BUDS.
MY IDEALS...
...WILL LIVE ON IN THE MAGIC KNIGHTS OF THE NEXT ERA.

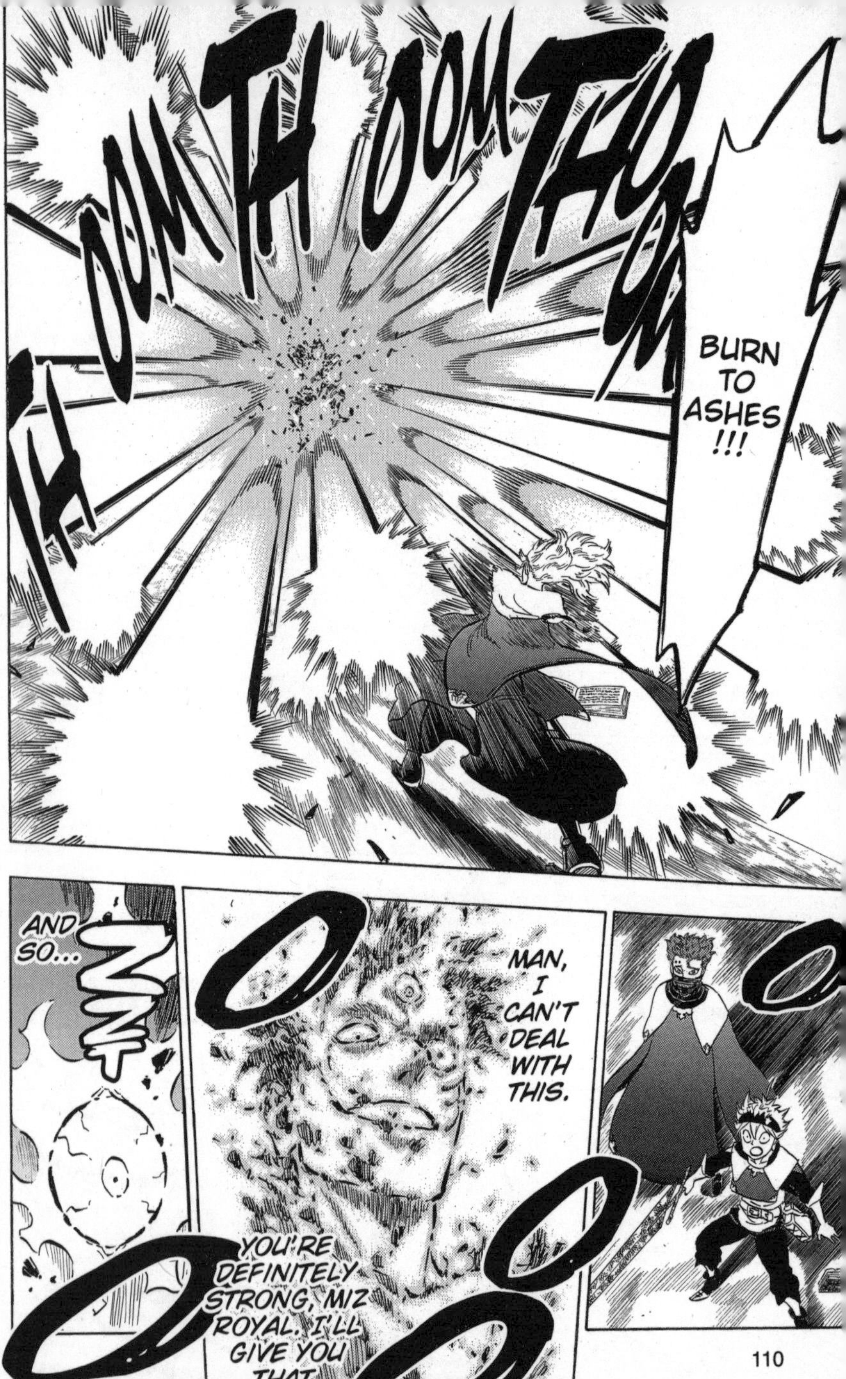
THOOM THOOM THOOM
BURN TO ASHES!!!
MAN, I CAN'T DEAL WITH THIS.
YOU'RE DEFINITELY STRONG, MIZ ROYAL. I'LL GIVE YOU THAT.
AND SO...
ZMMT

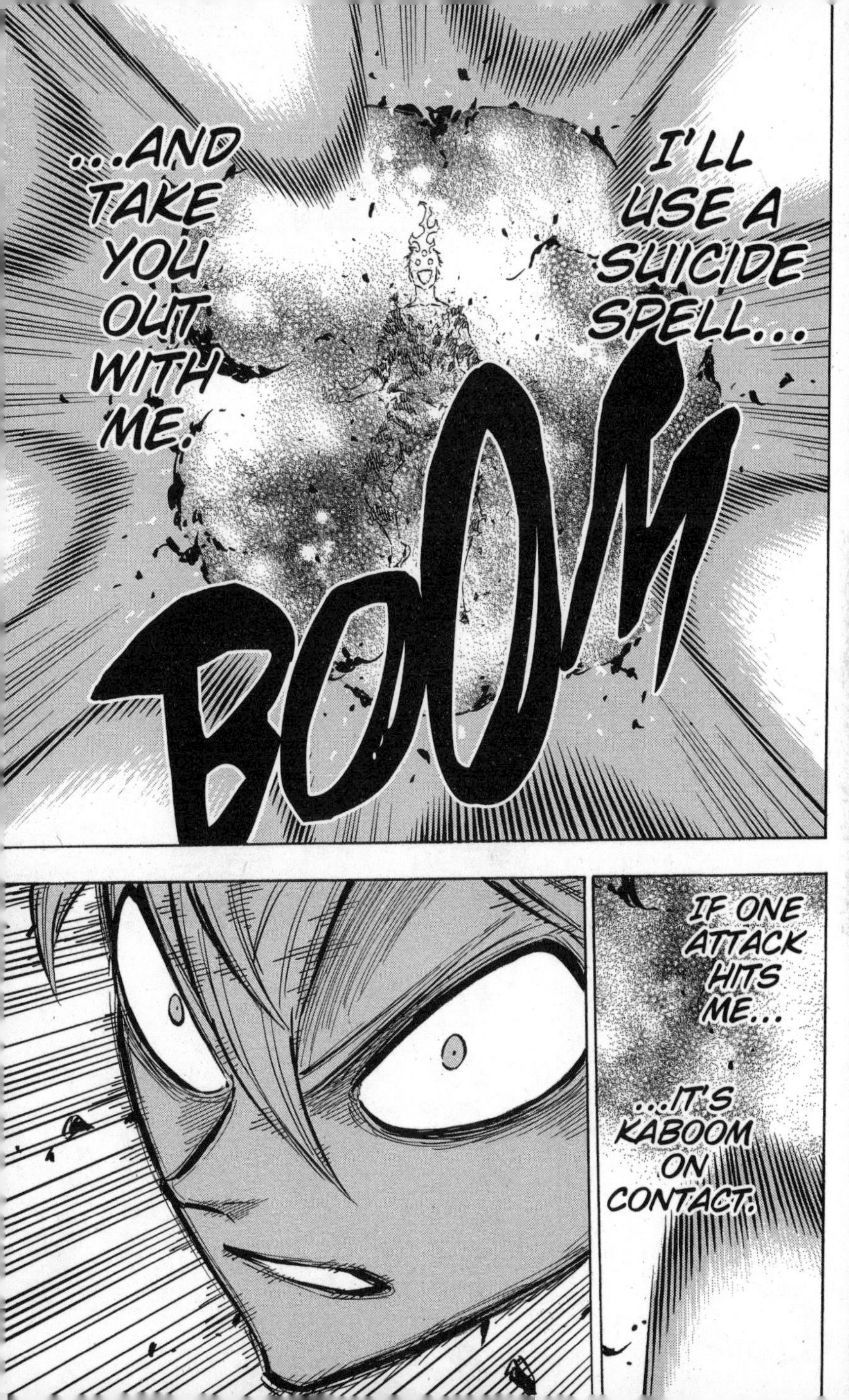
I'LL USE A SUICIDE SPELL...
...AND TAKE YOU OUT WITH ME.
BOOM
IF ONE ATTACK HITS ME...
...IT'S KABOOM ON CONTACT.

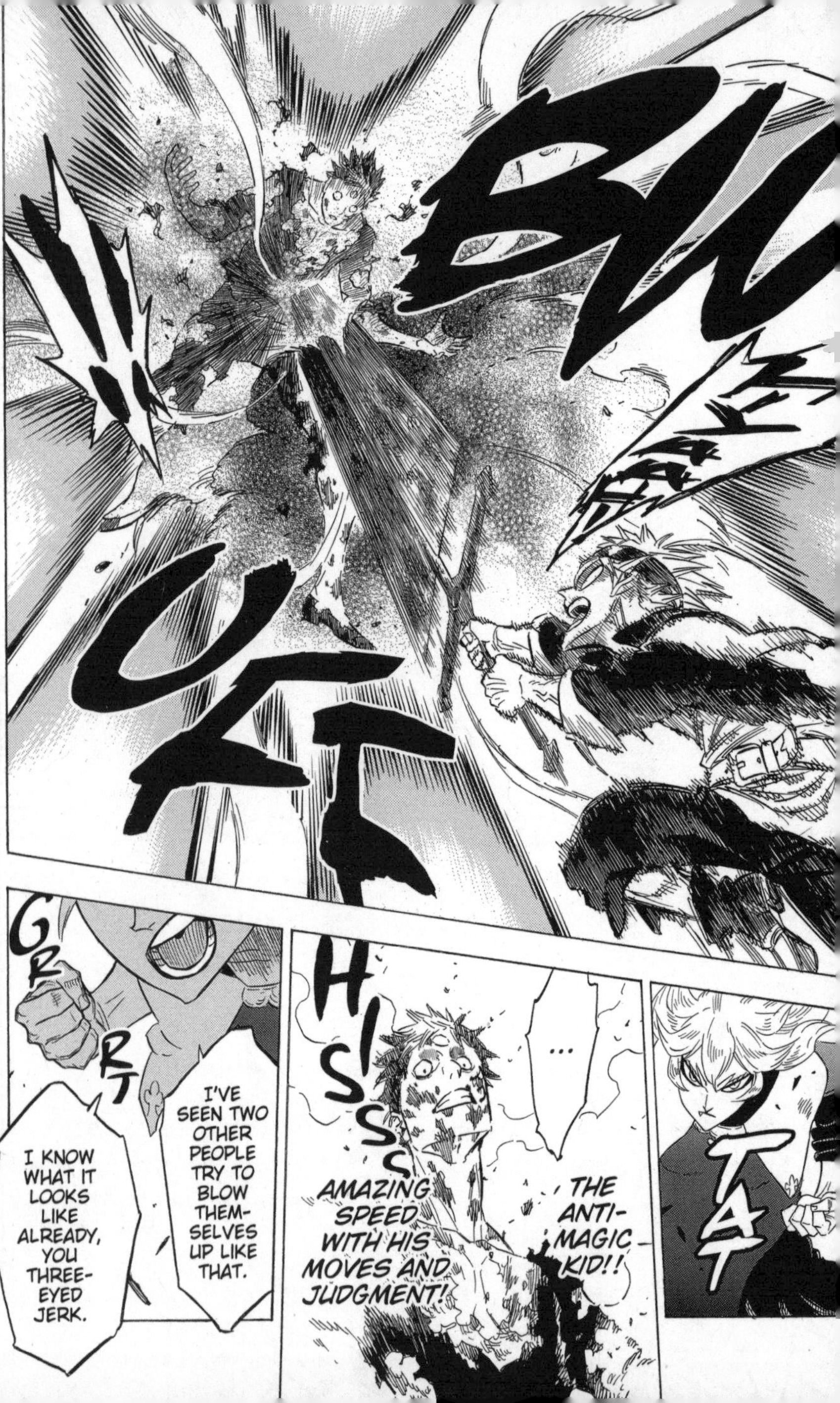
!!
TAT
...
THE ANTI-MAGIC KID!!
AMAZING SPEED WITH HIS MOVES AND JUDGMENT!
HISSS
GRRT
I'VE SEEN TWO OTHER PEOPLE TRY TO BLOW THEMSELVES UP LIKE THAT.
I KNOW WHAT IT LOOKS LIKE ALREADY, YOU THREE-EYED JERK.

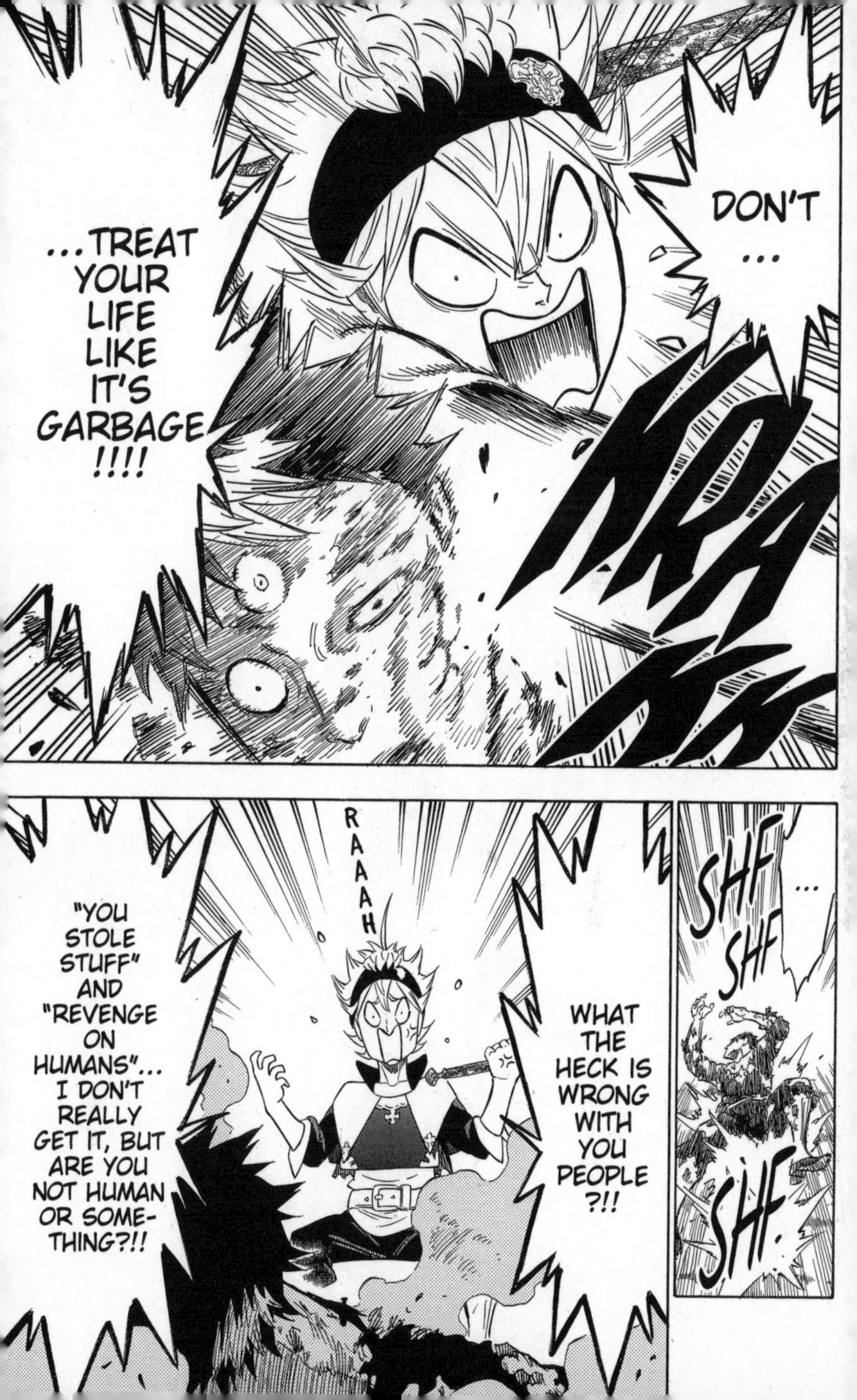
DON'T ...
...TREAT YOUR LIFE LIKE IT'S GARBAGE!!!!
SHF ...
SHF
SHF
RAAAAH
WHAT THE HECK IS WRONG WITH YOU PEOPLE?!!
"YOU STOLE STUFF" AND "REVENGE ON HUMANS"... I DON'T REALLY GET IT, BUT ARE YOU NOT HUMAN OR SOME-THING?!!

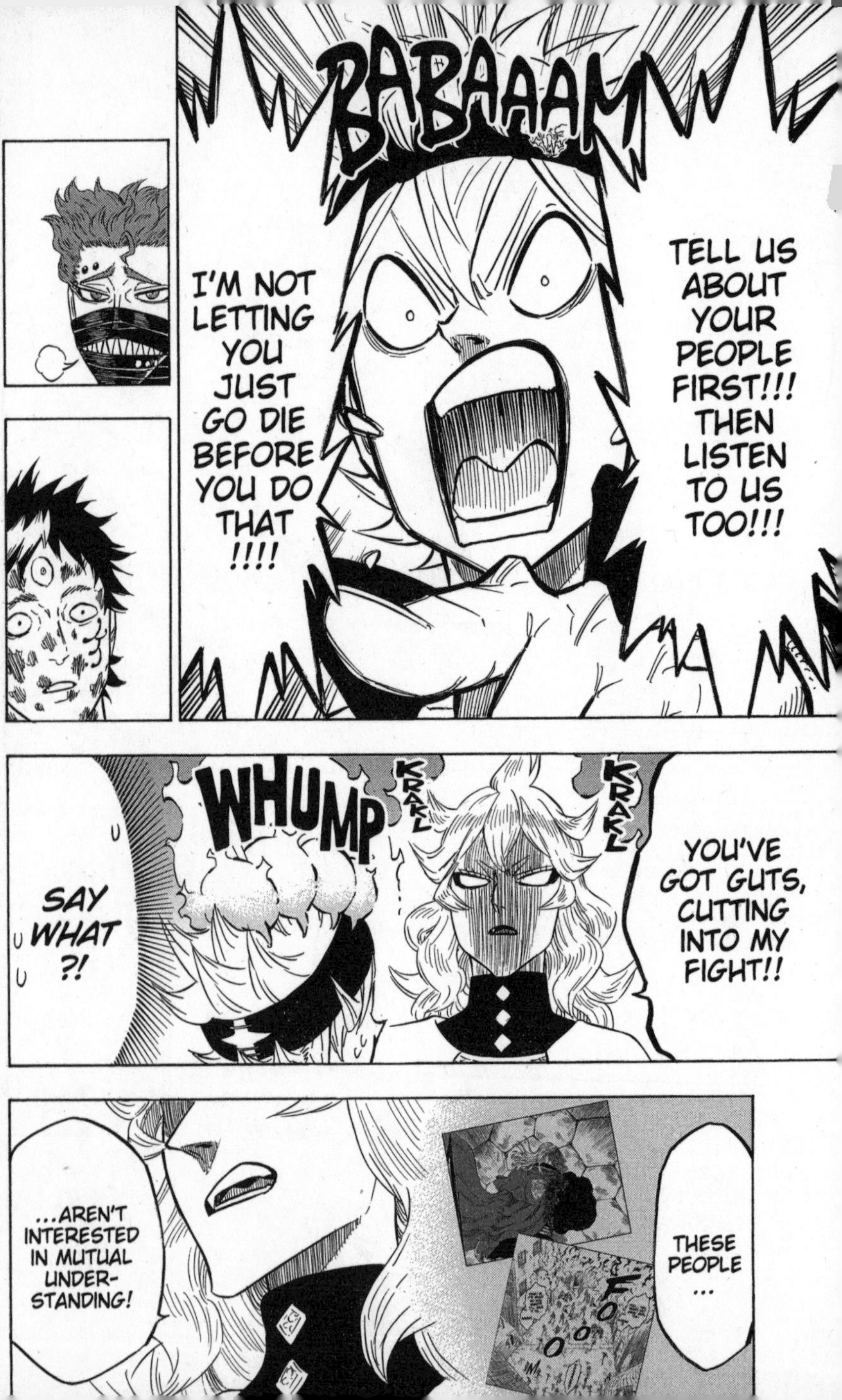
BABAAAM
TELL US ABOUT YOUR PEOPLE FIRST!!! THEN LISTEN TO US TOO!!!
I'M NOT LETTING YOU JUST GO DIE BEFORE YOU DO THAT!!!!
KRAKL
YOU'VE GOT GUTS, CUTTING INTO MY FIGHT!!
KRAKL
WHUMP
SAY WHAT?!
THESE PEOPLE...
FOOOO
...AREN'T INTERESTED IN MUTUAL UNDER-STANDING!

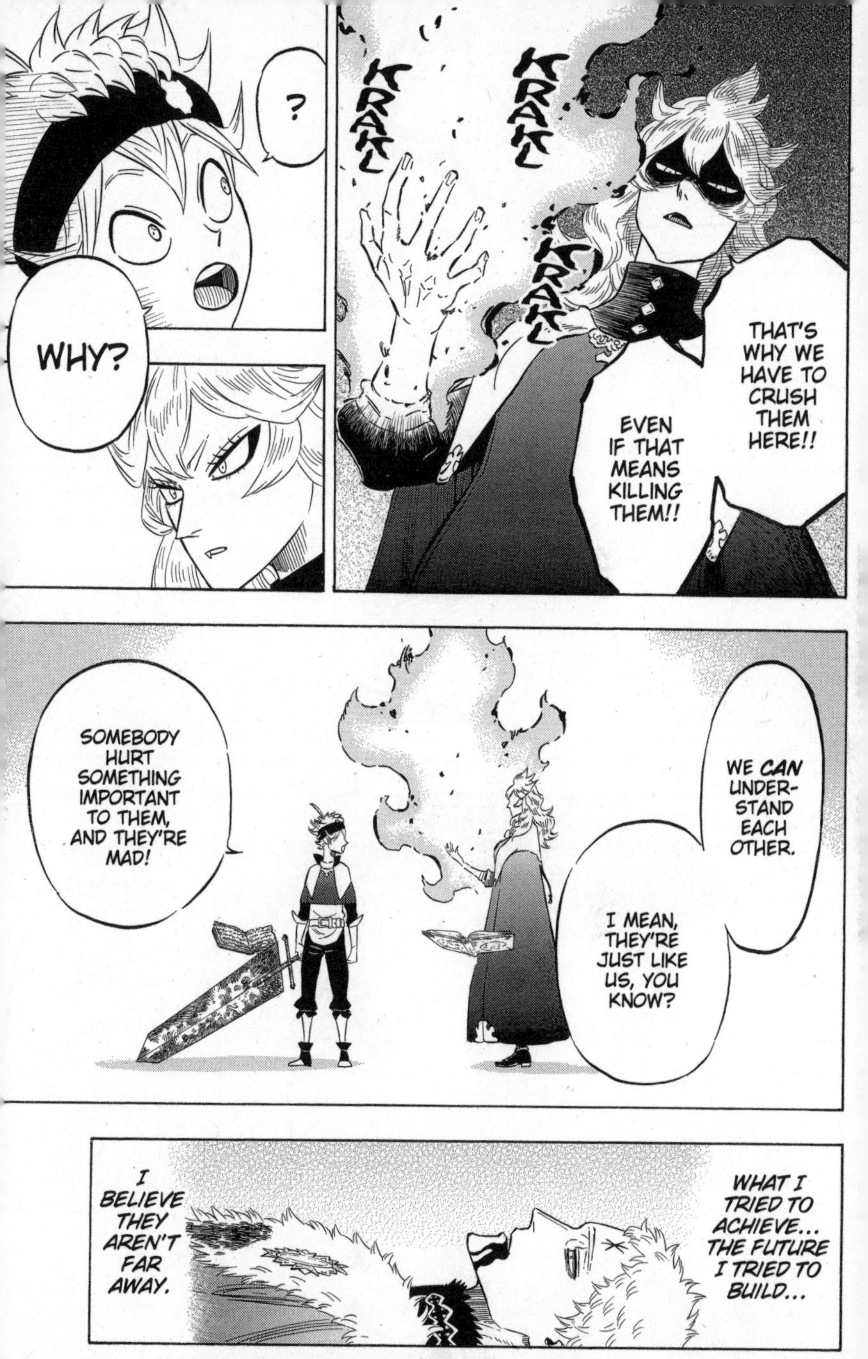
KRAKL
KRAKL
KRAKL
THAT'S WHY WE HAVE TO CRUSH THEM HERE!!
EVEN IF THAT MEANS KILLING THEM!!
?
WHY?
WE *CAN* UNDER-STAND EACH OTHER.
I MEAN, THEY'RE JUST LIKE US, YOU KNOW?
SOMEBODY HURT SOMETHING IMPORTANT TO THEM, AND THEY'RE MAD!
WHAT I TRIED TO ACHIEVE... THE FUTURE I TRIED TO BUILD...
I BELIEVE THEY AREN'T FAR AWAY.

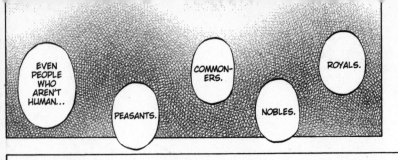

ROYALS.
NOBLES.
COMMON-ERS.
PEASANTS.
EVEN PEOPLE WHO AREN'T HUMAN...
A COUNTRY WITHOUT DISCRIMINATION OR HATRED.
THE NEW FUTURE I'LL BUILD WITH YOU.
A FREE COUNTRY, WHERE EVERYBODY CAN APPRECIATE EACH OTHER AND JOKE AND LAUGH TOGETHER.
THAT'S THE SORT OF COUNTRY I WANT TO BUILD ONCE I'M THE WIZARD KING!!

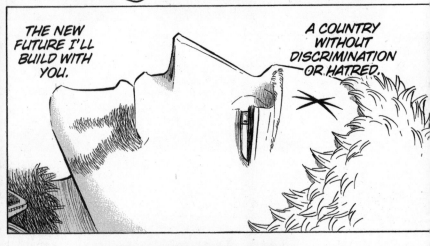

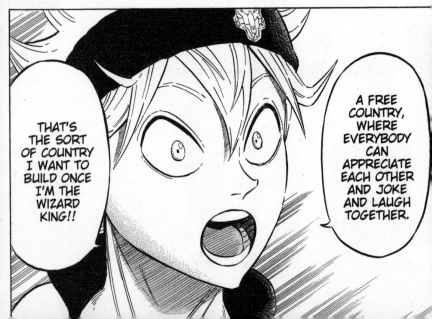

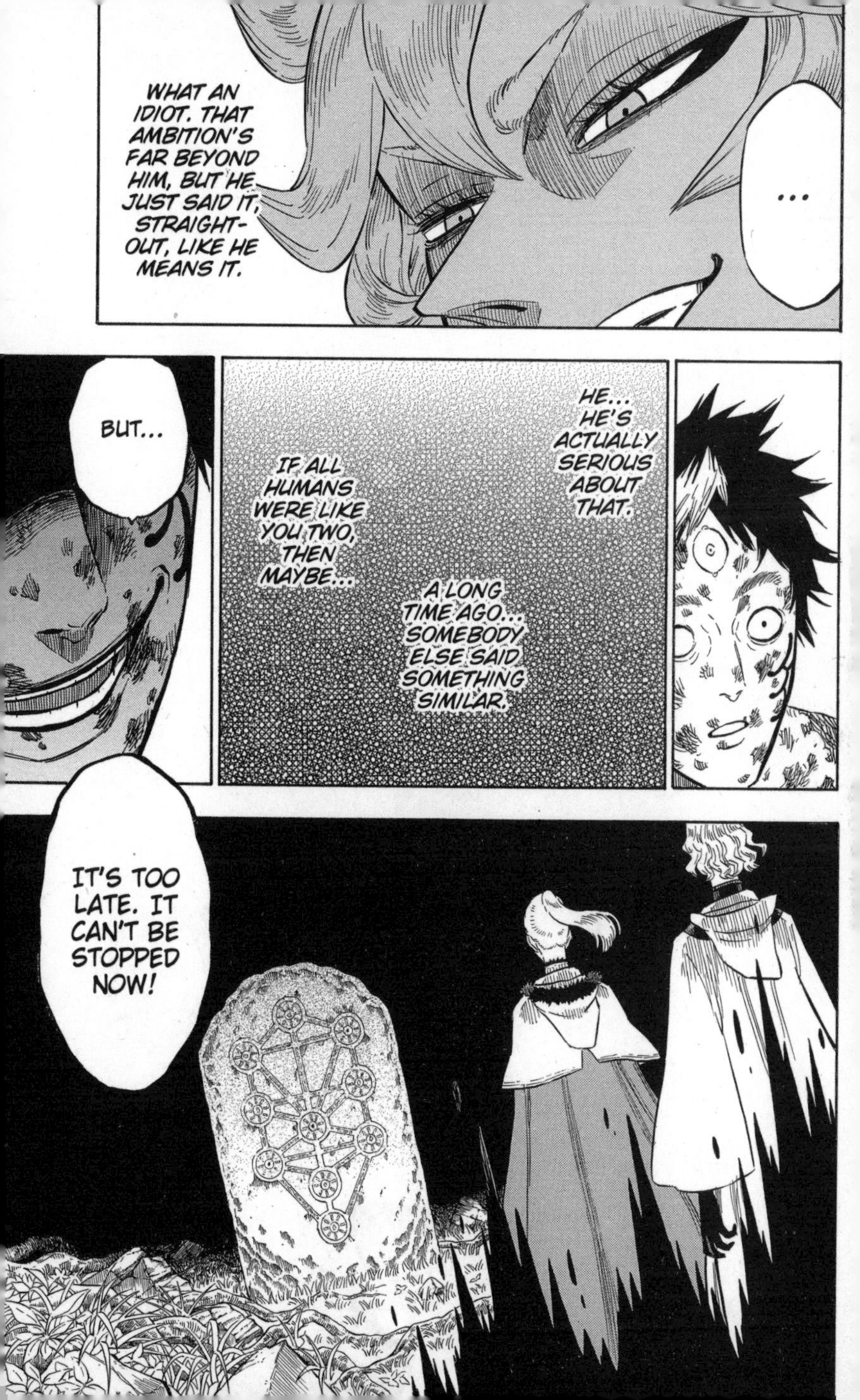

...
WHAT AN IDIOT. THAT AMBITION'S FAR BEYOND HIM, BUT HE JUST SAID IT, STRAIGHT-OUT, LIKE HE MEANS IT.
HE... HE'S ACTUALLY SERIOUS ABOUT THAT.
A LONG TIME AGO... SOMEBODY ELSE SAID SOMETHING SIMILAR.
IF ALL HUMANS WERE LIKE YOU TWO, THEN MAYBE...
BUT...
IT'S TOO LATE. IT CAN'T BE STOPPED NOW!

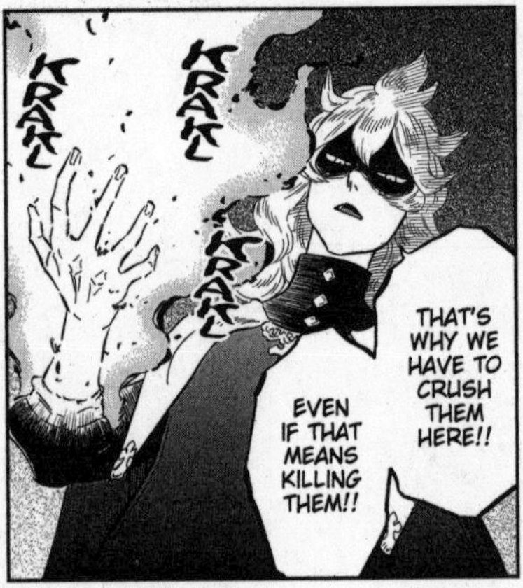
KRAK!
KRAK!
KRAK!
THAT'S WHY WE HAVE TO CRUSH THEM HERE!!
EVEN IF THAT MEANS KILLING THEM!!

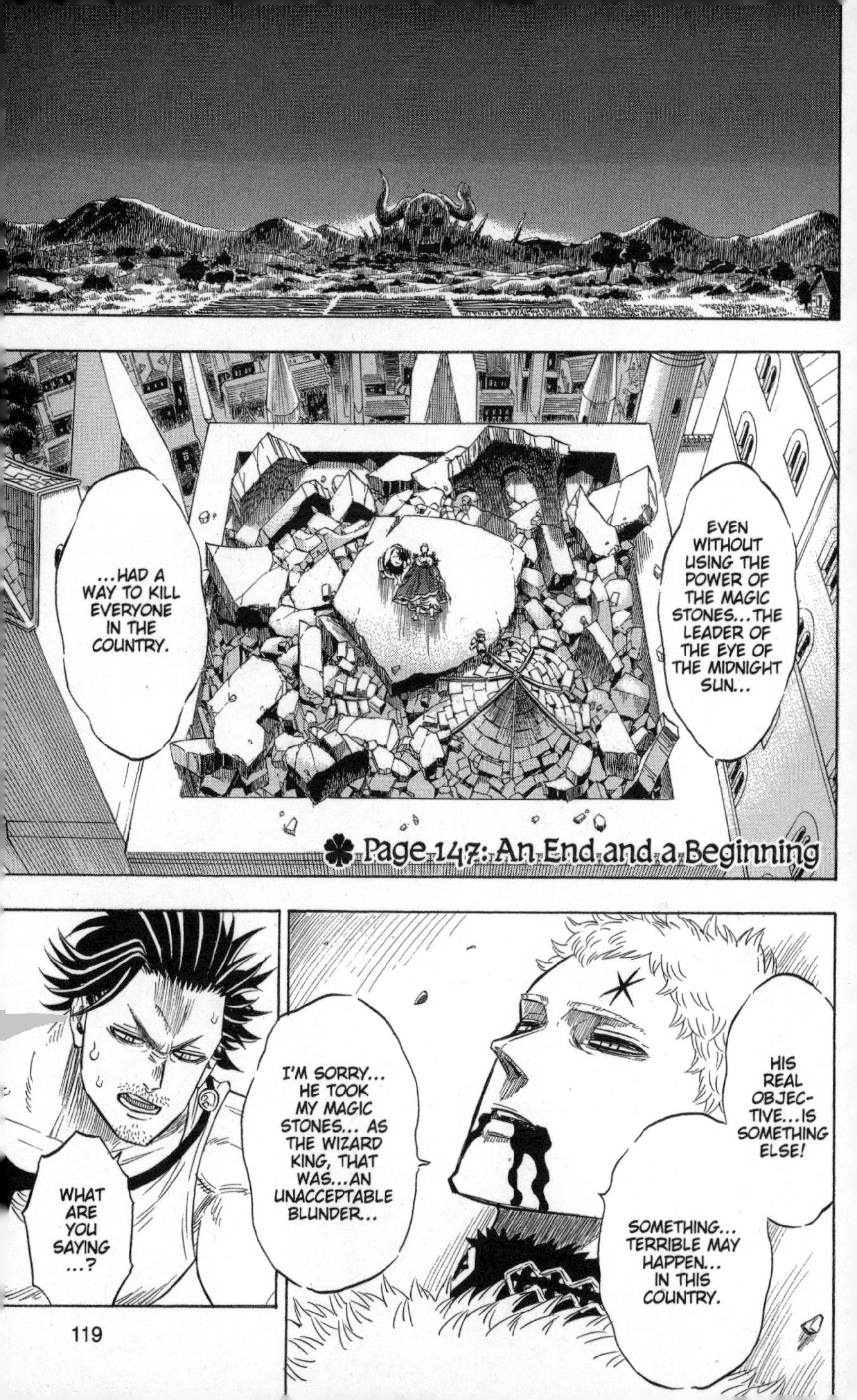
EVEN WITHOUT USING THE POWER OF THE MAGIC STONES...THE LEADER OF THE EYE OF THE MIDNIGHT SUN...
...HAD A WAY TO KILL EVERYONE IN THE COUNTRY.
Page 147: An End and a Beginning
HIS REAL OBJECTIVE...IS SOMETHING ELSE!
I'M SORRY... HE TOOK MY MAGIC STONES... AS THE WIZARD KING, THAT WAS...AN UNACCEPTABLE BLUNDER..
SOMETHING... TERRIBLE MAY HAPPEN... IN THIS COUNTRY.
WHAT ARE YOU SAYING ...?

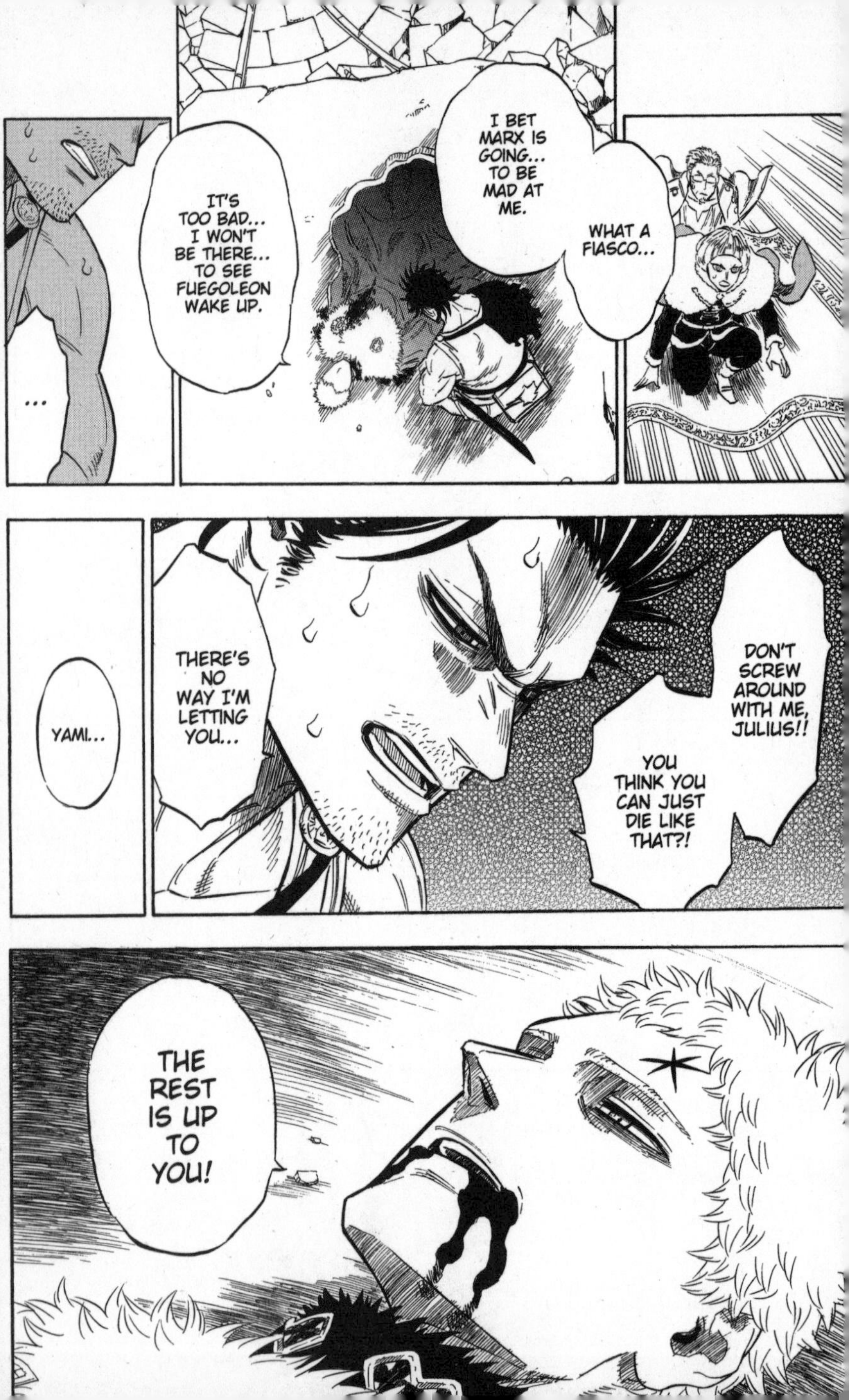
WHAT A FIASCO...
I BET MARX IS GOING... TO BE MAD AT ME.
IT'S TOO BAD... I WON'T BE THERE... TO SEE FUEGOLEON WAKE UP.
...
DON'T SCREW AROUND WITH ME, JULIUS!!
YOU THINK YOU CAN JUST DIE LIKE THAT?!
THERE'S NO WAY I'M LETTING YOU...
YAMI...
THE REST IS UP TO YOU!

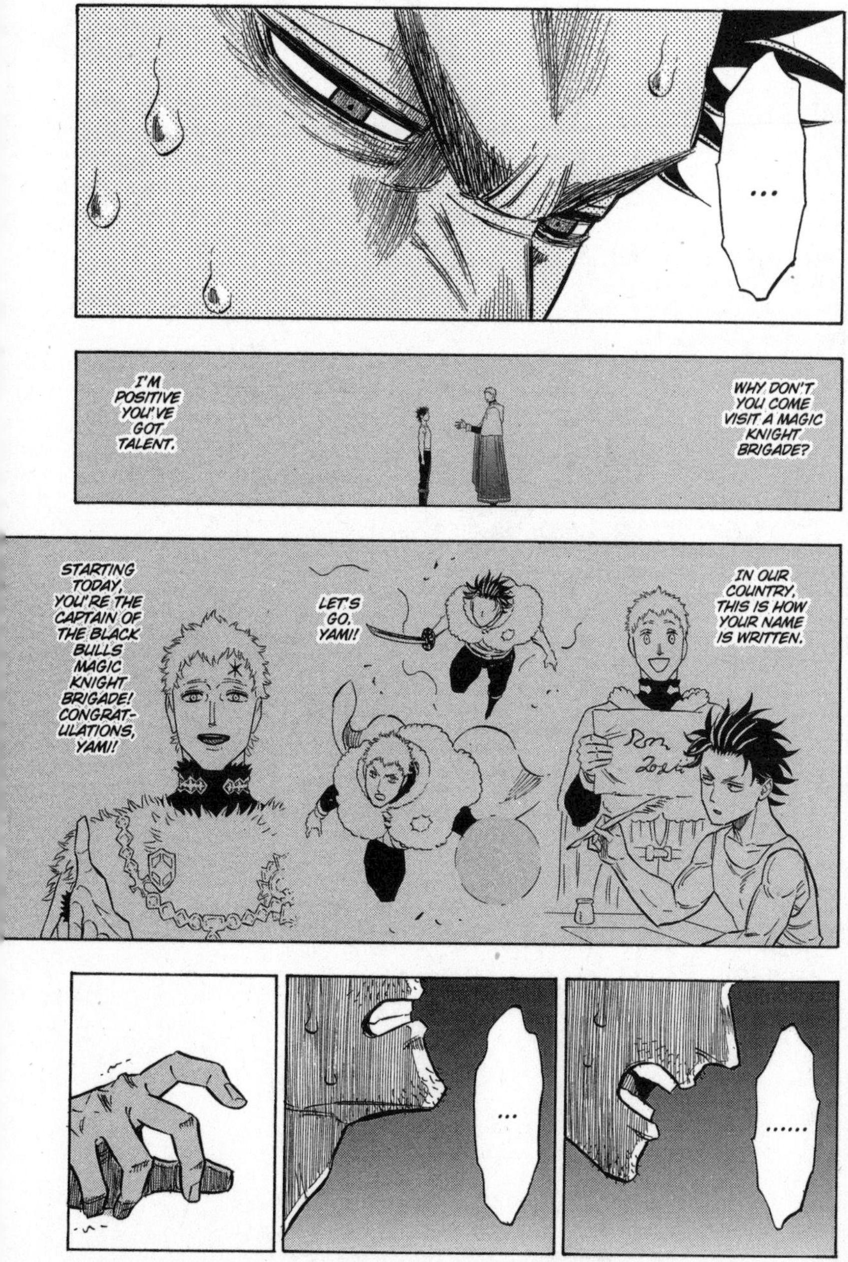
...
WHY DON'T YOU COME VISIT A MAGIC KNIGHT BRIGADE?
I'M POSITIVE YOU'VE GOT TALENT.
IN OUR COUNTRY, THIS IS HOW YOUR NAME IS WRITTEN.
LET'S GO, YAMI!
STARTING TODAY, YOU'RE THE CAPTAIN OF THE BLACK BULLS MAGIC KNIGHT BRIGADE! CONGRAT-ULATIONS, YAMI!
......
...

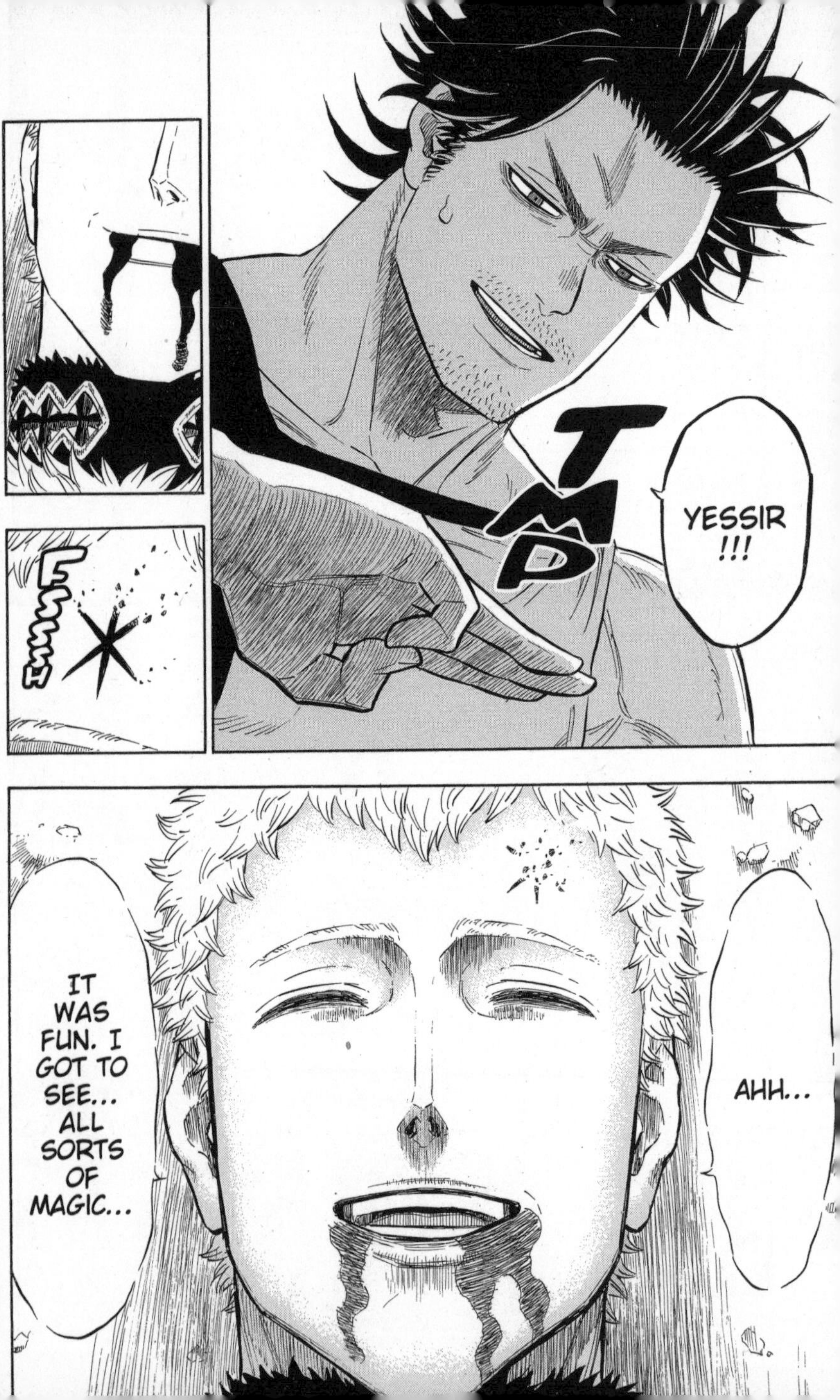
TMP
YESSIR !!!
FSSSH
AHH...
IT WAS FUN. I GOT TO SEE... ALL SORTS OF MAGIC...

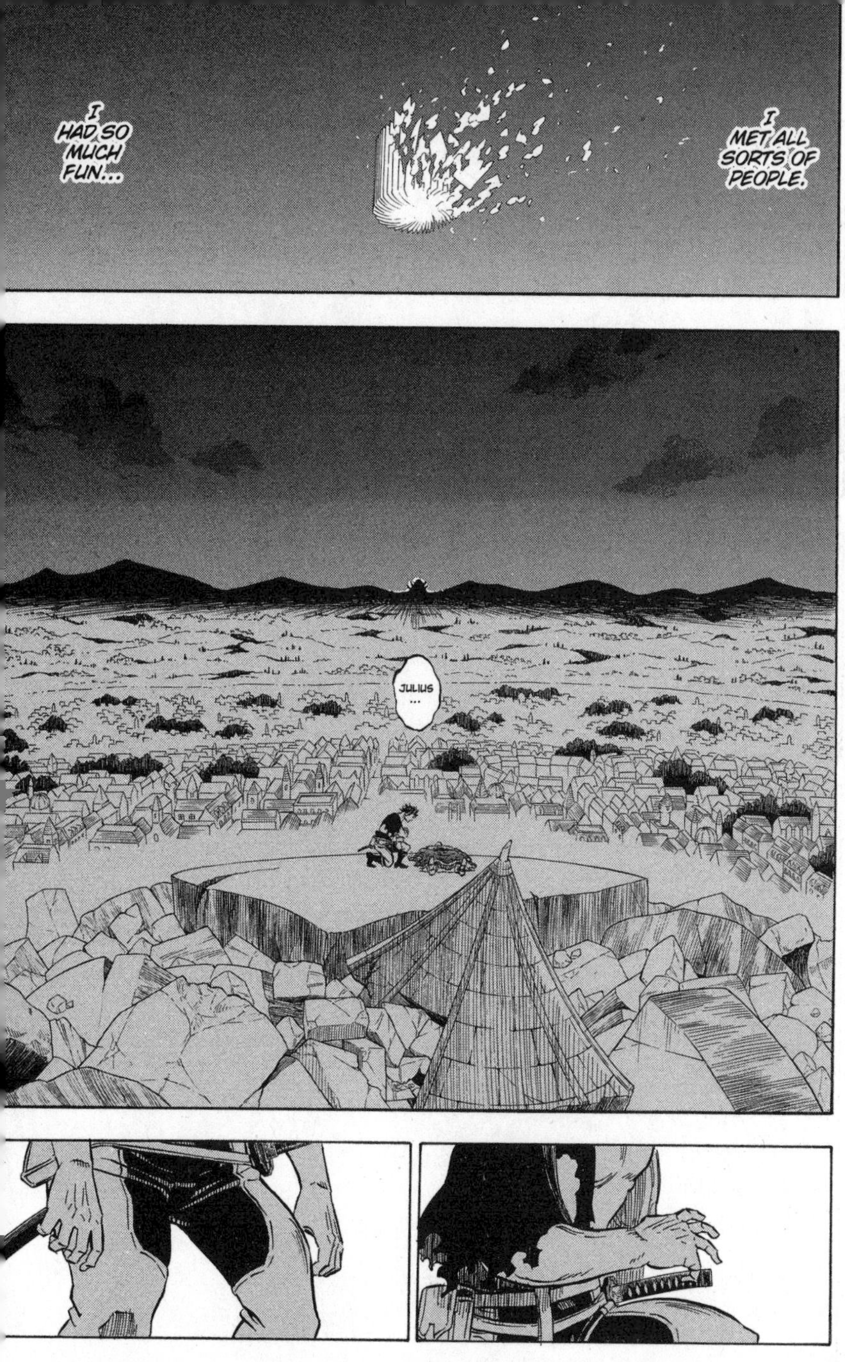
I MET ALL SORTS OF PEOPLE.
I HAD SO MUCH FUN...
JULIUS...

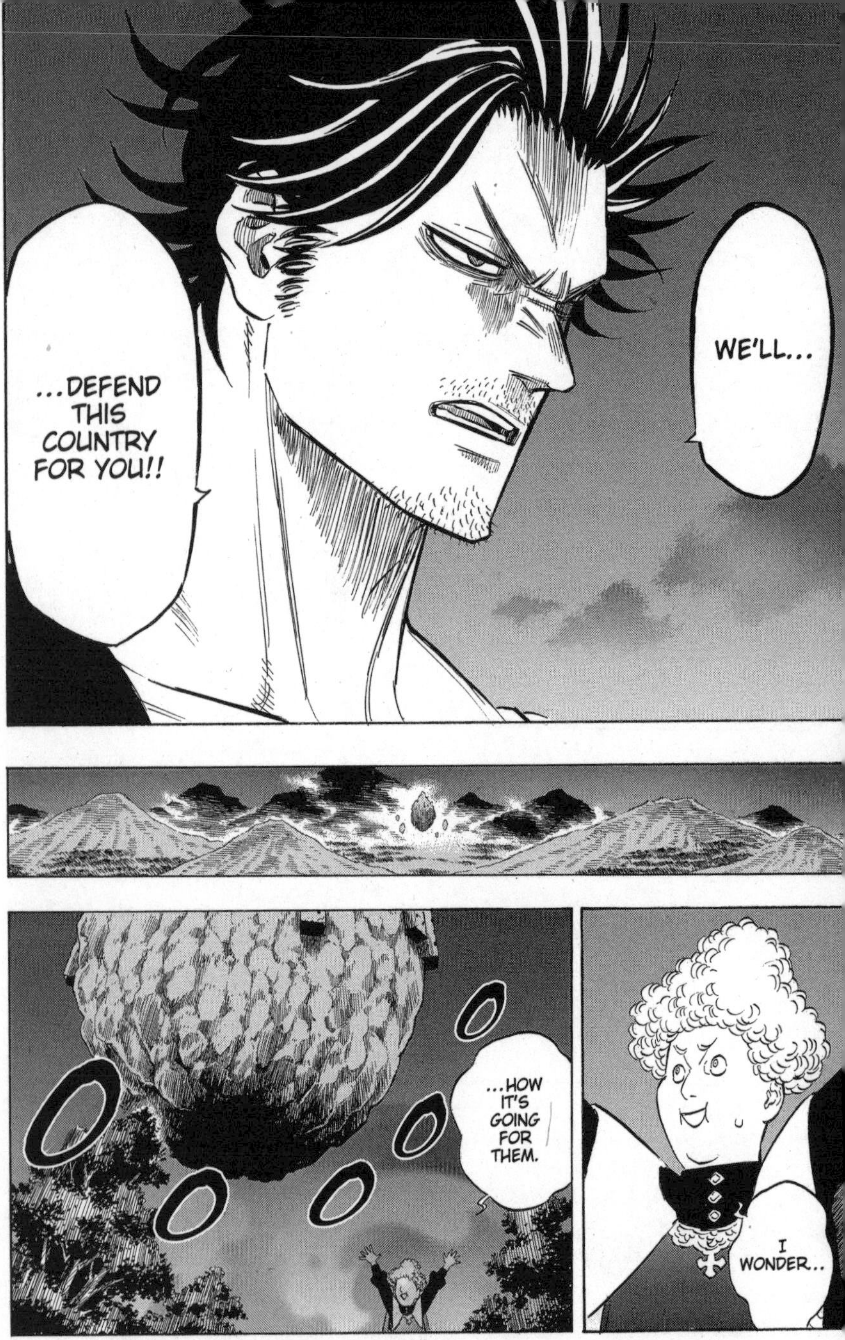
WE'LL...
...DEFEND THIS COUNTRY FOR YOU!!
I WONDER...
...HOW IT'S GOING FOR THEM.

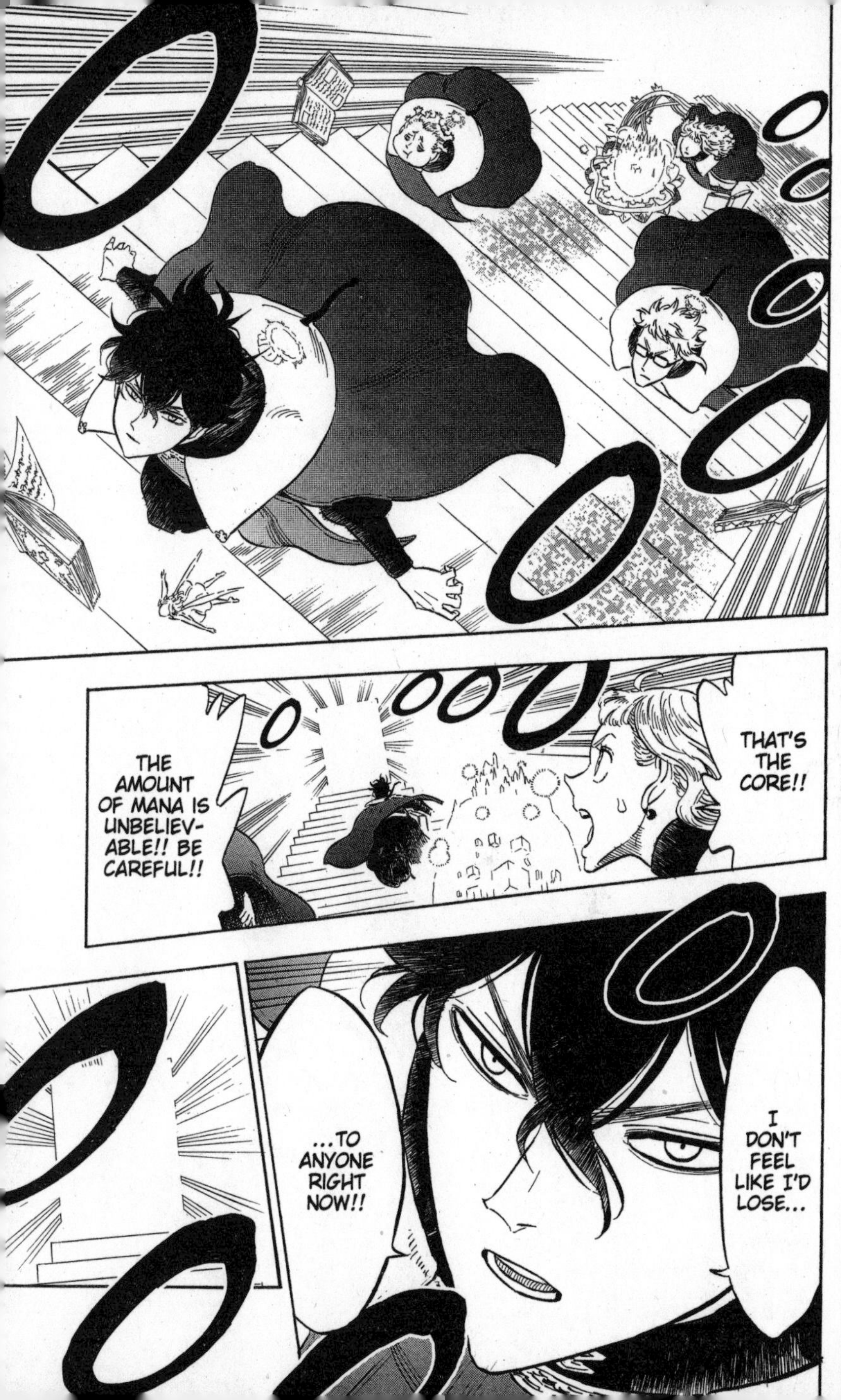
THAT'S THE CORE!!
THE AMOUNT OF MANA IS UNBELIEV-ABLE!! BE CAREFUL!!
I DON'T FEEL LIKE I'D LOSE...
...TO ANYONE RIGHT NOW!!

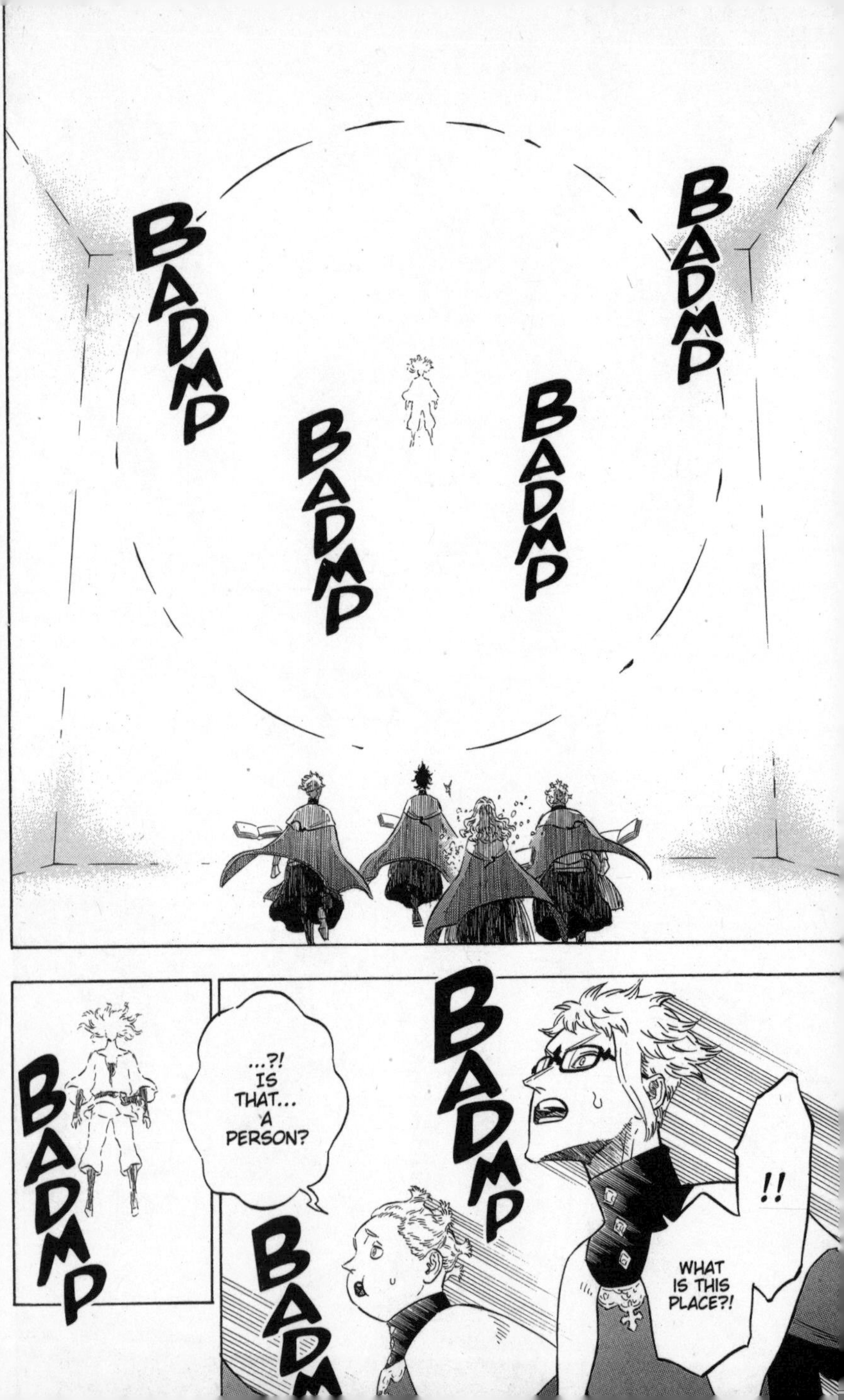
BADMP
BADMP
BADMP
BADMP
BADMP
!!
WHAT IS THIS PLACE?!
...?! IS THAT... A PERSON?
BADM
BADMP

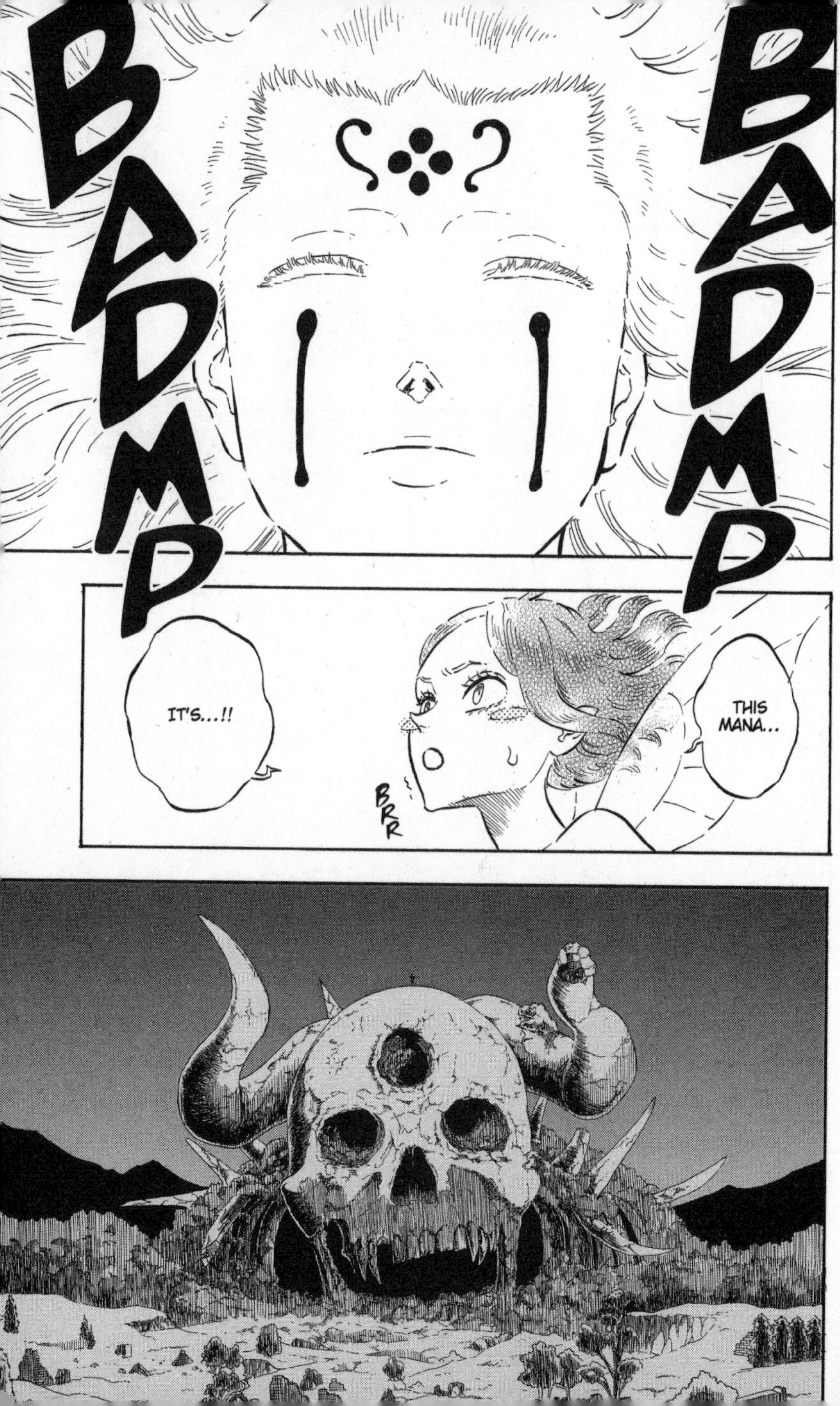
BADMP
BADMP
THIS MANA...
BRR
IT'S...!!

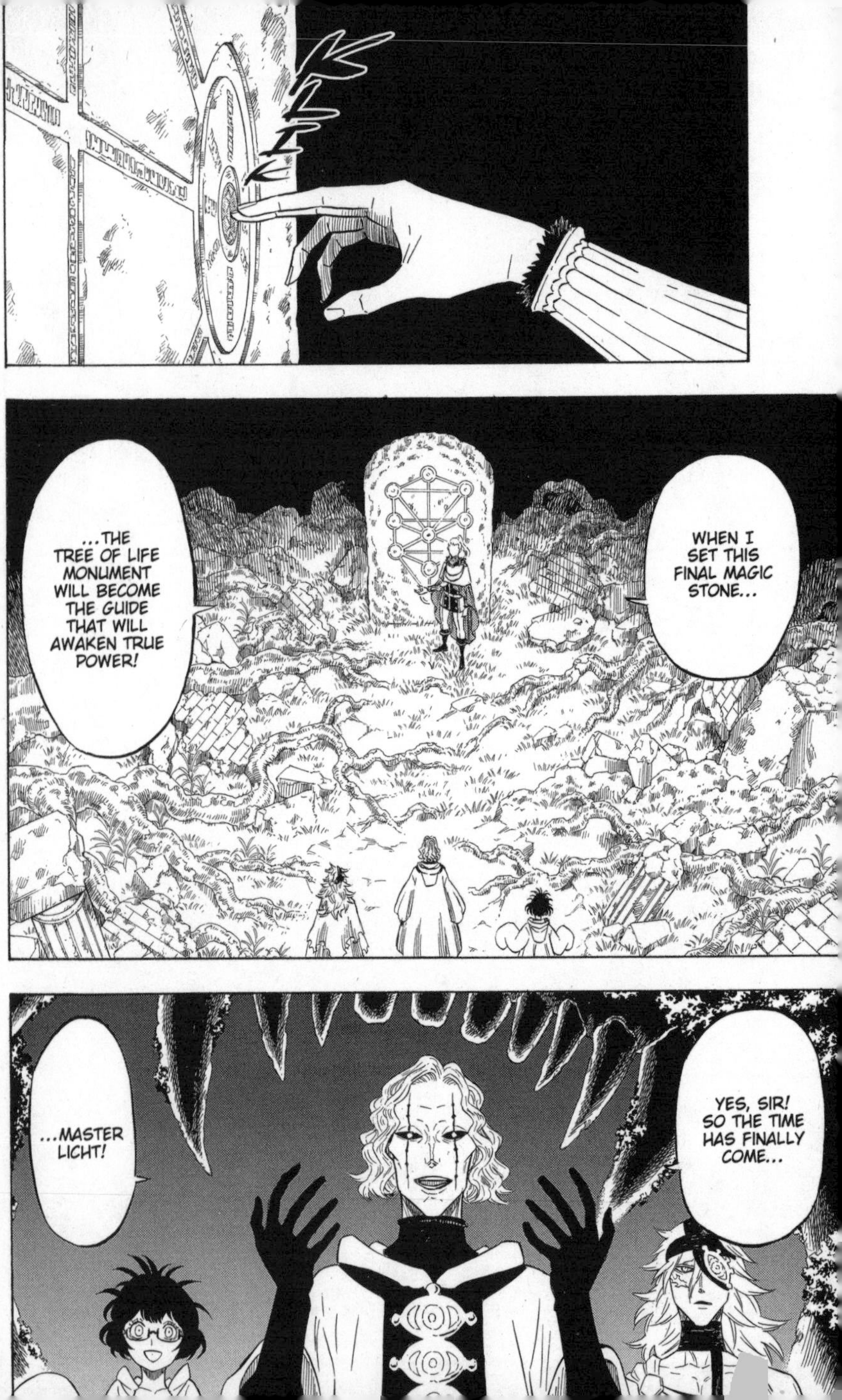
WHEN I SET THIS FINAL MAGIC STONE...
...THE TREE OF LIFE MONUMENT WILL BECOME THE GUIDE THAT WILL AWAKEN TRUE POWER!
YES, SIR! SO THE TIME HAS FINALLY COME...
...MASTER LICHT!

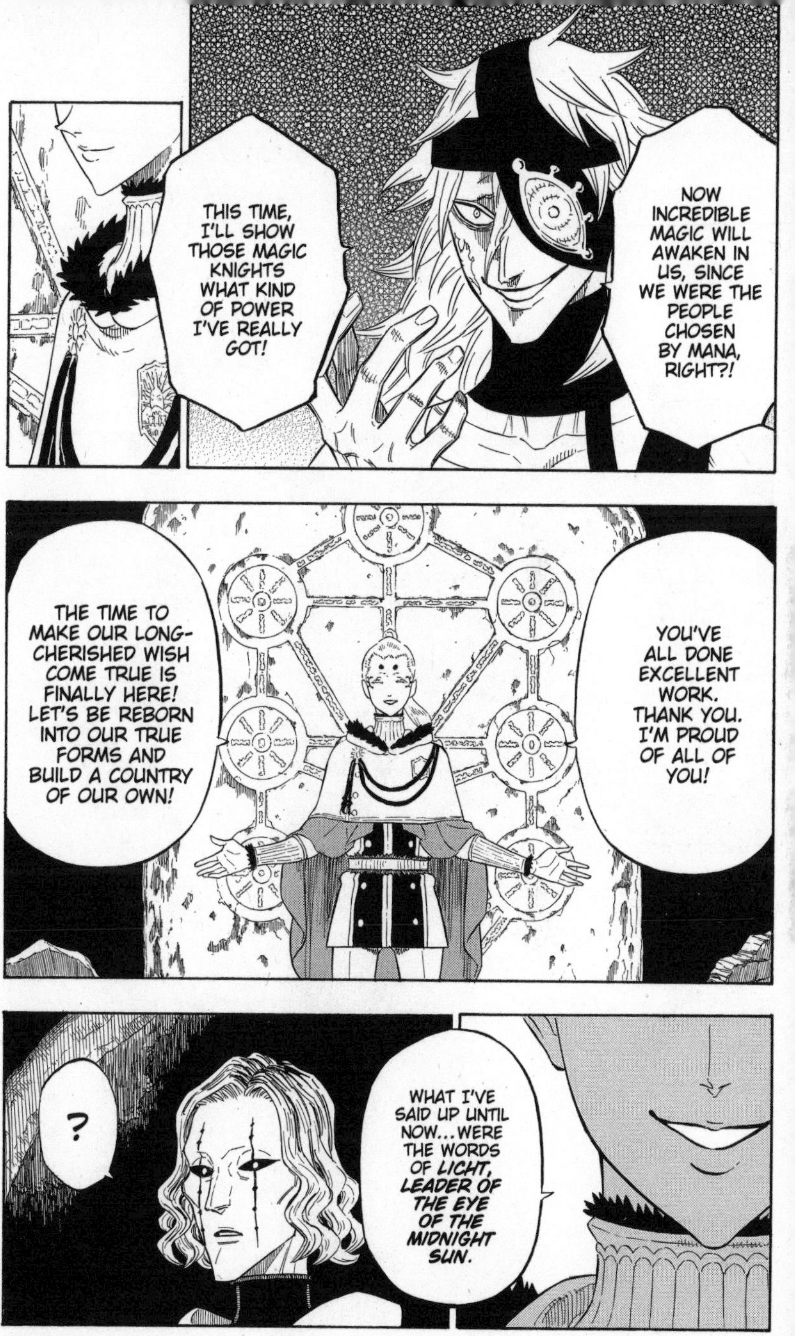
NOW INCREDIBLE MAGIC WILL AWAKEN IN US, SINCE WE WERE THE PEOPLE CHOSEN BY MANA, RIGHT?!
THIS TIME, I'LL SHOW THOSE MAGIC KNIGHTS WHAT KIND OF POWER I'VE REALLY GOT!
YOU'VE ALL DONE EXCELLENT WORK. THANK YOU. I'M PROUD OF ALL OF YOU!
THE TIME TO MAKE OUR LONG-CHERISHED WISH COME TRUE IS FINALLY HERE! LET'S BE REBORN INTO OUR TRUE FORMS AND BUILD A COUNTRY OF OUR OWN!
WHAT I'VE SAID UP UNTIL NOW... WERE THE WORDS OF *LICHT, LEADER OF THE EYE OF THE MIDNIGHT SUN.*
?

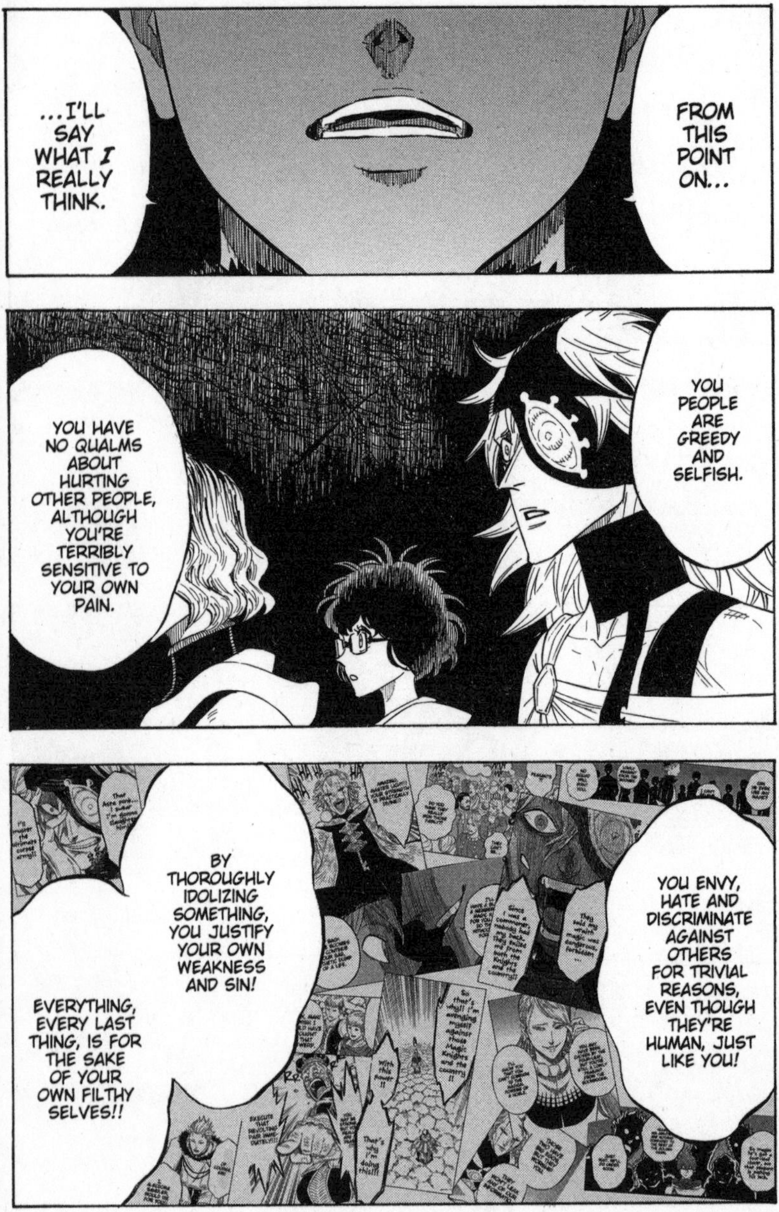
FROM THIS POINT ON...
...I'LL SAY WHAT I REALLY THINK.
YOU PEOPLE ARE GREEDY AND SELFISH.
YOU HAVE NO QUALMS ABOUT HURTING OTHER PEOPLE, ALTHOUGH YOU'RE TERRIBLY SENSITIVE TO YOUR OWN PAIN.
YOU ENVY, HATE AND DISCRIMINATE AGAINST OTHERS FOR TRIVIAL REASONS, EVEN THOUGH THEY'RE HUMAN, JUST LIKE YOU!
BY THOROUGHLY IDOLIZING SOMETHING, YOU JUSTIFY YOUR OWN WEAKNESS AND SIN!
EVERYTHING, EVERY LAST THING, IS FOR THE SAKE OF YOUR OWN FILTHY SELVES!!

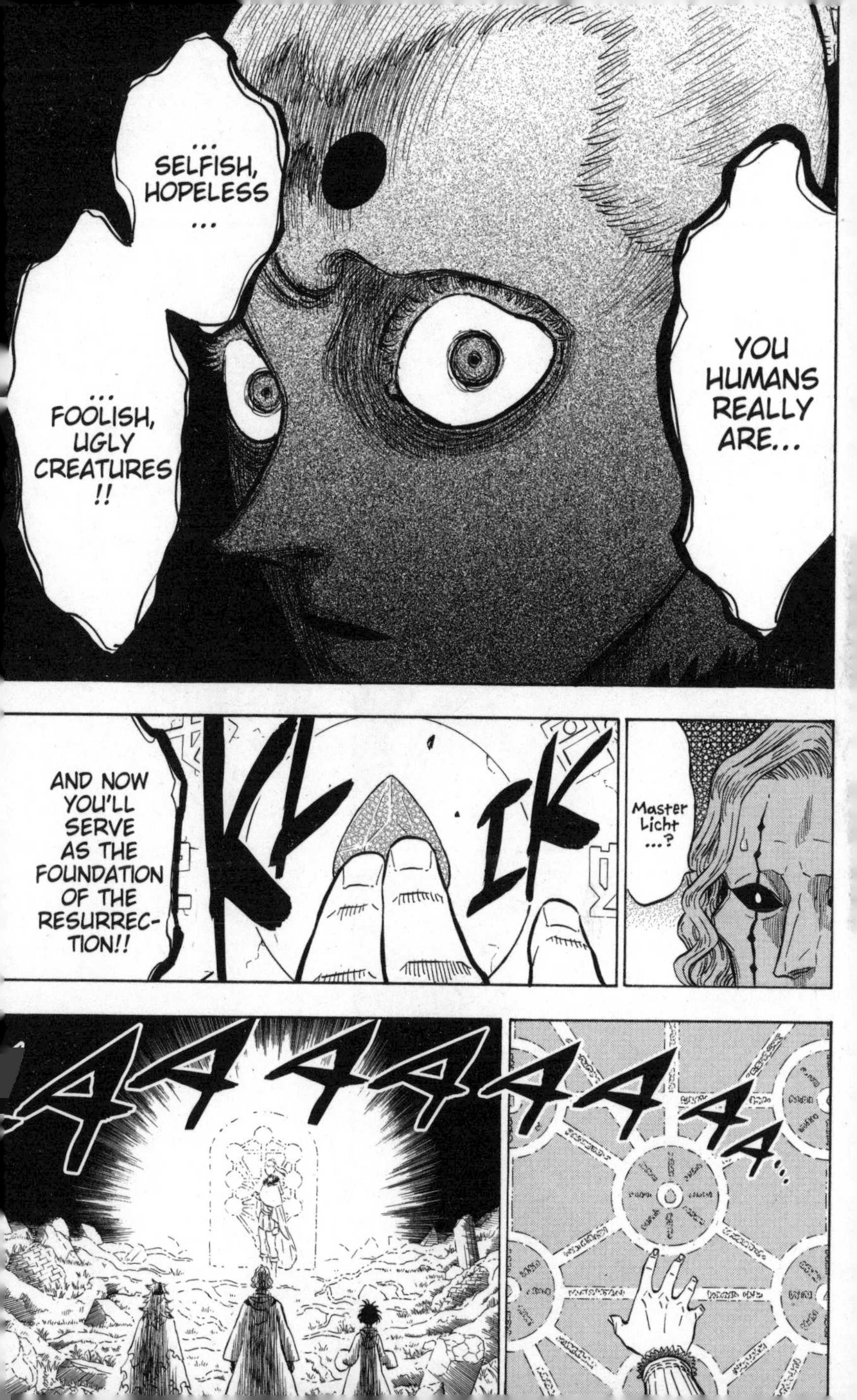
YOU HUMANS REALLY ARE...
...SELFISH, HOPELESS...
...FOOLISH, UGLY CREATURES!!
Master Licht...?
KLIK
AND NOW YOU'LL SERVE AS THE FOUNDATION OF THE RESURREC-TION!!
AAAAAAAAA...

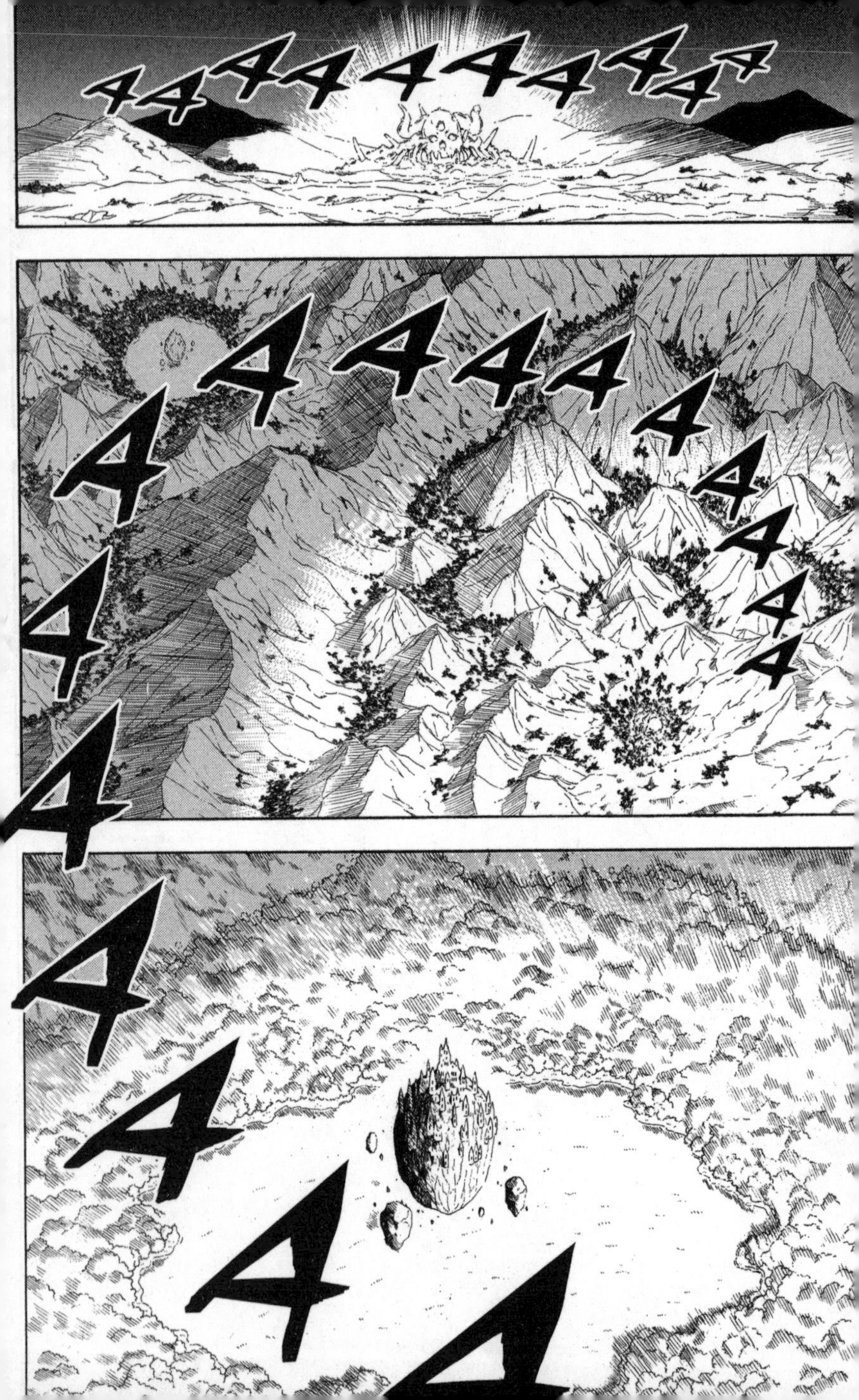

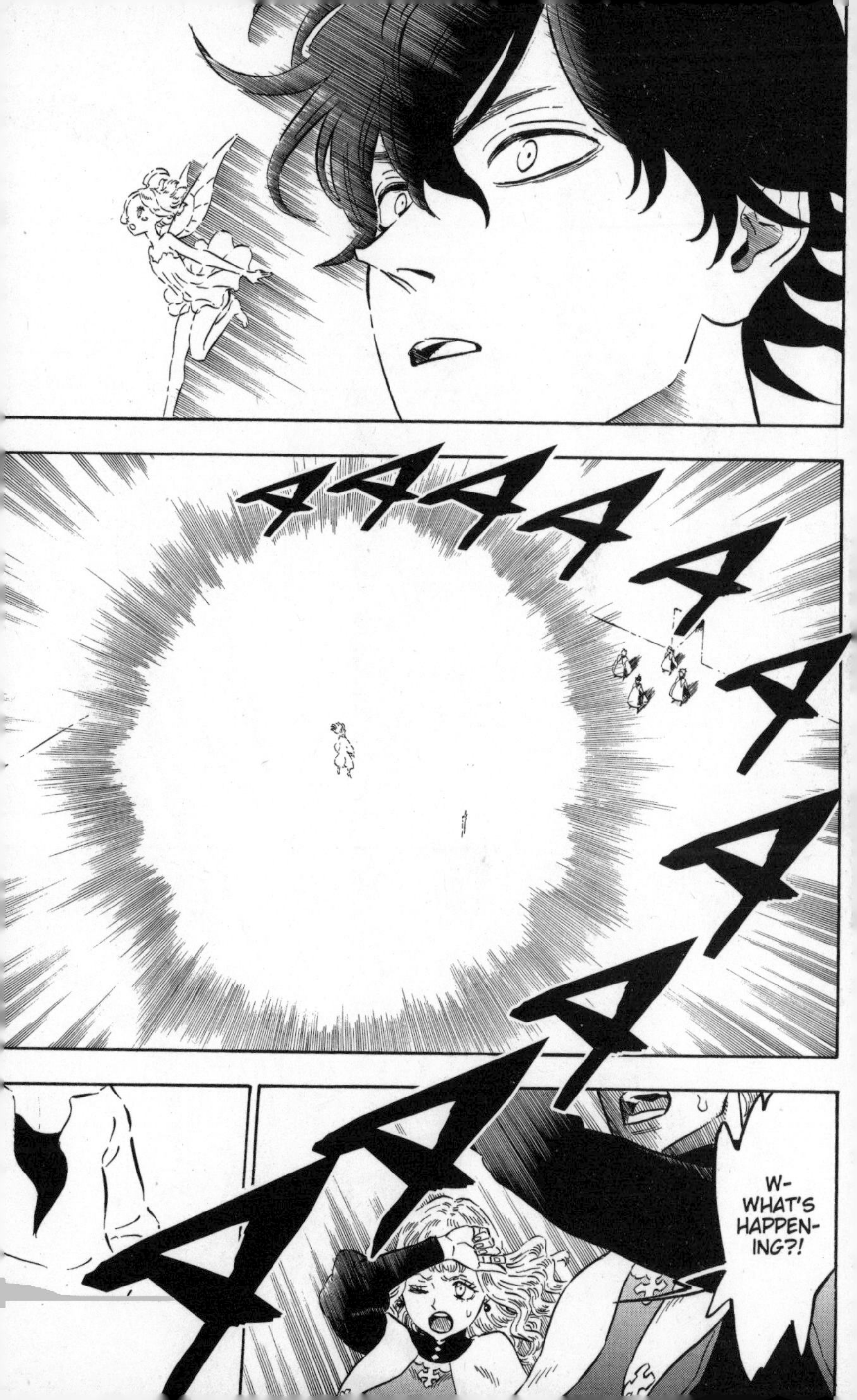
AAAAAAAAAAAA
W- WHAT'S HAPPEN-ING?!

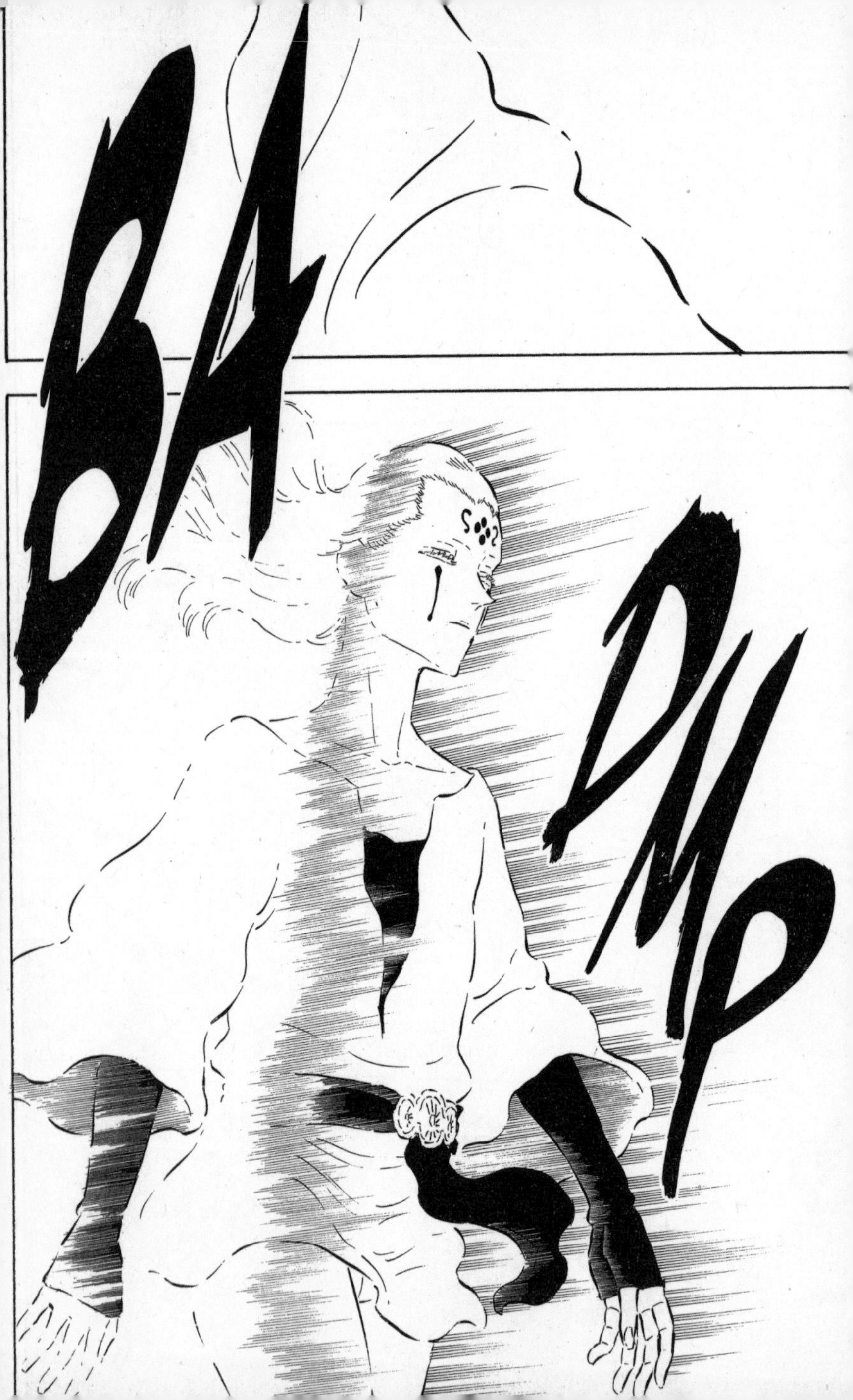
BA
DMP

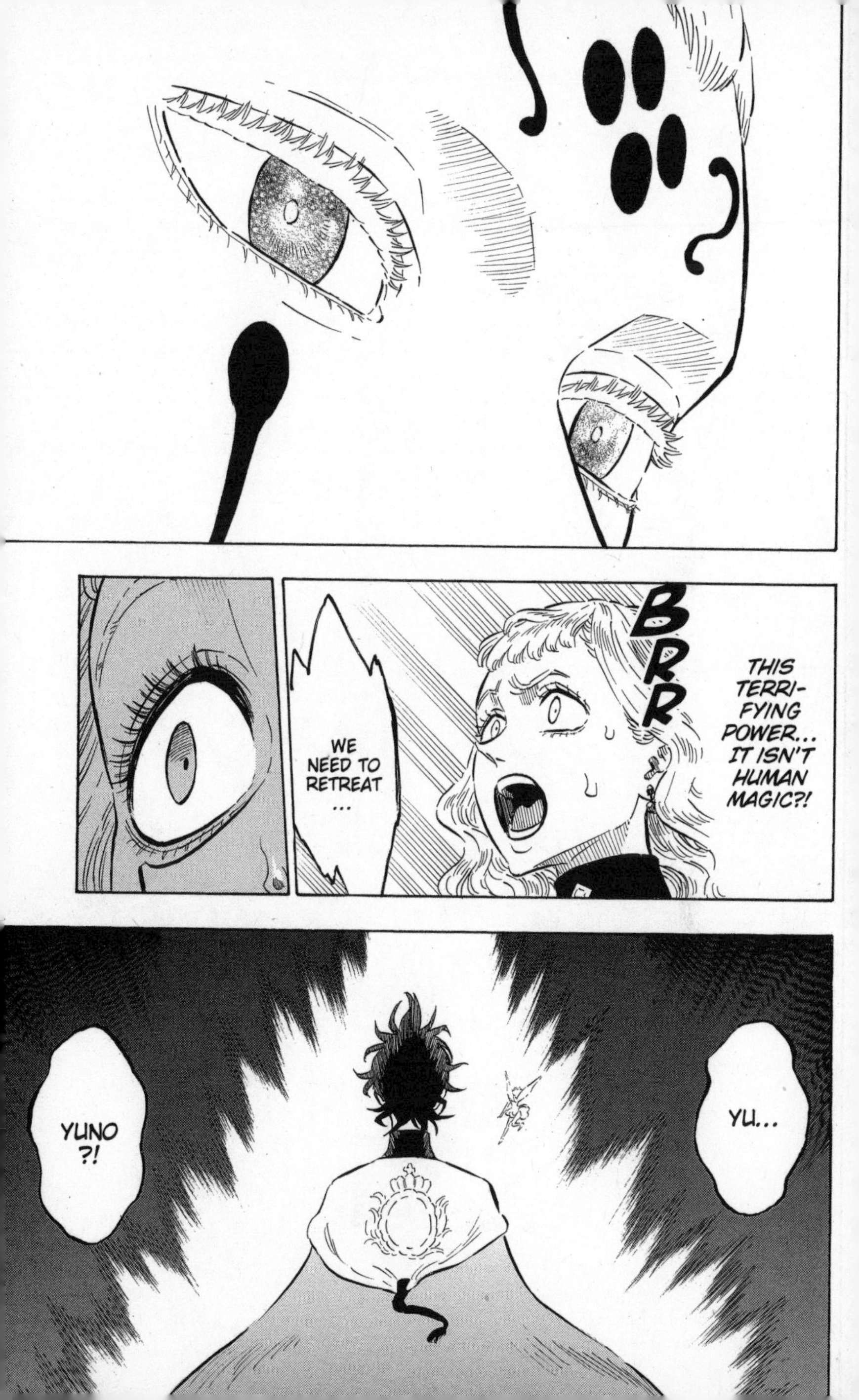

BRR
THIS TERRI-FYING POWER... IT ISN'T HUMAN MAGIC?!
WE NEED TO RETREAT...
YU...
YUNO ?!

✿ Page 148: Until Now

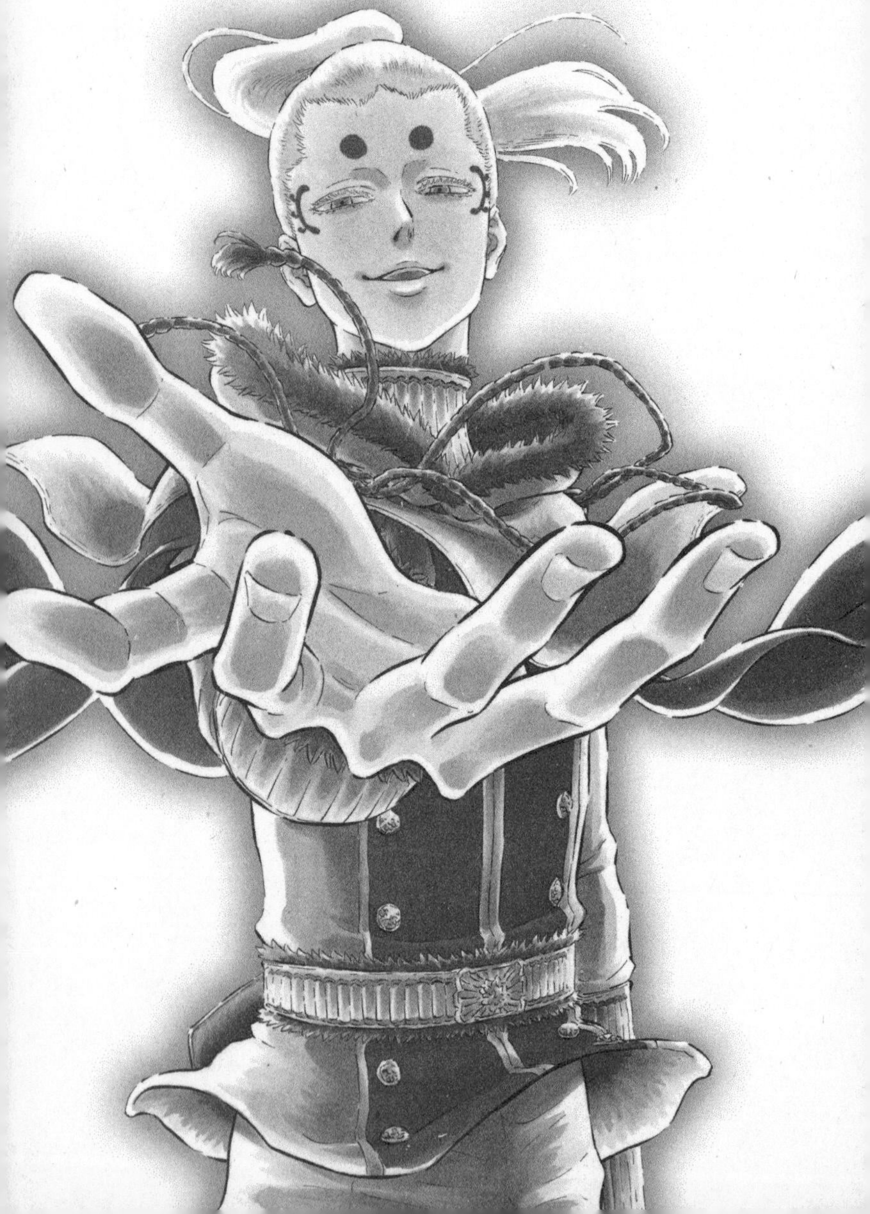

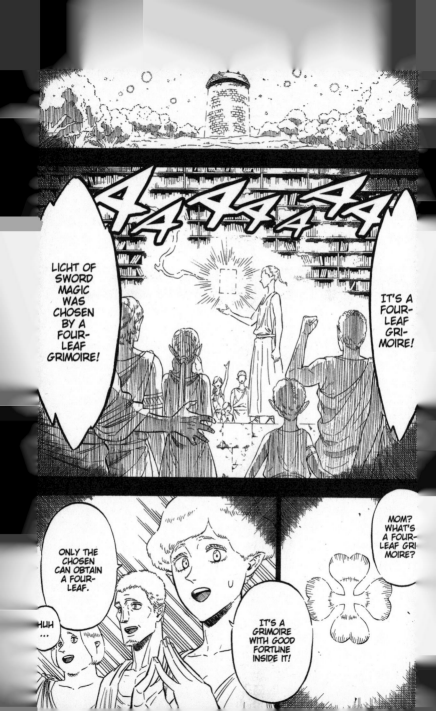

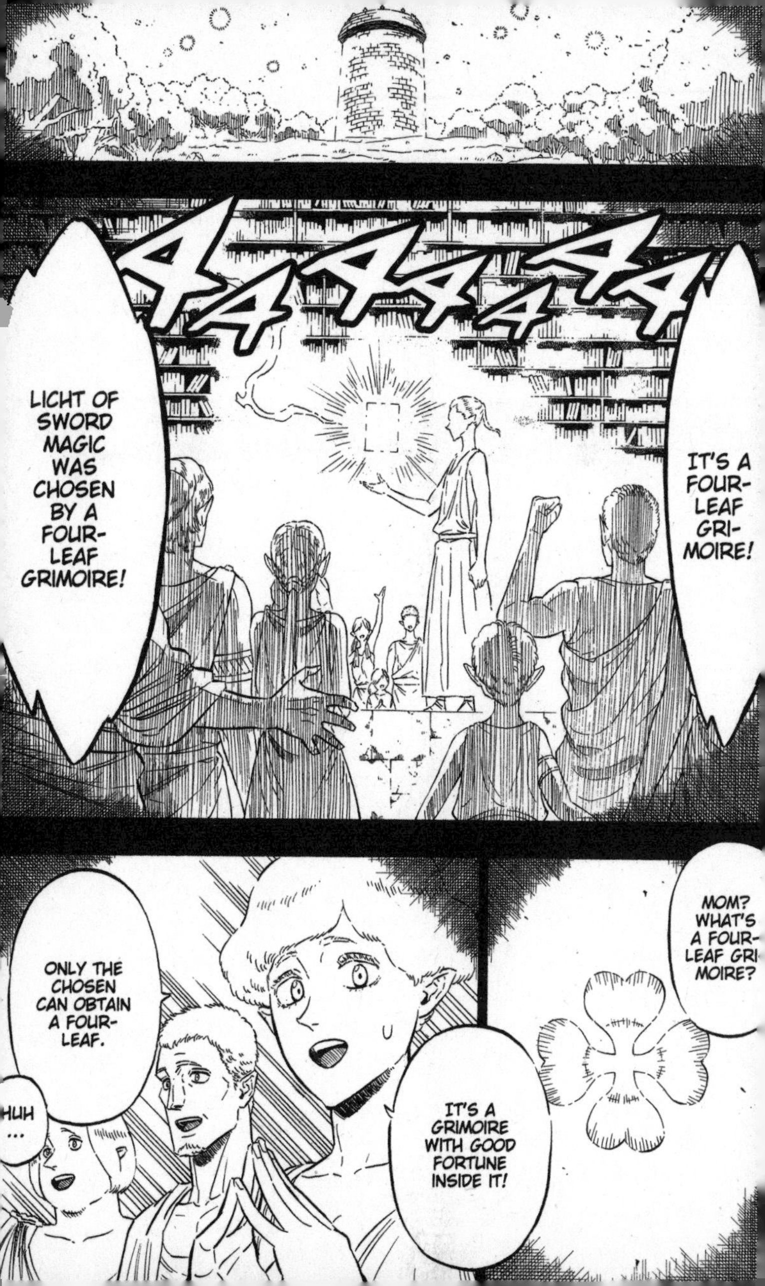
IT'S A FOUR-LEAF GRIMOIRE!
LICHT OF SWORD MAGIC WAS CHOSEN BY A FOUR-LEAF GRIMOIRE!
MOM? WHAT'S A FOUR-LEAF GRIMOIRE?
IT'S A GRIMOIRE WITH GOOD FORTUNE INSIDE IT!
ONLY THE CHOSEN CAN OBTAIN A FOUR-LEAF.
HUH...

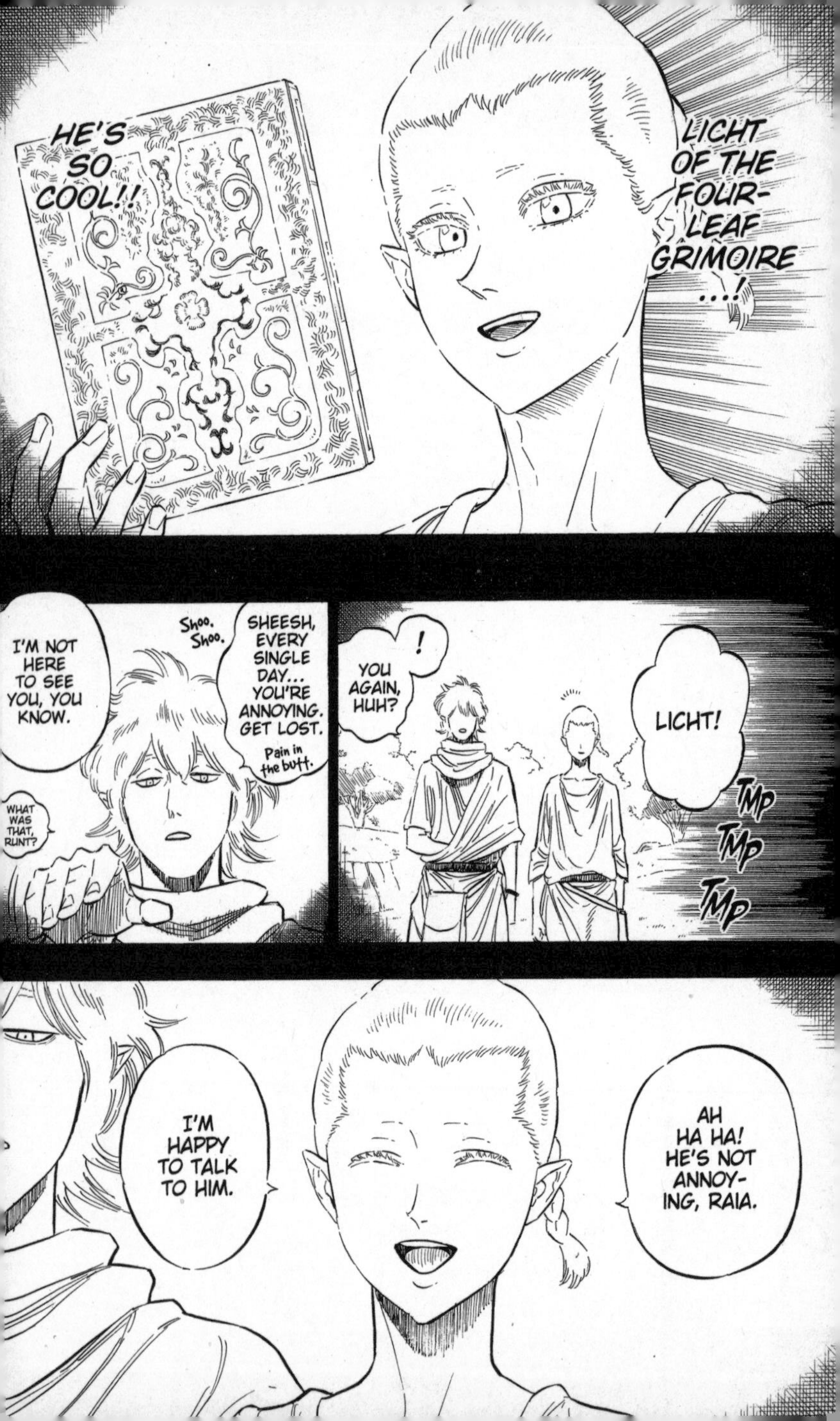
LICHT OF THE FOUR-LEAF GRIMOIRE ...!
HE'S SO COOL!!
LICHT!
TMP TMP TMP
!
YOU AGAIN, HUH?
SHEESH, EVERY SINGLE DAY... YOU'RE ANNOYING. GET LOST.
Shoo. Shoo.
Pain in the butt.
I'M NOT HERE TO SEE YOU, YOU KNOW.
WHAT WAS THAT, RUNT?
AH HA HA! HE'S NOT ANNOYING, RAIA.
I'M HAPPY TO TALK TO HIM.

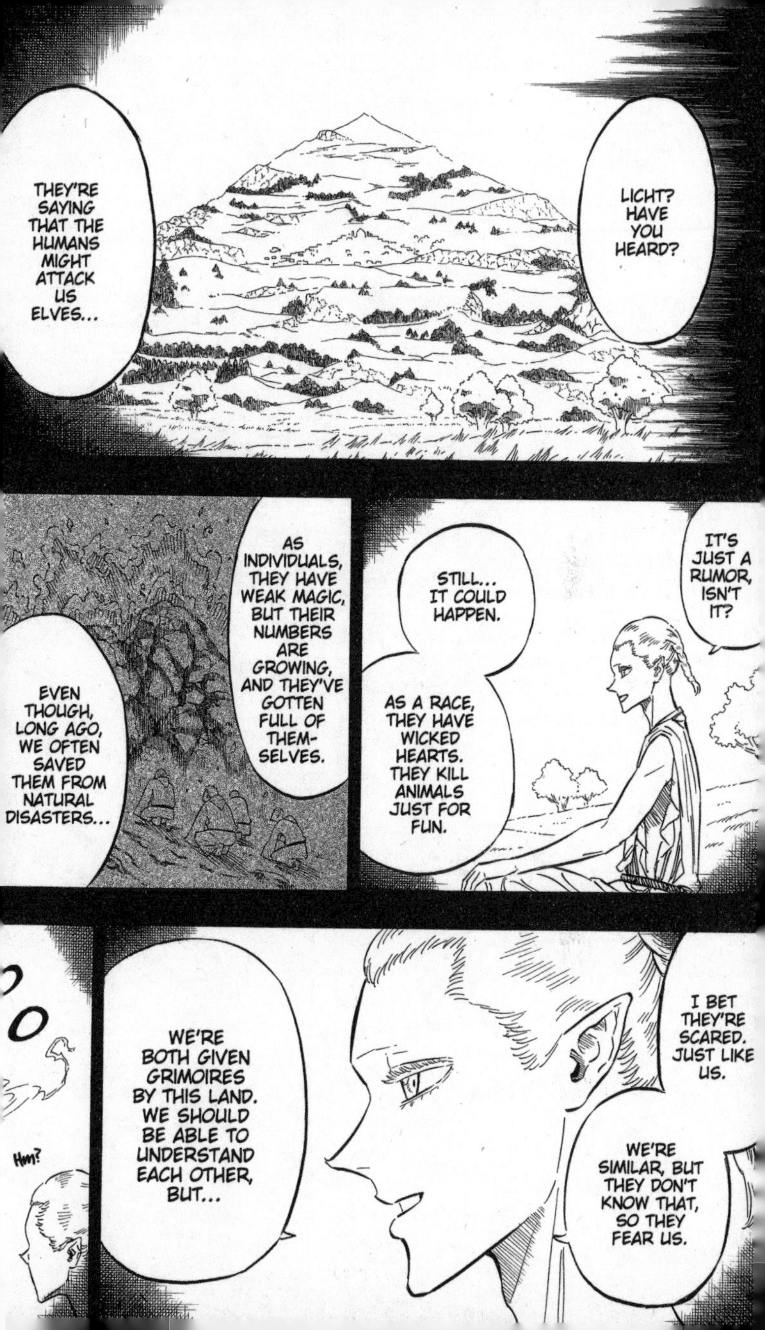
LICHT? HAVE YOU HEARD?
THEY'RE SAYING THAT THE HUMANS MIGHT ATTACK US ELVES...
IT'S JUST A RUMOR, ISN'T IT?
STILL... IT COULD HAPPEN.
AS A RACE, THEY HAVE WICKED HEARTS. THEY KILL ANIMALS JUST FOR FUN.
AS INDIVIDUALS, THEY HAVE WEAK MAGIC, BUT THEIR NUMBERS ARE GROWING, AND THEY'VE GOTTEN FULL OF THEM-SELVES.
EVEN THOUGH, LONG AGO, WE OFTEN SAVED THEM FROM NATURAL DISASTERS...
I BET THEY'RE SCARED. JUST LIKE US.
WE'RE SIMILAR, BUT THEY DON'T KNOW THAT, SO THEY FEAR US.
WE'RE BOTH GIVEN GRIMOIRES BY THIS LAND. WE SHOULD BE ABLE TO UNDERSTAND EACH OTHER, BUT...
Hm?

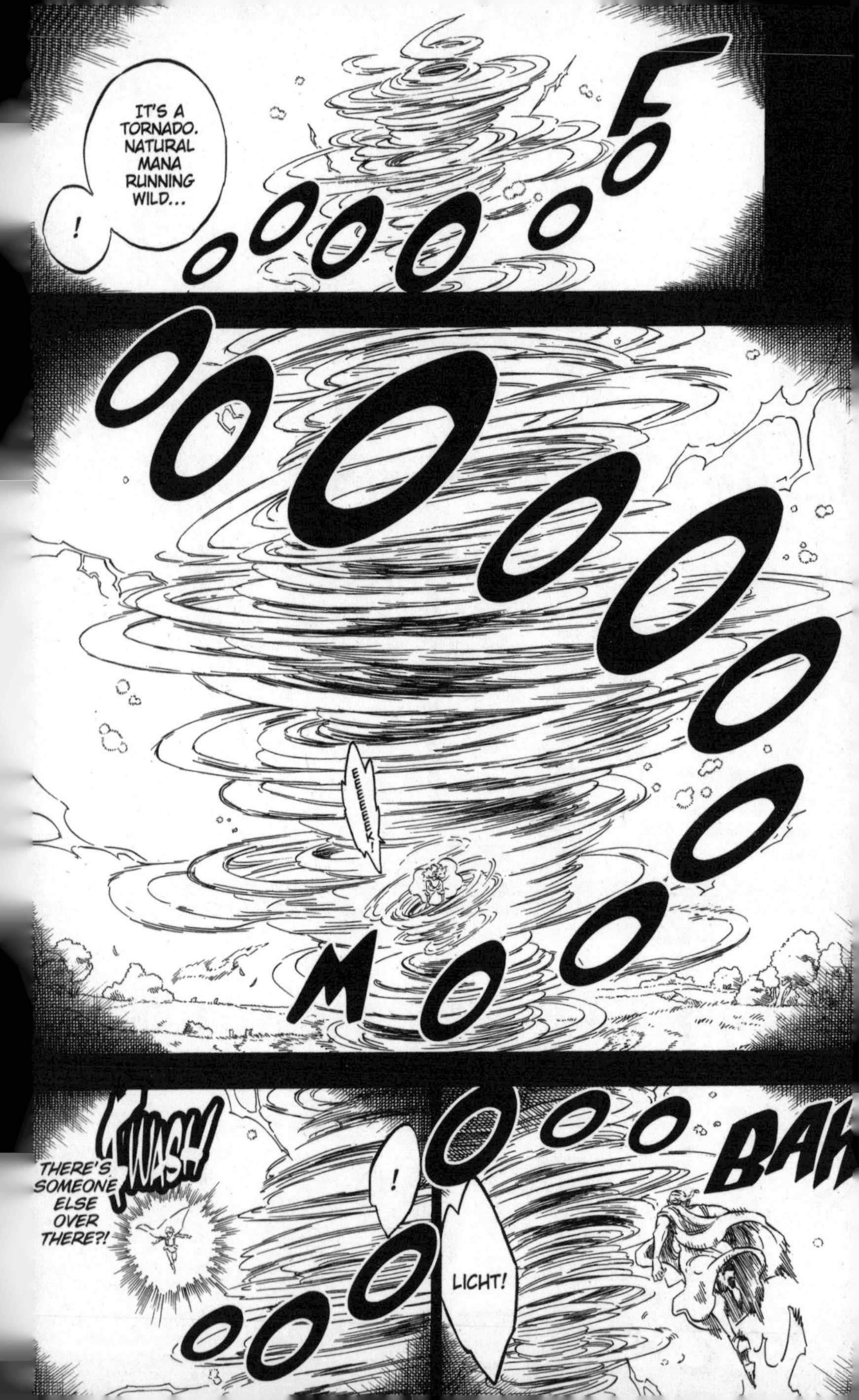
IT'S A TORNADO. NATURAL MANA RUNNING WILD...
!
EEEEEEEK!
BAH
!
LICHT!
WASH!
THERE'S SOMEONE ELSE OVER THERE?!

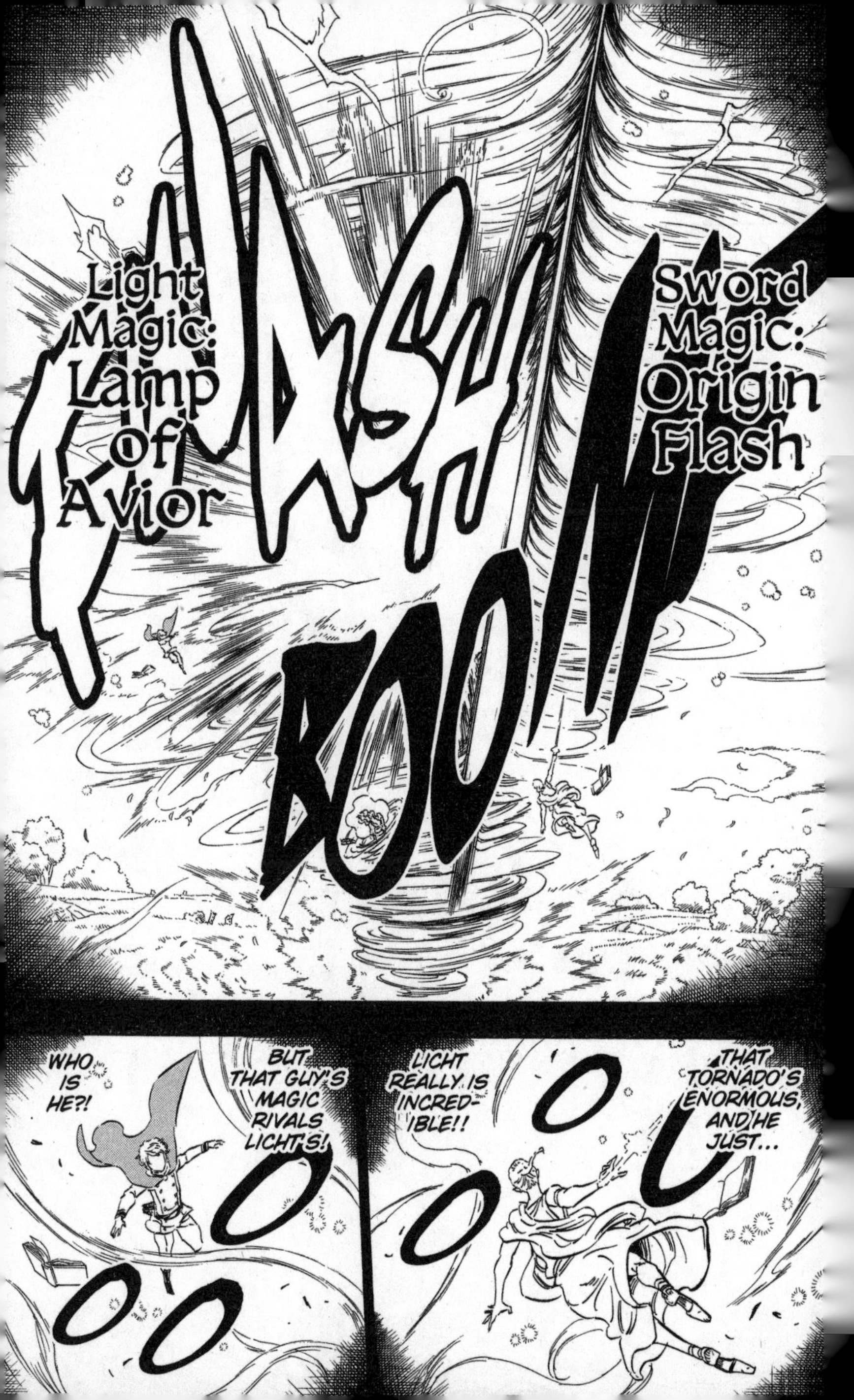
Sword Magic: Origin Flash
Light Magic: Lamp of Avior
BOOM
THAT TORNADO'S ENORMOUS, AND HE JUST...
LICHT REALLY IS INCRED-IBLE!!
BUT THAT GUY'S MAGIC RIVALS LICHT'S!
WHO IS HE?!

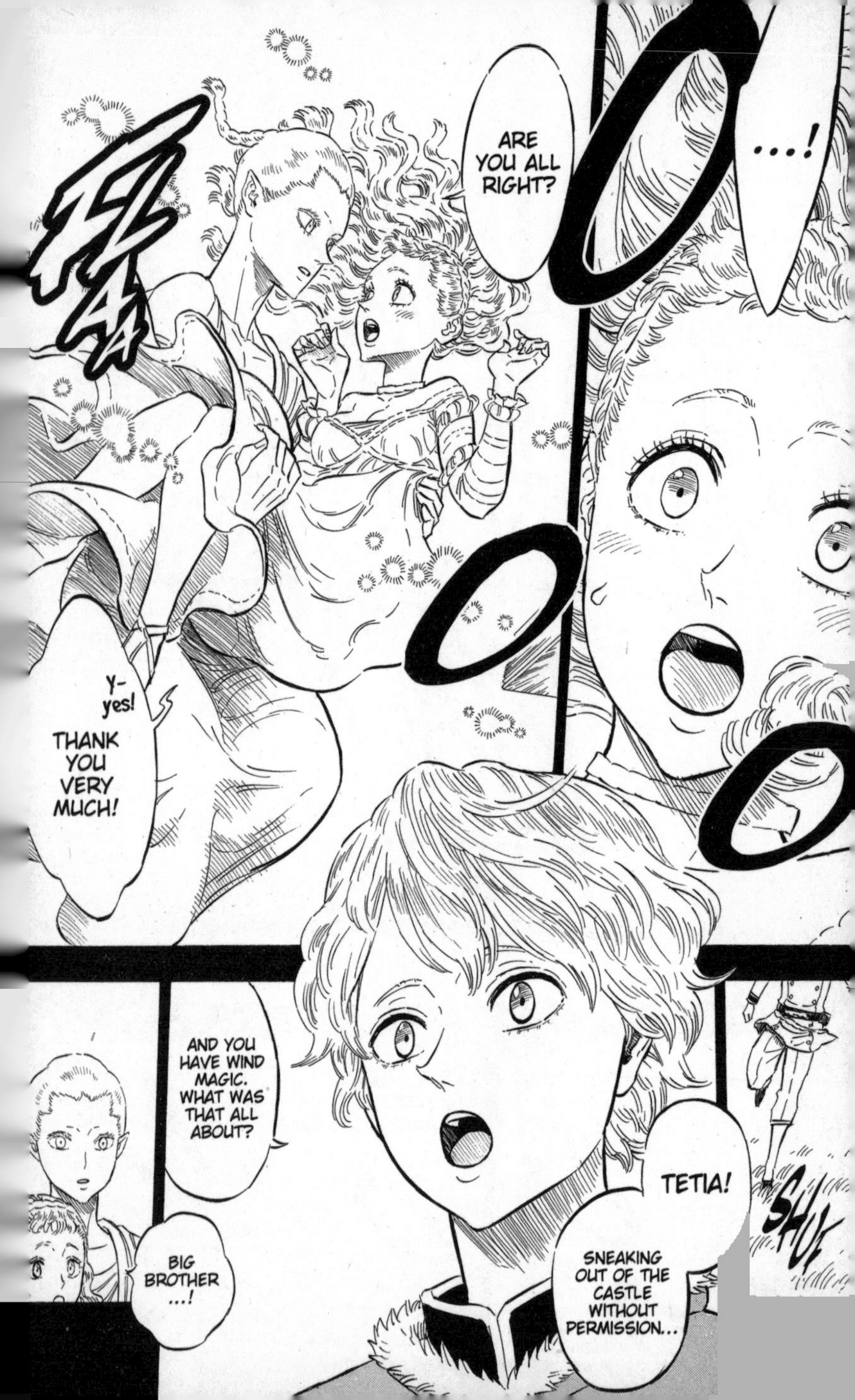
...!
ARE YOU ALL RIGHT?
Y-yes! THANK YOU VERY MUCH!
SHU
TETIA!
SNEAKING OUT OF THE CASTLE WITHOUT PERMISSION...
AND YOU HAVE WIND MAGIC. WHAT WAS THAT ALL ABOUT?
BIG BROTHER ...!

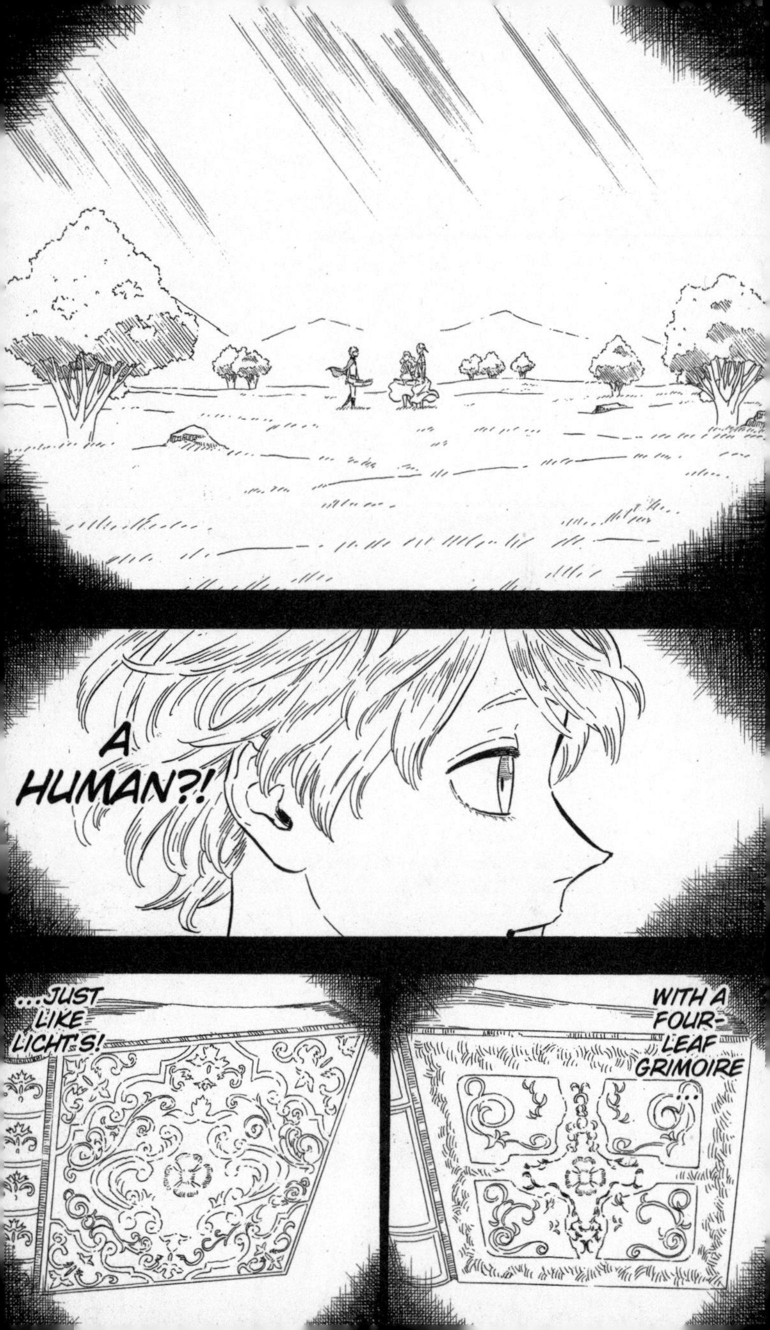
A HUMAN?!
WITH A FOUR-LEAF GRIMOIRE...
...JUST LIKE LICHT'S!

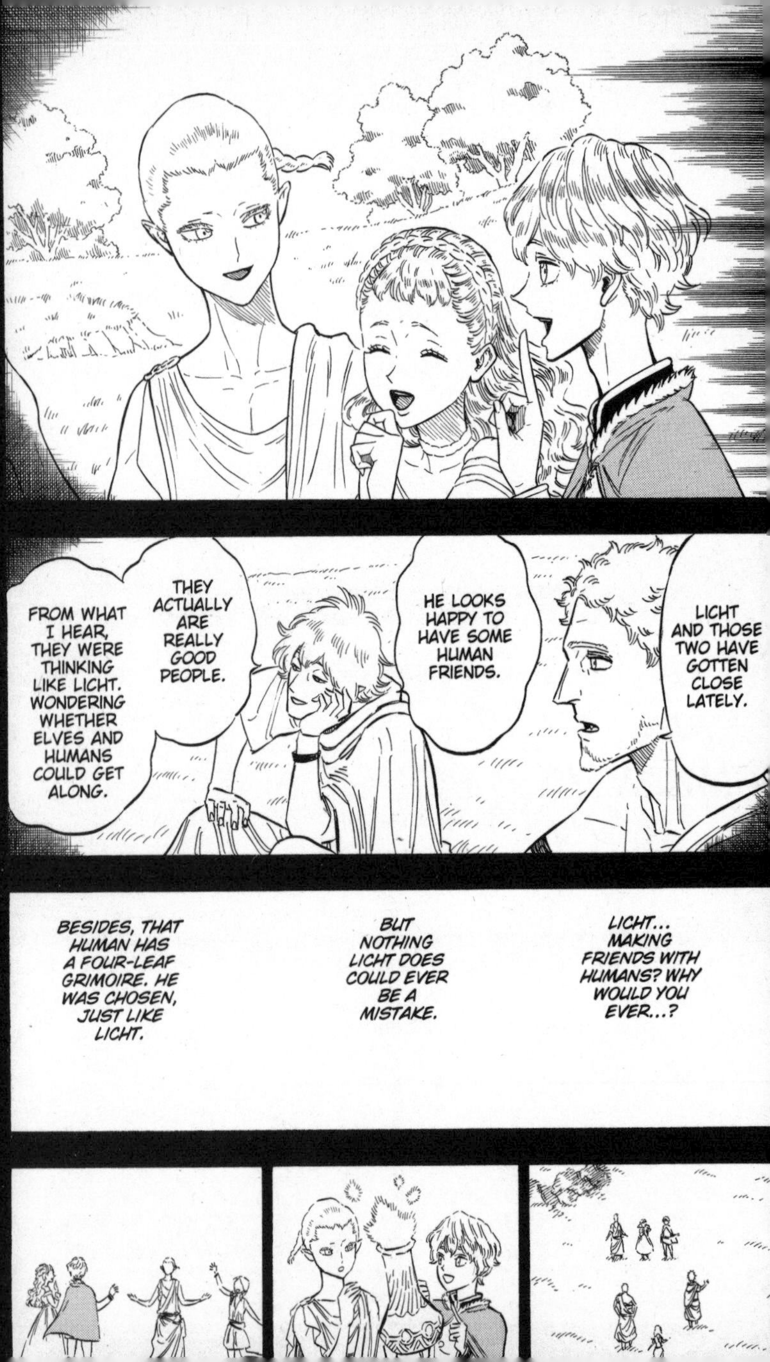
LICHT AND THOSE TWO HAVE GOTTEN CLOSE LATELY.
HE LOOKS HAPPY TO HAVE SOME HUMAN FRIENDS.
THEY ACTUALLY ARE REALLY GOOD PEOPLE.
FROM WHAT I HEAR, THEY WERE THINKING LIKE LICHT. WONDERING WHETHER ELVES AND HUMANS COULD GET ALONG.
LICHT... MAKING FRIENDS WITH HUMANS? WHY WOULD YOU EVER...?
BUT NOTHING LICHT DOES COULD EVER BE A MISTAKE.
BESIDES, THAT HUMAN HAS A FOUR-LEAF GRIMOIRE. HE WAS CHOSEN, JUST LIKE LICHT.

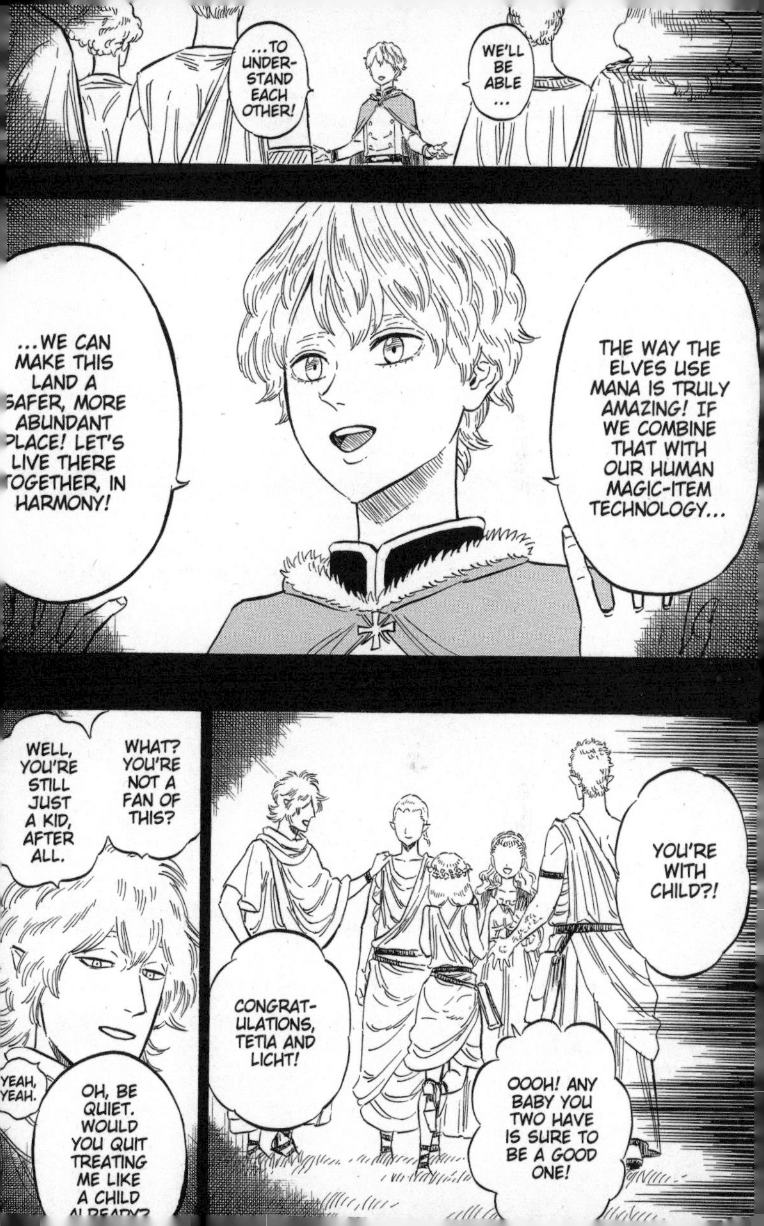
WE'LL BE ABLE...
...TO UNDERSTAND EACH OTHER!
THE WAY THE ELVES USE MANA IS TRULY AMAZING! IF WE COMBINE THAT WITH OUR HUMAN MAGIC-ITEM TECHNOLOGY...
...WE CAN MAKE THIS LAND A SAFER, MORE ABUNDANT PLACE! LET'S LIVE THERE TOGETHER, IN HARMONY!
YOU'RE WITH CHILD?!
CONGRATULATIONS, TETIA AND LICHT!
OOOH! ANY BABY YOU TWO HAVE IS SURE TO BE A GOOD ONE!
WHAT? YOU'RE NOT A FAN OF THIS?
WELL, YOU'RE STILL JUST A KID, AFTER ALL.
OH, BE QUIET. WOULD YOU QUIT TREATING ME LIKE A CHILD ALREADY?
YEAH, YEAH.

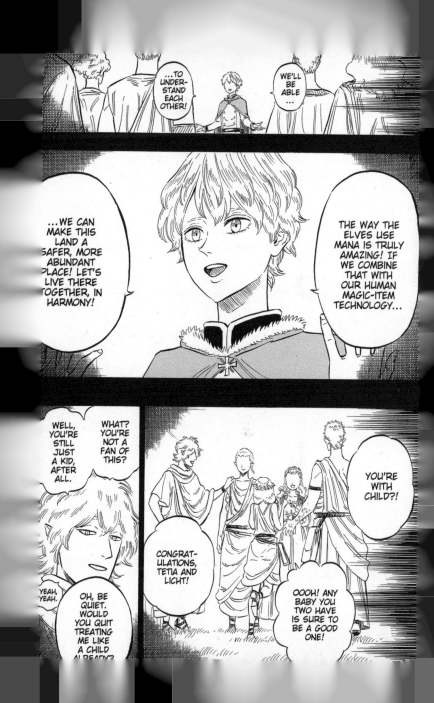

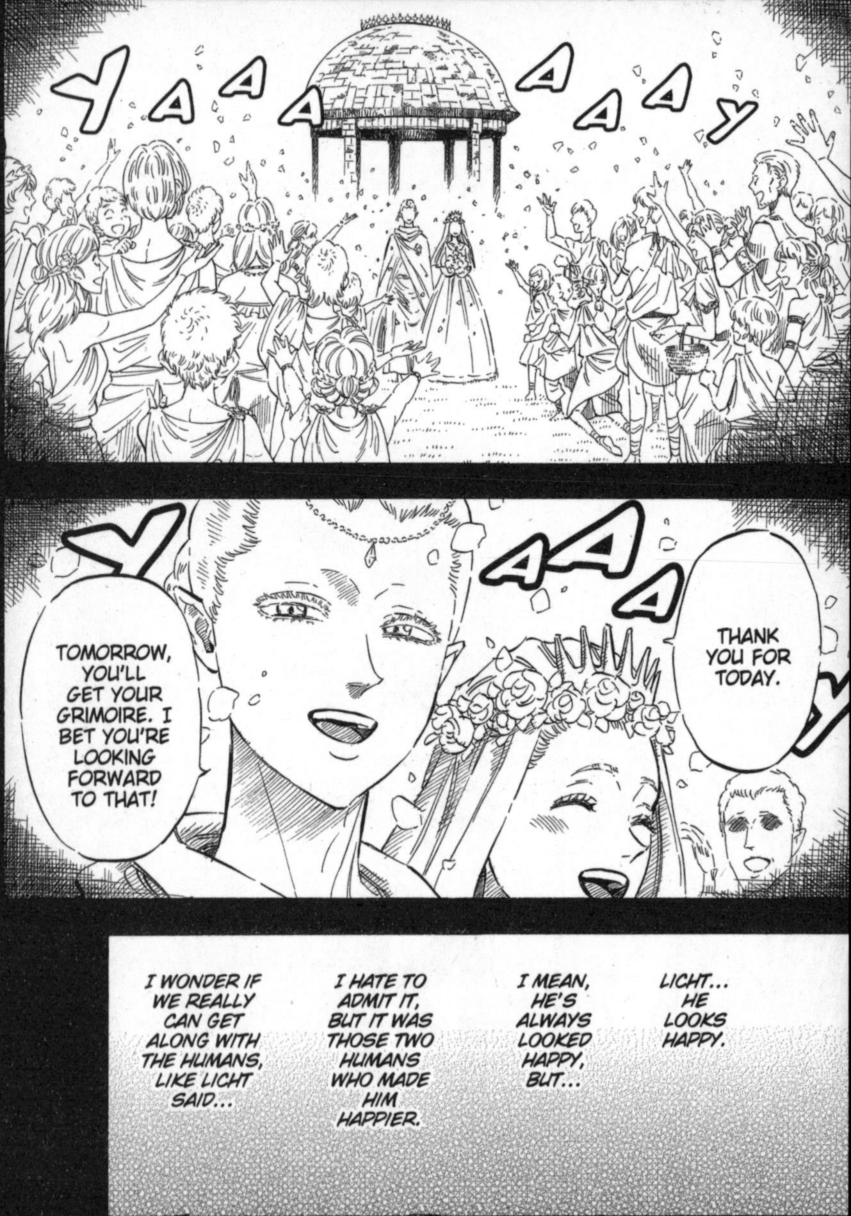
YAAAAAAAY
YAAAY
THANK YOU FOR TODAY.
TOMORROW, YOU'LL GET YOUR GRIMOIRE. I BET YOU'RE LOOKING FORWARD TO THAT!
LICHT... HE LOOKS HAPPY.
I MEAN, HE'S ALWAYS LOOKED HAPPY, BUT...
I HATE TO ADMIT IT, BUT IT WAS THOSE TWO HUMANS WHO MADE HIM HAPPIER.
I WONDER IF WE REALLY CAN GET ALONG WITH THE HUMANS, LIKE LICHT SAID...

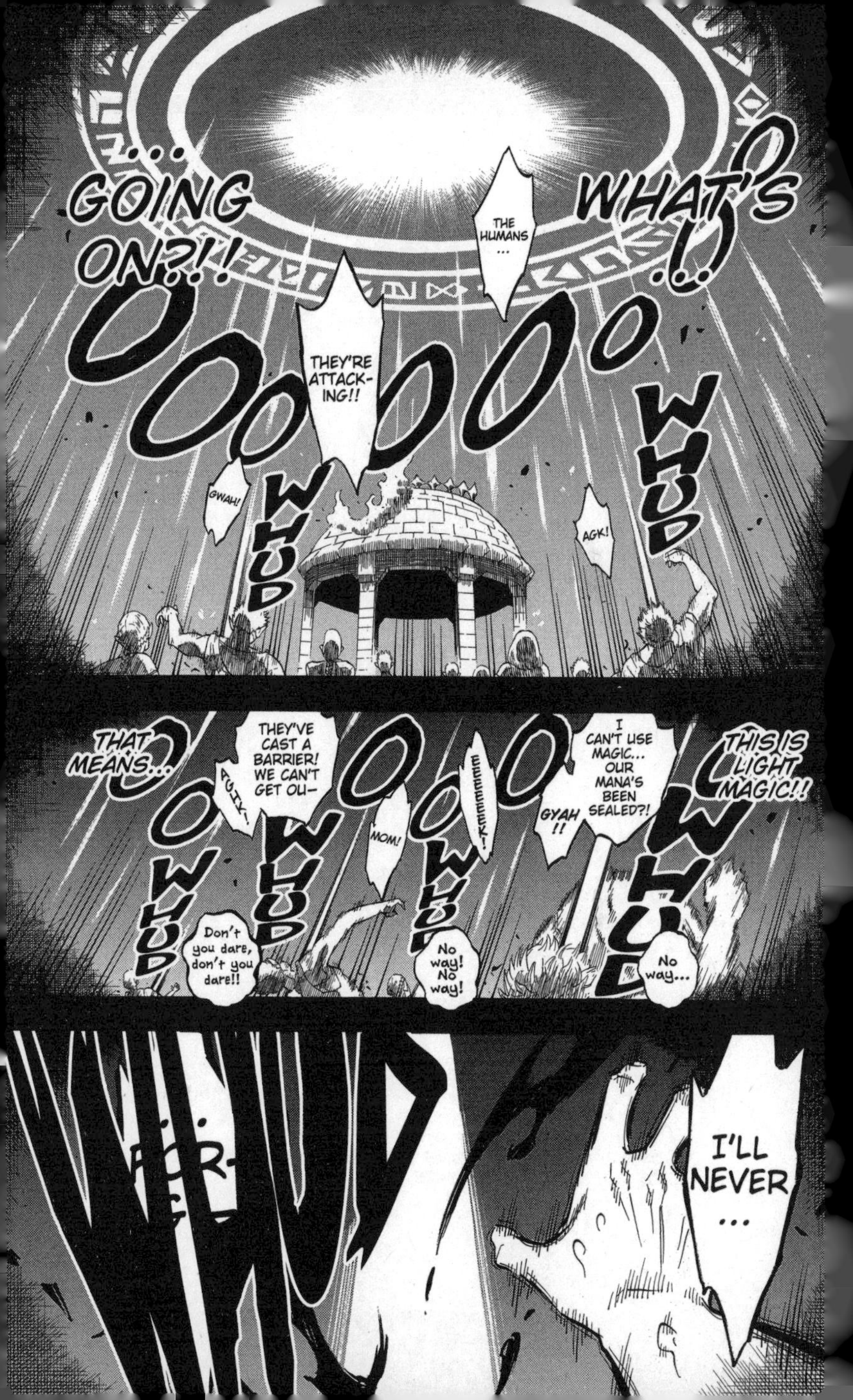
WHAT'S...
THE HUMANS...
...GOING ON?!!
THEY'RE ATTACKING!!
OOOOO
WHUD
AGK!
GWAH!
WHUD
THIS IS LIGHT MAGIC!!
WHUD
I CAN'T USE MAGIC... OUR MANA'S BEEN SEALED?!
GYAH!!
No way...
OOO
EEEEEEK!
WHUD
No way! No way!
MOM!
THEY'VE CAST A BARRIER! WE CAN'T GET OU–
WHUD
AGIK!
THAT MEANS...
WHUD
Don't you dare, don't you dare!!
I'LL NEVER...
WHUD
...FOR-G

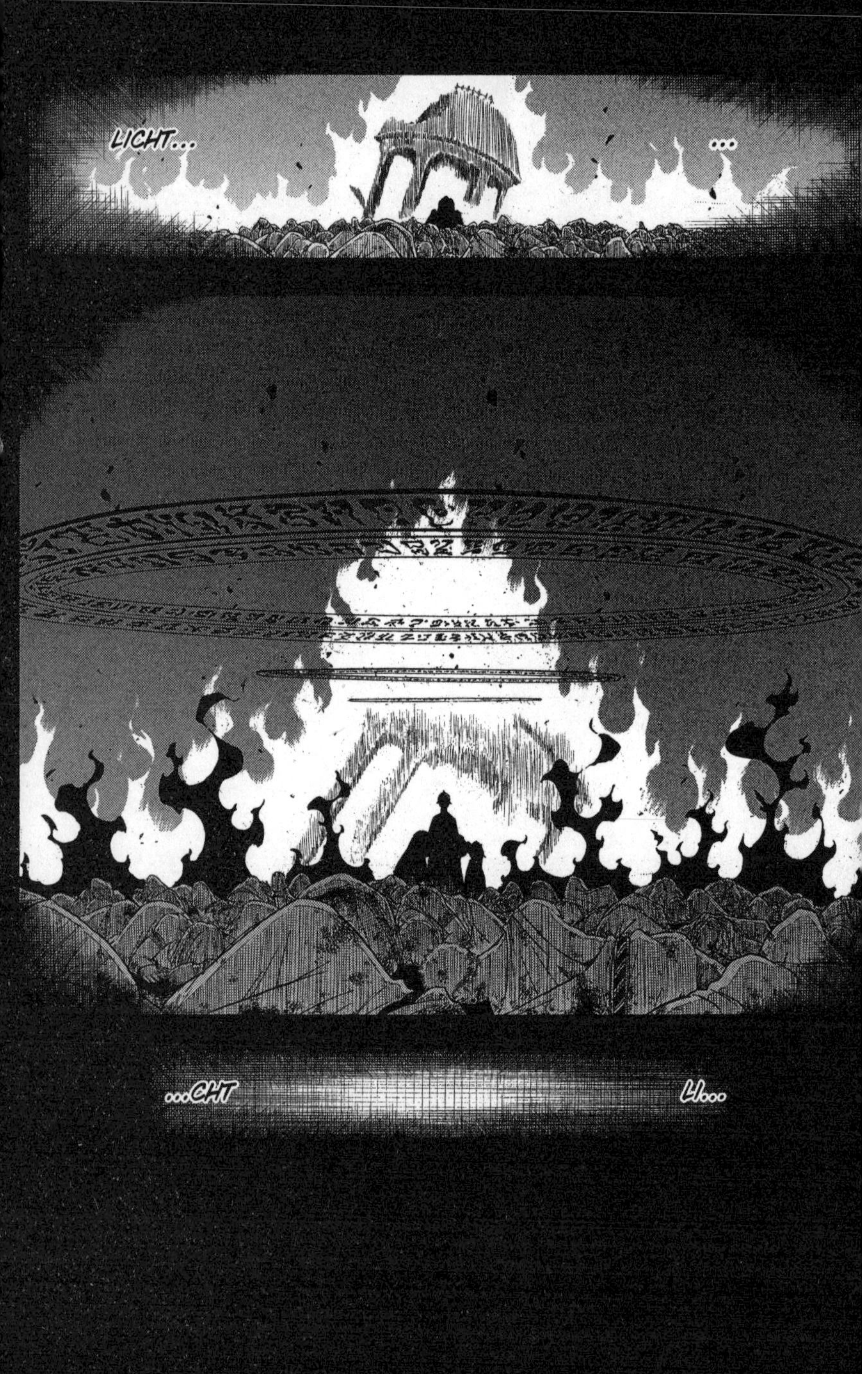
...
LICHT...
LI...
...CHT

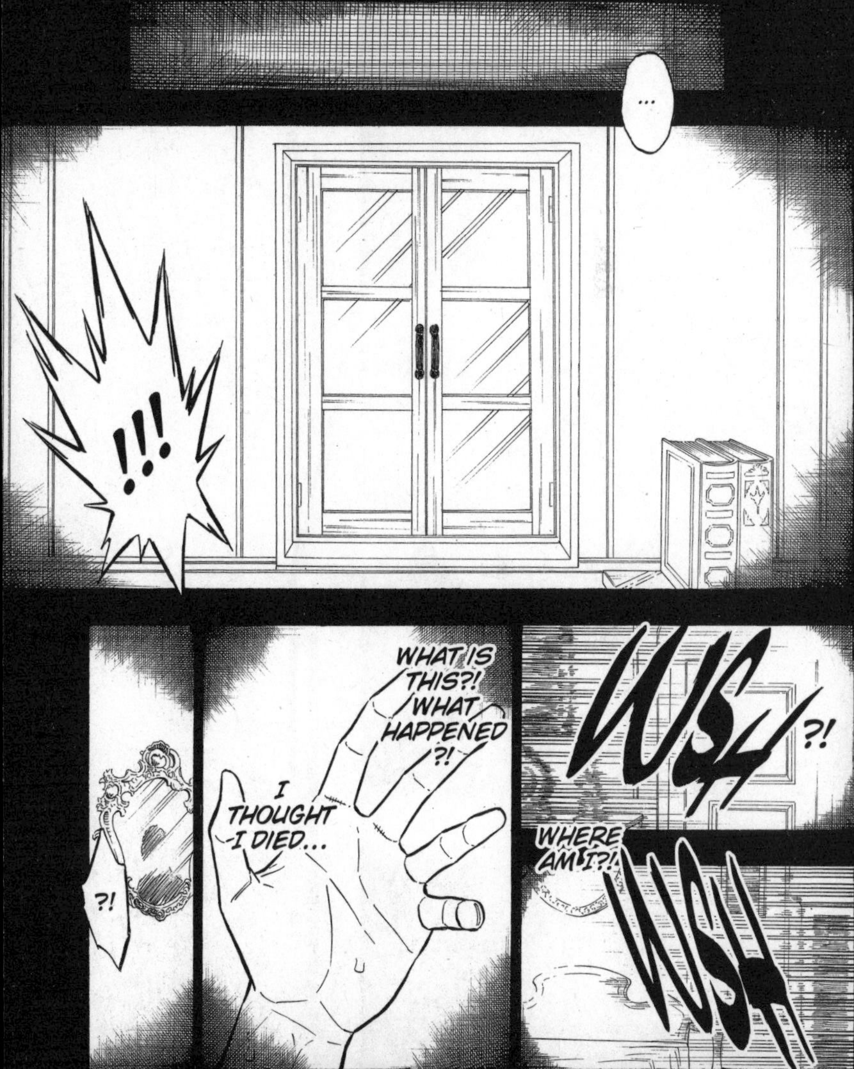
...
!!!
WSH
?!
WHERE AM I?!
WSH
WHAT IS THIS?! WHAT HAPPENED?!
I THOUGHT I DIED...
?!

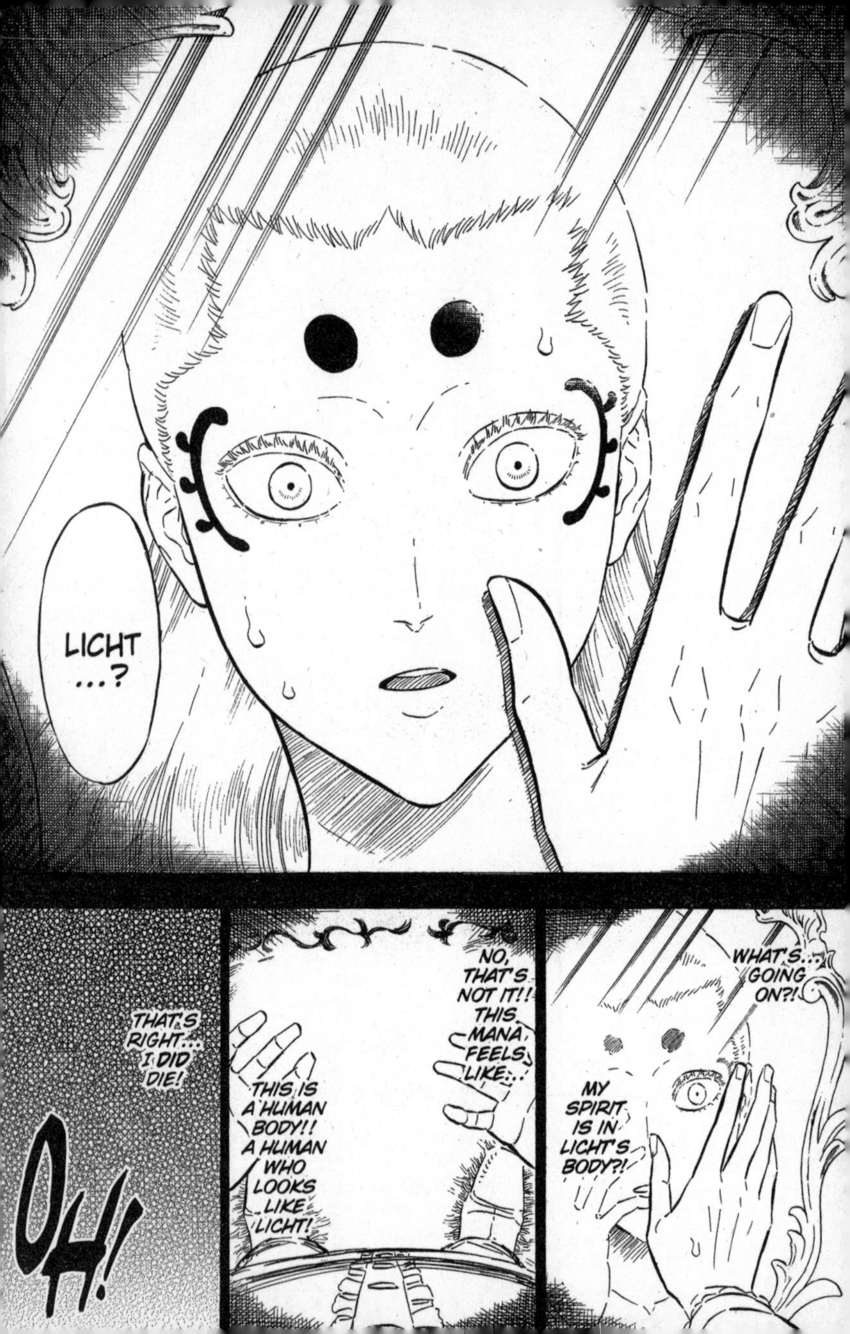
LICHT ...?
WHAT'S... GOING ON?!
MY SPIRIT IS IN LICHT'S BODY?!
NO, THAT'S NOT IT!! THIS MANA FEELS LIKE...
THIS IS A HUMAN BODY!! A HUMAN WHO LOOKS LIKE LICHT!
THAT'S RIGHT... I DID DIE!
OH!

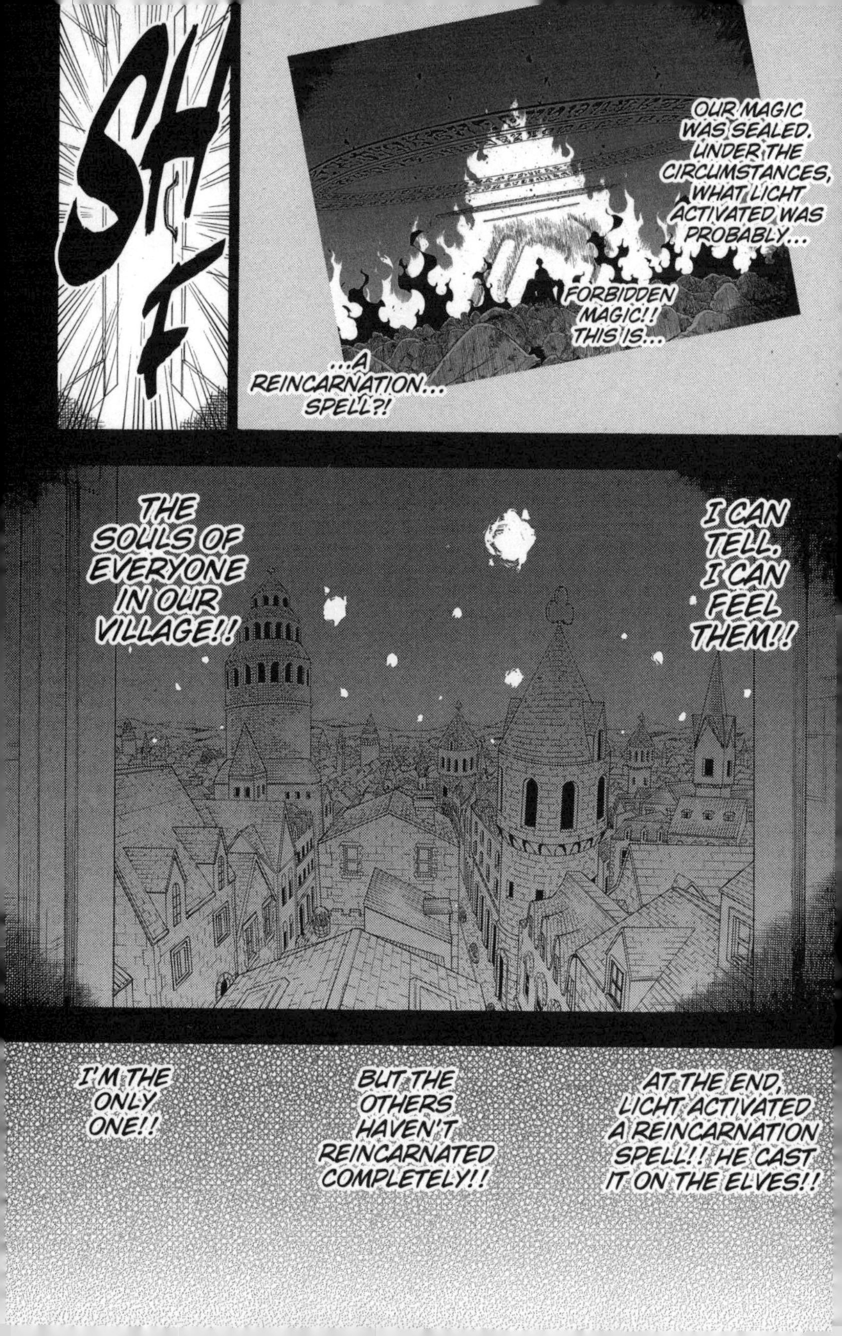
OUR MAGIC WAS SEALED. UNDER THE CIRCUMSTANCES, WHAT LICHT ACTIVATED WAS PROBABLY...
FORBIDDEN MAGIC!! THIS IS...
...A REINCARNATION... SPELL?!
SHF
I CAN TELL. I CAN FEEL THEM!!
THE SOULS OF EVERYONE IN OUR VILLAGE!!
AT THE END, LICHT ACTIVATED A REINCARNATION SPELL!! HE CAST IT ON THE ELVES!!
BUT THE OTHERS HAVEN'T REINCARNATED COMPLETELY!!
I'M THE ONLY ONE!!

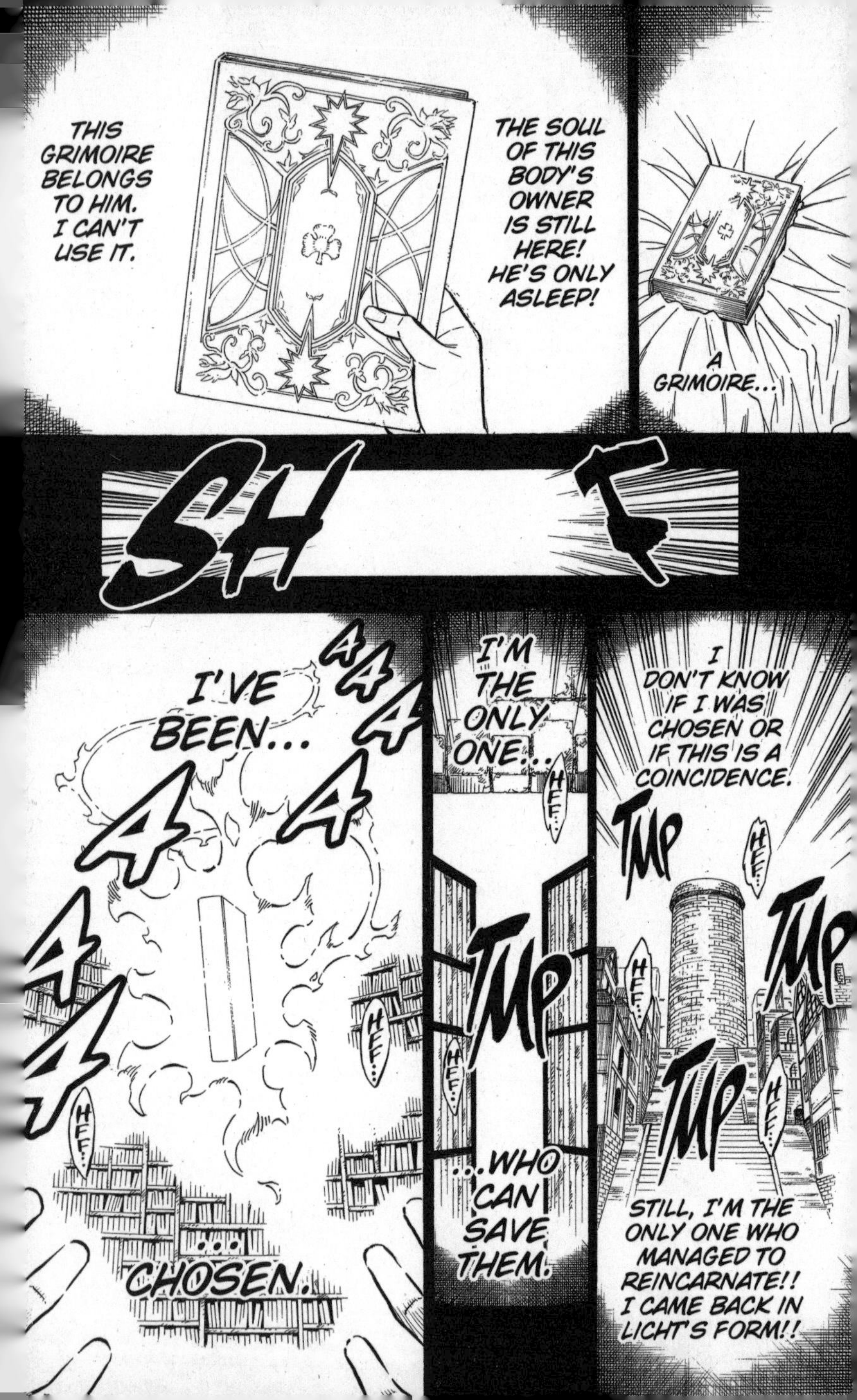
A GRIMOIRE...
THE SOUL OF THIS BODY'S OWNER IS STILL HERE! HE'S ONLY ASLEEP!
THIS GRIMOIRE BELONGS TO HIM. I CAN'T USE IT.
SH T
I DON'T KNOW IF I WAS CHOSEN OR IF THIS IS A COINCIDENCE.
TMP
HFF...
TMP
HFF...
TMP
HFF...
STILL, I'M THE ONLY ONE WHO MANAGED TO REINCARNATE!! I CAME BACK IN LICHT'S FORM!!
I'M THE ONLY ONE...
HFF...
TMP
HFF...
...WHO CAN SAVE THEM.
AAAA
I'VE BEEN...
AAAA
HFF...
HFF...
...CHOSEN.

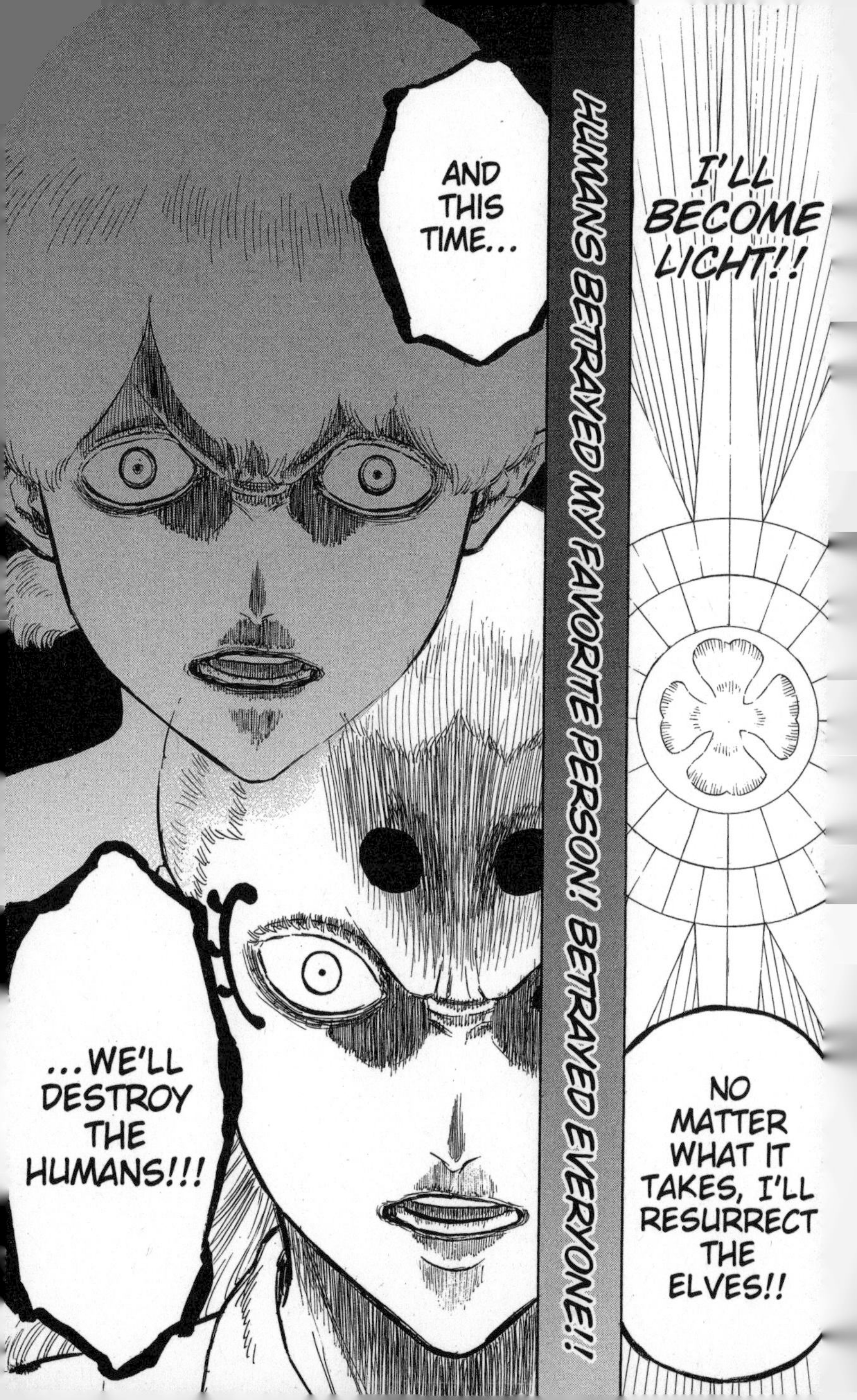

I'LL BECOME LIGHT!!
NO MATTER WHAT IT TAKES, I'LL RESURRECT THE ELVES!!
HUMANS BETRAYED MY FAVORITE PERSON! BETRAYED EVERYONE!!
AND THIS TIME...
...WE'LL DESTROY THE HUMANS!!!

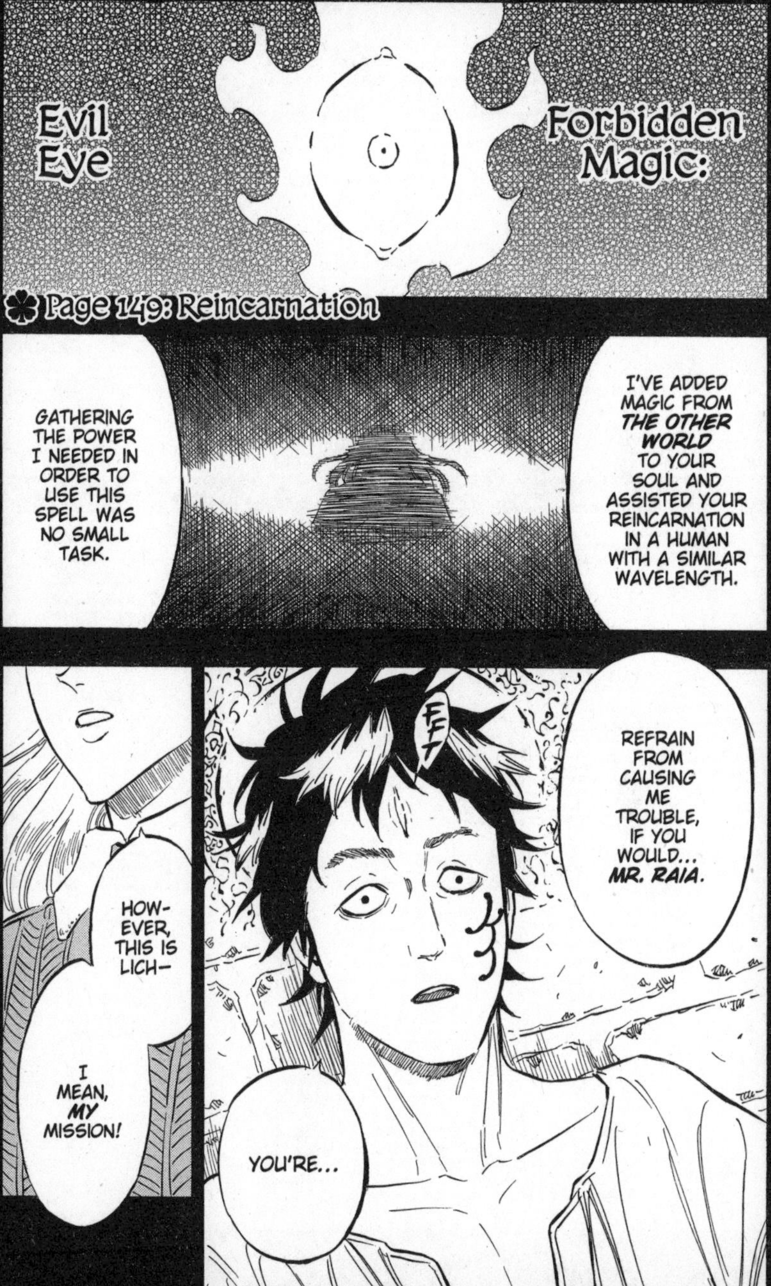
Forbidden Magic:
Evil Eye
Page 149: Reincarnation
I'VE ADDED MAGIC FROM THE OTHER WORLD TO YOUR SOUL AND ASSISTED YOUR REINCARNATION IN A HUMAN WITH A SIMILAR WAVELENGTH.
GATHERING THE POWER I NEEDED IN ORDER TO USE THIS SPELL WAS NO SMALL TASK.
FFT
REFRAIN FROM CAUSING ME TROUBLE, IF YOU WOULD... MR. RAIA.
YOU'RE...
HOW-EVER, THIS IS LICH-
I MEAN, MY MISSION!

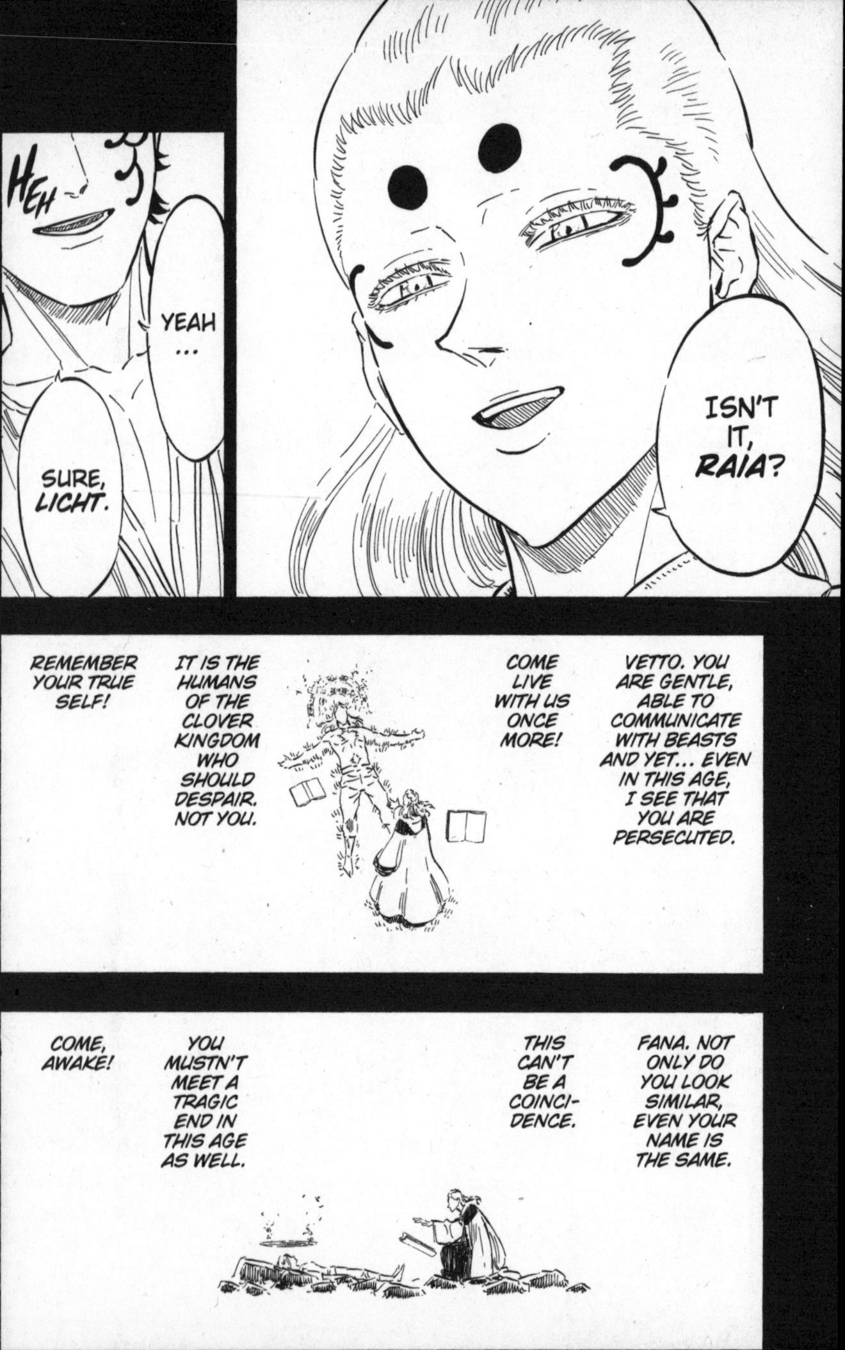
ISN'T IT, RAIA?
HEH
YEAH ...
SURE, LICHT.
VETTO. YOU ARE GENTLE, ABLE TO COMMUNICATE WITH BEASTS AND YET... EVEN IN THIS AGE, I SEE THAT YOU ARE PERSECUTED.
COME LIVE WITH US ONCE MORE!
IT IS THE HUMANS OF THE CLOVER KINGDOM WHO SHOULD DESPAIR. NOT YOU.
REMEMBER YOUR TRUE SELF!
FANA. NOT ONLY DO YOU LOOK SIMILAR, EVEN YOUR NAME IS THE SAME.
THIS CAN'T BE A COINCI-DENCE.
YOU MUSTN'T MEET A TRAGIC END IN THIS AGE AS WELL.
COME, AWAKE!

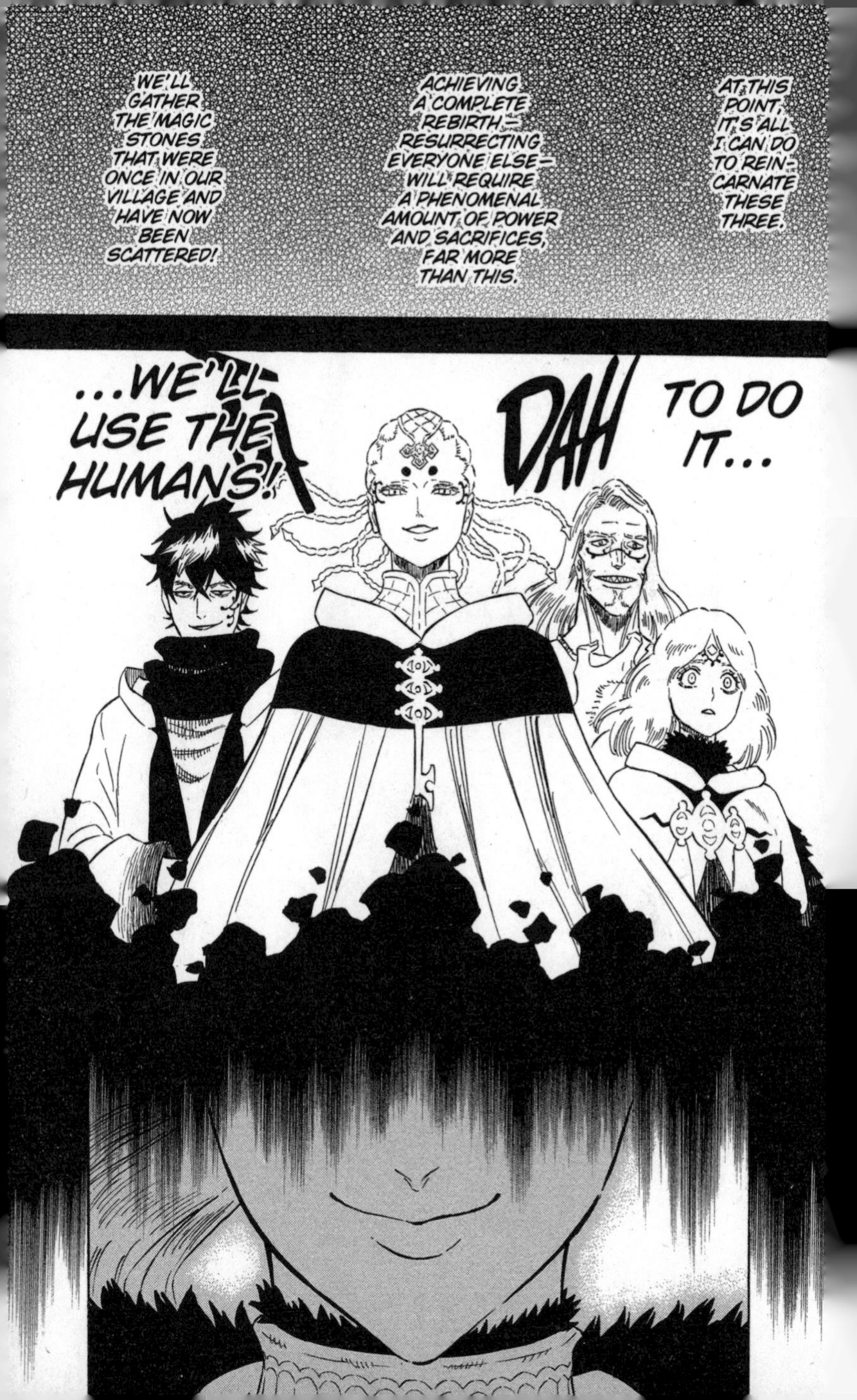
AT THIS POINT, IT'S ALL I CAN DO TO REINCARNATE THESE THREE.
ACHIEVING A COMPLETE REBIRTH— RESURRECTING EVERYONE ELSE— WILL REQUIRE A PHENOMENAL AMOUNT OF POWER AND SACRIFICES, FAR MORE THAN THIS.
WE'LL GATHER THE MAGIC STONES THAT WERE ONCE IN OUR VILLAGE AND HAVE NOW BEEN SCATTERED!
TO DO IT...
DAH
...WE'LL USE THE HUMANS!!

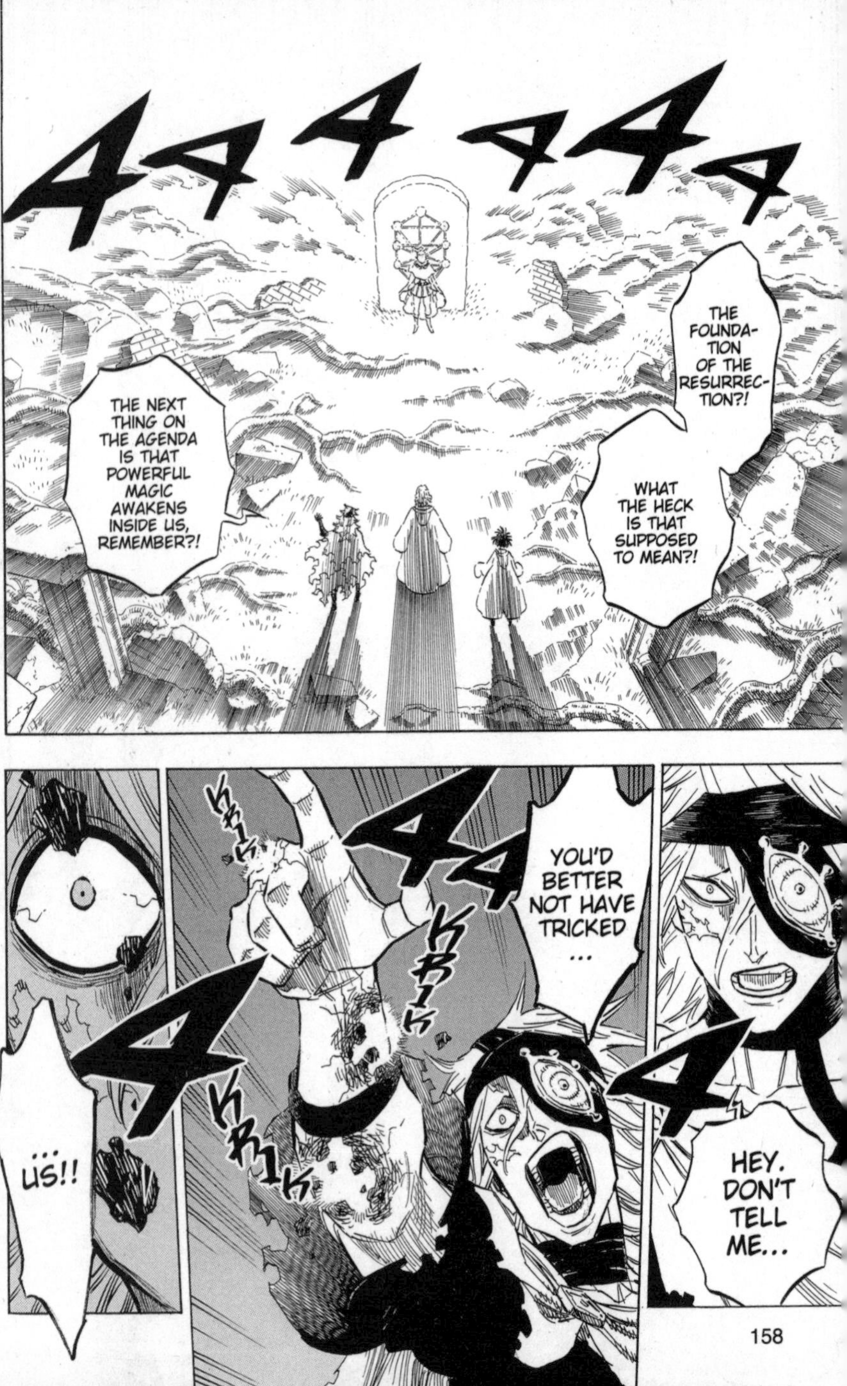
THE FOUNDATION OF THE RESURRECTION?!
WHAT THE HECK IS THAT SUPPOSED TO MEAN?!
THE NEXT THING ON THE AGENDA IS THAT POWERFUL MAGIC AWAKENS INSIDE US, REMEMBER?!
HEY. DON'T TELL ME...
YOU'D BETTER NOT HAVE TRICKED ...
KRIK KRIK KRIK
... US!!

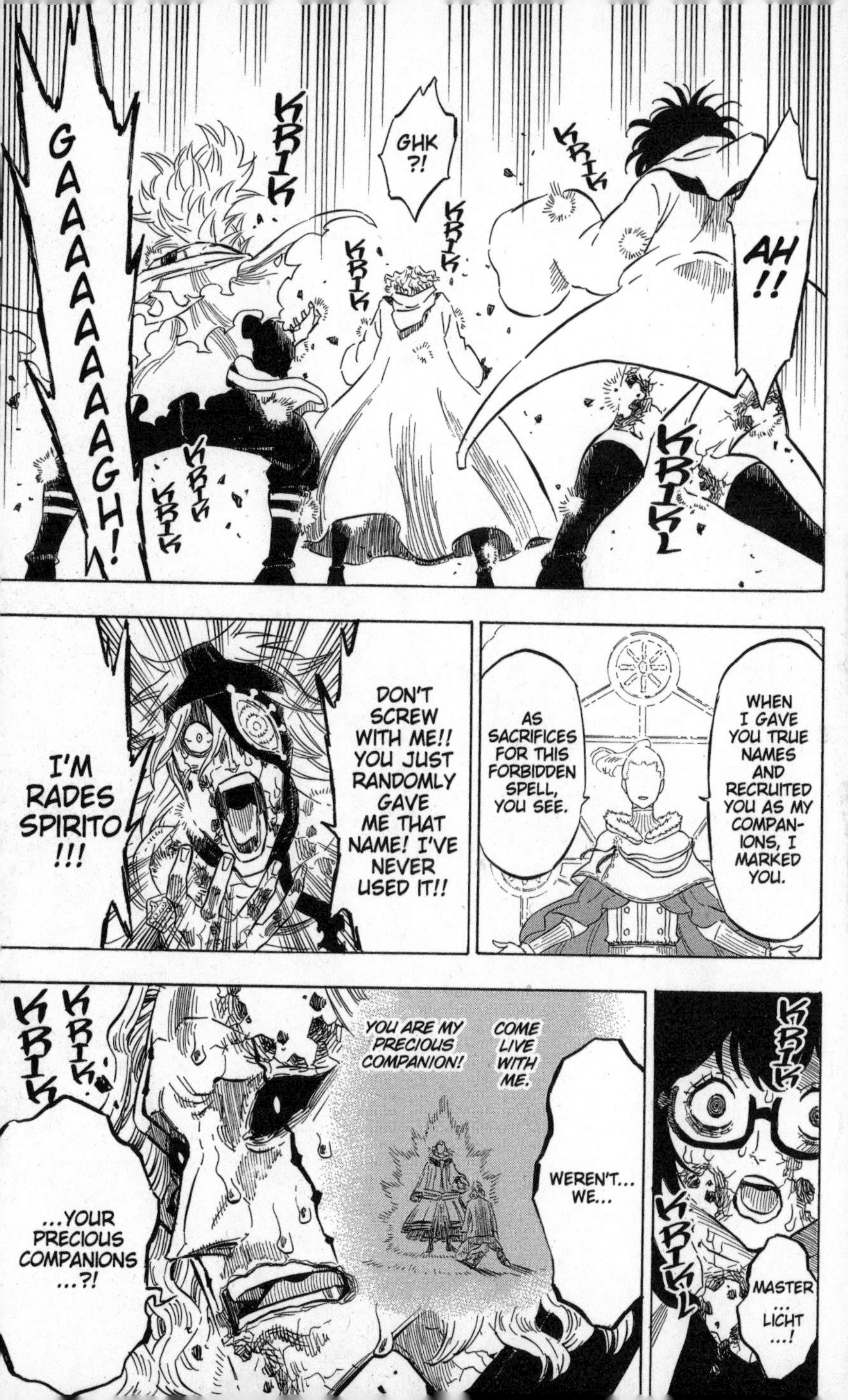
AH!!
KRIK
KRIK
GHK?!
KRIK
KRIK
KRIK
KRIK
GAAAAAAAAAAGH!
WHEN I GAVE YOU TRUE NAMES AND RECRUITED YOU AS MY COMPANIONS, I MARKED YOU.
AS SACRIFICES FOR THIS FORBIDDEN SPELL, YOU SEE.
DON'T SCREW WITH ME!! YOU JUST RANDOMLY GAVE ME THAT NAME! I'VE NEVER USED IT!!
I'M RADES SPIRITO!!!
KRIK
KRIK
MASTER... LICHT...!
COME LIVE WITH ME.
YOU ARE MY PRECIOUS COMPANION!
WEREN'T... WE...
...YOUR PRECIOUS COMPANIONS...?!
KRIK
KRIK

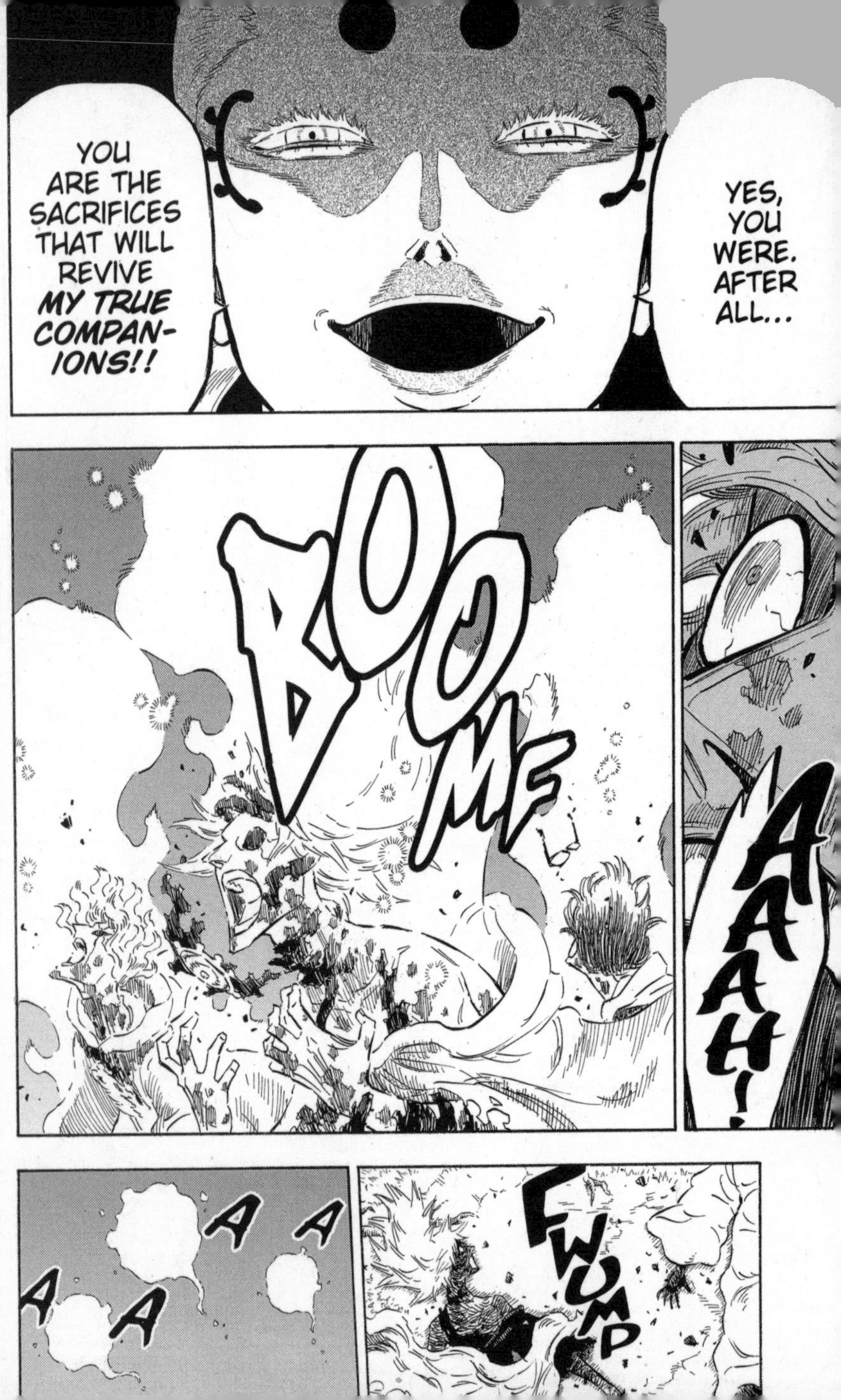
YES, YOU WERE. AFTER ALL...
YOU ARE THE SACRIFICES THAT WILL REVIVE *MY TRUE COMPANIONS!!*
AAAH!!
BOOOMF
FWUMP
AAAA

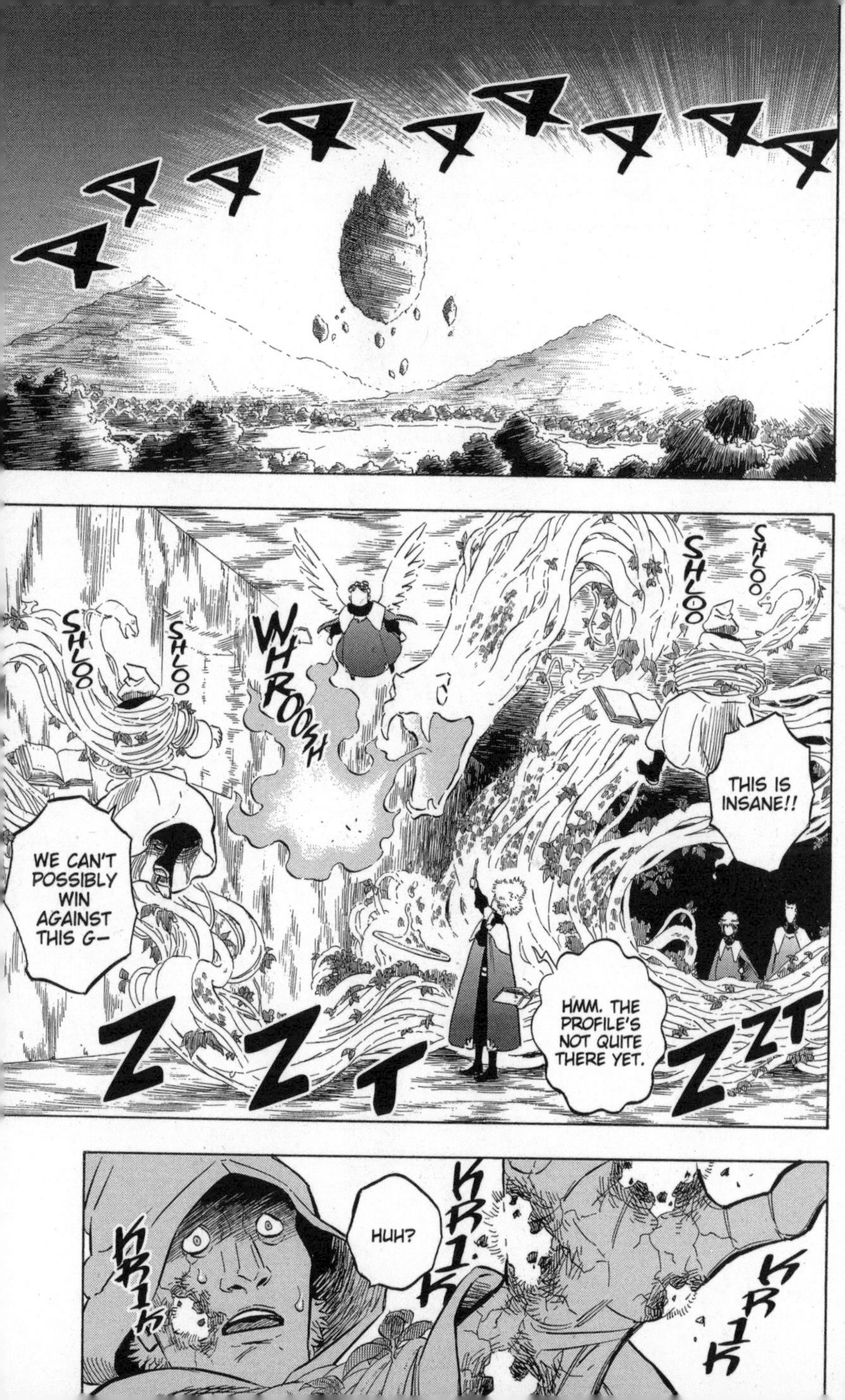
AAAAAAAAA
SHLOO
SHLOO
THIS IS INSANE!!
WHROOOSH
SHLOO
SHLOO
HMM. THE PROFILE'S NOT QUITE THERE YET.
WE CAN'T POSSIBLY WIN AGAINST THIS G—
ZZZZZT
KRIK
HUH?
KRIK
KRIK

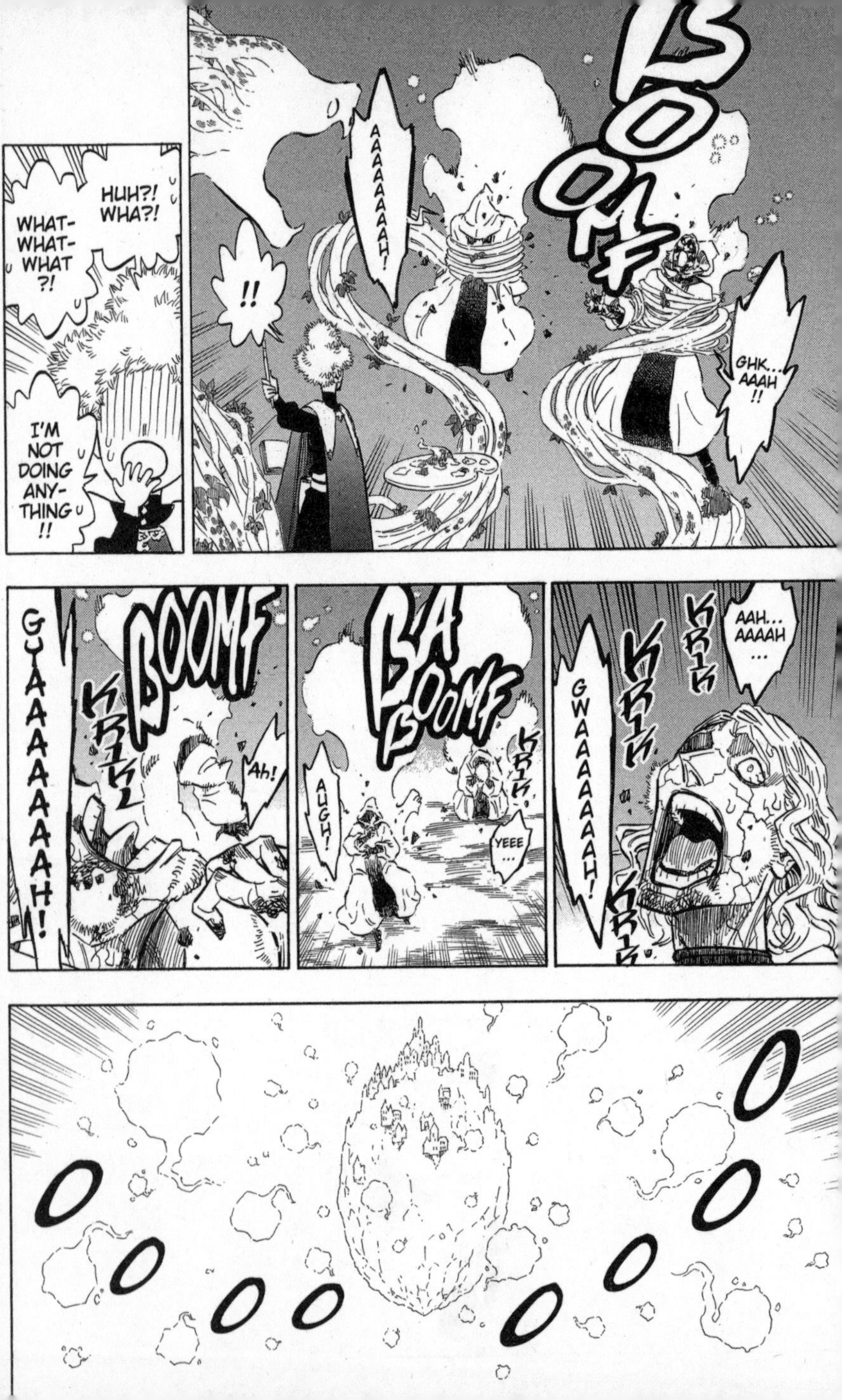
BOOOMF
GHK... AAAH!!
AAAAAAAAH!
!!
HUH?! WHA?!
WHAT-WHAT-WHAT?!
I'M NOT DOING ANYTHING!!
AAH... AAAAH...
KRIK KRIK KRIK
GWAAAAAAAAAH!
BA BOOMF
KRIK
YEEE...
AUGH!
BOOMF
Ah!
KRIK
GUAAAAAAAAAAAH!
OOOOOOOOOOO

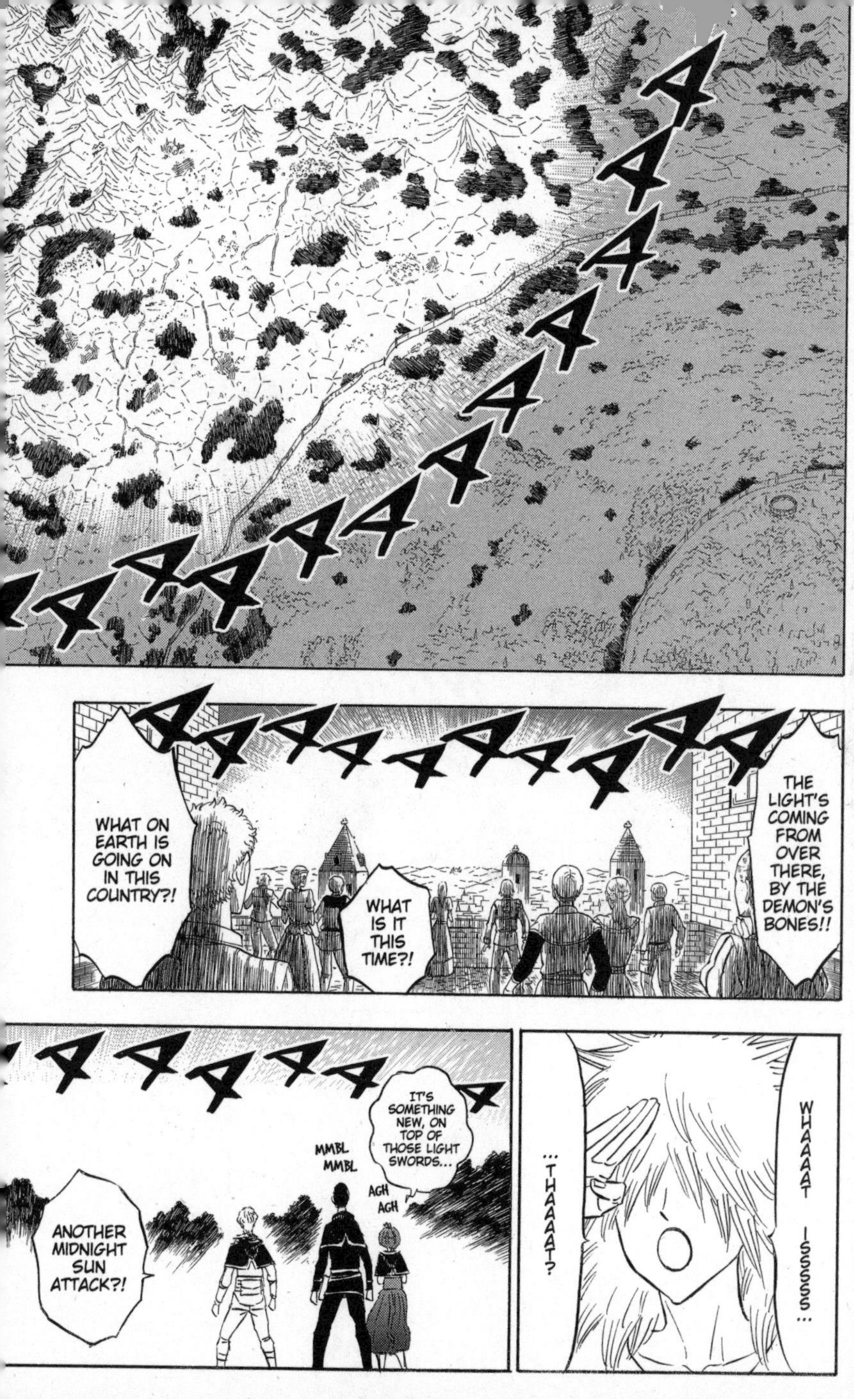
AAAAAAAAAAAAA
AAAAAAAAAAAA
THE LIGHT'S COMING FROM OVER THERE, BY THE DEMON'S BONES!!
WHAT IS IT THIS TIME?!
WHAT ON EARTH IS GOING ON IN THIS COUNTRY?!
WHAAAAT ISSSSS...
...THAAAAT?
AAAAAA
IT'S SOMETHING NEW, ON TOP OF THOSE LIGHT SWORDS...
AGH AGH
MMBL MMBL
ANOTHER MIDNIGHT SUN ATTACK?!

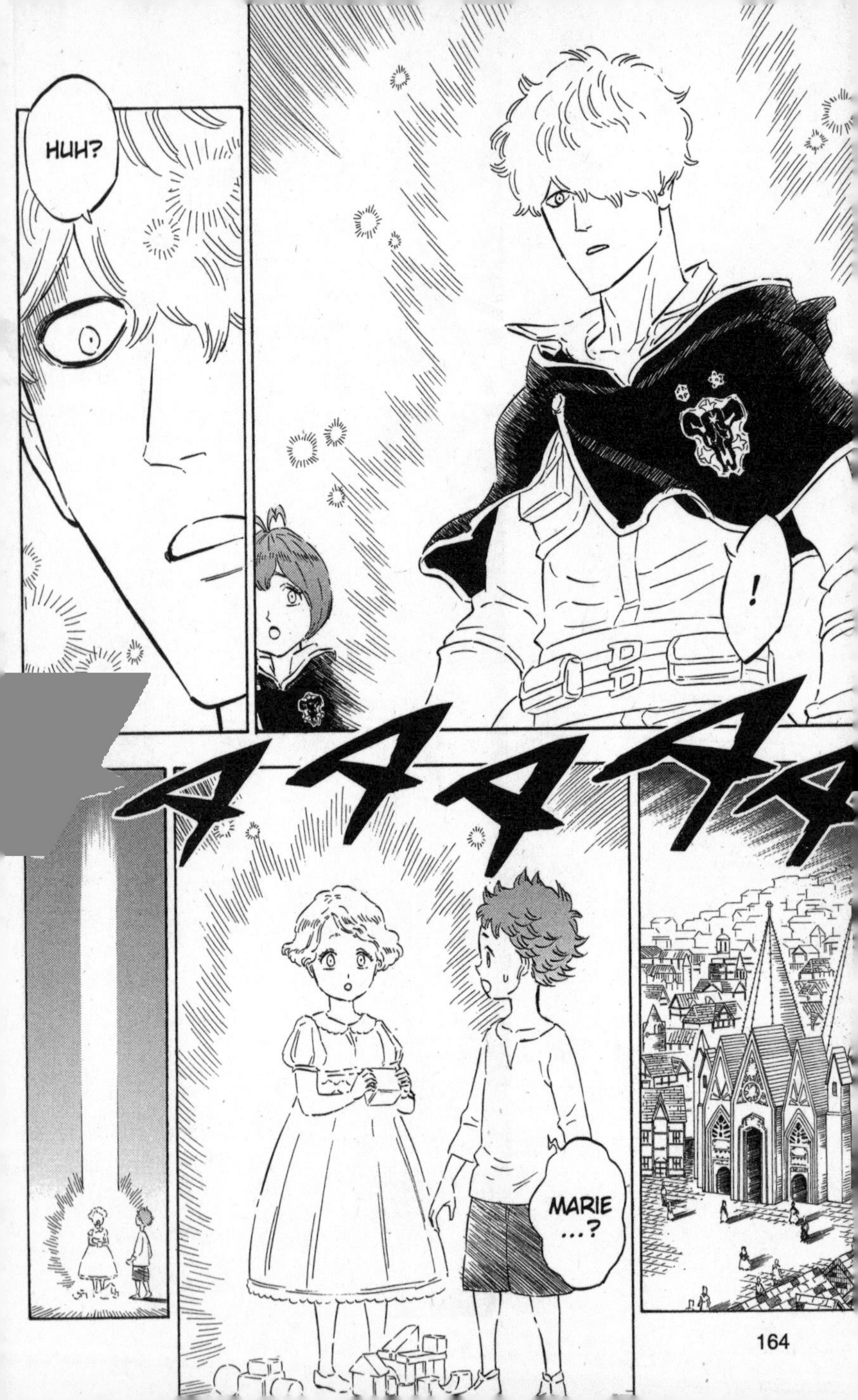
!
HUH?
MARIE ...?

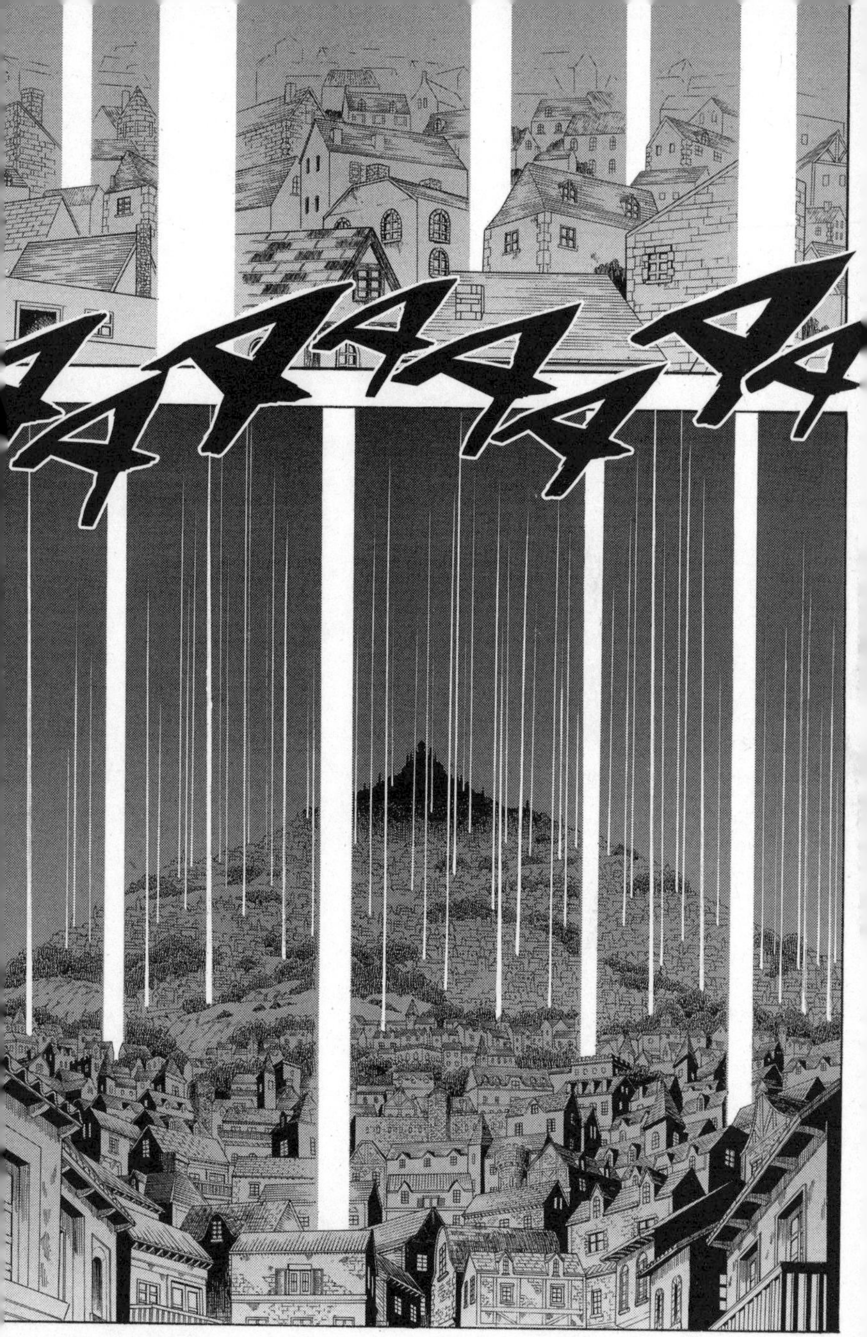
AAAAAAAAA

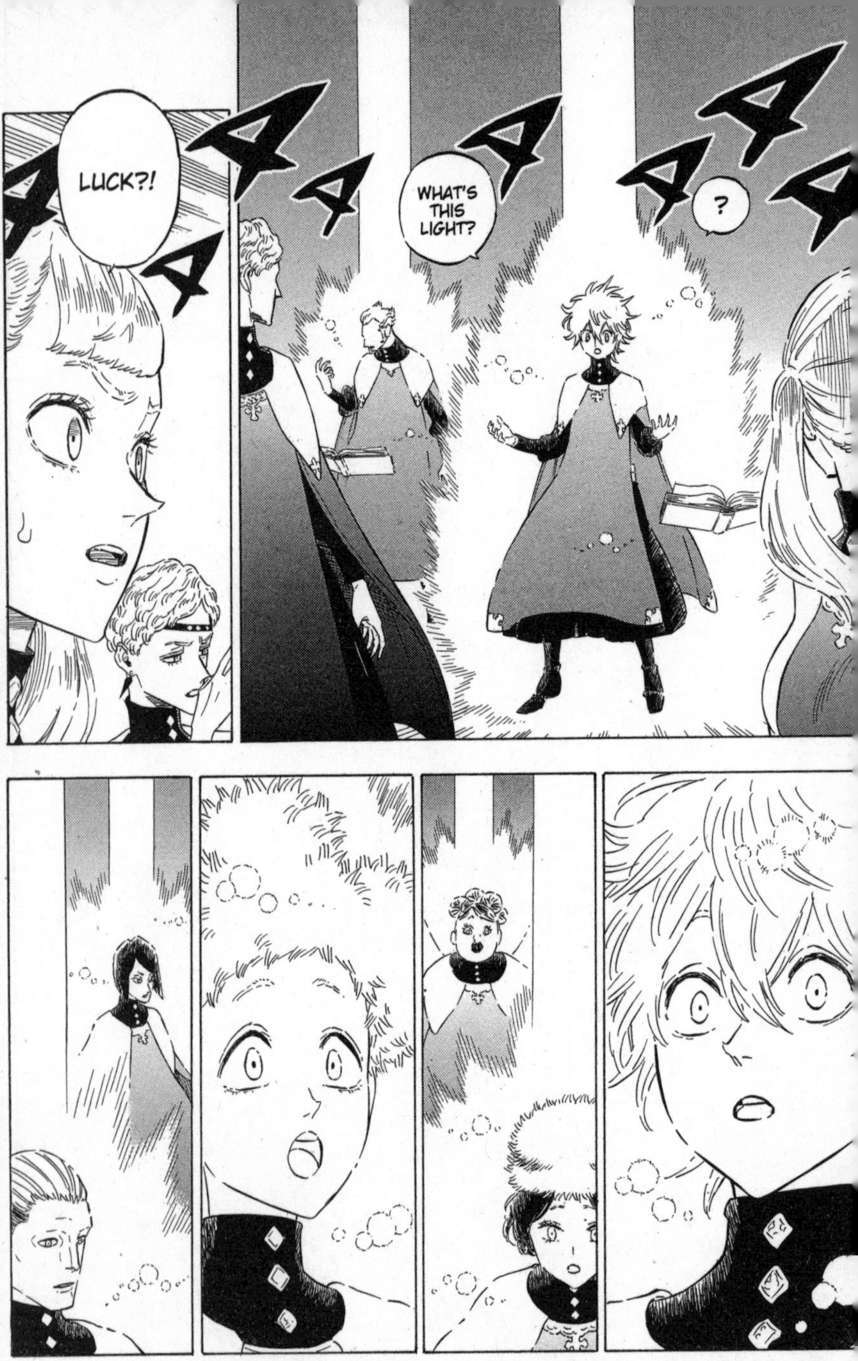
?
WHAT'S THIS LIGHT?
LUCK?!

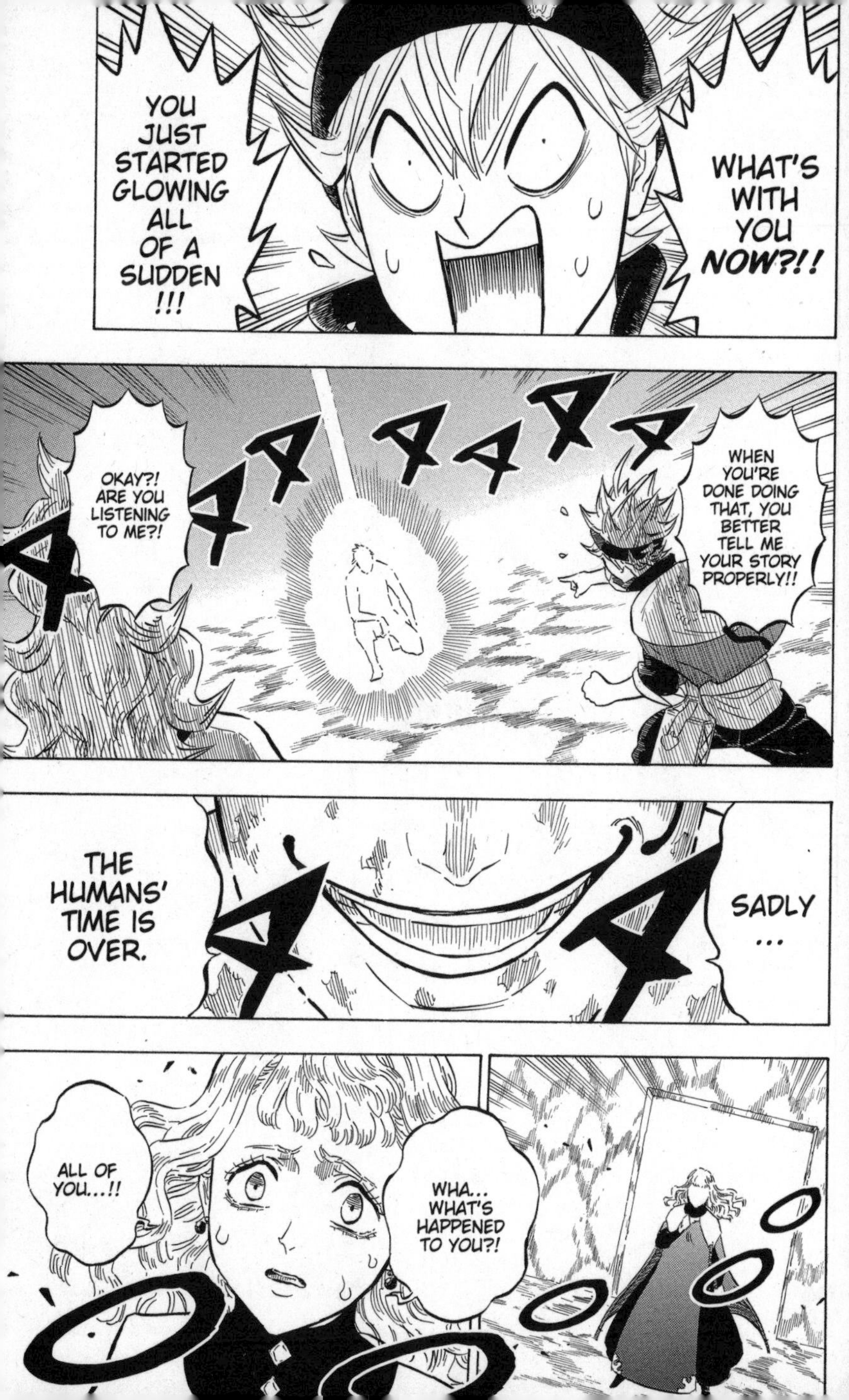
WHAT'S WITH YOU NOW?!!
YOU JUST STARTED GLOWING ALL OF A SUDDEN!!!
WHEN YOU'RE DONE DOING THAT, YOU BETTER TELL ME YOUR STORY PROPERLY!!
OKAY?! ARE YOU LISTENING TO ME?!
SADLY...
THE HUMANS' TIME IS OVER.
WHA... WHAT'S HAPPENED TO YOU?!
ALL OF YOU...!!

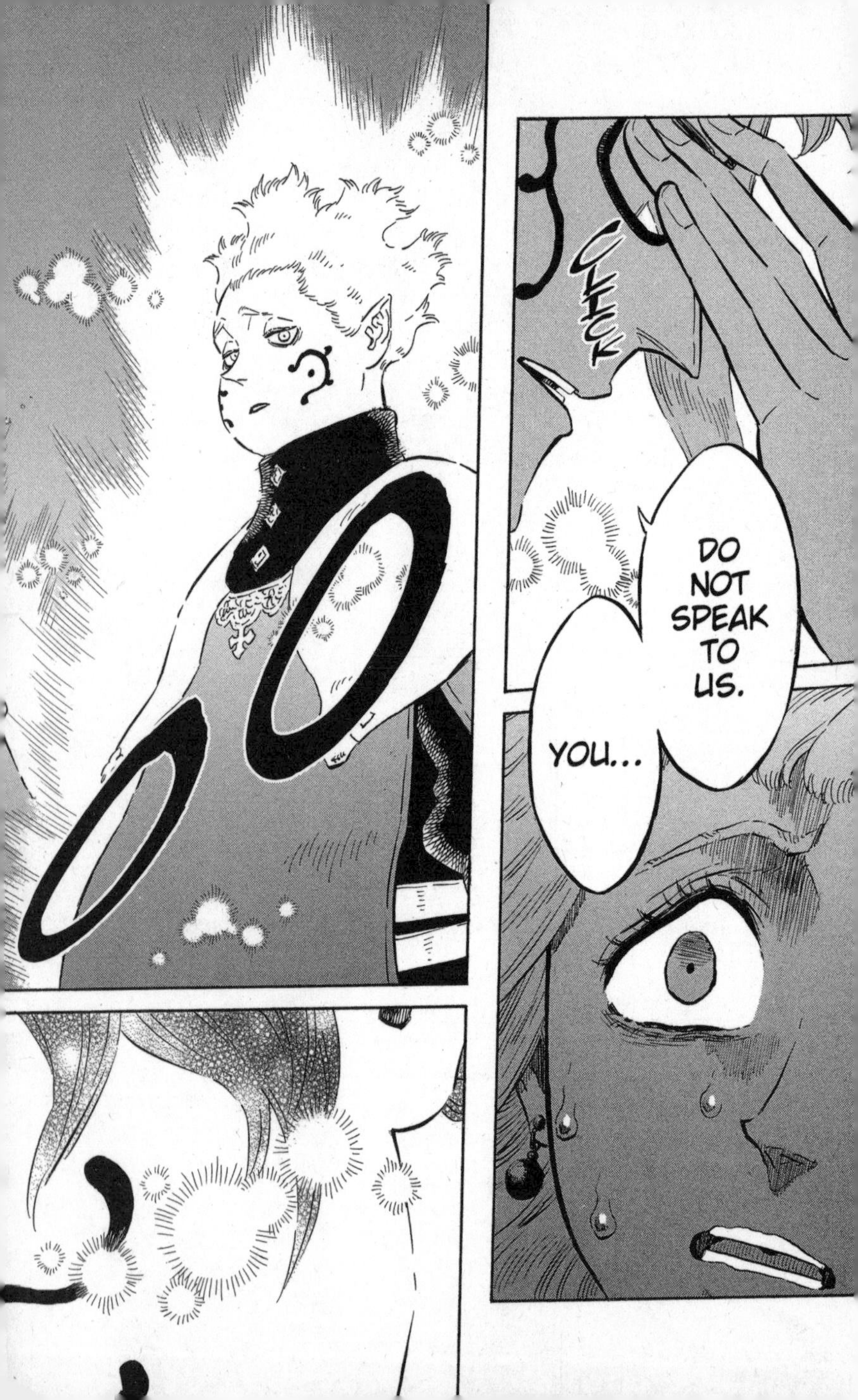
CLICK
YOU...
DO NOT SPEAK TO US.

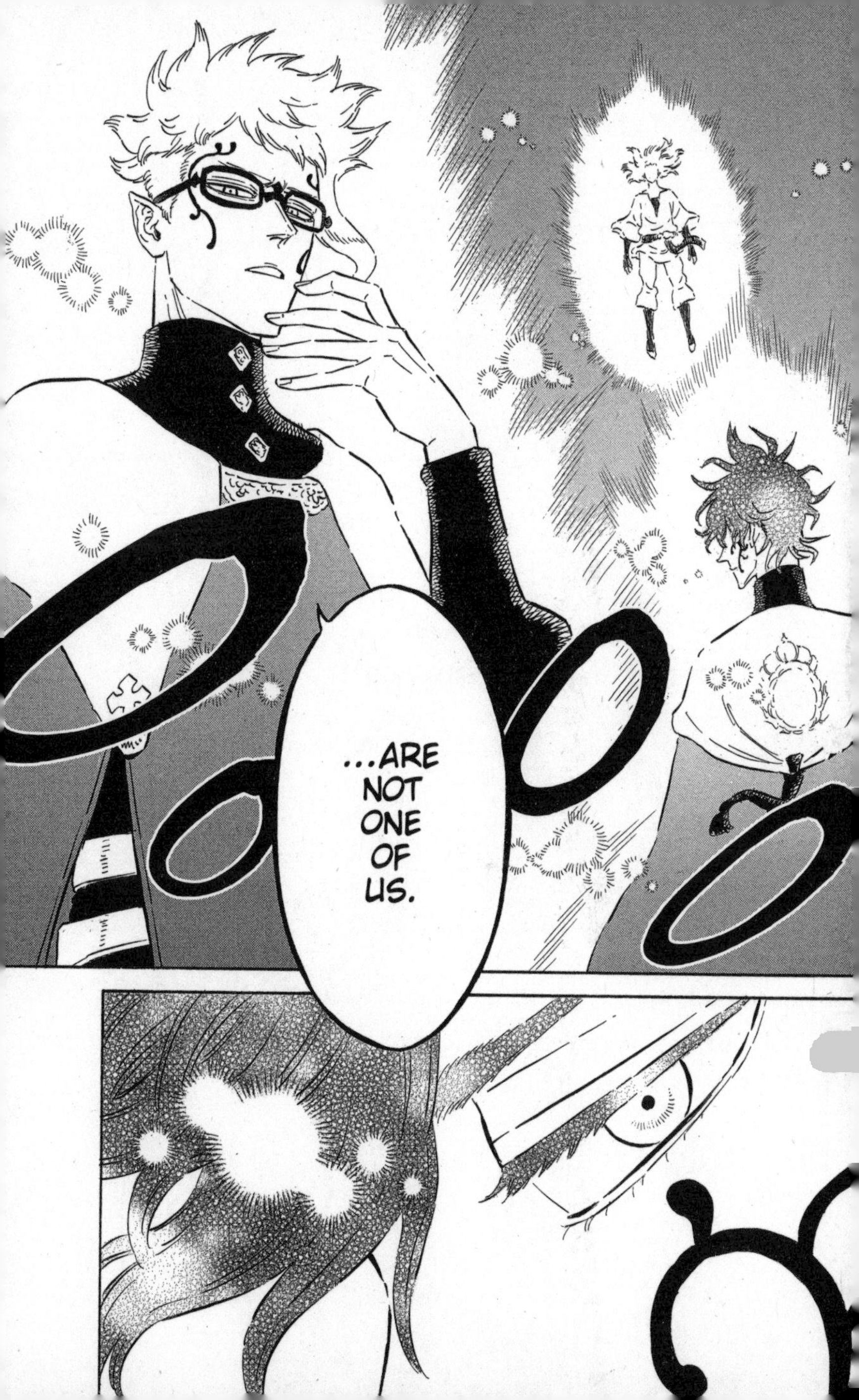
...ARE NOT ONE OF US.

VANISH...

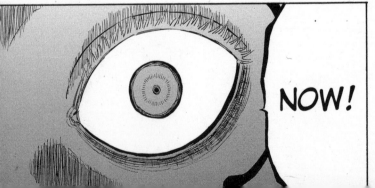

NOW!

...HUMANS.

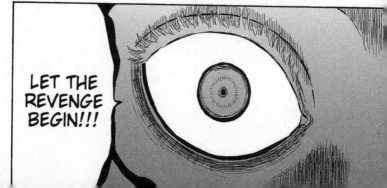

LET THE REVENGE BEGIN!!!

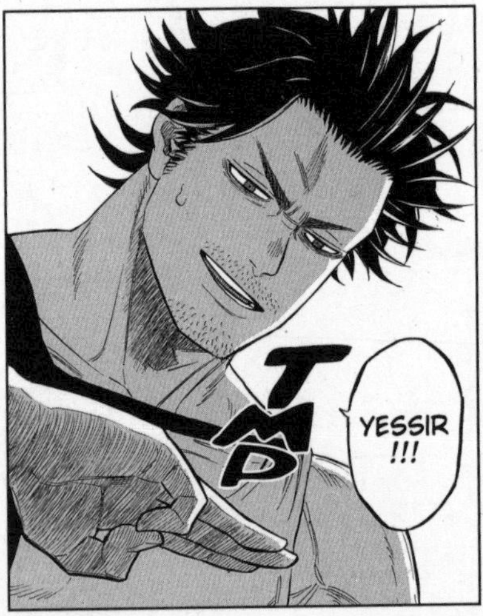
YESSIR !!!
TMP

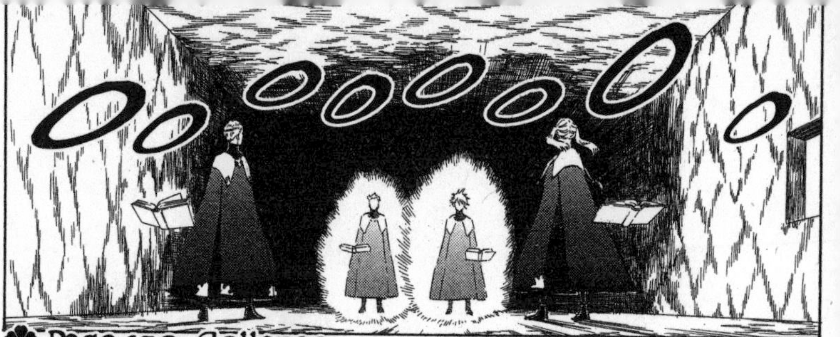

Page 150: Collapse

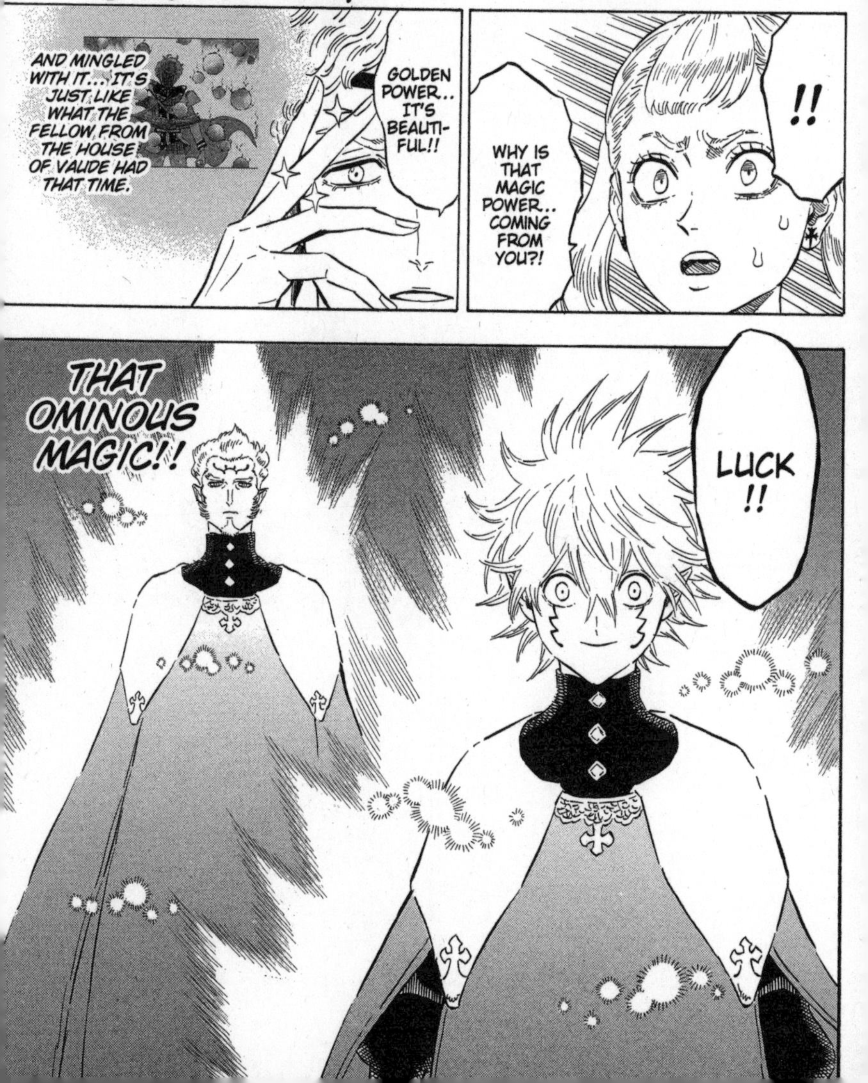
!!
WHY IS THAT MAGIC POWER.. COMING FROM YOU?!
GOLDEN POWER.. IT'S BEAUTIFUL!!
AND MINGLED WITH IT... IT'S JUST LIKE WHAT THE FELLOW FROM THE HOUSE OF VAUDE HAD THAT TIME.
LUCK!!
THAT OMINOUS MAGIC!!

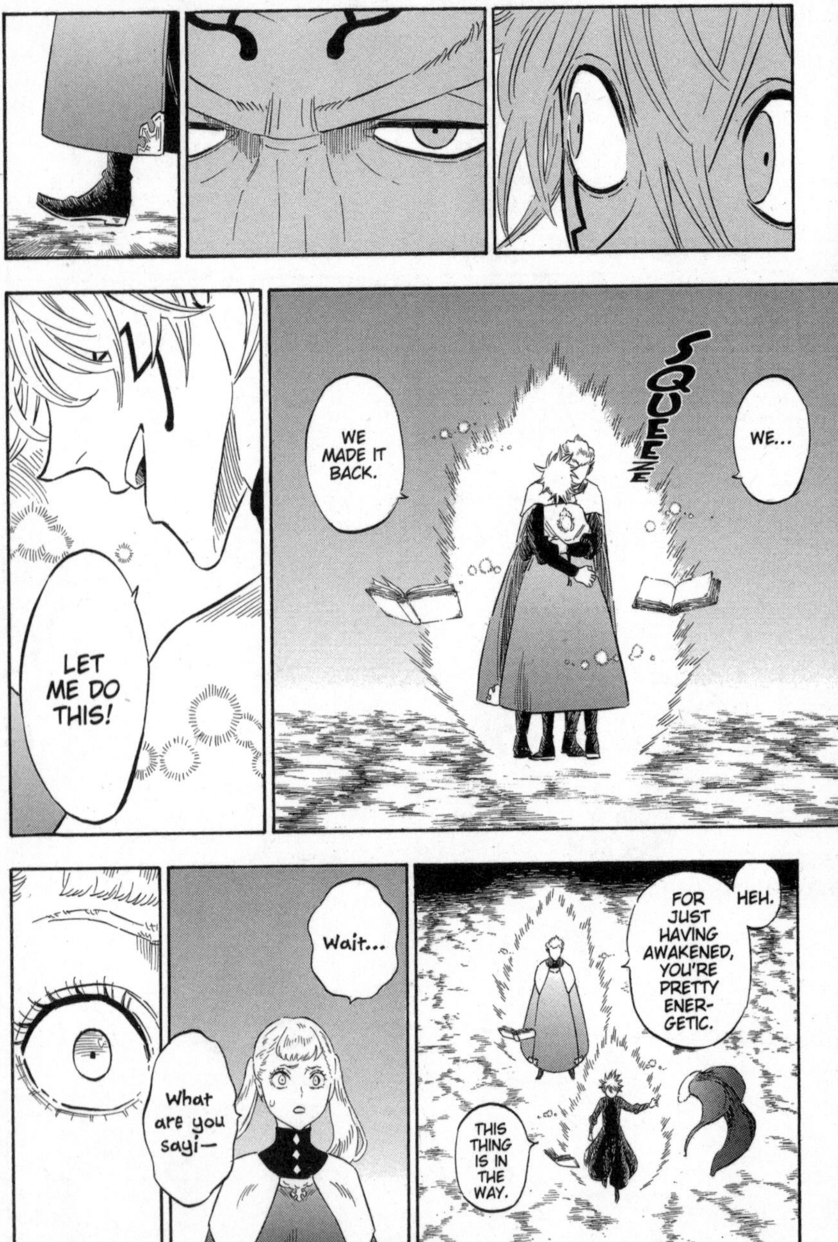
WE...
SQUEEEZE
WE MADE IT BACK.
LET ME DO THIS!
HEH.
FOR JUST HAVING AWAKENED, YOU'RE PRETTY ENERGETIC.
THIS THING IS IN THE WAY.
Wait...
What are you sayi—

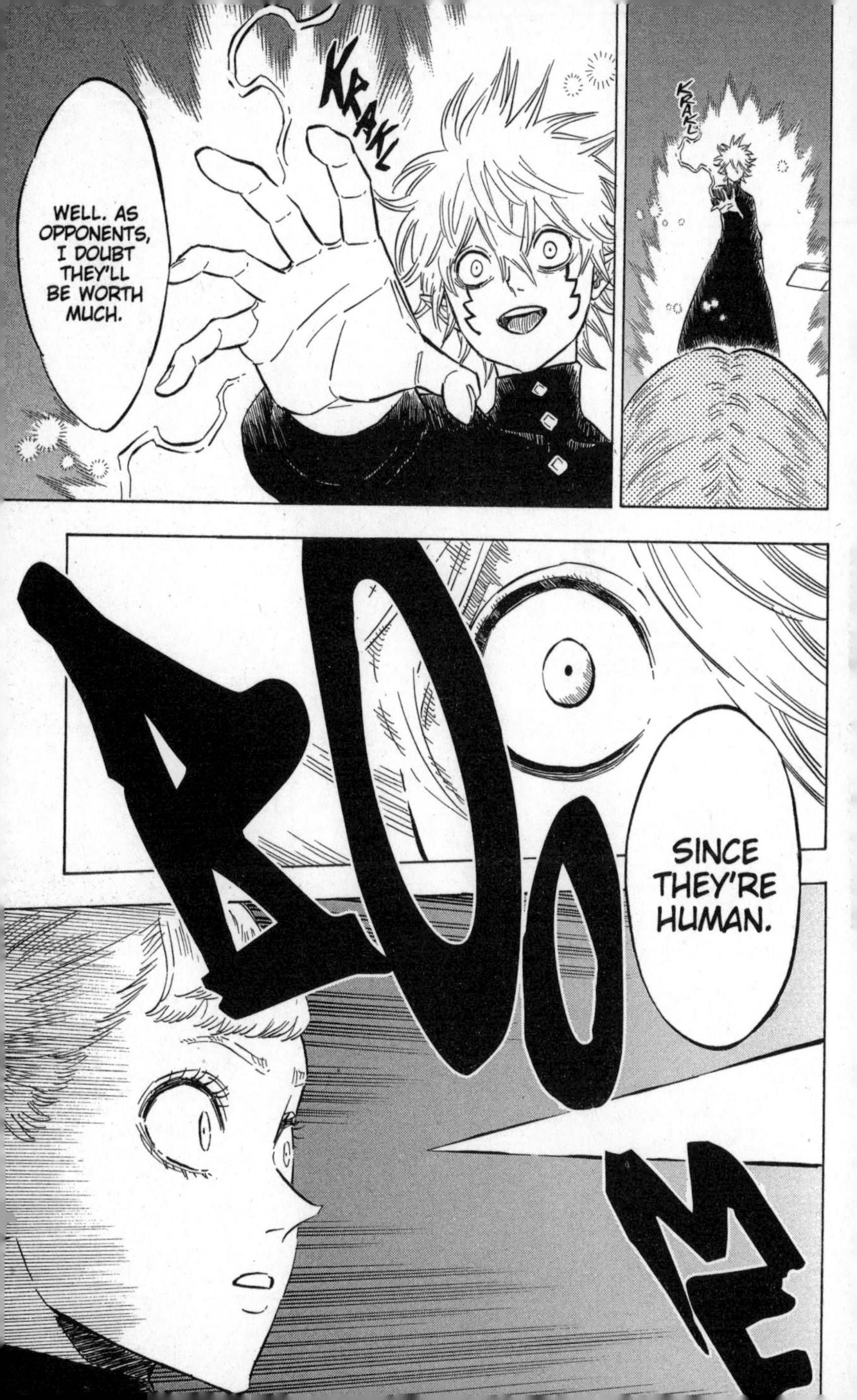
KRAKL
KRAKL
WELL. AS OPPONENTS, I DOUBT THEY'LL BE WORTH MUCH.
SINCE THEY'RE HUMAN.

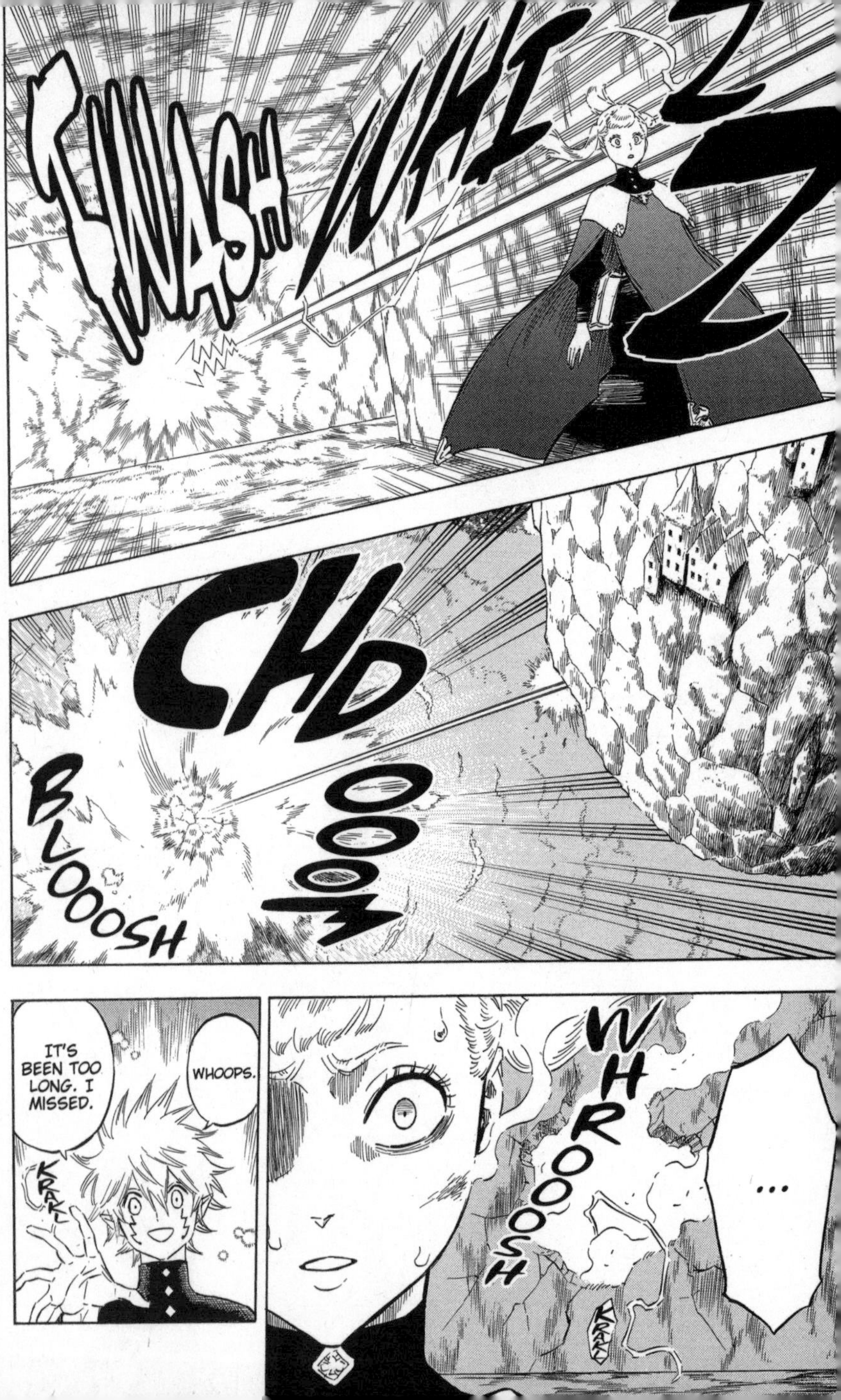
WHIZZ
FWASH
CHDOOOOM
BLOOOOSH
...
WHROOOOSH
KRAKL
WHOOPS.
IT'S BEEN TOO LONG. I MISSED.
KRAKL

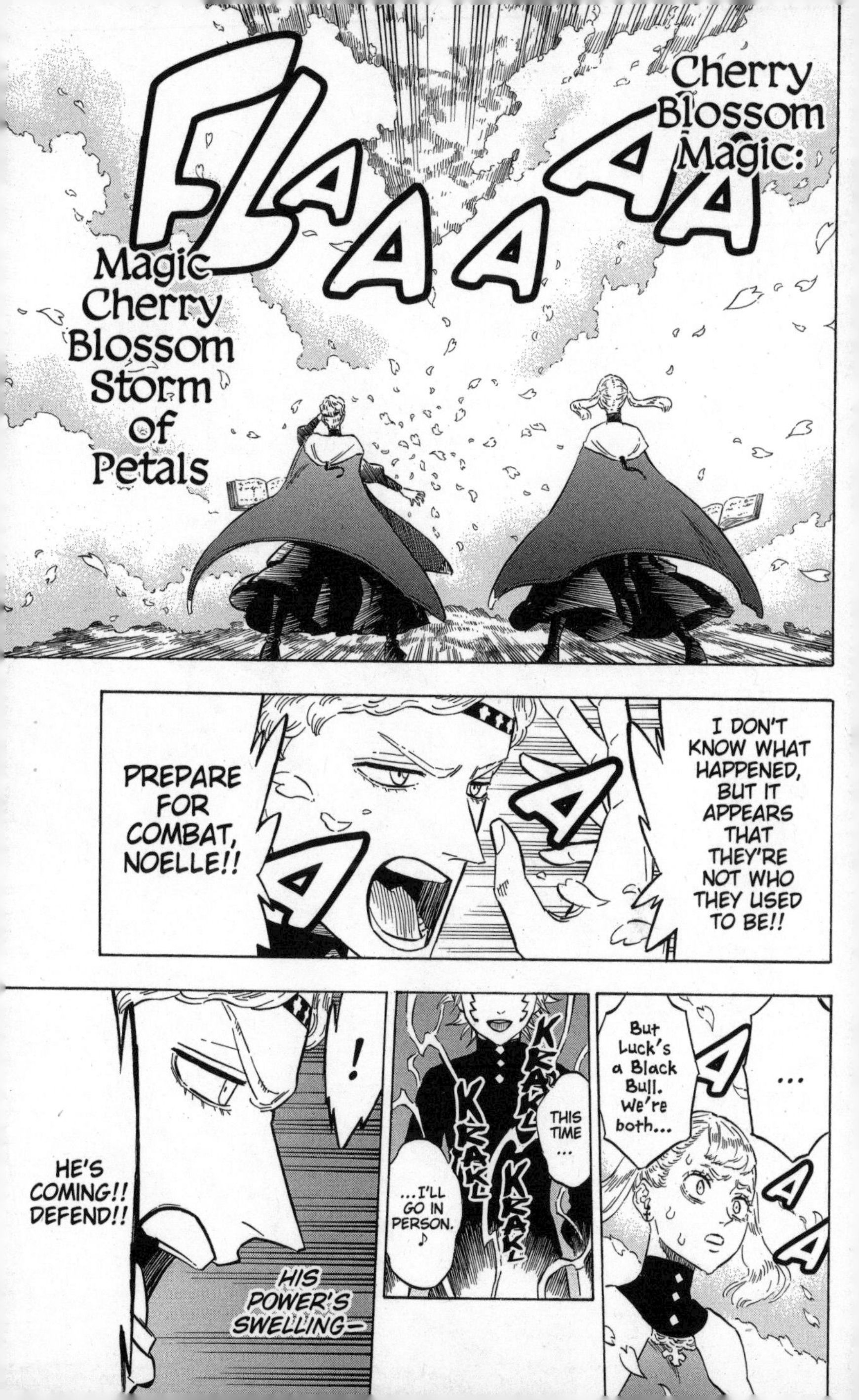
Cherry Blossom Magic:
FLAAAAAA
Magic Cherry Blossom Storm of Petals
I DON'T KNOW WHAT HAPPENED, BUT IT APPEARS THAT THEY'RE NOT WHO THEY USED TO BE!!
AA
PREPARE FOR COMBAT, NOELLE!!
...
But Luck's a Black Bull. We're both...
AAA
THIS TIME...
KRAKL KRAKL KRAKL KRAKL
...I'LL GO IN PERSON. ♪
!
HE'S COMING!! DEFEND!!
HIS POWER'S SWELLING—

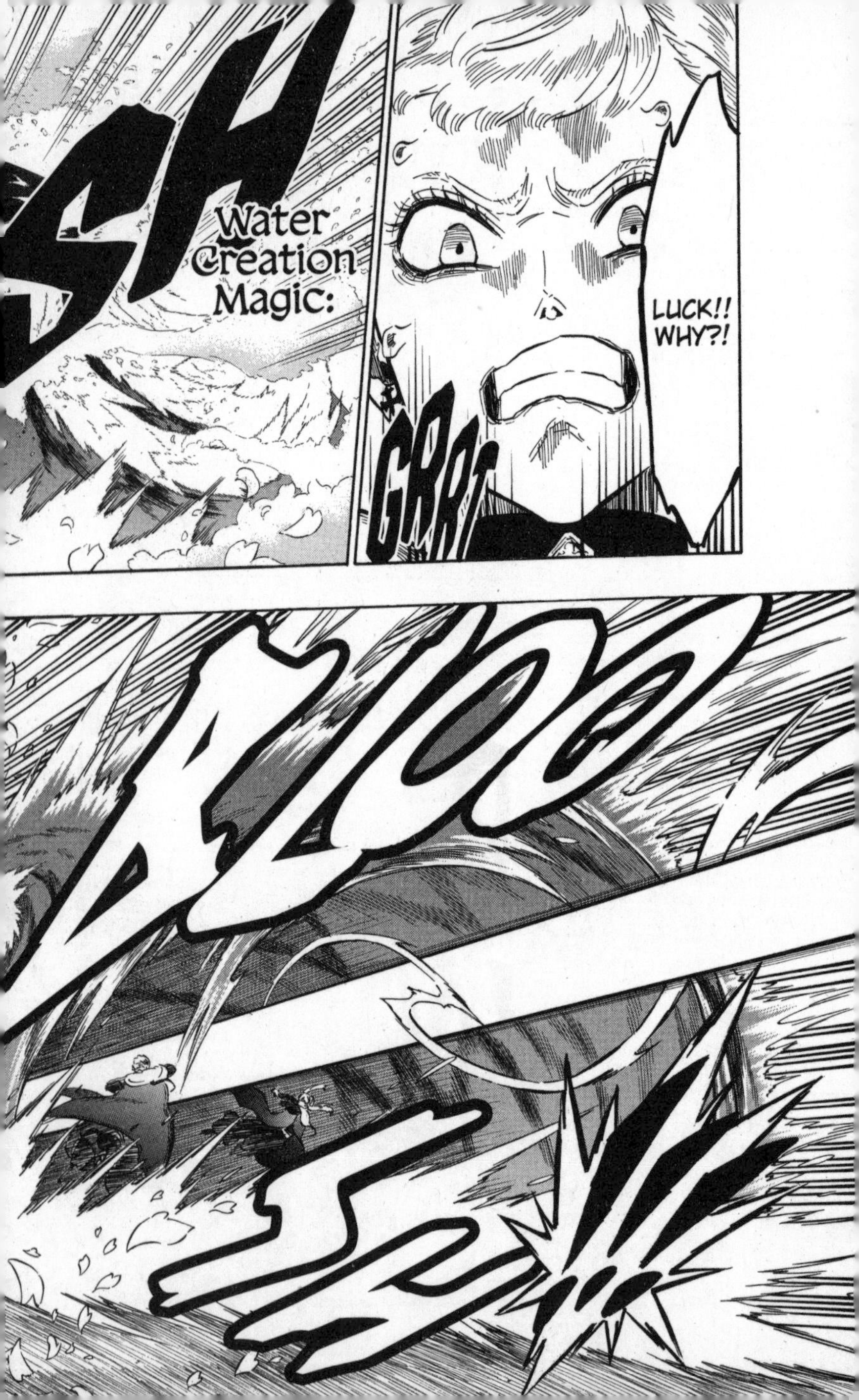
LUCK!! WHY?!
GRR
SH
Water Creation Magic:

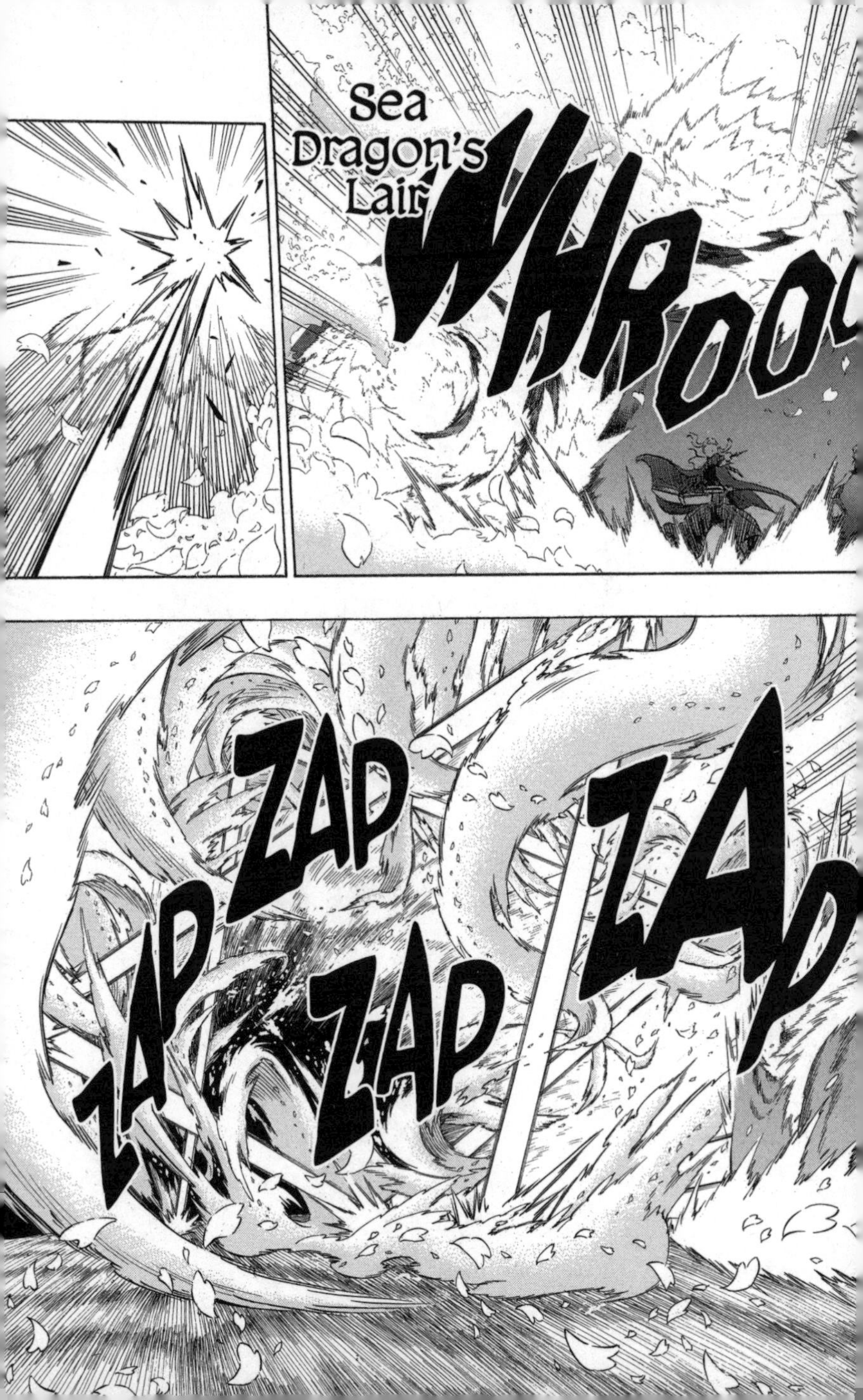
Sea Dragon's Lair
WHROOO
ZAP
ZAP
ZAP
ZAP

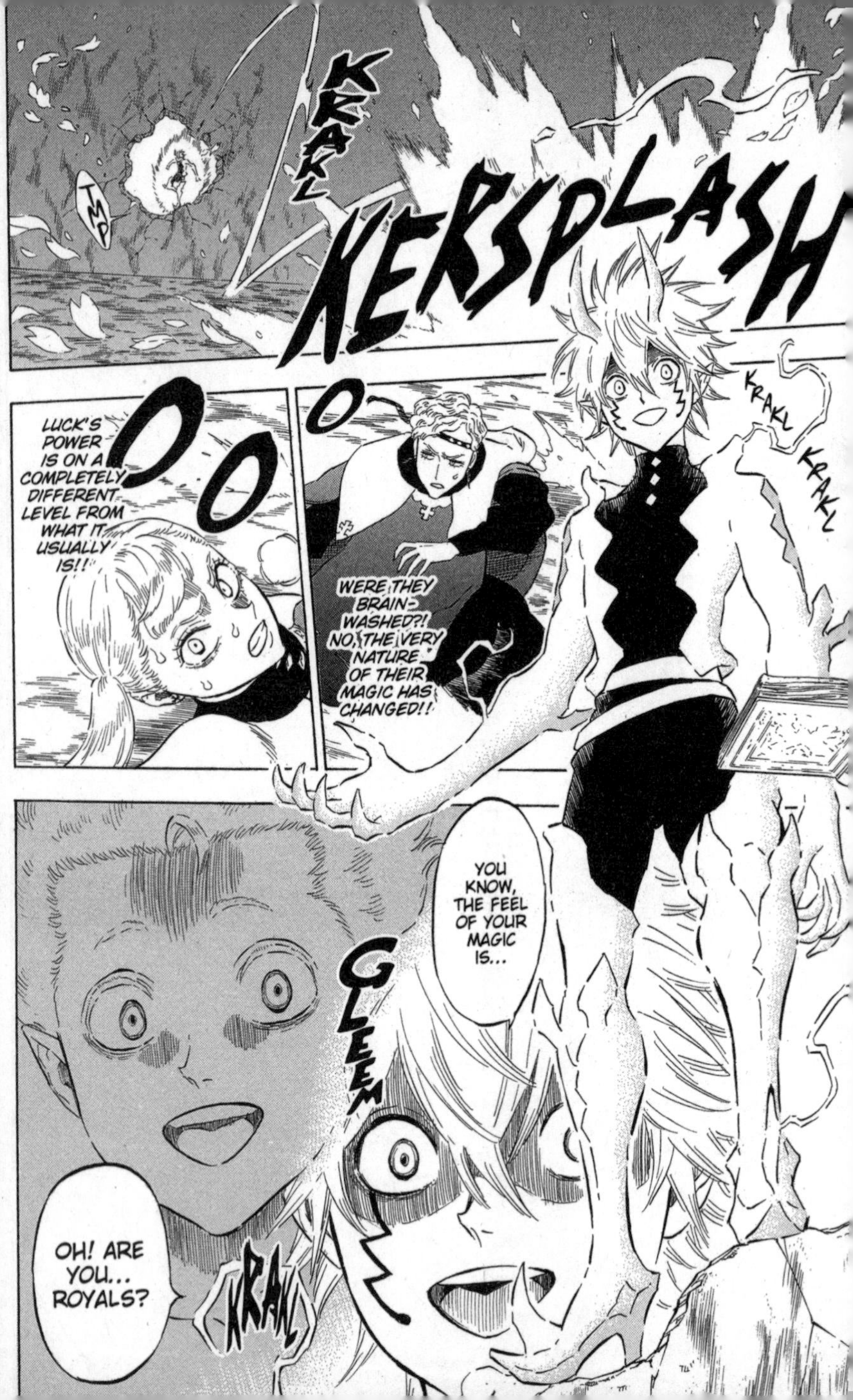
KERSPLASH
KRAKL
TMP
KRAKL
KRAKL
WERE THEY BRAIN-WASHED?! NO, THE VERY NATURE OF THEIR MAGIC HAS CHANGED!!
LUCK'S POWER IS ON A COMPLETELY DIFFERENT LEVEL FROM WHAT IT USUALLY IS!!
YOU KNOW, THE FEEL OF YOUR MAGIC IS...
GLEEM
OH! ARE YOU... ROYALS?
KRAKL

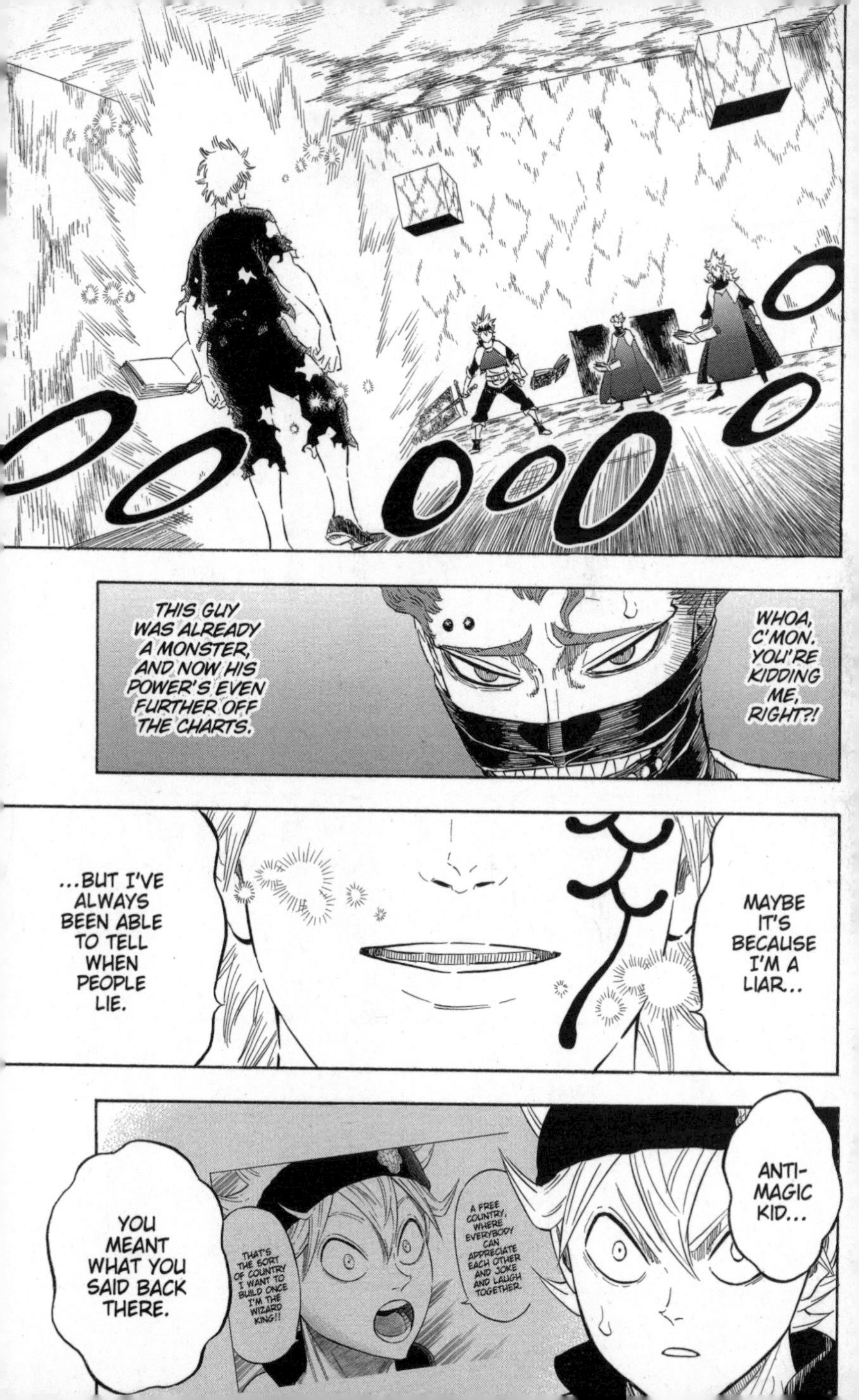
WHOA, C'MON. YOU'RE KIDDING ME, RIGHT?!
THIS GUY WAS ALREADY A MONSTER, AND NOW HIS POWER'S EVEN FURTHER OFF THE CHARTS.
MAYBE IT'S BECAUSE I'M A LIAR...
...BUT I'VE ALWAYS BEEN ABLE TO TELL WHEN PEOPLE LIE.
ANTI-MAGIC KID...
A FREE COUNTRY, WHERE EVERYBODY CAN APPRECIATE EACH OTHER AND JOKE AND LAUGH TOGETHER.
THAT'S THE SORT OF COUNTRY I WANT TO BUILD ONCE I'M THE WIZARD KING!!
YOU MEANT WHAT YOU SAID BACK THERE.

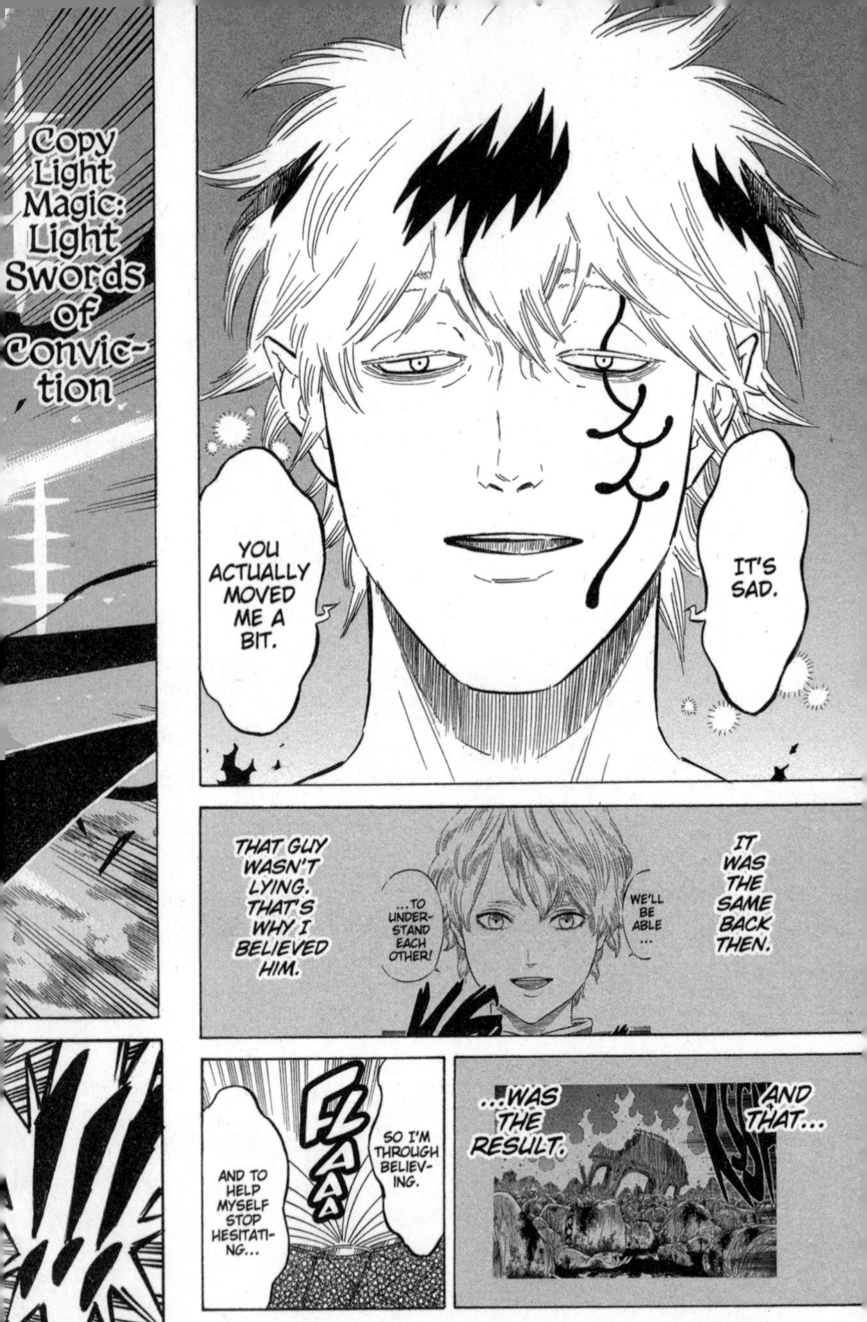
IT'S SAD.
YOU ACTUALLY MOVED ME A BIT.
IT WAS THE SAME BACK THEN.
WE'LL BE ABLE...
...TO UNDERSTAND EACH OTHER!
THAT GUY WASN'T LYING. THAT'S WHY I BELIEVED HIM.
Copy Light Magic: Light Swords of Conviction
AND THAT...
...WAS THE RESULT.
SO I'M THROUGH BELIEVING.
FLAAAA
AND TO HELP MYSELF STOP HESITATING...

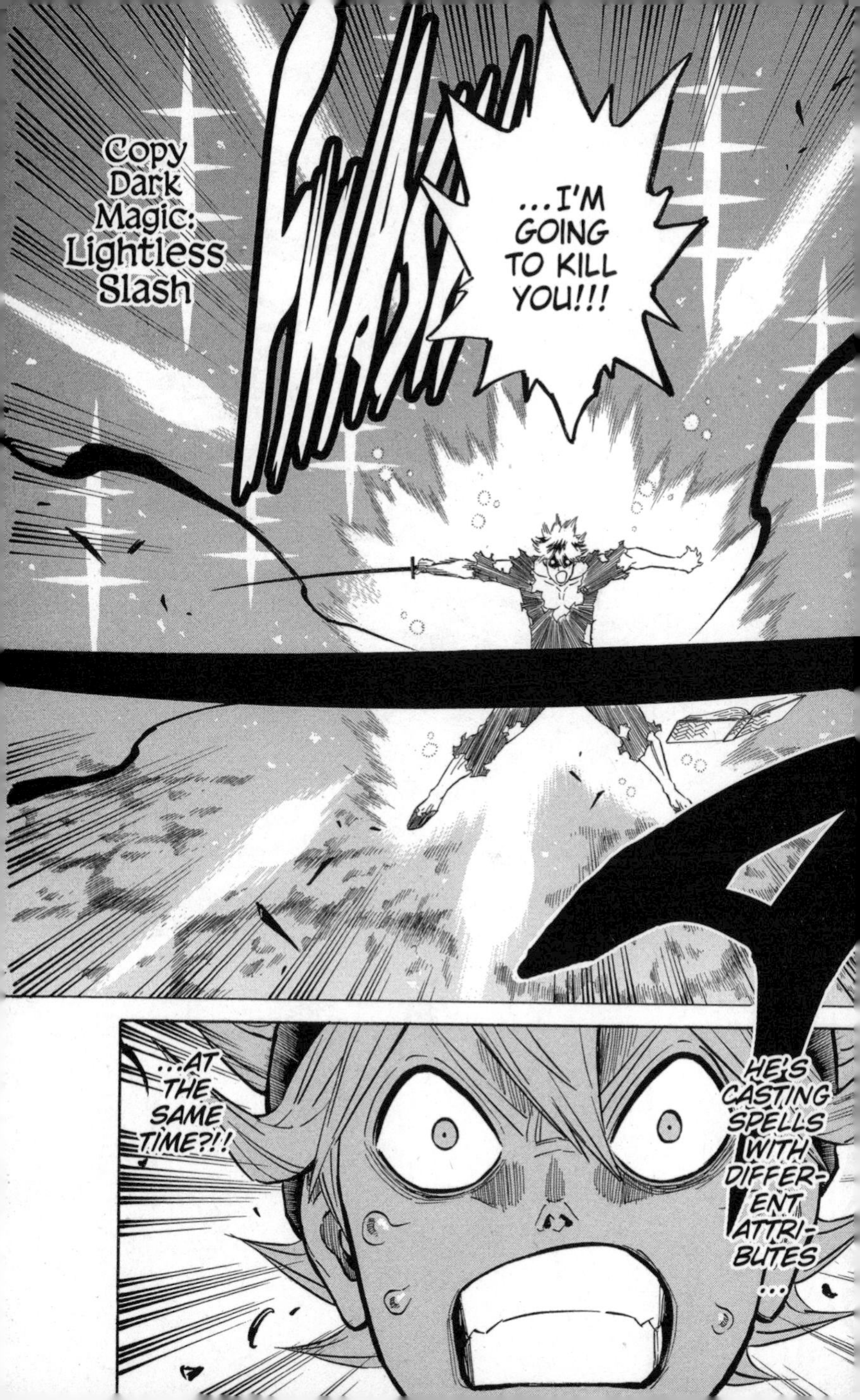
...I'M GOING TO KILL YOU!!!
Copy Dark Magic: Lightless Slash
HE'S CASTING SPELLS WITH DIFFERENT ATTRIBUTES...
...AT THE SAME TIME?!!

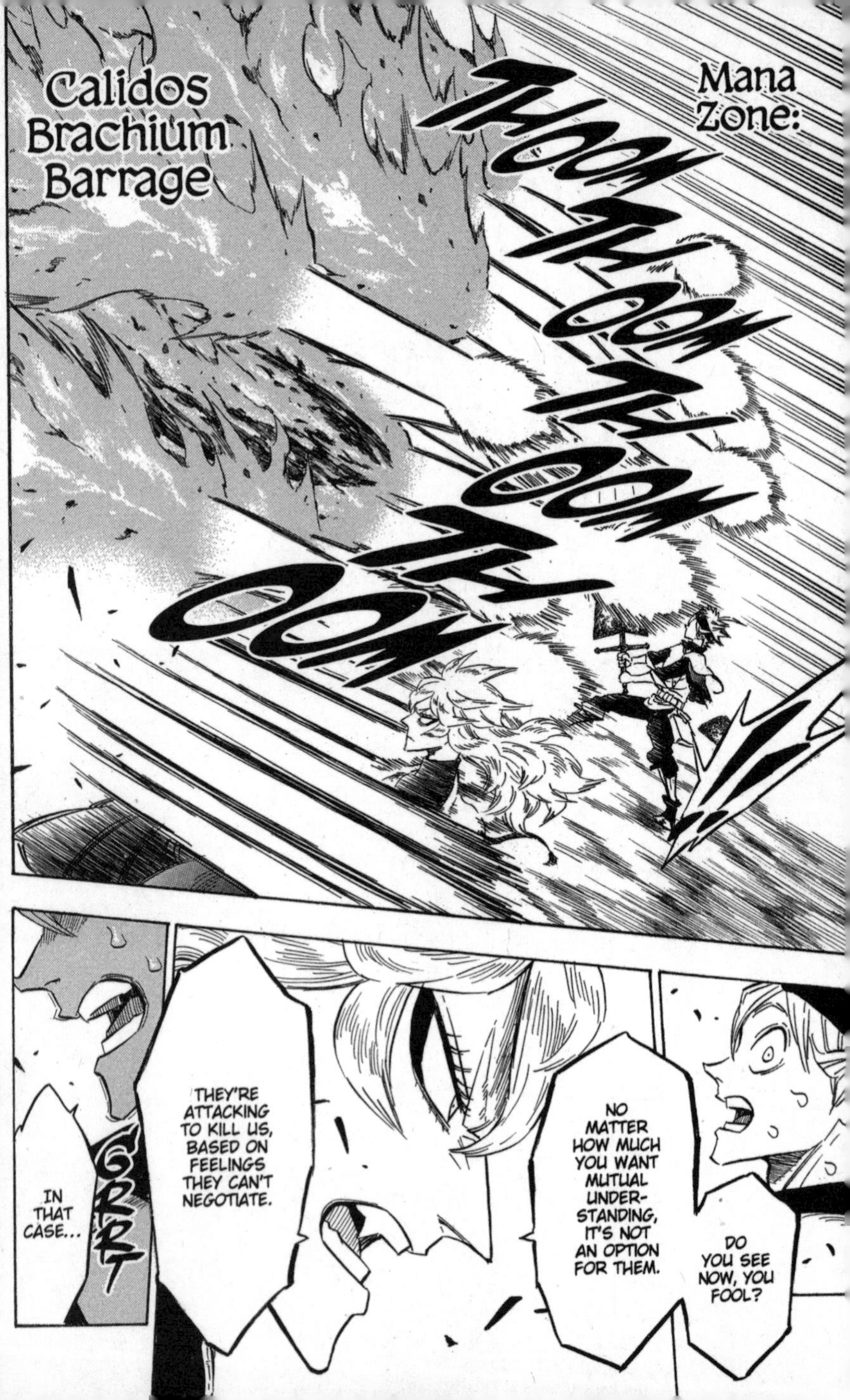
Mana Zone:
Calidos Brachium Barrage
THOOM THOOM THOOM THOOM!!
DO YOU SEE NOW, YOU FOOL?
NO MATTER HOW MUCH YOU WANT MUTUAL UNDER-STANDING, IT'S NOT AN OPTION FOR THEM.
THEY'RE ATTACKING TO KILL US, BASED ON FEELINGS THEY CAN'T NEGOTIATE.
GRRRT
IN THAT CASE...

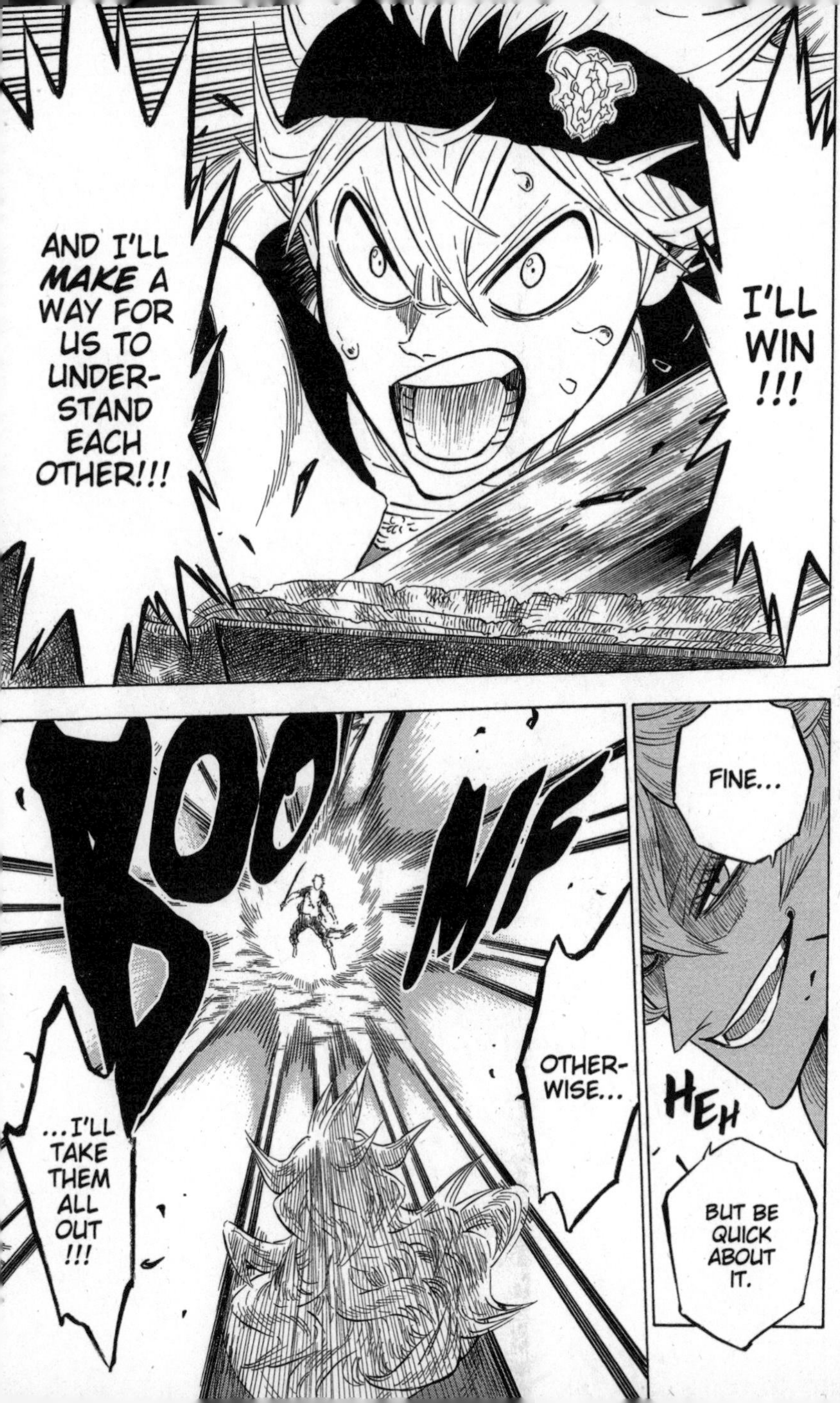
I'LL WIN!!!
AND I'LL *MAKE* A WAY FOR US TO UNDERSTAND EACH OTHER!!!
FINE...
HEH
BUT BE QUICK ABOUT IT.
BOOOMF
OTHERWISE...
...I'LL TAKE THEM ALL OUT!!!

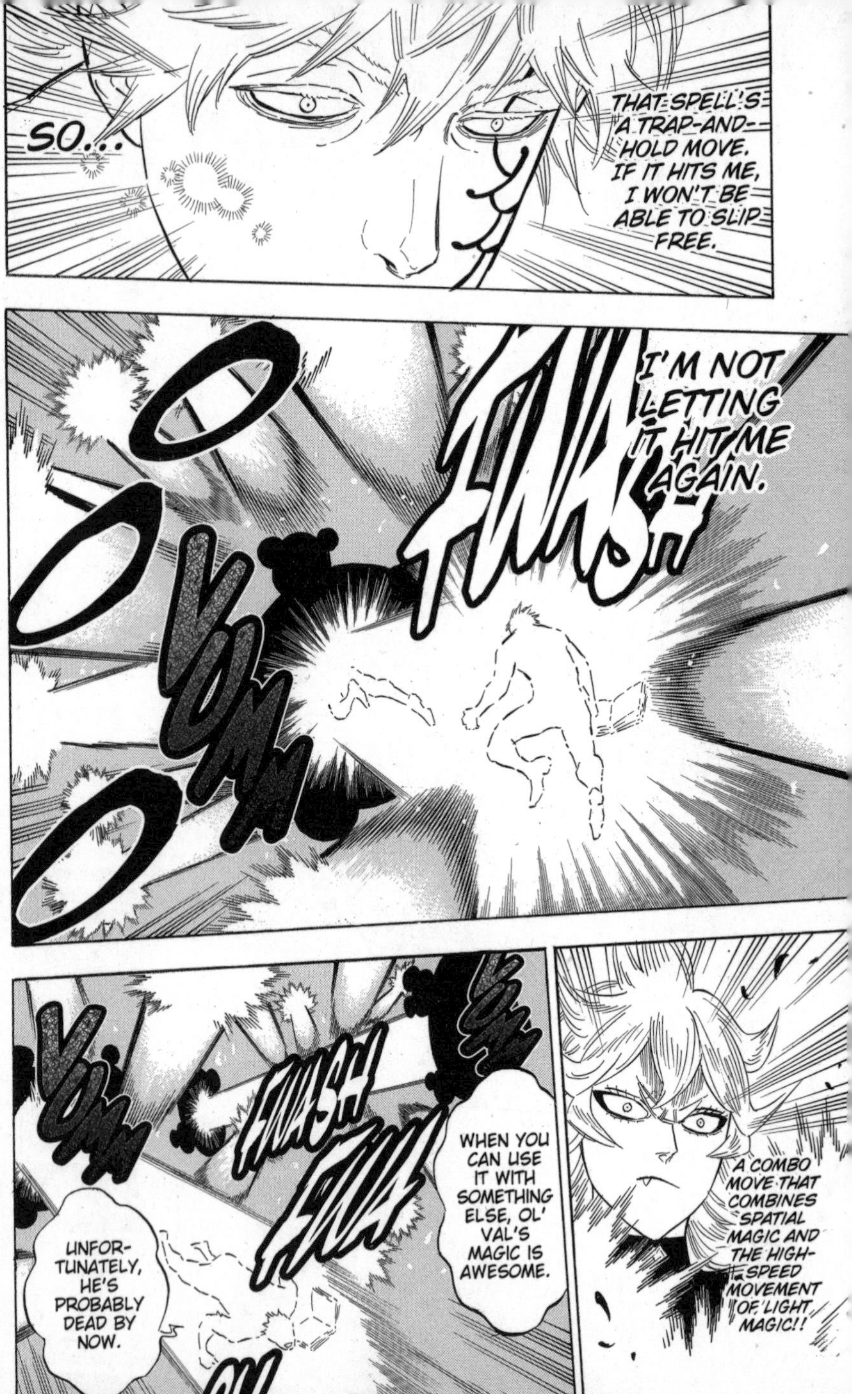
THAT SPELL'S A TRAP-AND-HOLD MOVE. IF IT HITS ME, I WON'T BE ABLE TO SLIP FREE.
SO...
I'M NOT LETTING IT HIT ME AGAIN.
A COMBO MOVE THAT COMBINES SPATIAL MAGIC AND THE HIGH-SPEED MOVEMENT OF LIGHT MAGIC!!
FWASH
WHEN YOU CAN USE IT WITH SOMETHING ELSE, OL' VAL'S MAGIC IS AWESOME.
UNFORTUNATELY, HE'S PROBABLY DEAD BY NOW.

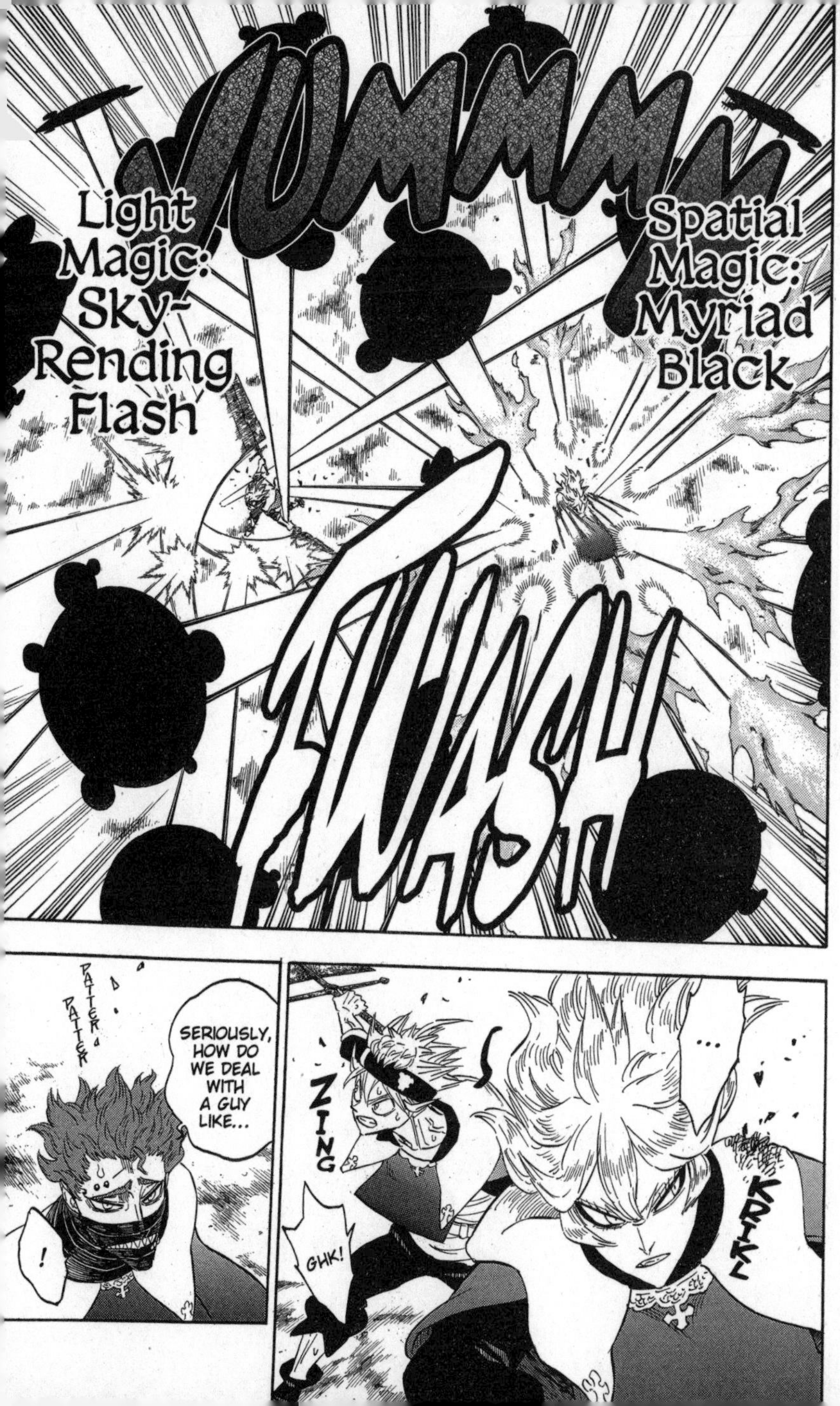
Spatial Magic: Myriad Black
Light Magic: Sky-Rending Flash
...
KRIK!
ZING
GHK!
PATTER PATTER
SERIOUSLY, HOW DO WE DEAL WITH A GUY LIKE...
!

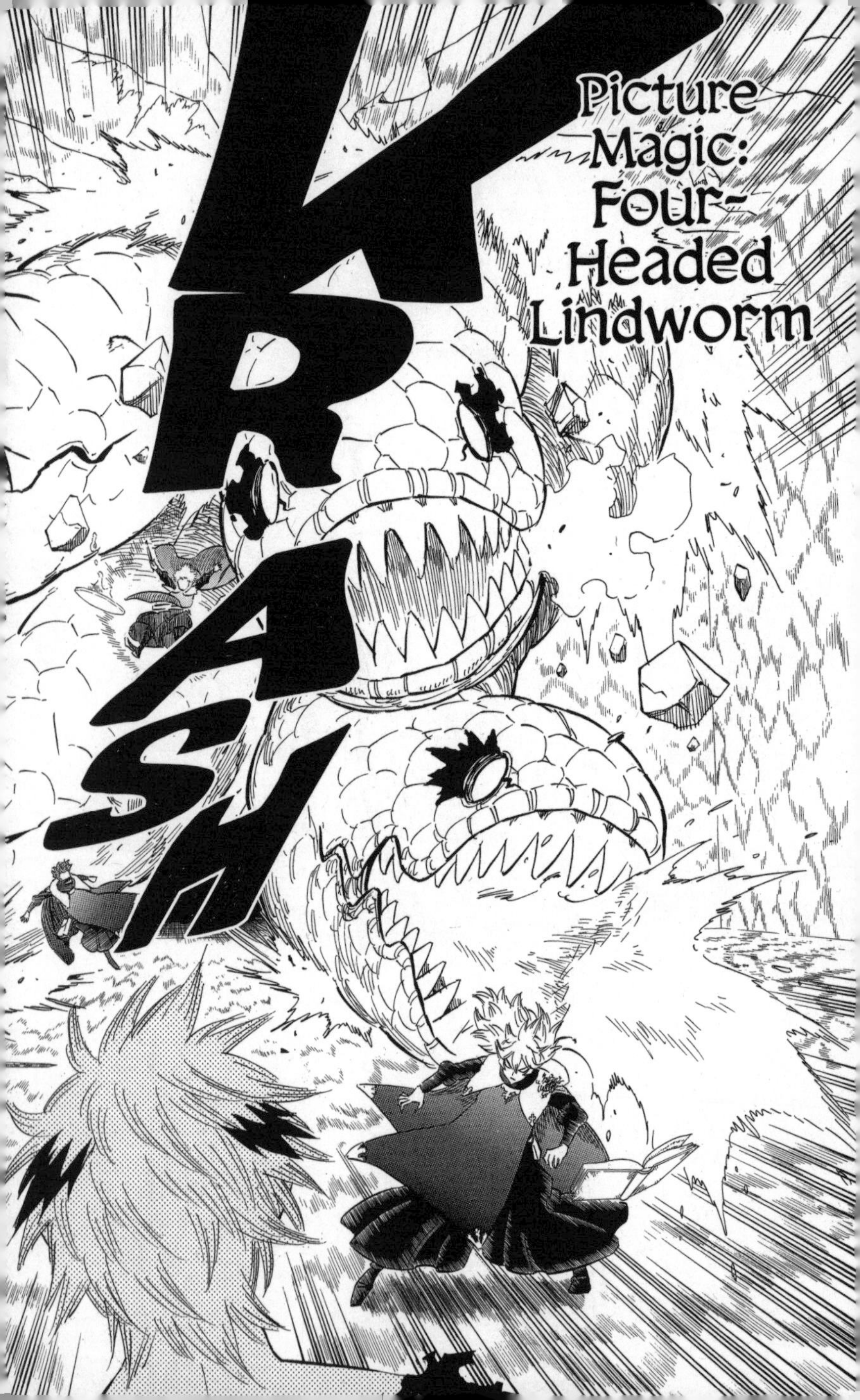
Picture Magic: Four-Headed Lindworm
KRASH

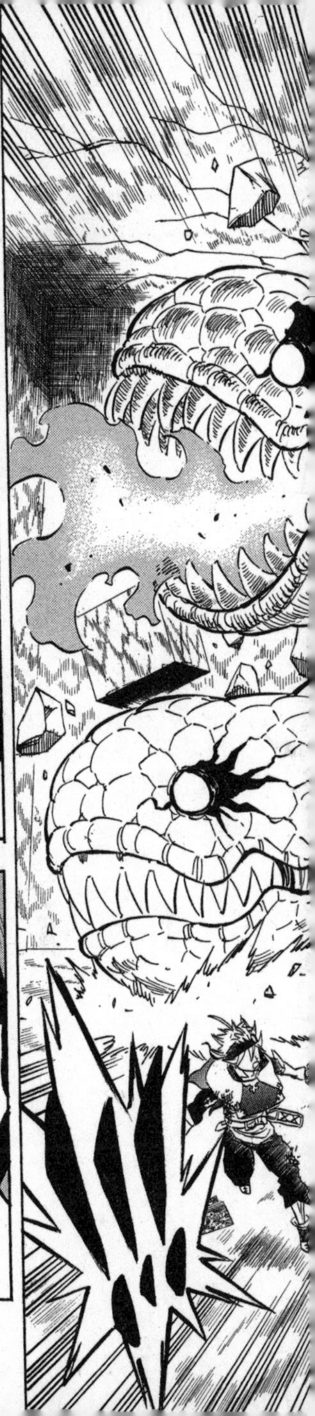

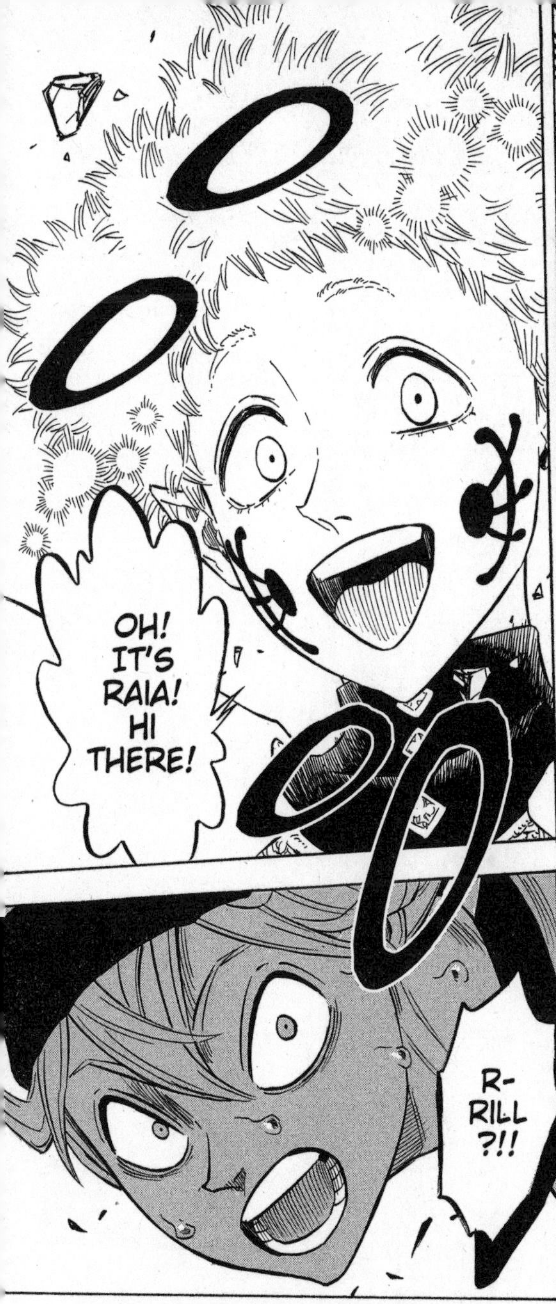
OH! IT'S RAIA! HI THERE!
R-RILL?!!

TO BE CONTINUED IN VOLUME 17!

The Blank Page Brigade

This volume's topic: What's your favorite curry fixing, and what does your family put in theirs?

My favorite fixing: Melt-in-your-mouth carrots
My family uses: Roly-poly eggplant chunks

Kazuhiro Wakao

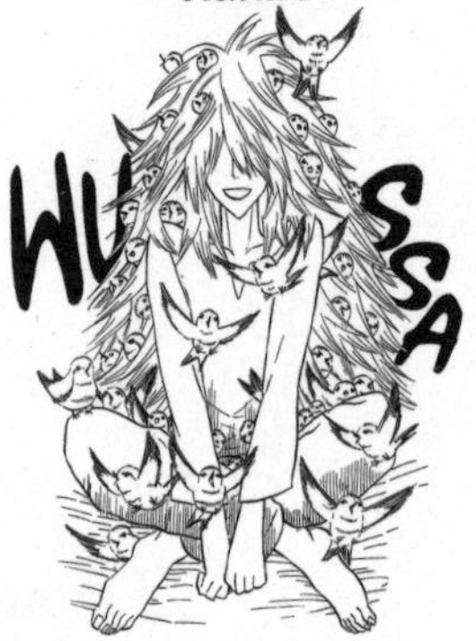

WU
SSA

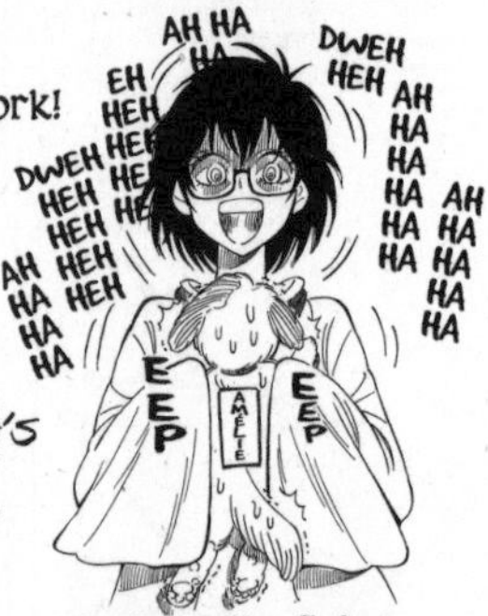

AH HA HA
DWEH HEH
EH HEH HEH HEH HEH
DWEH HEH HEH
AH HA HA HA HA
AH HA HA HA HA HA HA
AH HA HA HA HA HA
AMELIE
EEP
EEP

My favorite fixing: Tons of tomatoes
My family uses: Tons of tomatoes

Shūtarō Koga

My favorite fixing: Humongous! Chunks! of Pork!
My family uses: Chikuwa fish cakes

Yōtarō Hayakawa

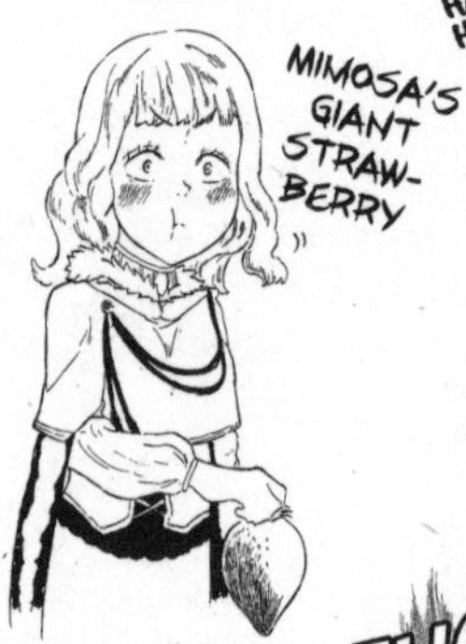

MIMOSA'S GIANT STRAW-BERRY

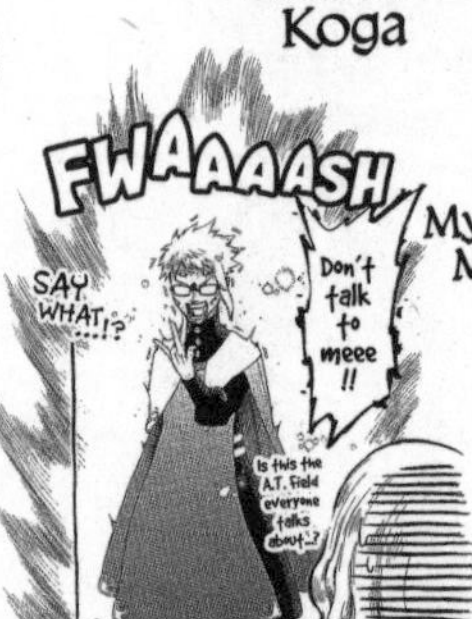

FWAAAASH
Don't talk to meee!!
SAY WHAT!?
Is this the A.T. Field everyone talks about...?

My favorite fixing: Tuna
My family uses: Tuna

Kōki Ishikawa

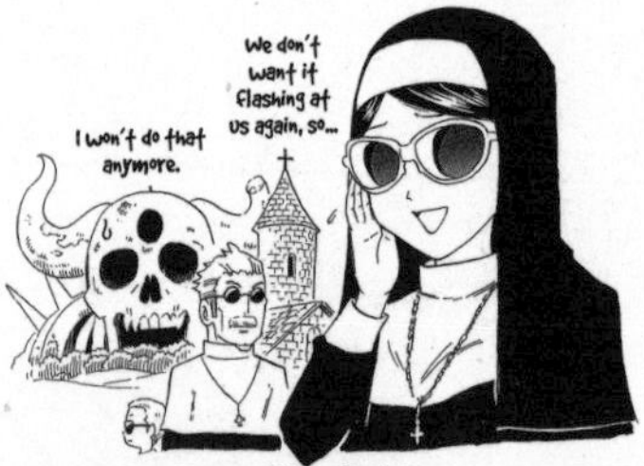

We don't want it flashing at us again, so...
I won't do that anymore.

My favorite fixing: Crispy sausages
My family uses: Tomatoes

Teruaki Mizuno

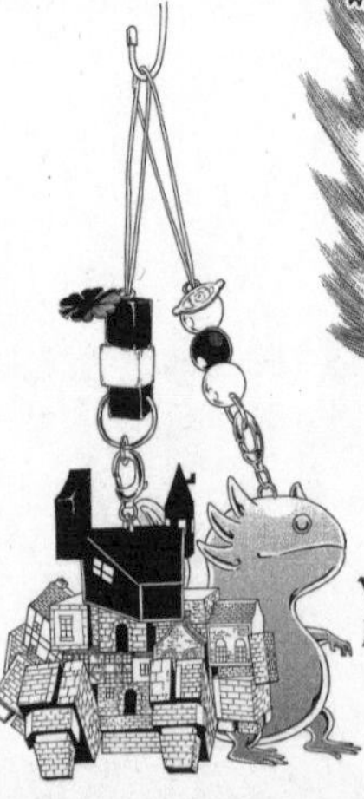

My favorite fixing: Veggies in big chunks
My family uses: Pork

Hayato Gotō

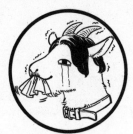

My favorite fixing:
Roly-poly veggies
My family uses:
Roly-poly veggies
©

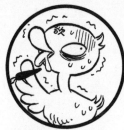

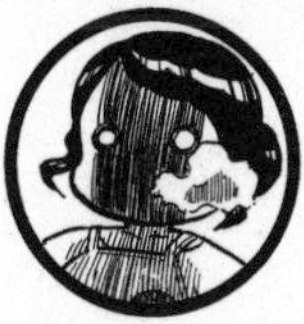

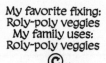

My favorite fixing:
Onions that are still
a bit crunchy
My family uses:
Mild curry that's
tailored to my
physical and
emotional
condition

Captain Tabata

My favorite fixing:
Potato salad
My family uses:
Delicious rice
from back home

Editor Toide

My favorite
fixing: Nothing
in particular...
My family
uses: I can't
remember...

Designer
Iwai

My favorite fixing:
Large-cut potatoes
My family uses:
Grilled veggies

Comics
Editor
Koshimura

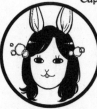

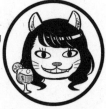

AFTERWORD

♣

In this volume, we hit the reincarnation, one of the series' major turning points! Now that I'm actually drawing it, it's giving me all sorts of trouble!! Even so, I'll psych myself up and gooooo!

They've also simultaneously released a character book of sorts, for which I'm very grateful at a time like this!

It has lots of information that hasn't shown up in the main story yet, so definitely check it out as well!

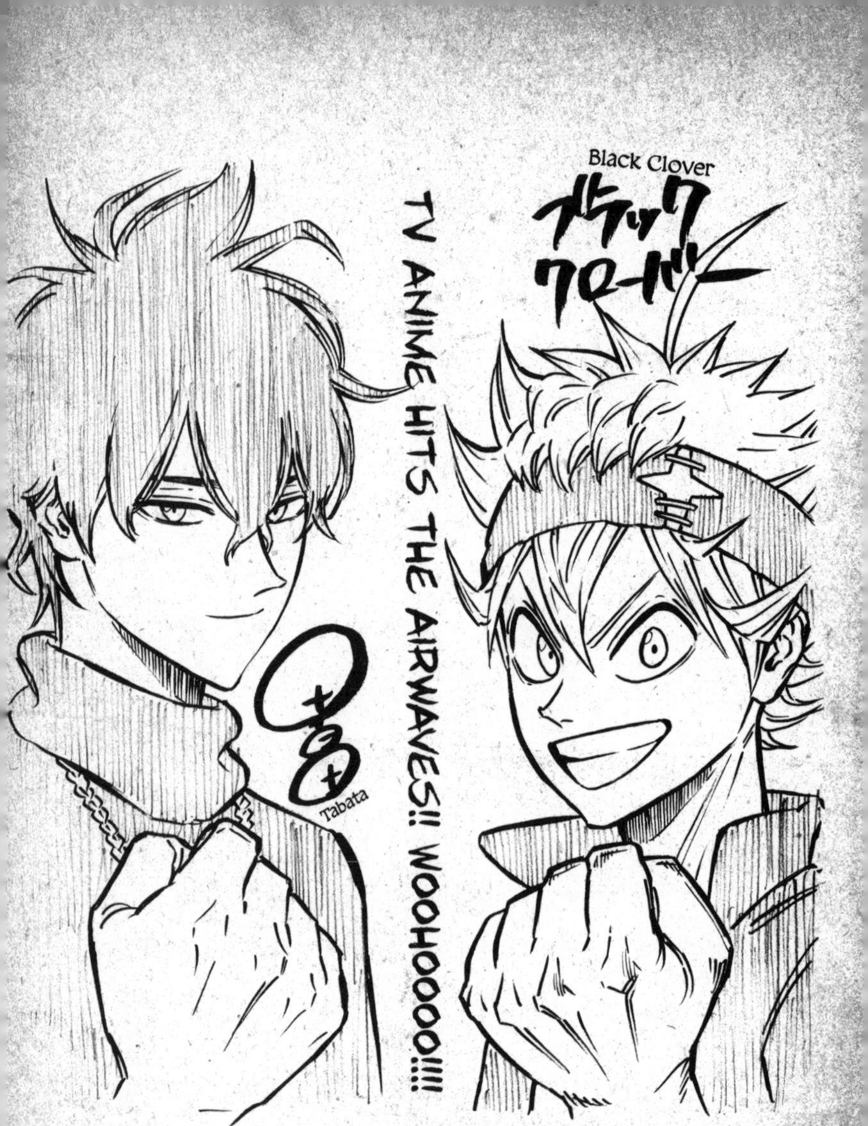
Black Clover
ブラッククローバー
TV ANIME HITS THE AIRWAVES!! WOOHOOOOO!!!!
Tabata

An autograph board I drew before
the anime began airing!
It already feels like so long ago...

Special Bonus Materials

Early design
sketches for
Rill! He was more
mature than he
is now!

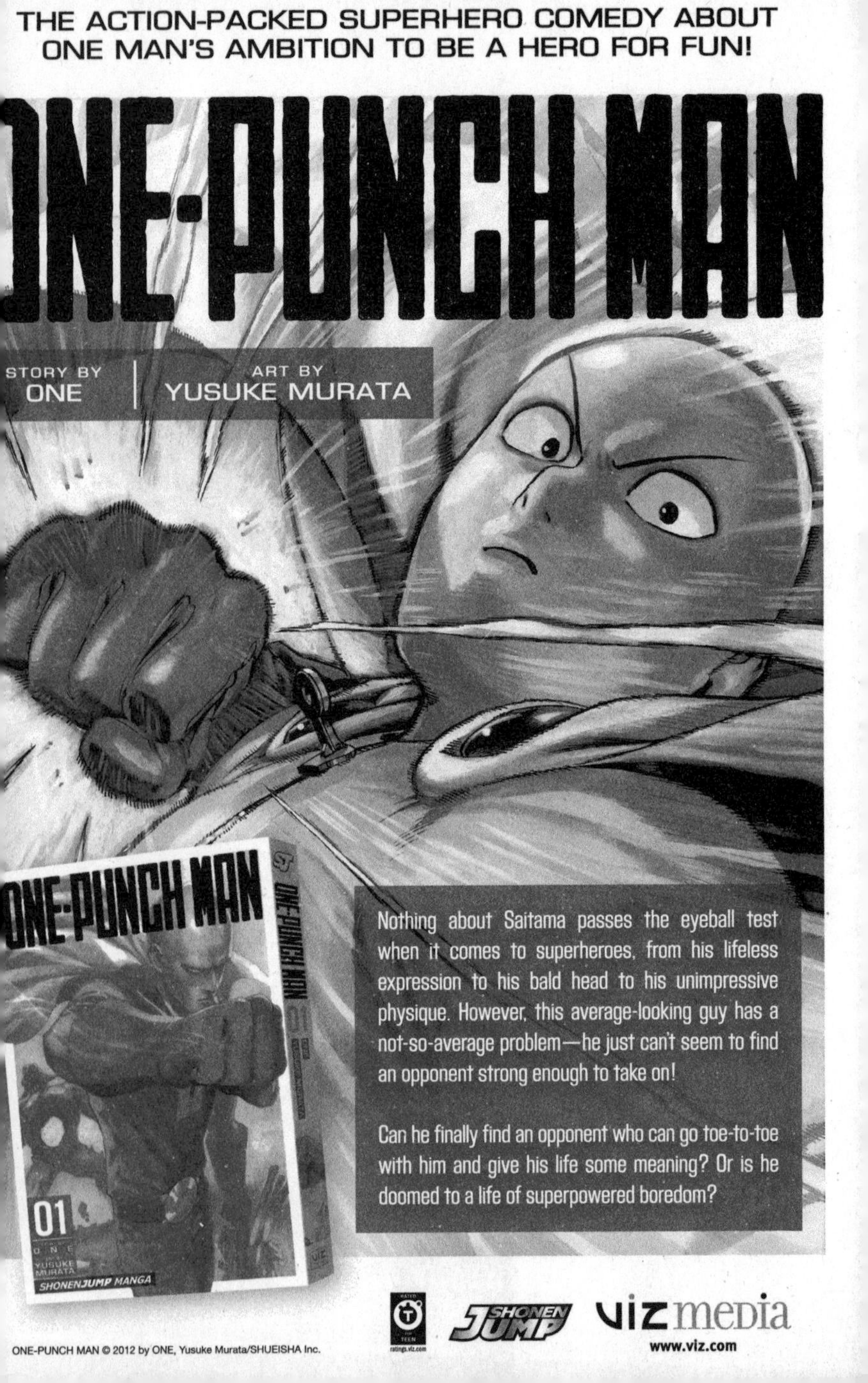
THE ACTION-PACKED SUPERHERO COMEDY ABOUT ONE MAN'S AMBITION TO BE A HERO FOR FUN!
ONE-PUNCH MAN
STORY BY ONE
ART BY YUSUKE MURATA
Nothing about Saitama passes the eyeball test when it comes to superheroes, from his lifeless expression to his bald head to his unimpressive physique. However, this average-looking guy has a not-so-average problem—he just can't seem to find an opponent strong enough to take on!
Can he finally find an opponent who can go toe-to-toe with him and give his life some meaning? Or is he doomed to a life of superpowered boredom?
ONE-PUNCH MAN
01
ONE
YUSUKE MURATA
SHONENJUMP MANGA
SHONEN JUMP
viz media
www.viz.com
ONE-PUNCH MAN © 2012 by ONE, Yusuke Murata/SHUEISHA Inc.

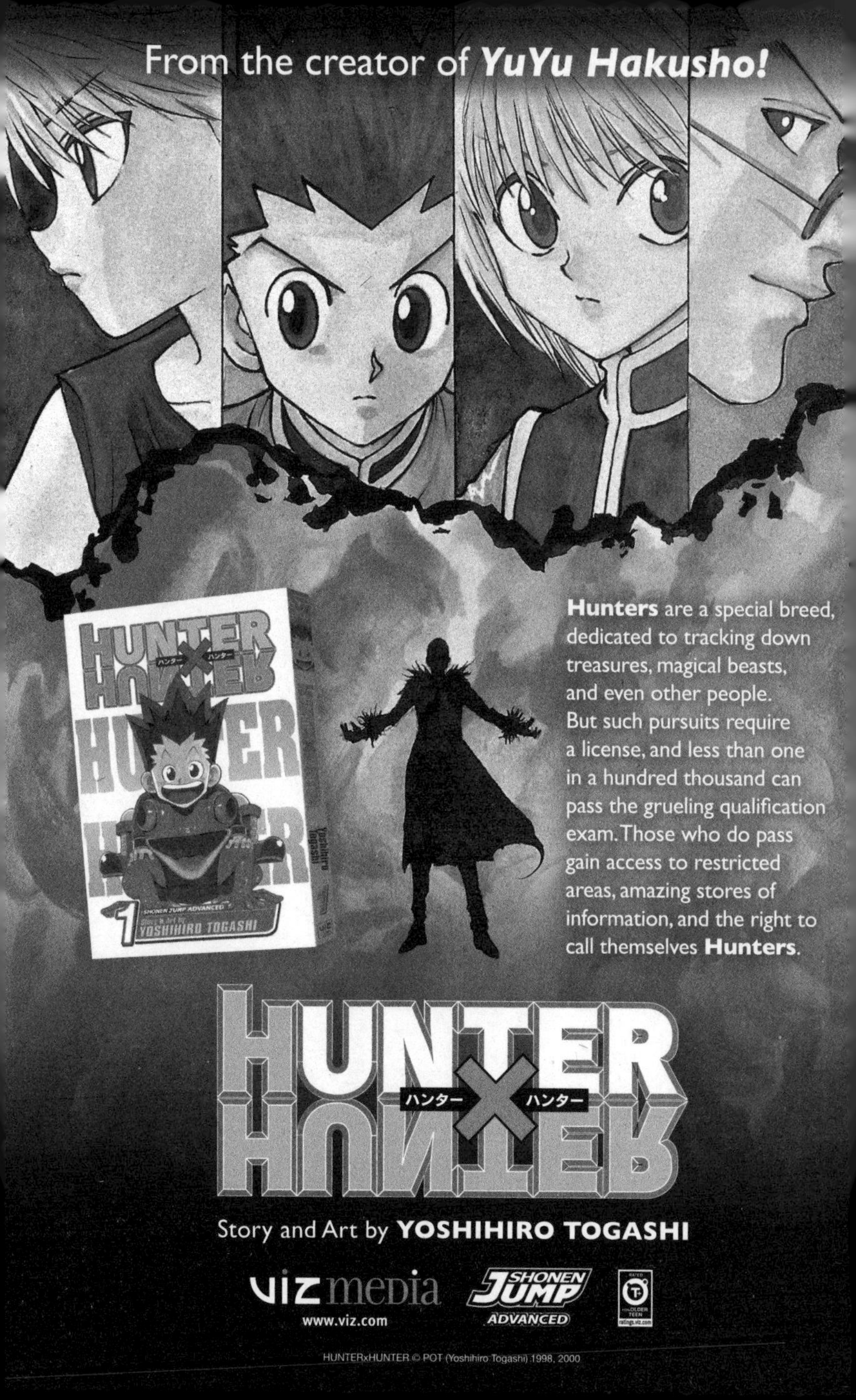
From the creator of YuYu Hakusho!
HUNTER × HUNTER
ハンター ハンター
SHONEN JUMP ADVANCED
1
YOSHIHIRO TOGASHI
Yoshihiro Togashi
Hunters are a special breed, dedicated to tracking down treasures, magical beasts, and even other people. But such pursuits require a license, and less than one in a hundred thousand can pass the grueling qualification exam. Those who do pass gain access to restricted areas, amazing stores of information, and the right to call themselves Hunters.
HUNTER × HUNTER
ハンター ハンター
Story and Art by YOSHIHIRO TOGASHI
VIZ media
www.viz.com
SHONEN JUMP ADVANCED
RATED T+ FOR OLDER TEEN
ratings.viz.com
HUNTERxHUNTER © POT (Yoshihiro Togashi) 1998, 2000

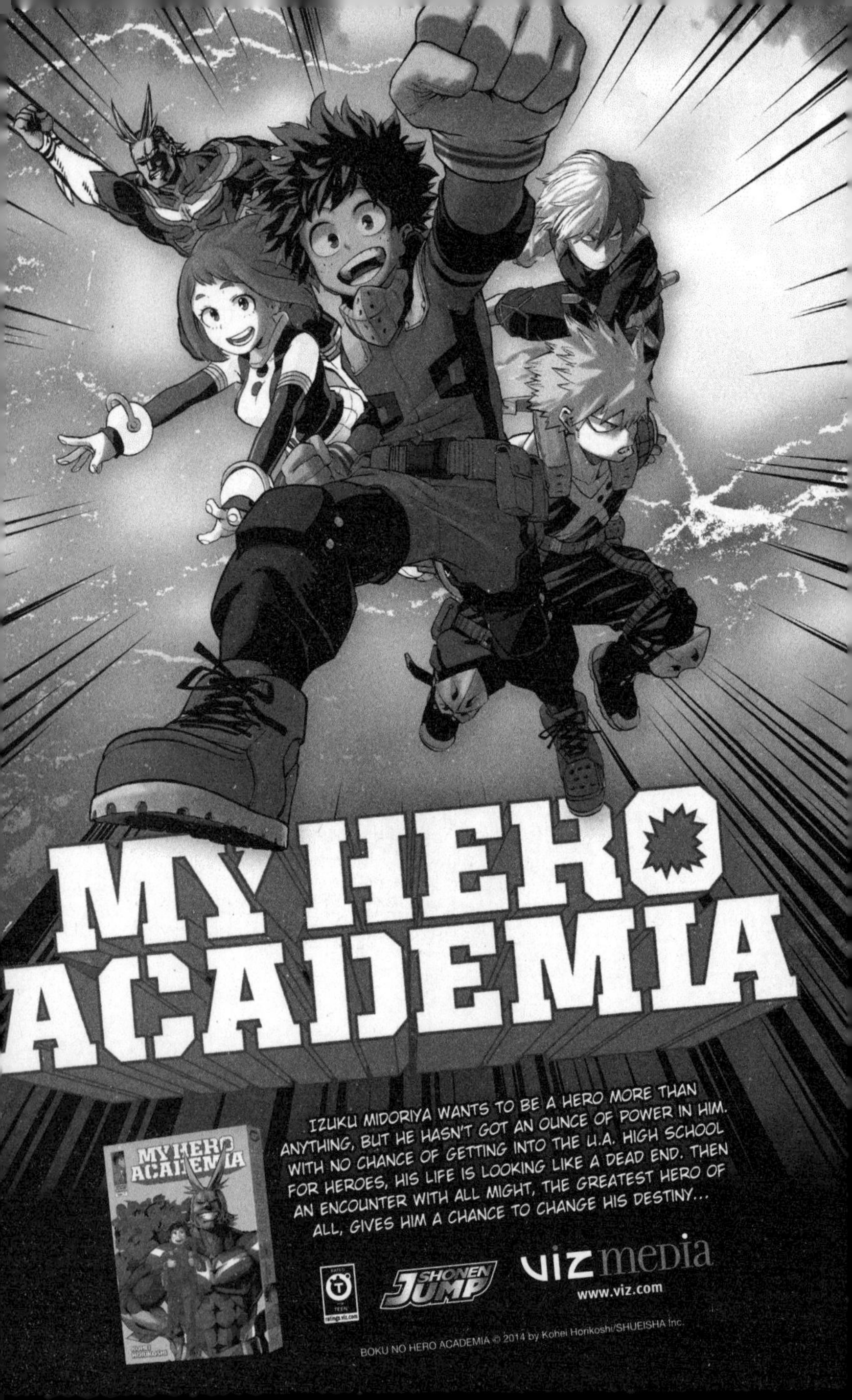
MY HERO ACADEMIA
IZUKU MIDORIYA WANTS TO BE A HERO MORE THAN ANYTHING, BUT HE HASN'T GOT AN OUNCE OF POWER IN HIM. WITH NO CHANCE OF GETTING INTO THE U.A. HIGH SCHOOL FOR HEROES, HIS LIFE IS LOOKING LIKE A DEAD END. THEN AN ENCOUNTER WITH ALL MIGHT, THE GREATEST HERO OF ALL, GIVES HIM A CHANCE TO CHANGE HIS DESTINY...
MY HERO ACADEMIA
SHONEN JUMP
viz media
www.viz.com
BOKU NO HERO ACADEMIA © 2014 by Kohei Horikoshi/SHUEISHA Inc.

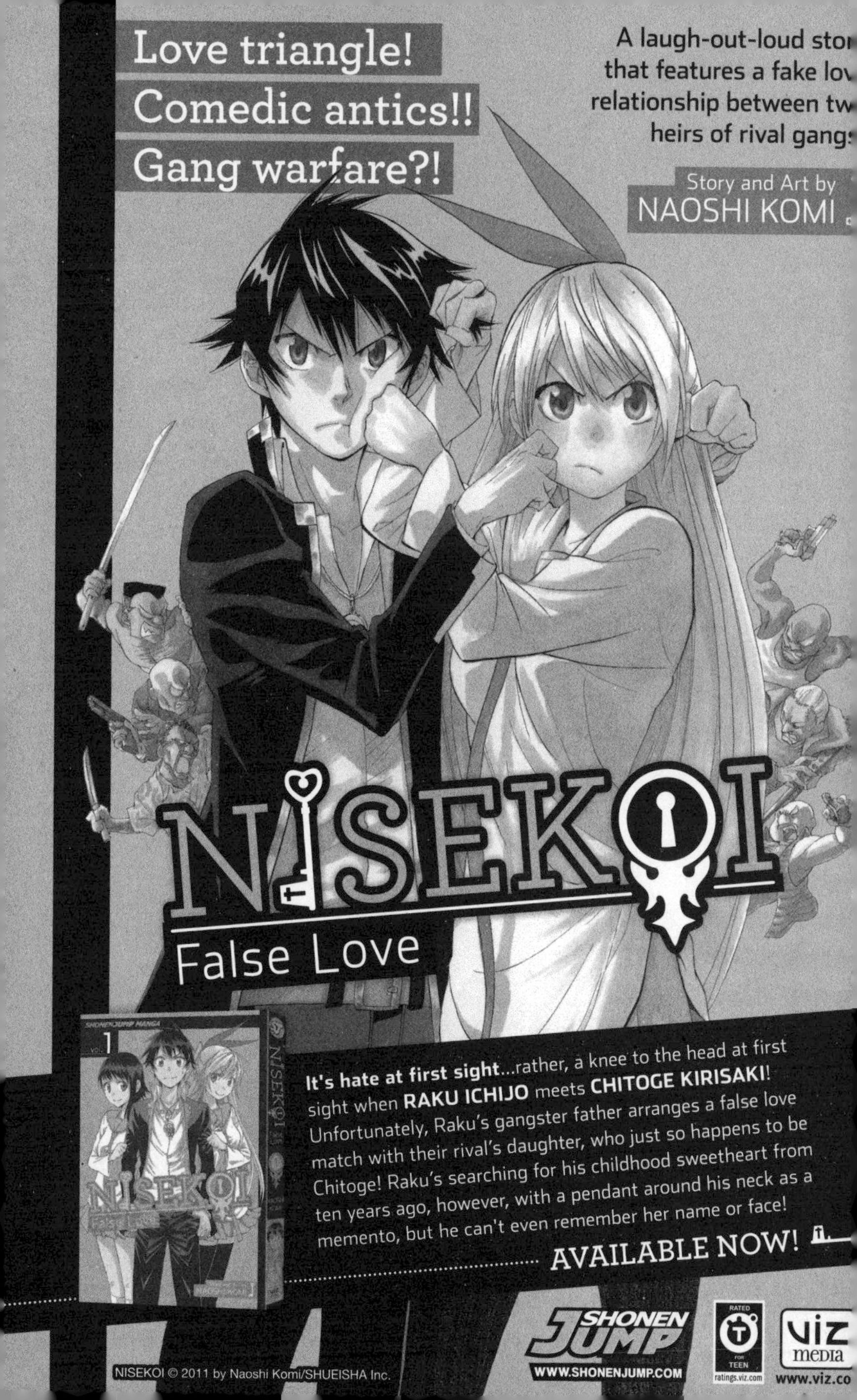

Love triangle!
Comedic antics!!
Gang warfare?!
A laugh-out-loud stor
that features a fake lov
relationship between tw
heirs of rival gang
Story and Art by
NAOSHI KOMI
NISEKOI
False Love
SHONEN JUMP MANGA
VOL. 1
It's hate at first sight...rather, a knee to the head at first
sight when RAKU ICHIJO meets CHITOGE KIRISAKI!
Unfortunately, Raku's gangster father arranges a false love
match with their rival's daughter, who just so happens to be
Chitoge! Raku's searching for his childhood sweetheart from
ten years ago, however, with a pendant around his neck as a
memento, but he can't even remember her name or face!
AVAILABLE NOW!
SHONEN JUMP
WWW.SHONENJUMP.COM
RATED T FOR TEEN
ratings.viz.com
VIZ media
www.viz.co
NISEKOI © 2011 by Naoshi Komi/SHUEISHA Inc.

ASTRA
LOST IN SPACE

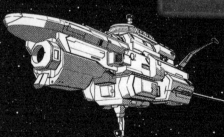

CAN EIGHT TEENAGERS FIND THEIR WAY HOME FROM 5,000 LIGHT-YEARS AWAY?

t's the year 2063, and interstellar space travel has become he norm. Eight students from Caird High School and one hild set out on a routine planet camp excursion. While here, the students are mysteriously transported 5,000 ight-years away to the middle of nowhere! Will they ever nake it back home?!

ASTRA
LOST IN SPACE
Story and Art by KENTA SHINOHARA

VIZ

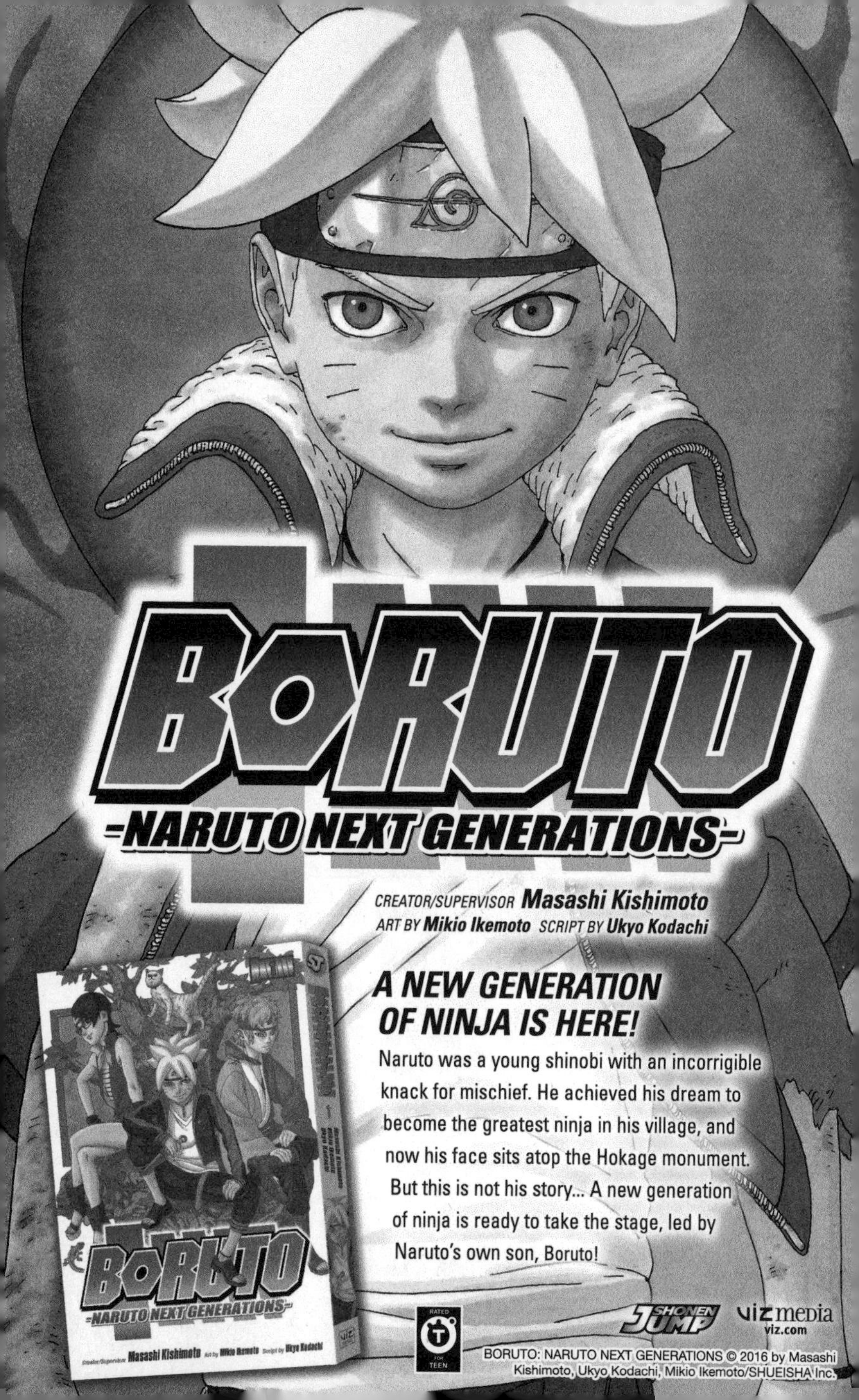
BORUTO
-NARUTO NEXT GENERATIONS-
CREATOR/SUPERVISOR Masashi Kishimoto
ART BY Mikio Ikemoto SCRIPT BY Ukyo Kodachi
A NEW GENERATION OF NINJA IS HERE!
Naruto was a young shinobi with an incorrigible knack for mischief. He achieved his dream to become the greatest ninja in his village, and now his face sits atop the Hokage monument. But this is not his story... A new generation of ninja is ready to take the stage, led by Naruto's own son, Boruto!
BORUTO
-NARUTO NEXT GENERATIONS-
Masashi Kishimoto
RATED T FOR TEEN
SHONEN JUMP
VIZ media
viz.com
BORUTO: NARUTO NEXT GENERATIONS © 2016 by Masashi Kishimoto, Ukyo Kodachi, Mikio Ikemoto/SHUEISHA Inc.

Stop

YOU'RE READING
THE WRONG WAY!

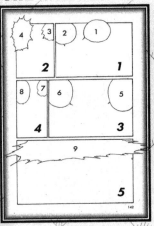

BLACK CLOVER

reads from right to left, starting
in the upper-right corner. Japanese
is read from right to left, meaning
that action, sound effects, and
word-balloon order are completely
reversed from English order.